剑桥雅思高分指南系列

外研社·剑桥

雅思考试培训教程

●●● 高德立 编著

剑桥雅思

阅读高分指南

CAMBRIDGE IELTS Objective Reading

外语教学与研究出版社
FOREIGN LANGUAGE TEACHING AND RESEARCH PRESS
北京 BEIJING

图书在版编目(CIP)数据

剑桥雅思阅读高分指南/ 高德立编著. — 北京：外语教学与研究出版社，2010.1（2013.3 重印）
（剑桥雅思高分指南系列）
ISBN 978-7-5600-9287-4

Ⅰ. ①剑… Ⅱ. ①高… Ⅲ. ①英语—阅读教学—高等教育—自学参考资料 Ⅳ. ①H319.4

中国版本图书馆 CIP 数据核字（2010）第 014702 号

出 版 人：蔡剑峰
责任编辑：丁　宁　赵　婧
封面设计：刘　冬
版式设计：张苏梅
出版发行：外语教学与研究出版社
社　　址：北京市西三环北路 19 号（100089）
网　　址：http://www.fltrp.com
印　　刷：北京市鑫霸印务有限公司
开　　本：880×1230　1/16
印　　张：19.5
版　　次：2010 年 1 月第 1 版　2013 年 3 月第 4 次印刷
书　　号：ISBN 978-7-5600-9287-4
定　　价：35.90 元

*　　*　　*

购书咨询：(010)88819929　　电子邮箱：club@fltrp.com
如有印刷、装订质量问题，请与出版社联系
联系电话：(010)61207896　　电子邮箱：zhijian@fltrp.com

物料号：192870001

写在前面的话

阅读技巧常常被等同于应试技巧，等同于取巧，这其实是一种误解。阅读技巧是国内外教学专家们（尤其是英美教学专家）经过多年研究，总结出来的科学的阅读技能。掌握了这种技巧，在具有一定的词汇量和语法知识的基础上（国内高中英语或以上水平），读者就能在阅读中更迅速、更有效地获取信息，享受阅读的乐趣。有乐趣就促进多读，多读又促进理解，理解好了又更有乐趣，这样相辅相成，英语水平的提高自然水到渠成。

雅思阅读考试与传统考试有所不同，重点在于测试考生提取、理解、分析信息的能力，不直接考查语法和词汇，而是考查考生综合运用语言的能力。在这种考试中，掌握阅读技巧比死记硬背更有用武之地。

市面上关于英语阅读和雅思阅读的书出了不少，有些太繁琐，太学术化，适合指导教师作为教学参考资料，专业有余而趣味不足；有些还是按照传统的思路编写——提供文章，罗列单词表，分析难句；还有一些只针对某一种阅读考试设计内容，显然把阅读技巧狭隘化了。针对这种情况，本书把阅读技巧的学习和使用结合起来，先学习技巧，再运用到雅思阅读考试中。笔者根据多年的英语阅读和雅思教学经验，将本书分为“阅读技巧学习篇”和“雅思阅读考试实践篇”两大部分。第一部分分为九章，详细介绍了各种英语阅读技巧，并结合雅思题型讲解阅读技巧在雅思阅读考试中的应用。第二部分分为五章，包括雅思考试的测试要求、题型分类、具体题型以及雅思阅读考试真题破解等内容。

科学的阅读技巧适用于任何类型的阅读考试。本书介绍的技巧同样适用于其他类型的英语考试，包括高考、大学英语考试、专业英语考试、新托福、GRE 和 GMAT 等。除此之外，阅读技巧也适用于生活、学习和工作。通过学习阅读技巧可以一举多得，使学习者（包括高中生、大学非英语专业学生、英语专业学生、研究生和需要参加雅思等留学考试的考生）能够突破英语阅读的“瓶颈”，终生受用。同时，英语教师也可借鉴此书，提高教学水平。

最后，笔者希望与广大考生共同分享英语阅读的经验，切实提高考生的英语阅读水平，从而在雅思阅读考试中获取高分！

高德立

目录

阅读技巧学习篇

雅思阅读考试实践篇

阅读技巧

学习篇

To Be Filed

1 寻读——提取细节信息快捷方便

1.1 寻读技巧概述

不同的阅读目的决定不同的阅读动作。要在文本中迅速找到所需的细节信息是不必通读全文的，因为这些信息在文中是孤立存在的，不与其他信息发生横向的联系。信息的性质决定阅读的方式，逐字、逐句、逐行的阅读不能达到快速从文本中找到所需信息的目的。在这里，提高速度是首要问题。

严格说来，寻读（scanning）并不是阅读，而是通过眼睛的快速移动来搜寻信息。在寻读开始前，必须确定寻找目标，比如在词典中查生词，在报纸分类广告中找工作、租房、买房、找各种娱乐活动信息、确定旅游地点等，或在期刊杂志、书籍和百科全书目录中很快找到要读的文章、章节和信息。在阅读考试中，针对要求回答细节信息的题目，考生则要先读问题，确定寻找目标，再记住与所需信息有关的关键词，然后快速移动眼球，发现与信息相关的关键词在文中的位置，阅读上下文，就会找到所需内容。用这种方法来寻找细节信息，回答关于细节信息的问题，会大大提高答题速度，为完成其他类型的题目争取更多的时间。

1.2 寻读技巧专项训练

基本上每个人都会查词典，但你有没有想过，学会查词典就相当于掌握了寻读这个快捷提取信息的技巧。寻读本身是一种学习的技能；把它用在阅读考试中，它就变成了阅读技能；用在生活和工作中，它又成为了生活和工作技能。

请看查词典的步骤：第一，先确定目标（即要查哪个单词），譬如查 flu 这个单词；第二，根据字母顺序查到这个单词的首字母 f 在词典中的位置；第三，再根据字母顺序查到这个词在哪一页。若在页眉上查到了 flub（如下图所示），你会推断出 flu 必然就在这一页。这时候，快速移动眼球，很快就会发现 flu 是在该页右下角的倒数第二个词条。你是不会从这一页的左上角开始一行一行地读，慢慢地读到右下角才发现 flu 这个词条的，因为 flu 是单个的孤立信息，与别的词条不发生横向联系。因此要通过眼睛的快速搜寻，立刻定位，这就是寻读。

热身练习

查阅下图，回答问题。

flop /flɑp/ *n* [U] • *He fell with a flop* (= he dropped heavily) *on the bed.*

flop FAILURE /flɑp/ *n* [C usually sing] *infml* a failure • *The movie was a complete flop.*

flop /flɑp/ *v* [I] **-pp-** • *Her first book flopped, but her second became a bestseller.*

flophouse /ˈflɑp·hɑʊs/ *n* [C] *pl* **flophouses** /ˈflɑp,hɑʊ·zəz, -səz/ a cheap, usually dirty, hotel • *That area of Manhattan used to be full of flophouses.*

floppy /ˈflɑp·i/ *adj* soft and easily bent; not able to maintain a firm shape or position • *a floppy hat* ◦ *a dog with big, floppy ears* • A **floppy disk** is a round piece of plastic that can bend which is protected by a plastic cover and used to store computer information.

flora /ˈflɔːr·ə, ˈfloʊr·ə/ *n* [U] *specialized* all the plants of a particular area or period of time • *the flora of the Hawaiian Islands* • Compare FAUNA.

floral /ˈflɔːr·əl, ˈfloʊr·əl/ *adj* made of flowers, or decorated with a flowery pattern • *a floral display* ◦ *floral curtains/wallpaper*

florid RED /ˈflɔːr·əd, ˈflɑr·əd/ *adj slightly fml* (of a person's face) too red, esp. in a way that is unhealthy • *a florid complexion*

florid DECORATED /ˈflɔːr·əd, ˈflɑr·əd/ *adj* with too much decoration or detail • *a florid architectural style* ◦ *florid prose/speech*

florist /ˈflɔːr·əst, ˈflɑr-/ *n* [C] a person who sells cut flowers and plants for inside the house

floss /flɑs, flɔːs/ *v* [T] to clean between (your teeth) using **dental floss** (= thin thread made especially for this purpose)

floss /flɑs, flɔːs/ *n* [C/U] **dental floss**, see at DENTAL

flotilla /floʊˈtɪl·ə/ *n* [C] a large group of boats or small ships, esp. military ships

flounce /flɑʊns/ *v* [I always + adv/prep] to walk quickly with large noticeable movements, esp. to attract attention or show that you are angry • *"Don't expect any help from me!" she said, as she flounced out of the room.*

flounder MOVE AWKWARDLY /ˈflɑʊn·dər/ *v* [I] to move awkwardly or to be in an awkward or difficult situation • *She floundered around in the water.* ◦ *He lost the next page of his speech and floundered for a few seconds.* ◦ *His business was flourishing, but his marriage was floundering.*

flounder FISH /ˈflɑʊn·dər/ *n* [C/U] *pl* **flounder** a flat fish that is used as food

flour /flɑʊr/ *n* [U] powder made from grain, esp. wheat, used for making bread, cakes, pasta, pastry, etc. • *wheat/rye flour* ◦ *three cups of flour*

flour /flɑʊr/ *v* [T] to put a thin layer of flour on (something) • *Flour the board, then roll out the dough.*

flourish SUCCEED /ˈflɜr·ɪʃ/ *v* [I] to grow or develop successfully • *Parts of the city continue to flourish.* ◦ *This is the perfect environment for our company to flourish and expand in.*

flourish WAVE /ˈflɜr·ɪʃ/ *v* [T] to move (something) in your hand in order to make people look at it • *She ran up to her father, flourishing her diploma.*

flourish /ˈflɜr·ɪʃ/ *n* [C] • *I pulled into the driveway with a flourish* (= a noticeable movement).

flout /flɑʊt/ *v* [T] to intentionally disobey (a rule or law), or to intentionally avoid (behavior that is usual or expected) • *They think they can flout the law and get away with it.* ◦ *He conducted business in his pajamas to flout convention.*

flow /floʊ/ *v* [I] (esp. of liquids, gases, or electricity) to move in one direction, esp. continuously and easily • *Air flows over an aircraft's wing faster than it flows under it.* ◦ *Lava from the volcano was flowing down the hillside.* ◦ *An electrical current flows from positive to negative.* ◦ *Many rivers flow into the Pacific Ocean.* ◦ *With fewer cars on the roads, traffic is flowing* (= moving forward) *more smoothly than usual.* • Something can be said to flow if it hangs down loosely and attractively: *Her long, red hair flowed down over shoulders.* ◦ (*fig.*) *My thoughts flow more easily* (= I can think more easily) *if I work on a word processor.*

flow /floʊ/ *n* [C usually sing] • *This drug increases the flow of blood to the heart.* ◦ (*fig.*) *Music interrupted the flow of the conversation* (= the regular exchange between speakers).

flower /ˈflɑʊ·ər, flɑʊr/ *n* [C] the part of a plant that is often brightly colored and sometimes has a pleasant smell, or a plant that grows these parts • *to cut/gather/pick flowers* ◦ *a bunch/bouquet/vase of flowers* ◦ *These flowers bloom in the late spring.* • A **flowerbed** is an area of ground or part of a garden where flowers are planted. • A **flowerpot** is a container usually made of clay or plastic in which a plant is grown. • The related adjective is FLORAL.

flower /ˈflɑʊ·ər, flɑʊr/ *v* [I] • *Our shrubs flower* (= produce flowers) *in late summer.*

flowered /ˈflɑʊ·ərd, flɑʊrd/ *adj* decorated with pictures of flowers • *flowered curtains* ◦ *a flowered dress*

flowery /ˈflɑʊ·ə·ri, ˈflɑʊr·i/ *adj* covered with pictures of flowers • *a flowery blouse* • (*disapproving*) If a speech or writing style is flowery, it uses too many complicated or unusual words or phrases.

flown /floʊn/ *past participle of* FLY

flu /fluː/, *esp. medical* **influenza** /,ɪn·fluːˈen·zə/ *n* [U] an infectious illness like a very bad cold that also causes a fever • *Robby has a bad case of the flu.*

flub /flʌb/ *v* [I/T] **-bb-** *infml* to fail or make a mistake, esp. when performing • *He really flubbed badly by not catching the ball.* [I] ◦ *Sheila flubbed her lines in the second act.* [T]

(From *Cambridge Dictionary of American English*)

(1) What word is "flu" short for? ________

(2) What is the simple past form of the verb "flow"? ________

(3) "Flown" is the past participle (过去分词) of ________. A flow B fly C flee

(4) Flour is made from ________. A seeds B flowers C vegetables D grain

(5) What is a "flophouse"? ________

(6) Is "flowery" a noun or an adjective? ________

(7) Can "flounder" be used as a verb? If yes, what does it mean? ________

(8) As a verb, "flourish" has got two meanings. Find them out. ________

(9) Can "flour" be used as a verb? If yes, what does it mean? ________

(10) Can "flower" be used as a verb? If yes, what does it mean? ________

【参考答案】

(1) Influenza. (2) Flowed. (3) B (4) D (5) A cheap, usually dirty, hotel.
(6) An adjective. (7) Yes. To move awkwardly or to be in an awkward or difficult situation.
(8) To grow or develop successfully; to move (something) in your hand in order to make people look at it. (9) Yes. To put a thin layer of flour on (something). (10) Yes. To produce flowers.

1.2.1 杂志信息查询

在平时阅读杂志的时候，读者要快速决定在本期杂志中选择读哪篇文章和重点提取什么信息，因此也要用到寻读这一技巧。在雅思培训类试题中，就有类似的测试。使用寻读技巧，回答下面的问题。

要点：先仔细读问题，换言之，先确定寻读目标，再移动眼球搜寻，快速定位，找出答案。

(1) If you want to know something about finance, where might you begin your reading? ________

(2) Where could you find information on the new fuels from the farm? ________

(3) Where would you focus on to find something about China? ________

(4) On which page can you read about business? ________

(5) On which page can you begin to read about terrorists? ________

(6) Where could you find the information on the American affairs? ________

(7) If you want to read the article *A European Sahara*, on which page can you begin to read it? ________

(8) If you want to know something new in life, where would you focus on to find it? ________

(9) On which page is the main article in the magazine? ________

【参考答案】

(1) Page 40. (2) Page 42. (3) Page 30. (4) Page 36. (5) Page 14.
(6) Page 24. (7) Page 18. (8) Page 57. (9) Page 42.

Top of the Week

Newsweek

Fuels From The Farm

With the price of oil skyrocketing and new technologies coming on-stream, biofuels are posing **the first real threat** to petroleum. **Page 42**

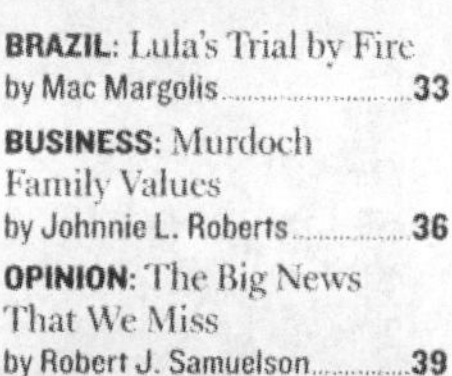

STILL SHINING. Neil Diamond returns with raw songwriting

DEADLY: Police nab several suspects in the London attacks

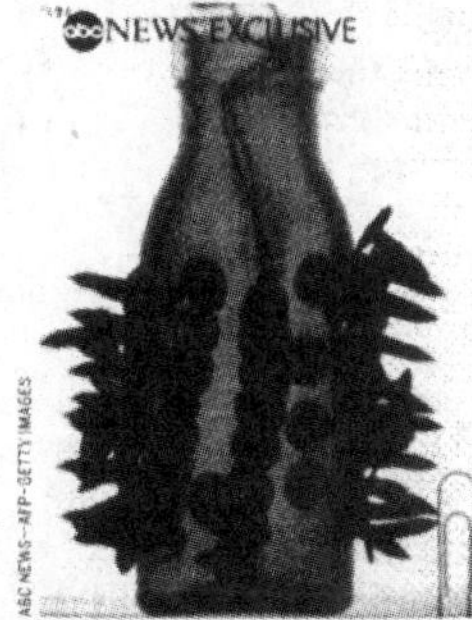

COVER: Photo illustration by NEWSWEEK. Photographs by Getty Images.

(From *Newsweek*, August 8, 2005)

运用寻读技巧回答下列问题。在下面《时代》杂志的目录页上，找出问题中的信息出现在哪一页的文章中。

30 Everyone knows chubbiness is bad for your health, but dropping pounds alone won't necessarily fix things

TIME

August 8, 2005

Vol. 166, No. 6

COVER: *Photograph by Photonica/Getty Images*

18 ▲ Thailand's troubled south looks and feels like a war zone

26 Nervous days for the U.S. space program

(From *Time,* August 8, 2005)

(1) On which page is the main article in the magazine? ________

(2) If you want to know the readers' response, which page should you turn to? ________

(3) If you want to know something about the shuttle *Discovery*, on which page should you find it? ________

(4) If you are concerned about Thailand's troubled south, which page would you read? ________

(5) Which page would you read to find the information on London bombings? ________

【参考答案】

(1) Page 30.　　(2) Page 6.　　(3) Page 26.　　(4) Page 18.　　(5) Page 24.

1.2.2 租售房源信息查询

在国外留学或移民，第一个要解决的就是住宿问题。找房子最好的方式之一是看报纸上的租房和售房广告，这时就可以用到寻读技巧。具体步骤如下：先确定自己的需求，如地点、租金、房型、居住环境、附近交通及购物情况等，然后用寻读技巧在报纸广告栏快速搜寻自己需要的房子，再进行比较，做出取舍。从各类广告中提取所需信息是雅思培训类阅读测试的重点之一，很有必要进行重点训练。

看下面的广告，回答问题。

(1) You want to find a flat in Kensington, which company should you contact with and how?

____

(2) You can only pay about 400 pounds a week for rent, in which ad(s) can you find the suitable flat?

____

(3) If you want a one-bedroom furnished apartment, which ad should you read?

____

(4) You want your flat with the river view of the Thames and all the conveniences of the city, which ad should you read?

____

(5) For more rental information, which website should you visit?

____

【参考答案】

(1) Rickman Properties; call 020 7937 9777, or visit www.rickmanproperties.co.uk.

(2) Ads 5 and 6. (3) Ad 2. (4) Ad 6. (5) primelocation.com

1.2.3 广告招聘信息查询

找工作的主要渠道之一是看报纸上的招聘广告。要迅速选定一个适合自己的工作，其要点是：先看自身条件，再看招聘单位的要求，二者要匹配才行。要想在繁多的工作信息中找到适合自己的工作，用寻读这一技巧最节省时间。

看下面的广告，回答问题。

①

A Beauty and Health Corporate is looking for

Analyst Programmer/Programmer

for its POS system. Details of the requirements and responsibilities for the post are given as below:

- Higher Diploma / Degree in Computing Studies or equivalent
- Must have minimum 2 years working experience in Microsoft .NET C#, Crystal Report and MSSQL
- Must possess good knowledge in database concepts and Object Oriented Concepts
- Familiar with Data migration
- Practical programming experience in POS development will be advantage
- Responsible for system development maintenance and user support
- Candidate with less experience will be considered as Programmer

Interested parties please e-mail resume to **admin.recruit@gmail.com**

Winsor (H.K.) Ltd.

②

We are inviting high caliber candidates for the following position:

Estate Manager (Maintenance) [Ref: EM(M)]

(1) A practising member of one of the following professional institutions:
- The HK Institute of Surveyors (Building Division);
- The Royal Institution of Chartered Surveyors (Building Division);
- The HK Institute of Architects;
- The Royal Institution of British Architects;
- The Institute of Civil Engineers;
- The Institute of Structural Engineers;
- The HK Institution of Engineers (Civil, Structural, Geotechnical, Building Services, Electrical and Mechanical Disciplines);
- The Chartered Institution of Building Services Engineers;
- The Institution of Electrical Engineers;
- The Institution of Mechanical Engineers, and

(2) A minimum of 5 years' post qualification experience in building maintenance

Immediate available. Interested parties, pls. send resume with expected salary to **Kong Shum Union Property Management Co., Ltd., PO Box No. 86312, Gillies Avenue Post Office, Kln.** or by e-mail to: **admin2@kongshum.com.hk**.

(All personal data collected will be used for recruitment purpose only.)

③

Inside Sales Account Manager
(Shanghai-based, Cisco Products)

Vision-X, Inc. is now hiring Inside Sales Managers(ISAM) targeting markets in Hong Kong. ISAM will close sale and develop revenue through telephone contact with end users, and partner with CISCO field sales to achieve revenue targets within a given territory in Hong Kong.

Job location is Shanghai. Company Websites: www.vxiusa.com

Requirements:
- College degree or equivalent
- Native Hong Kong resident a must
- 2-4 years' sales experience
- Solid knowledge of computer hardware and network
- Excellent negotiation and communication skills
- Fluent Cantonese, Mandarin and English

Contact information:
Email: vxihr@vxichina.com
Add: Fushan Rd 455 Rd. 7th Floor
Pudong District, Shanghai 200122 Tel: 86-21-50544518

④

Established CPA firm looking for high caliber candidates for the following posts:-

CLERK
- With or without working experience
- Knowledge in accountancy would be an advantage
- Selected candidates will work under the CPA firm or its related companies

AUDIT INTERMEDIATE
- University Graduate in Accountancy and relevant audit experience
- Knowledge of accounting software preferred

Please apply with full resume, expected salary and recent photo to **504 - 505 Dominion Centre, 43-59 Queen's Road East, Hong Kong** or e-mail to: **denise.chu@lycf.com.hk**

⑤

Hon Wah Middle School

Our school is a DSS Secondary School. We are now looking for **Native English Teacher (NET) and English Language Teacher** to join our team in September 2005.

Application should include a covering letter indicating the position applied for and full resume and a one-page personal statement of education philosophy. **Post by mail before 5 August 2005 to the Principal, Hon Wah Middle School, 10 Ching Lin Terrace, West Point, H.K. or by fax 28176453.**

(Personal data collected will be used for recruitment purpose only.)

⑥

THE HONG KONG INSTITUTE OF BANK

Executive Officer (Beijing) / Executive Officer (Hong Kong
- University Graduate with AHKIB is preferred
- 5-8 years working experience in a bank or financial institution
- Project management exposure
- Experience in training management is preferred
- Fluent spoken English and Putonghua
- Good writing skill in both English and Chinese
- Excellent communication and networking skill

The position will be responsible for the Institute's development and training activities. F Executive Officer (China), travel to the Mainland is required.

Executive Assistant / Senior Secretary
- University graduate with 3 or more years of experience in supporting exec
- Fluent spoken English and Putonghua
- Good writing skill in both English and Chinese
- Excellent presentation and communication skill

The position will responsible for composing memos and documents for meeting an work closely with the CEO and Management office on corporate affairs and business re

Please send your resume with expected salary to **Email: hkib@hkib.org / Fa**

Part-Time Assistant Wanted

⑦
- Fluent Cantonese & English
- Legal knowledge / Gurkha training preferred
- Any Nationality guard / retired police welcome

Fax resume to **S.C. Mgt Service Ltd** at **2366 8636** / or call **2359 9550**.

REQUIRED English Speaking Office Assistant at TST pref. with working exp. computer literate resume at fax 23675125 (Feng Mao Ltd)

⑧

Lucky Plastic Factory Ltd. (ZAPTOYS) - A Global Toys Manufacturer in TST East invites applicants for the following post:-

ACCOUNTANT
- University graduate in Accounting or relevant Degree
- Must have at least 5 years solid experience in manufacturing & cost accounting & at least 2 years in administrative and human resources
- Experience & knowledge in PRC accounting practice, taxation standards preferred
- Proactive with excellent interpersonal, leadership, organizational & communication skills
- Fluent in both written / spoken English & Mandarin

Responsibilities:-
- Manage daily accounting, administrative & HR activities
- Develop & implement procedures & internal control systems
- Prepare & control company's budget
- Prepare effective management reports
- Frequent travel to Shenzhen is required

Interested parties, please send full resume with expected salary by fax: **2312-3829** or by email to **recruit@zaptoy.com** for the attention to The HR Manager.

(Personal data collected for recruitment purpose only)

⑨

Teachers are required for next academic term. Applicants should possess relevant qualification degrees, CM/GM. Teachers required:-

1) Business Studies & Economics (AS/AL)
2) English & Use of English (AS level)

Employment term: september 2005 to the end of Easter 2006, with possibility of renewal. Interested parties please fax resume to **2838 6141** / email to **rhsbss@hotmail.com.**

Our reg. No. E.D.1/21151/59. (Data collected will be used for recruitment purpose only)

⑩

GMP Project Manager

Requirement by a pharm. related group, Applicants should have experience in setting up a GMP Plant, good remuneration. Please send resume to **admin.recruit@gmail.com** .

Winsor (H.K.) Ltd.

⑪

A Hong Kong - Beijing textile joi requires a self motivated, hones

SALES EXECUTI

The right candidate should hav
- 5 years experience in sale of denim with proven sales recor
- preferably be a textile graduate Hong Kong Polytechnic Unive recognised textile college. This not a pre-requisite for the pos
- good command of English and
- you will be stationed in Hong will be required to make occas to our factory in Beijing.

Attractive salary will be offered t candidate, Please send to **Box Post** for application form.

⑫

Health Food Production
- Strong sense and solid knowledg industries, diploma holder in food preferred.
- Independent, energetic, creative wi communication and interpersonal q
- Motivated and not afraid of hardwork to travel to Beijing.
- Previous experience in food prod good command of English and Chine an advantage.

Please send resume to **admin.recruit@**

Winsor (H.K.) Ltd.

⑬

Two English Spe Personal Assist

needed by boss who works at hom familiar with PC & Windows, Intere please e-mail resume and expecte **admin.recruit@gmail.com.**

Winsor (H.K.) Ltd.

⑭

Marketing Off

A large retail health product corp above vacancies. Applicants sh related experience. Good remune bonus.

Interested parties please e-mail r expected salary to **admin.recruit@ Winsor (H.K.) Ltd.**

Suppose you have got a degree in computer science and 3 years' work experience in computer programming, which ad would you choose to read in detail?

【参考答案】

The first ad.

1.2.4 税收信息查询

在国外生活和工作，同样要考虑缴纳个人所得税（income tax）的问题。用寻读技巧快速提取有关税收的信息是非常有效的。阅读下面的信息，回答问题。

How To Get California Tax Information

In Person

Addresses of Franchise Tax Board district offices are shown below. You can get information, California tax forms, and you can resolve problems on your account. Our district offices are open Monday through Friday from 8:00 a.m. to 5:00 p.m.

District Offices	Address
Bakersfield	1430 Truxtun Avenue
El Monte	9660 Flair Drive
Fresno	2550 Mariposa Street
Long Beach	245 West Broadway
Los Angeles	Office to be relocated*
Oakland	1970 Broadway
Sacramento	1912 I Street
San Bernardino	215 North D Street
San Diego	Office to be relocated*
San Francisco	345 Larkin Street
San Jose	96 North Third Street
Santa Ana	600 West Santa Ana Blvd.
Santa Barbara	360 South Hope Avenue
Santa Rosa	50 D Street
Stockton	31 East Channel Street
Van Nuys	6150 Van Nuys Blvd.

*For address information, call our F.A.S.T. toll-free phone number at 1-800-338-0505 (enter code 214 after you reach the number).

Letters

We can serve you quickly if you call us or visit a district office for information to complete your California income tax return, or to find out about your tax refund. However, you may want to write to us if you are replying to a notice we sent you, or to get a reply in writing.

If you write to us, be sure to include your social security number and your daytime and evening telephone numbers in your letter. Send your letter to:

Franchise Tax Board
P.O. Box 942840
Sacramento, CA 94240-0040

We will acknowledge your letter within six to eight weeks. In some cases, we may need to call you for additional information.

Your Rights As A Taxpayer

Our goal at the Franchise Tax Board is to make certain that your rights are protected, so that you will have the highest confidence in the integrity, efficiency and fairness of our state tax system. FTB Pub. 4058, California Taxpayers' Bill of Rights, includes information on your rights as a California taxpayer, the Taxpayers' Rights Advocate Program and how you can request written advice from the Franchise Tax Board on whether a particular transaction is taxable. You can order FTB Pub. 4058 by writing or calling the Franchise Tax Board.

Where To Get Income Tax Forms

In person – You can get California tax forms at the Franchise Tax Board district offices listed at left. Most libraries, post offices and banks also provide free California tax booklets during the filing season. Many libraries and some quick print businesses have copies of forms and schedules for you to photocopy (you may have to pay a nominal fee). Note that employees at libraries, post offices, banks and quick print businesses cannot provide tax information or assistance.

By phone – For 1990 California tax forms, call our toll-free number listed under 'F.A.S.T.' Toll-Free Phone Service." For prior year California tax forms, call our toll-free number listed under "Regular Toll-Free Phone Service."

By mail – Use the order blank below to request forms. Print or type your name and address on the lines below. On the back of the order blank, check the boxes for those forms you need. We will send you two copies of each tax form and one copy of each set of instructions you order. Please allow two weeks to receive your order. Address your envelope to:

Franchise Tax Board
Tax Forms Request Unit
P.O. Box 942840
Sacramento, CA 94240-0070

- - - - - - - - - - - - - - - - - - - -

Franchise Tax Board
Tax Forms Request
P.O. Box 942840
Sacramento, CA 94240-0070

Name ____________________

Number and street ____________________

City or town, State and ZIP code ____________________

FORMS REQUEST

Enter your name and address on this label. It will be used to speed your order for forms to you.

(1) You live in San Jose and want to get tax information in person, where and when would you go to get it?

____

(2) How many ways can you use to get tax information?

____

(3) Where can you get income tax forms in person?

____

【参考答案】

(1) San Jose district office, 96 North Third Street; Monday through Friday from 8:00 a.m. to 5:00 p.m.

(2) Three (in person, by phone, or by mail).

(3) Get forms from Franchise Tax Board district offices, most libraries, post offices and banks, or photocopy them at libraries and some quick print businesses.

1.2.5 天气信息查询

在日常生活中，可以从报纸上的天气预报栏中了解到本地和国内其他地区的天气情况。在这种情况下，寻读技巧就能派上用场了。下页是《泰晤士报》2005 年 8 月 5 日星期五的天气预报栏，阅读并回答下面的问题。

(1) What was the weather like in southeast England on August 5?

____

(2) What was the weather like in the U.K. on August 5?

____

Weather Forecast, Aug. 5, 2005

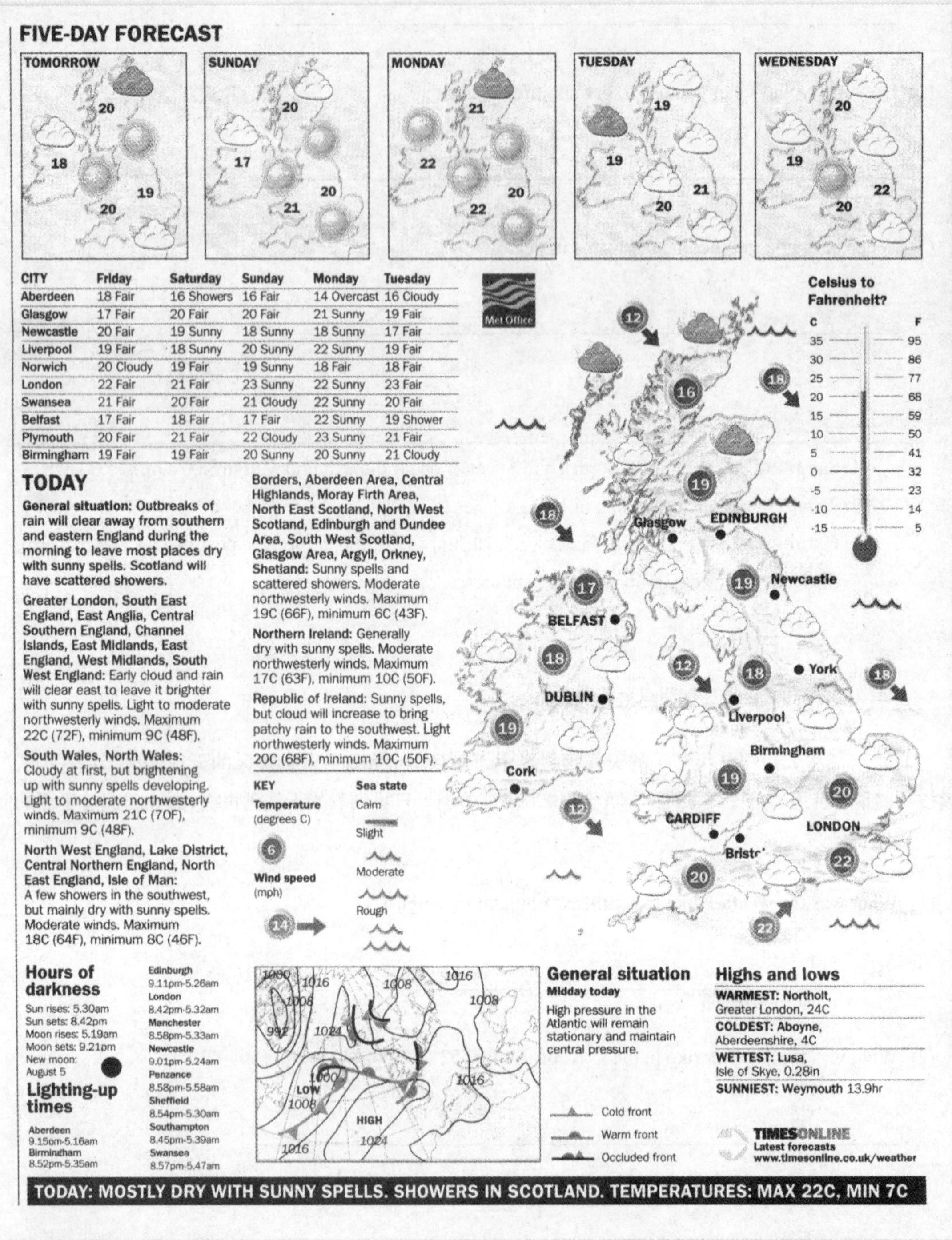

FIVE-DAY FORECAST

CITY	Friday	Saturday	Sunday	Monday	Tuesday
Aberdeen	18 Fair	16 Showers	16 Fair	14 Overcast	16 Cloudy
Glasgow	17 Fair	20 Fair	20 Fair	21 Sunny	19 Fair
Newcastle	20 Fair	19 Sunny	18 Sunny	18 Sunny	17 Fair
Liverpool	19 Fair	18 Sunny	20 Sunny	22 Sunny	19 Fair
Norwich	20 Cloudy	19 Fair	19 Sunny	18 Fair	18 Fair
London	22 Fair	21 Fair	23 Sunny	22 Sunny	23 Fair
Swansea	21 Fair	20 Fair	21 Cloudy	22 Sunny	20 Fair
Belfast	17 Fair	18 Fair	17 Fair	22 Sunny	19 Shower
Plymouth	20 Fair	21 Fair	22 Cloudy	23 Sunny	21 Fair
Birmingham	19 Fair	19 Fair	20 Sunny	20 Sunny	21 Cloudy

TODAY

General situation: Outbreaks of rain will clear away from southern and eastern England during the morning to leave most places dry with sunny spells. Scotland will have scattered showers.

Greater London, South East England, East Anglia, Central Southern England, Channel Islands, East Midlands, East England, West Midlands, South West England: Early cloud and rain will clear east to leave it brighter with sunny spells. Light to moderate northwesterly winds. Maximum 22C (72F), minimum 9C (48F).

South Wales, North Wales: Cloudy at first, but brightening up with sunny spells developing. Light to moderate northwesterly winds. Maximum 21C (70F), minimum 9C (48F).

North West England, Lake District, Central Northern England, North East England, Isle of Man: A few showers in the southwest, but mainly dry with sunny spells. Moderate winds. Maximum 18C (64F), minimum 8C (46F).

Borders, Aberdeen Area, Central Highlands, Moray Firth Area, North East Scotland, North West Scotland, Edinburgh and Dundee Area, South West Scotland, Glasgow Area, Argyll, Orkney, Shetland: Sunny spells and scattered showers. Moderate northwesterly winds. Maximum 19C (66F), minimum 6C (43F).

Northern Ireland: Generally dry with sunny spells. Moderate northwesterly winds. Maximum 17C (63F), minimum 10C (50F).

Republic of Ireland: Sunny spells, but cloud will increase to bring patchy rain to the southwest. Light northwesterly winds. Maximum 20C (68F), minimum 10C (50F).

KEY

Hours of darkness

Sun rises: 5.30am
Sun sets: 8.42pm
Moon rises: 5.19am
Moon sets: 9.21pm
New moon: August 5

Lighting-up times

Aberdeen 9.15pm-5.16am
Birmingham 8.52pm-5.35am
Edinburgh 9.11pm-5.26am
London 8.42pm-5.32am
Manchester 8.58pm-5.33am
Newcastle 9.01pm-5.24am
Penzance 8.58pm-5.58am
Sheffield 8.54pm-5.30am
Southampton 8.45pm-5.39am
Swansea 8.57pm-5.47am

General situation

Midday today

High pressure in the Atlantic will remain stationary and maintain central pressure.

Cold front
Warm front
Occluded front

Highs and lows

WARMEST: Northolt, Greater London, 24C

COLDEST: Aboyne, Aberdeenshire, 4C

WETTEST: Lusa, Isle of Skye, 0.28in

SUNNIEST: Weymouth 13.9hr

TIMESONLINE
Latest forecasts
www.timesonline.co.uk/weather

TODAY: MOSTLY DRY WITH SUNNY SPELLS. SHOWERS IN SCOTLAND. TEMPERATURES: MAX 22C, MIN 7C

【参考答案】

(1) Early cloud and rain will clear east to leave it brighter with sunny spells. Light to moderate northwesterly winds. Temperatures: Max 22 °C, Min 9 °C.

(2) Mostly dry with sunny spells. Showers in Scotland. Temperatures: Max 22 °C, Min 7 °C.

在雅思阅读测试中，有些题目要求考生从原文中迅速提取信息，完成各种表格(适用于A类和G类考生)。试从上图的天气预报中找出信息，完成下面的表格。

City	Friday	Saturday	Sunday	Monday	Tuesday	Hours of darkness & lighting-up times
London	22 Fair				23 Fair	8:42 pm—5:32 am
Aberdeen		16 Showers				
Newcastle			18 Sunny			
Swansea				22 Sunny		

【参考答案】

City	Friday	Saturday	Sunday	Monday	Tuesday	Hours of darkness & lighting-up times
London	22 Fair	21 Fair	23 Sunny	22 Sunny	23 Fair	8:42 pm—5:32 am
Aberdeen	18 Fair	16 Showers	16 Fair	14 Overcast	16 Cloudy	9:15 pm—5:16 am
Newcastle	20 Fair	19 Sunny	18 Sunny	18 Sunny	17 Fair	9:01 pm—5:24 am
Swansea	21 Fair	20 Fair	21 Cloudy	22 Sunny	20 Fair	8:57 pm—5:47 am

1.2.6 电话信息查询

在国外旅游，要事先了解某个旅游景点的吃、住、行和景点介绍等信息，最便捷的方法之一就是打电话。电话号码及相关信息通常会印在旅游杂志和免费的小册子上，这些旅游指南在车站和机场很容易找到。试用寻读技巧在下面的一页杂志中找出相关旅游景点的电话。

(1) Niagara County — Niagara Falls: ____________________

(2) Top of the Falls Restaurant: ____________________

(3) The Hillside Mansion and Spa: ____________________

(4) Four Season Recreation: ____________________

(5) Edgewood Resort: ____________________

(6) Watertown Chamber of Commerce: ____________________

READER'S RESPONSE

So much to see & do along the Seaway Trail . . . Great places to stay, dine, shop and tour — These fine businesses can provide you with additional information for your next visit to our region. Give them a call — they can answer any questions you may have. See their advertisements throughout Journey; the page numbers are marked for your convenience.

CHAUTAUQUA COUNTY

Chautauqua-Allegheny Region: Lakes, trails, museums, wineries, antiques, lighthouses, skiing, cultural events and more! Call (716) 753-4304, (716) 945-2034, 1-800-242-ILNY • *pg. 5*

Sheraton Harborfront Inn: On Lake Erie in Chautauqua Wine Country. Restaurant, lounge, indoor and outdoor pools, fitness center, fishing charters. (716) 366-8350 • *pg. 4*

ERIE COUNTY

Buffalo-Erie County: a sophisticated, charming, attractive city offering limitless opportunity to enjoy world class dining, entertainment, shopping and professional sports. (NYS) 800-458-8969/ (USA) 800-235-6979 • *pg. 8*

NIAGARA COUNTY

Ames Department Stores: Located throughout New York State with low discount prices for family, home and car. • *pg. 32*

Artpark - Historic Lewiston: NY State Park for visual and performing arts. Live theater, workshops, resident artists. (716) 745-3377; Winter: (716) 754-9001 • *pg. 19*

Maid of the Mist: Sail into the mist of Niagara Falls! Book your tour on the unforgettable Maid of the Mist. (716) 284-8897 • *pg. 17*

Niagara County - Niagara Falls: The Falls, Aquarium, Old Fort Niagara, Power Project, Erie Barge Canal, Festival of Lights, Parks, Boating, Fishing & More! 1-800-338-7890 • *pg. 10*

Niagara County Sportfishing: Lake Ontario's finest four seasons fishery. Spring/summer/fall salmon; year-round trout, bass, muskie, & walleye. Info: 1-800-338-7890; Hotline: (716) 433-5606 • *pg. 25*

Niagara Power Project: Visit the Power Authority's Visitor Center in Niagara Falls, NY. Minutes from the Falls & Historic Lewiston. Free. (716) 285-3211 • *pg. 2*

Summit Park Mall: The Summit Park Mall is Niagara County's largest shopping center...featuring 100 stores and services including a food court. • *pg. 20*

The Tonawandas on the Canal & River: Herschell Carrousel Museum, Long Homestead, Riviera Theater, Canal Fest '90, cruises, boat racing. (716) 692-5120 • *pg. 13 & 14*

Top of the Falls Restaurant: The only American restaurant overlooking Niagara Falls. Enjoy a spectacular view from any table. (716) 285-3311 • *pg. 17*

WHLD: 1270 AM — The Sound of the Falls. The Best in Big Band, Contemporary and Ethnic Music! • *pg. 15*

ORLEANS COUNTY

Orleans County: "Home of the King" Salmon, Cobblestone Museum and "Miss Apple Grove" — Mule drawn Erie Canal packet boat tours. (716) 589-7004 Ext. 220 • *pg. 24*

MONROE COUNTY

Rochester "A Welcome Surprise": Museums, Mansions, Music... & More! For more information contact Rochester Visitor's & Convention Bureau. (716) 546-3070 • *pg. 26*

The Hillside Mansion and Spa: Luxury Lodging, fine dining . . . impeccable, historic, breathtaking, secluded. 1-800-544-2249 • *pg. 28*

WAYNE COUNTY

Wayne County, The Place for enjoying the Trail: Water sports, trophy fishing, outdoor sports & events year-round, plus sightseeing, historic sites & more! 800-527-6510 • *pg. 30*

Wayne County Museums: Over 10 museums capture history and culture of Wayne County — from coverlets to lighthouse to old jail. 800-527-6510 • *pg. 31*

CAYUGA COUNTY

Sterling Renaissance Festival: Weekends — July 7 - August 19. Recreation of English Festival c.1585. Entertainment, games, crafts, & unusual foods & merriment for all ages. (315) 947-5783 • *pg. 35*

OSWEGO COUNTY

The Energy Center is a great joint presentation of the NY Power Authority and Niagara Mohawk Power Corporation. For information call (315) 342-4117 • *pg. 2*

Savor the sunsets, sail the seas, ramble along the river, fish near our fort & ***Catch the Excitement of Oswego!*** (315) 342-5600 • Page *pg. 37*

Trophy, Fair and More! *in Oswego County* — including campgrounds, historic sites, museums, exciting events and attractions. 1-800-248-4FUN or 1-800-248-LURE • *pg. 33*

Four Season Recreation. Fishing, x-country skiing, snowmobiling. Call (315) 298-2213 or write: Pulaski/ Eastern Shore Chamber of Commerce, Pulaski, NY 13142 (315) 298-2213 • *pg. 39*

JEFFERSON COUNTY

1000 Islands, 1000 Vacations: boat tours, Boldt Castle, trophy fishing, camping, museums, pageants, festivals, golfing. 1-800-5ISLAND (NYS) OR 1-800-8ISLAND (eastern US) • *pgs. 43, 60, 61 & 70*

Alexandria Bay Chamber of Commerce: Heart of the 1000 Islands! Make Alexandria Bay your vacation spot in 1990. For info, call (315) 482-9531 or (NYS) 800-541-2110 • *pg. 64*

Bonnie Castle Resort: A year round resort, complete facilities — luxury accommodations, riverview dining, night club — complete recreation (NYS) 1-800-521-5514 or (315) 482-4511 • *pg. 69*

Give Cape Vincent a Try for your vacation, fishing trip or permanent home. We are sure you will enjoy it. (315) 654-2495 • *pg. 59*

Clayton, NY: Free 32 page vacation guide. Call: 1-800-252-9806 • *pg. 62-63*

Edgewood Resort: Complete resort with 160 rooms overlooking Alexandria Bay. Waterfront dining and fabulous nightly entertainment in two great lounges. (315) 482-9922 • *pg. 68*

Henderson Harbor: Charter fishing at its best, sailing, marinas, great restaurants, comfortable inns. Rural beauty, friendly people. (315) 938-5521 • *pg. 40*

Madison Barracks: A resort community. You are cordially invited to view our luxury townhouses. An architectural depiction of the War of 1812. (315) 646-2066 • *pg. 44*

Norstar Bank: Over 400 service banks in the northeast. Use our automated teller machine locations. In NYS 1-800-228-1281 • *pg. 36*

Riveredge: Unique 122 room hotel-resort and convention facilities, 60 slip dockage (water, power, telephone, cable tv) all season health facilities. (315) 482-9917 • *pg. 65*

The Salmon Run Mall: Located in Watertown, features over 95 fine shops, restaurants, and services. Phone (315) 788-9210 for information. • *pg. 57*

Shipyard Museum: Celebrating the tradition of antique boating in the 1000 Islands. Annual Boat Show and Auction. (315) 686-4104 • *pg. 58*

Uncle Sam Boat Tours & Thomson Resorts: Lunch, dinner and two-nation tours. Waterfront dining, banquet facilities, and two resorts. • 1-800-ALEX BAY • *pg. 67*

Watertown Chamber of Commerce: Whitewater rafting, historic walking tour, Snowtown USA, Farmers Market, Sci-Tech Center, shopping, restaurants, and more! (315) 788-4400 • *pg. 56*

ST. LAWRENCE COUNTY

Massena: International Community with Bridge to Canada, shopping, Robert Moses Power Project & Visitor's Center. (315) 769-2535 • *pg. 76*

Ogdensburg: International Bridge to Canada, Remington Museum, Marina. Wide selection of restaurants and accommodations. Greater Ogdensburg Chamber of Commerce. (315) 393-3620 • *pg. 72-74*

Come to the Power Authority's St. Lawrence-FDR Project, Massena: Our visitor center offers entertaining exhibits and breathtaking views. FREE ADMISSION. *(315) 764-0226 • pg. 2*

St. Lawrence County: For further information contact St. Lawrence County Chamber of Commerce, Drawer A, Canton, NY 13617 or call (315) 386-4000. *pg. 71*

For great day trips and a look at the scenic Seaway Trail see "Trailscapes" beginning on page 45.

【参考答案】

(1) 1-800-338-7890　(2) (716) 285-3311　(3) 1-800-544-2249

(4) (315) 298-2213　(5) (315) 482-9922　(6) (315) 788-4400

1.2.7 电视节目查询

看电视节目预告来选择想看的电视节目和频道，也要用到寻读技巧。浏览下面的电视节目预告，回答下列电影分别在什么频道和时间播出。

MOVIES

101 HBO	102 CINEMAX	103 STAR MOVIES
6.00 Bad Boys. 1995, Action. Martin Lawrence, Will Smith. **7.50** Funny About Love. 1990, Comedy. Gene Wilder, Christine Lahti. **9.40** Intolerable Cruelty. 2003, Comedy. George Clooney, Catherine Zeta-Jones. **11.20** Scrooged. 1988, Comedy. Bill Murray, Karen Allen. **1.10** Indiana Jones And The Temple Of Doom. 1984, Action. Harrison Ford, Kate Capshaw. **3.15** Moto X Kids. 2004, Family. Bobby Preston, Brandon Alexander. **4.40** Suspect. 1987, Thriller. Cher, Dennis Quaid. **6.45** The Challenge. 2003, Family. Ashley Olsen, Mary Kate Olsen	**6.00** The Birds II: Land's End. 1994, Horror. Brad Johnson, Chelsea Field. **7.30** Nothing In Common. 1986, Comedy. Tom Hanks, Jackie Gleason. **9.30** Billy Madison. 1995, Comedy. Adam Sandler, Darren McGavin. **11.15** Altered Species. 2001, Thriller. Guy Vieg, Allen Lee Haff. **12.45** Everything That Rises. 1998, Drama. Dennis Quaid, Bruce McGill. **2.30** Torn Curtain. 1966, Thriller. Paul Newman, Julie Andrews. **4.45** Nuts. 1987, Drama. Barbra Streisand, Richard Dreyfuss. **6.45** Caught In The Headlights. 2004, Action. Erika Eliniak, Stacy Keach.	**6.20** The Kid Stays In The Picture. 2002, Documentary. Robert Evans, Woody Allen. **7.55** Twelve Days Of Christmas Eve. 2004, Comedy. Steven Weber, Molly Shannon. **9.30** Drumline. 2002, Comedy. Nick Cannon, Orlando Jones. **11.30** The Chamber. 1996, Thriller. Chris O'Donnell, Gene Hackman. **1.30** Sonny. 2002, Crime. James Franco, Brenda Blethyn. **3.15** Air Rage. 2001, Action. Ice-T, Cyril O'Reilly. **5.00** Baby For Sale. 2004, Drama. Dana Delaney, Hart Bochner. **6.45** Die Another Day. 2002, Action. Pierce Brosnan, Halle Berry.
8.20 Dragonheart. 1996, Fantasy. Dennis Quaid, David Thewlis. A dragonslayer teams up with the last remaining dragon to defeat an evil king.	**8.15** The Making Of Battlestar Galactica.	
10.00 Sex And The City: A Farewell. **10.55** What A Girl Wants. 2003, Comedy. Amanda Bynes, Colin Firth, Kelly Preston, Jonathan Pryce. An American girl travels to Britain to be reunited with her father.	**9.00** The Tuxedo. 2002, Sci-fi. Jackie Chan, Jennifer Love Hewitt. A chauffeur poses as a secret agent with the assistance of a special gadget-laden suit. **10.40** The Birds II: Land's End. 1994, Horror. Brad Johnson, Chelsea Field, James Naughton.	**9.00** Six Days Seven Nights. 1998, Romance. Harrison Ford, Anne Heche. A pilot and a magazine editor crash-land on an uncharted deserted island. **10.45** Stepmom. 1998, Family. Julia Roberts, Susan Sarandon, Ed Harris. (See highlights)
12.40 Intolerable Cruelty. 2003, Comedy. George Clooney, Catherine Zeta-Jones, Geoffrey Rush, Billy Bob Thornton. **2.20** Mack The Knife. 1990, Crime. Raul Julia, Richard Harris, Julie Walters. **4.20** Dragonheart. 1996, Fantasy. Dennis Quaid, David Thewlis, Peter Postlethwaite.	**12.05** Billy Madison. 1995, Comedy. Adam Sandler, Darren McGavin. **1.30** Everything That Rises. 1998, Drama. Dennis Quaid, Bruce McGill, Meat Loaf. **3.00** Caught In The Headlights. 2004, Action. Erika Eliniak, Stacy Keach, Kim Coates. **4.30** 20 Million Miles To Earth. 1957, Sci-fi. William Hooper.	**12.50** The Chamber. 1996, Thriller. Chris O'Donnell, Gene Hackman, Faye Dunaway. **2.45** Jill Rips. 2000, Thriller. Dolph Lundgren, Danielle Brett. **4.15** Sexual Life. 2005, Drama. Eion Bailey, Elizabeth Banks. **5.45** Die Another Day. 2002, Action. Pierce Brosnan, Halle Berry, Toby Stephens.

(1) *Dragonheart:* ____________________

(2) *Sex and the City:* ____________________

(3) *Stepmom:* ____________________

(4) *Intolerable Cruelty:* ____________________

【参考答案】

(1) HBO; 8:20 and 4:20 (2) HBO; 10:00 (3) Star Movies; 10:45 (4) HBO; 12:40

浏览下面的电视节目预告，找出下列纪录片分别在什么频道和时间播出。

DOCUMENTARIES

	52 NATIONAL GEOGRAPHIC	53 DISCOVERY	54 DISCOVERY T & L
	6.00 Blue Realm. **7.00** Dogs With Jobs. **7.30** Hayden Turner's Wildlife Challenge. **8.00** Wildlife Detectives. **8.30** Hayden Turner's Wildlife Challenge. **9.00** Top Cat. **10.00** The Strange Case Of Peking Man. **11.00** Eternal Enemies. **12.00** Croc Chronicles. **12.30** Planet Wild. **1.00** Deep Jungle. **2.00** Interpol Investigates: Missing Link. **3.00** Air Crash Investigation: Flying Blind. **4.00** The Mafia: The Great Betrayal. **5.00** Tomb Robbers. **6.00** Dogs With Jobs: Zelda, Azili & Amy. **6.30** Hayden Turner's Wildlife Challenge: Wildbeest.	**6.00** Blueprint For Disaster: The Sampoong Collapse. **7.00** Dying To Be Apart. **8.00** Why Intelligence Fails: Unreliable Sources. **9.00** The Ultimate Guide: Dolphins. **10.00** Great Quakes: Mexico City. **11.00** Sphinx – Mystery In Stone. **12.00** Battlefield Detectives: The Gallipoli Disaster. **1.00** Wild South America: Penguin Shores. **2.00** Case Studies In Forensics: Critical Evidence. **3.00** Dying To Be Apart. **4.00** Why Intelligence Fails: Unreliable Sources. **5.00** The Ultimate Guide: Dolphins. **6.00** Deadly Women: Greed.	**6.00** Planet Food. **7.00** Globe Trekker. **8.00** Far Flung Floyd. **8.30** Made To Order. **9.00** Travellers. **10.00** World's 50 Greatest Places. **11.00** World's Sexiest Destinations For Couples. **12.00** Surfing The Menu. **12.30** Floyd Around The Med: France. **1.00** Globe Trekker: Venezuela. **2.00** Travellers: London. **3.00** Meshach Taylor's Hidden Caribbean: Jamaica; Barbados. **4.00** Great Country Inns: Lahaina Inn, Hawaii; Mansion Inn, Pennsylvania. **5.00** Ice Cream Palaces. **6.00** Faking It: Briefcase To Bodyslam.
7PM	**7.00** Africa's Secret Seven. **8.00** Yum Cha.	**7.00** Rides: Rods. **8.00** Genius Sperm Bank.	**7.00** Globe Trekker: Northern Italy. **8.00** Surfing The Menu: Hunter Valley. **8.30** Kylie Kwong – Cooking With Heart & Soul: Shellfish.
9PM	**9.00** Nazi Expedition. [See highlights] **10.00** Air Crash Investigation: Flying On Empty. **11.00** The Mafia: The Godfathers.	**9.00** Reptiles: Turtles – Life In A Shell. **10.00** The Secrets Of Megalightning. **11.00** Human Mutants: The Dangerous Womb.	**9.00** Globe Trekker. **10.00** Made To Order: Fashion Plate. **10.30** A Place In France – Indian Summer. **11.00** Adventure Golf: Florida. **11.30** Travel Gear.
12AM	**12.00** Harem Conspiracy. **1.00** Nazi Expedition. **2.00** Air Crash Investigation: Flying On Empty. **3.00** The Mafia: The Godfathers. **4.00** Harem Conspiracy. **5.00** Yum Cha.	**12.00** Science At The Edge: Breaking Nature's Rules. **1.00** Mythbusters: Barrel Of Bricks. **2.00** Deadly Women: Obsession. **3.00** Rides: Rods. **4.00** Genius Sperm Bank. **5.00** Reptiles: Turtles – Life In A Shell.	**12.00** Surfing The Menu: Hunter Valley. **12.30** Floyd Around The Med: France. **1.00** Globe Trekker: Northern Italy. **2.00** Travellers: London. **3.00** Meshach Taylor's Hidden Caribbean: Jamaica; Barbados. **4.00** Great Country Inns. **5.00** Ice Cream Palaces.

(1) *Africa's Secret Seven:* ____________________

(2) *Genius Sperm Bank:* ____________________

(3) *The Secrets of Megalightning:* ____________________

(4) *The Mafia: The Godfathers:* ____________________

【参考答案】

(1) National Geographic; 7:00 pm
(2) Discovery; 8:00 pm and 4:00 am
(3) Discovery; 10:00 pm
(4) National Geographic; 11:00 pm and 3:00 am

1.2.8 地图信息查询

选择自驾车出游，要先看地图和计划旅程。下列表格是雅思考试的常见题型。看下面的地图，用寻读技巧查出从俄勒冈州（Oregon）的波特兰市（Portland）到下列各城市的公路里程，完成下面的表格。

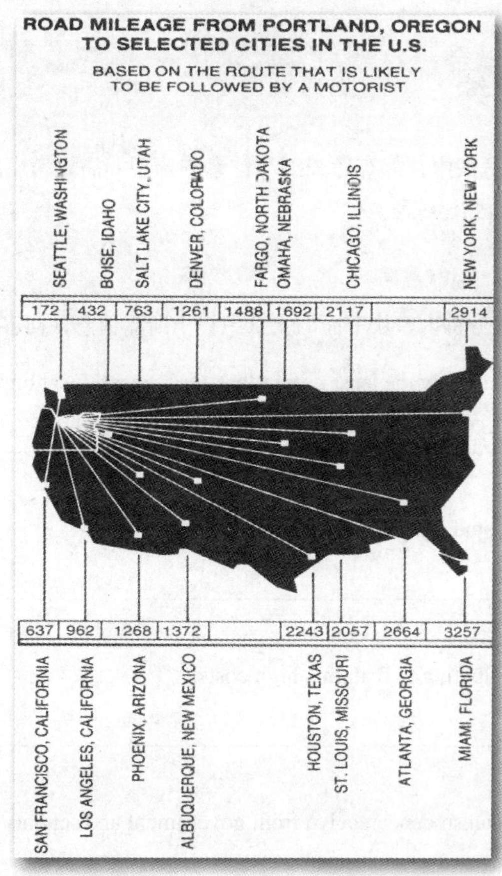

From Portland to	Road mileage
New York	
	1,268
	2,664
Seattle	
Houston	

【参考答案】

From Portland to	Road mileage
New York	2,914
Phoenix	1,268
Atlanta	2,664
Seattle	172
Houston	2,243

1.3 寻读技巧强化训练

在雅思或英语四、六级考试中，都有考查细节信息的题型，需要考生在文章中使用寻读技巧对信息进行快速定位。现在不妨先做做强化练习。

A. 试用寻读技巧，在 1 分钟内，从下面的文章中找出所需信息，回答下列问题。

(1) Which country's students pay the least tuition fees for higher education? How much?

____

(2) How much do British students pay for higher education a year?

____

(3) Give two factors contributing to Britain's high costs.

____

(4) How much do American students receive from government and schools?

____

Overseas study ranked by universities' costs

looking abroad

A RECENT report by the Educational Policy Institute, UK, gave a detailed comparison of international higher education costs. The report was part of the global higher education rankings.

It found that Finnish students pay the least for higher education tuition fees. One year in Finland costs an average of £1,820 pounds (£1=US$1.88). Next comes the Netherlands, where one year costs £1,826. After that comes Sweden, with £2,186. The rest of Europe range from £2,914 to £4,030.

Britain ranks as the third most expensive in the world, after Japan and New Zealand. Japanese students pay an average of £8,900 a year.

British students pay an average of almost £7,000 a year for their education, including tuition and living costs.

A number of factors contribute to Britain's high costs. First of all, there are limited grants (financial support from government and schools). Then the living costs can be very high and there is the large number of students living in London to deal with. It's one of the most expensive cities in the world.

The report also said that British students receive a grant of £597, on average, compared with £275 for Finland. American students receive around £2,120.

THE OBSERVER

【参考答案】

(1) Finnish students; £1,820 per year.　　(2) Almost £7,000.

(3) Limited grants and high living costs.　　(4) Around £2,120.

B. 在1分钟内，运用寻读技巧，从下面的文章中找出所需信息，回答下列问题。

UK graduates' degrees losing value

looking abroad

THE financial value of a university degree in Britain has fallen sharply over the past decade as more graduates enter the job market. This is according to a study by academics at the University of Swansea.

The study shows that graduates can expect to earn ￡150,000 more over the course of their careers than those who do not go to university. However, the figure predicted by the government last year was ￡400,000.

The study found that female graduates benefit more from higher education. On average they earn ￡158,000 more than non-graduates during their working lives, while university-educated men earn ￡142,000 more.

Male arts graduates came bottom in the study, earning less in their careers than those who started work without a degree.

Maths and computing graduates fared best, earning ￡225,000 more on average than non-graduates. The study also found that the university where a student studied and the class of their degree had a significant impact on earnings.

One of the authors of the study said the rate of return was still a real and sizable benefit if one chose the right subject and the right university.

THE GUARDIAN

￡1=15 yuan

(1) How much more does the study show that graduates can expect to earn than non-graduates?

____

(2) Which kind of graduates earned less in their careers than non-graduates?

____

(3) Which kind of graduates fared best?

____

(4) What influenced earnings greatly?

____

【参考答案】

(1) £150,000. (2) Male arts graduates. (3) Maths and computing graduates.
(4) The university where a student studies and the class of their degree.

C. 请在下面的文章中，快速找出下列问题的答案。

Dealing with Africa's debt

THE world's richest countries agreed Saturday on a historic deal to write off more than US$40 billion in debt of the world's poorest nations.

The debt relief package was backed by finance ministers from the Group of Eight industrialized nations. It is part of a British-led effort to lift Africa out of poverty.

Africa has about 800 million people, 80 per cent of them living in rural areas lacking in public services.

Life expectancy at birth in Africa is only 47 years. The infant mortality rate is 106 per 1,000 births.

The HIV/AIDS pandemic has badly affected development there. Twelve countries have infection rates of 10 per cent.

Sub-Saharan Africa accounts for more than 60 per cent of the 40 million people infected with HIV worldwide.

In March, a UN study predicted that more than 80 million Africans could die from AIDS by 2025.

The impact of AIDS on economic growth has been severe. Below are latest figures showing the poorest countries. Most of them are from Africa.

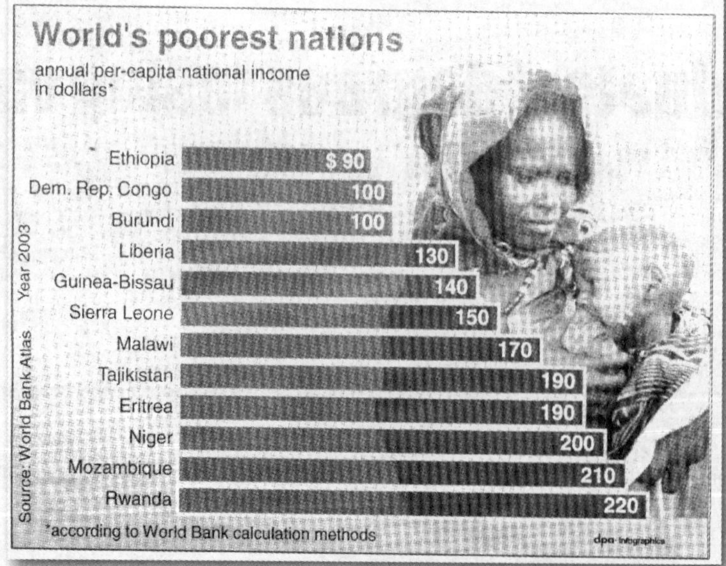

(1) How many African people live in the countryside lacking in public services?

____

(2) How long do African people live averagely?

____

(3) How many infants die among 1,000 births in Africa?

____

(4) How many people have been infected with HIV in Sub-Saharan Africa?

____

(5) How many Africans would die from AIDS by 2025?

____

(6) Which country is the poorest in the world?

____

【参考答案】

(1) 640 million. (2) 47 years. (3) 106. (4) More than 24 million.

(5) More than 80 million. (6) Ethiopia.

2 略读——提取总体信息迅速准确

2.1 略读技巧概述

“不同的阅读目的决定不同的阅读动作”是上一章节提出的概念，此概念至关重要。然而知易行难，人是有惯性的，一旦熟悉了一种动作，要开始另一种就不那么容易了。上一章谈的是寻读，即先不读，快速定位后，再阅读信息；本章谈的则是略读（skimming），即要粗略快速地读完整段文章，然后再找出或总结出段落大意。因为此时所找信息的性质发生了变化，从单个孤立的信息变成了相互关联的信息。信息的覆盖面大了，不读就没有对整体内容的认识，也就无法进行整段的总结。但是，这种读法是粗略的而不是仔细的，是“粗读”而不是“细读”。这种快速阅读的技能能够帮助学生迅速在阅读中提取总体信息，在阅读考试中，做到快而准；在国外读书时，能够应付教授布置的大量阅读任务；在自己的学习中，做到博览群书。但是，从“不读”到“读”是一个转变。在实践中，部分学生往往该“不读”的读，该“读”的不读。时刻牢记“不同的阅读目的决定不同的阅读动作”是最好的解决办法。下面通过练习来介绍略读的方法。

根据阅读专家的分析，阅读一段文字，只要读懂几个关键词，就能知道这段文字的大意。下面是剑桥大学教授设计的阅读练习，这个例子证明了他们分析的正确性。

You are skimming through an article in which most of the words are unknown to you. Here are the ones you may already know.

professor	Institute of Biochemistry	hard-working man	results of experiments	published
confession	invention	different results	fraud	regrets it

Can you guess, from these few words, what the article is about?

(1) It is about a well-known professor who has just published his confessions.

(2) It is about a scientist who has admitted inventing the results of his experiments.

(3) It is about a scientist who has killed himself because he couldn't get the same results as everybody else.

(4) It is about a scientist who regrets the publication of the results of his experiments.

上面这道题的答案是选项（2）。这个练习说明，在阅读一段文字时，是不用读懂每一个单词的；只要有一定的词汇量（3,000 左右的核心词汇，即高中英语水平），就能大致读懂这段文字的意思。换句话说，就是知道了 what the paragraph is about。而略读的目的就是要读懂这段文字的大意。

下面谈谈略读的具体方法。

眼睛快速地、自左向右一行一行地移动，在移动中抓住关键词（key words），同时忽略生词和语法结构，用这种方法就可以读得快、读得懂。这是为什么呢？在词汇学中关键词叫实义词（content words），包括名词、动词、数词、形容词、副词和作形容词用的分词等。这些词是用来传达意义的，而且在句子中出现频率较低，特别显眼。语法词（grammar words）在词汇学中叫功能词（function words），包括介词、冠词、系动词、助动词和连词等，这些词是用来搭建句子结构的，在句子中出现频率较高。功能词在英语中是固定的，我们在中学阶段已全部学完，因此十分熟悉，阅读中不必在这些词上停留。请看下面的例子。

———————————→ 眼球移动的方向

There are **swuude saada** and **huuda** in the **teeda**.

a. n. n. n.

这句话一看就知道是“某处有某物”的句型。要是不认识加粗的词（这四个词在句子中正好是实义词），具体的什么地方有什么东西就不清楚了。可见实义词在传达意义上的重要性。

———————————→ 眼球移动的方向

Being **able** to **determine** the **main idea** of a **passage** is **one** of the most **useful reading skills**.

a. v. a. n. n. num. a. ger. n.

快速抓住了这句话的实义词，也就明白了句子的意思。用这种方法阅读至少可节省一半的时间，因为不必在功能词上停留，只是在实义词处稍作停留。

但是考生要适当地进行练习方可掌握这种方法，不能一蹴而就。练习方法如下：找一篇低于自己英语水平的英文文章，一次性快速读完。读时尽量记住文中的实义词，读完后把记住的实义词写下来。随着训练的增多，阅读速度会越来越快，记住的实义词也会越来越多。如果最后达到几秒就能读完一段并能记住和写下大部分实义词的程度，便大功告成。如果读者对这种练习感到枯燥，也可以在课外阅读中有意识地进行。掌握这种技能会对今后不同类型的阅读大有裨益，有志者不妨一试。

2.2 学会如何提取段落大意

除了知道怎样略读，还要懂得怎样提取段落大意，因此略读还要进一步发展到“总结提炼”这个层面上。

根据对说明文文本段落的分析，一段写得好的段落具备以下特征：多数段落包含主题句（topic sentence）、支持句（supporting sentence，可多可少，视需要而定）和（或）结束句（concluding sentence）。如下表：

TOPIC SENTENCE
SUPPORTING SENTENCE
SUPPORTING SENTENCE
SUPPORTING SENTENCE
...
(CONCLUDING SENTENCE)

通过进一步的分析可以发现，主题句的位置并不固定，可以在段首的第一句或第二句，也可以在段末最后一句，甚至可以在段中出现。有的段落干脆就没有主题句。

这种现象完全与人类的逻辑思维和写作需要有关。有的人喜欢开门见山，一开始就告诉读者这段的主题，然后再进一步描述、解释或论证这一主题，最后总结性地结束，首尾呼应（有时也可以没有结束句）。这种写法就是逻辑思维上的“演绎法（deductive method）”。

有的人喜欢先列举现象、原因或举出例子、罗列数据，然后再点出这段的主题。这种写法就是逻辑思维上的“归纳法（inductive method）”。

有的段落涉及两件事情，由于是紧密相关的，因此不好分段，于是段中就用一句作为过渡并点出主题。

有的段落单纯叙述过程，主题已在前面的段落点出，因此整段就没有主题句，需要读者总结，不过其主题一般不难看出。这种段落在科技文章中时有出现。

根据以上的分析，要找出大部分段落的大意，发现主题句是关键；而对于小部分没有主题句的段落，只能自己总结。因此，建议读者在用略读技巧进行快速阅读的过程中，注意主题句的位置，以便能更快、更准确地找出段落大意。那种只读首句和尾句的做法是不可取的，这种做法并不是建立在缜密的文本分析上的，容易产生误解。况且，段落中的信息是息息相关，环环紧扣，按逻辑发展的，读者只有把整段读完才能完整地理解段落的意思。不过，如果读者掌握了略读的技巧和总结提炼段落大意的技能，阅读中的快与准是不难达到的，而且这些技能是可以终身受用的。

总结提炼段落大意的技能需要进行必要的训练，下面的练习就是为此而设计的。这种练习与高考，大学英语四、六级，英语专业四、八级，新托福，GRE 和 GMAT 的阅读题型相似，并且与雅思阅读九种题型中的部分选择题（multiple choice）题型相似。练好了这项技能，应对各种阅读考试就会得心应手。

2.3 段落略读技巧专项训练

用略读技巧快速阅读下列段落，注意主题句的位置。如果有主题句，根据主题句选择表述段落大意的最佳答案；如果没有主题句，读完后则要自己总结，然后选择最佳答案。

2.3.1 例题分析

例题 1：

By the time the first European travellers on the American continent began to record some of their observations about Indians, the Cherokee people had developed an advanced culture that probably was exceeded only by the civilised tribes of the Southwest: Mayan and Aztec groups. The social structures of the Cherokee people consisted of a form of clan kinship in which there were seven recognised clans. All members of a clan were considered blood brothers and sisters and were bound by honour to defend any member of that clan from wrong. Each clan, the Bird, Paint, Deer, Wolf, Blue, Long Hair, and Wild Potato was represented in the civil council by a counsellor or counsellors. The chief of the tribe was selected from one of these clans and did not inherit his office from his kinsmen. Actually, there were two chiefs, a Peace chief and a War chief. The Peace chief served when the tribe was at peace, but the minute war was declared, the War chief was in command.

Select the statement which best expresses the main idea of the paragraph. ________

A The Cherokee chief was different in war time than in peace time.

B Before the arrival of the Europeans the Cherokees had developed a well-organised society.

C The Mayans and the Aztecs were part of the Cherokee tribe.

D Several Indian cultures had developed advanced civilisations before the Europeans arrived.

【参考答案】

B

分析：这段的主题句是第一句，之后从 Cherokees 的社会结构角度来解释说明他们的文明高度发达，因此最佳答案是 B。

例题 2：

The first invention of mankind was the wheel. Although no wheel forms are found in nature, undoubtedly the earliest "wheels" were smooth logs which were used for moving weights over the earth's surface. No one recorded who he/she was or when it happened, but when the "first inventor" placed a wheel on an axle, mankind began to roll from one place to another. Records of this type of wheel have been found among Egyptian relics dating back to 2000 B.C. and earlier Chinese civilisations are credited with independent invention of the same mechanism. The wheel so fascinated the mind of man that we have spent centuries building machines around it; yet in over 4,000 years we have not changed its basic design. All about us we see the spinning shafts, gears, flywheels, pulleys, and rotors which are the descendents of the first wheel. The roaring propeller of an aircraft engine, the whirling wheel of a giant steam turbine, and the hairspring of a tiny watch are examples of the rotary motion which characterises our mechanical world. **It is hard to conceive of continuous motion without the wheel.**

Select the statement which best expresses the main idea of the paragraph. ______

A The wheel is used today in industry and transportation.

B One of mankind's first inventions, the wheel, has remained important for 4,000 years.

C Man has changed the basic design of the wheel to meet the needs of the industrial society.

D Although we don't know exactly who invented the wheel, it is evident that the Egyptians and Chinese used it about 4,000 years ago.

【参考答案】

B

分析：这段写得很好，既有主题句（第一句），也有结束句（最后一句）。支持句说明人们怎样发明和使用轮子。主题句用的是过去时，结束句用的是现在时，要表达从过去到现在的一段时间，一定要使用现在完成时。根据主题句的意思，排除选项 A 与 D，再比较 B 与 C，C 的表述与文章内容相反，所以选项 B 是最佳答案。

例题 3：

At the University of Kansas Art Museum, investigators tested the effects of different coloured walls on two groups of visitors to an exhibit of paintings. For the first group the room was painted white; for the second, dark brown. Movement of each group was followed by an electrical system under the carpet. The experiment revealed that those who entered the dark brown room walked more quickly, covered more area, and spent less time in the room than the people in the white environment. Dark brown stimulated more activity, but the activity ended sooner. **Not only the choice of colours but also the general appearance of a room communicates and influences those inside.** Another experiment presented subjects with photographs of faces that were to be rated in terms of energy and well-being. Three groups of subjects were used; each was shown the same photos, but each group was in a different kind of room. One group was in an "ugly" room that resembled a messy storeroom. Another group was in an average room — a nice office. The third group was in a tastefully designed living room with carpeting and drapes. Results showed that the subjects in the beautiful room tended to give higher ratings to the faces than those in the ugly room did. Other studies suggest that students do better on tests taken in comfortable, attractive rooms than in ordinary-looking or ugly rooms.

Select the statement which best expresses the main idea of the paragraph. ______

A People in beautiful rooms tend to give higher ratings to photographs of faces than people in ugly rooms.

B The colour and general appearance of a room influence the behaviour and attitudes of the people in it.

C The University of Kansas has studied the effects of the colour of a room on people's behaviour.

D Beautifully decorated, light-coloured rooms make people more comfortable than ugly, dark rooms.

【参考答案】

B

分析：这段讲的是两个实验，这两个实验既有联系又有区别。段落中间的句子就好像一座桥梁，把两个实验连接了起来，指出房间的颜色和外观都会影响里面的人这个共同点，因此选项B是最佳答案。

例题4：

John Cabot was the first Englishman to land in North America. However, this man who legitimised England's claim to everything from Labrador to Florida, left no sea journal, no diary or log, not even a portrait or a signature. Until 1956 most learned encyclopedias and histories indicated that Cabot's first landfall in America was Cape Breton, Nova Scotia. Then a letter was discovered in the Spanish archives, making it almost certain that he had touched first at the northernmost tip of Newfoundland, within five miles of the site of Leif Ericson's ill-fated settlement at L'Anse aux Meadows. Researchers studying the voyages of Columbus, Cartier, Frobisher, and other early explorers had a wealth of first-hand material with which to work. **Those who seek to recreate the life and routes used by Cabot must make do with third-hand accounts, the disloyal and untruthful boasts of his son, Sebastian, and a few hard dates in the maritime records of Bristol, England.**

Select the statement which best expresses the main idea of the paragraph. ________

A John Cabot claimed all the land from Labrador to Florida for England.

B Much of what is known about Cabot is based on the words of his son, Sebastian, and on records in Bristol, England.

C The lack of first-hand accounts of Cabot's voyages has left historians confused about his voyages to North America.

D Historians interested in the life and routes used by Cabot recently discovered an error they made in describing his discovery of North America.

【参考答案】

C

分析：这段的第二句只提到Cabot什么都没留下，最后一句才进行总结：正因为如此，那些希望重现他的生活和探险路线的人只能依靠间接的材料。读者可以由此作出推断：重现显然是十分困难的，有困难就会有困惑，因此最佳答案是选项C。

2.3.2 专项训练

1. 下面进行进一步的练习。用略读技巧快速读完以下各段落，注意主题句的位置。如果有主题句，根据主题句选择表述段落大意的最佳答案；如果没有主题句，则读完后自己总结，然后选择最佳答案，最后根据答案作出分析。

Paragraph 1

Teaching is supposed to be a professional activity requiring long and complicated training as well as official certification. The act of teaching is looked upon as a flow of knowledge from a higher source to an empty container. The student's role is one of receiving information; the teacher's role is one of sending it. There is a clear distinction assumed between one who is supposed to know (and therefore not capable of being wrong) and another, usually younger person who is supposed not to know. However, teaching need not be the province of a special group of people, nor need it be looked upon as a technical skill. Teaching can be more like guiding and assisting than forcing information into a supposedly empty head. If you have a certain skill you should be able to share it with someone. You do not have to get certified to convey what you know to someone else or to help them in their attempt to teach themselves. All of us, from the very youngest children to the oldest members of our culture, should come to realise our own potential as teachers. We can share what we know, however little it might be, with someone who is in need of that knowledge or skill.

Select the statement which best expresses the main idea of the paragraph. ________

A The author believes that it is not difficult to be a good teacher.

B The author believes that every person has the potential to be a teacher.

C The author believes that teaching is a professional activity requiring special training.

D The author believes that teaching is a flow of knowledge from a higher source to an empty container.

Paragraph 2

Albert Einstein once attributed the creativity of a famous scientist to the fact that he "never went to school, and therefore preserved the rare gift of thinking freely." Undoubtedly there is truth in Einstein's observation; many artists and geniuses seem to view their schooling as a disadvantage. But such a truth is not a criticism of schools. It is the function of schools to civilise, not to train explorers. The explorer is always a lonely individual whether his or her pioneering be in art, music, science, or technology. The creative explorer of unmapped lands shares with the genius what William James described as the "faculty of perceiving in an unhabitual way." Insofar as schools teach perceptual patterns they tend to destroy creativity and genius. But if schools could somehow exist solely to cultivate genius, then society would break down. For the social order demands unity and widespread agreement, both traits that are destructive to creativity. There will always be conflict between the demands of society and the impulses of creativity and genius.

Select the statement which best expresses the main idea of the paragraph. ________

A Albert Einstein and other geniuses and artists have said that schools limit creativity and genius.

B Schools should be designed to encourage creativity.

C Explorers can be compared to geniuses because both groups look at the world differently from the way most people do.

D Schools can never satisfy the needs of both geniuses and society as a whole.

Paragraph 3

Perhaps the most startling theory to come out of kinesics, the study of body movement, was suggested by Professor Ray Birdwhistell. He believes that physical appearance is often culturally programmed. In other words, we learn our looks — we are not born with them. A baby has generally unformed facial features. A baby, according to Birdwhistell, learns where to set the eyebrows by looking at those around — family and friends. This helps explain why the people of some regions of the United States look so much alike. New Englanders or Southerners have certain common facial characteristics that cannot be explained by genetics. The exact shape of the mouth is not set at birth, it is learned thereafter. In fact, the final mouth shape is not formed until well after permanent teeth are set. For many, this can be well into adolescence. A husband and wife together for a long time often come to look somewhat alike. We learn our looks from those around us. This is perhaps why in a single country there are areas where people smile more than those in other areas. In the United States, for example, the south is the part of the country where the people smile most frequently. In New England they smile less, and in the western part of New York state still less. Many Southerners find cities such as New York cold and unfriendly, partly because people on Madison Avenue smile less than people on Peachtree Street in Atlanta, Georgia. People in densely populated urban areas also tend to smile and greet each other in public less than people in rural areas and small towns do.

Select the statement which best expresses the main idea of the paragraph. ________

A Ray Birdwhistell can tell which region of the United States a person is from by how much he or she smiles.

B Ray Birdwhistell is a leader in the field of kinesics.

C Ray Birdwhistell says that our physical appearance is influenced by the appearance of people around us.

D People who live in the country are more friendly than people who live in densely populated areas.

【参考答案】

(1) B (2) D (3) C

2. 下面继续进行第二组练习。用略读技巧快速读完段落，注意主题句的位置。如果有主题句，根据主题句选择表述段落大意的最佳答案；如果没有主题句，则读完后自己总结，然后选择最佳答案，最后根据答案作出分析。

Paragraph 1

The Bible, while mainly a theological document written with the purpose of explaining the nature and moral imperatives of the Christian and Jewish God, is secondarily a book of history and geography. Selected historical materials were included in the text for the purpose of illustrating and underlining the religious teaching of the Bible. Historians and archaeologists have learned to rely upon the amazing accuracy of historical memory in the Bible. The smallest references to persons and places and events contained in the accounts of the Exodus, for instance, or the biographies of such Biblical heroes as Abraham and Moses and David, can lead, if properly considered and pursued, to extremely important historical discoveries. The archaeologists' efforts are not directed at "proving" the correctness of the Bible, which is neither necessary nor possible, any more than belief in God can be scientifically demonstrated. It is quite the opposite, in fact. The historical clues in the Bible can lead the archaeologists to a knowledge of the civilisations of the ancient world in which the Bible developed and with whose religious concepts and practices the Bible so radically differed. It can be considered as an almost unfailing indicator, revealing to the experts the locations and characteristics of lost cities and civilisations.

Select the statement which best expresses the main idea of the paragraph. ________

A The holy writings of the world's religions can provide valuable geographical information.

B The Bible is primarily a religious document.

C The Bible was intended by its authors to be a record of the history of the ancient world.

D The Bible, though primarily a religious text, is a valuable tool for people interested in history.

Paragraph 2

At one time it was the most important city in the region — a bustling commercial centre known for its massive monuments, its crowded streets and commercial districts, and its cultural and religious institutions. Then, suddenly, it was abandoned. Within a generation most of its population departed and the once magnificent city became all but a ghost town. This is the history of a pre-Columbian city called Teotihuacan (the Aztec Indians' word for "the place the gods call home"), once a metropolis of as many as 200,000 inhabitants 33 miles northeast of present-day Mexico City and the focus of a far-flung empire that stretched from the arid plains of central Mexico to the mountains of Guatemala. Why did this city die? Researchers have found no signs of epidemic disease or destructive invasions. But they have found signs that suggest the Teotihuacanos themselves burned their temples and some of their other buildings. Excavations revealed that piles of wood had been placed around these structures and set afire. Some speculate that Teotihuacan's inhabitants may have abandoned the city because it had become "a clumsy giant ... too unwieldy to change with the times." But other archaeologists think that the ancient urbanites may have destroyed their temples and abandoned their city in rage against their gods for permitting a long famine.

Select the statement which best expresses the main idea of the paragraph. ________

A Teotihuacan, once the home of 200,000 people, was the centre of a large empire.

B Many archaeologists are fascinated by the ruins of a pre-Columbian city called Teotihuacan.

C Teotihuacan, once a major metropolitan area, was destroyed by an invasion.

D A still unsolved mystery is why the people of Teotihuacan suddenly abandoned their city.

Paragraph 3

In any archaeological study that includes a dig, the procedures are basically the same: 1) selecting a site; 2) hiring local workmen; 3) surveying the site and dividing it into sections; 4) digging trenches to locate levels and places to excavate; 5) mapping architectural features; 6) developing a coding system that shows the exact spot where an object is found; and 7) recording, tagging, cleaning and storing excavated materials. Neilson C. Debevoise, writing on an expedition to Iraq in the early 1930s, described the typical "route" of excavated pottery. Workers reported an object to staff members before removing it from the ground. The date, level, location and other important information were written on a piece of paper and placed with the object. At noon the objects were brought in from the field to the registry room where they were given a preliminary cleaning. Registry numbers were written with waterproof India ink on a portion of the object previously painted with shellac. The shellac prevented the ink from soaking into the object, furnished a good writing surface, and made it possible to remove the number in a moment. From the registry room objects were sent to the drafting department. If a clay pot, for example, was of a new type, a scale drawing was made on graph paper. Measurement of the top, greatest diameter, base, height, colour of the glaze, if any, the quality and texture of the body and the quality of the workmanship were recorded on paper with the drawing. When the drafting department had completed its work the materials were placed on the storage shelves, grouped according to type for division with the Iraqi government and eventually shipped to museums. Today, the steps of a dig remain basically the same, although specific techniques vary.

Select the statement which best expresses the main idea of the paragraph. ________

A For a number of years, archaeologists have used basically the same procedure when conducting a dig.

B Neilson C. Debevoise developed the commonly accepted procedure for organizing a dig.

C Archaeologists take great care to assure that all excavated objects are properly identified.

D A great deal of important historical and archaeological information can be provided by a dig.

Paragraph 4

The unprecedented expansion of modern architecture throughout the world must be considered one of the great events in the history of art. Within the space of the last generation, the contemporary movement has become the dominant style of serious building not only in the United States and Europe, where pioneers had been at work since the late nineteenth century, but also in nations such as Brazil and India, where almost no modern architecture existed until much later. Only the Gothic perhaps, among all the styles of the past, gained popular acceptance with anything like the speed of the modern. And like the Gothic — which required a full seventy-five years of experimentation before it produced the Cathedral of Chartres — the modern has continually improved its structural techniques, gained in scale, and revised its aesthetics as it has attempted to meet the full range of man's civilised needs.

Select the statement which best expresses the main idea of the paragraph. ________

A Gothic architecture gained popular acceptance faster than modern architecture did.

B Modern architecture has not changed fast enough to meet the needs of mankind.

C The rapid growth and development of modern architecture (as an art form) is nearly unequaled in the history of art.

D If architectural styles are to endure, they must develop and improve in an attempt to meet society's needs.

【参考答案】

(1) D (2) D (3) A (4) C

2.4 短文略读技巧专项训练

2.4.1 例题分析

短文阅读与段落阅读性质相同，只不过短文由数个段落组成，每段都有自己的中心内容，各段之间又有联系，形成一个整体，阐述或证明一个事物或观点。短文阅读训练有助于读者提高对文本的整体认识，对阅读考试（尤其是雅思阅读考试）、论文写作和进一步的大量阅读都很有帮助。

用略读技巧快速阅读下面的短文，试着找出各段的主题句，然后作出总结。

例题 1：

It is not often realised that women held a high place in southern European societies in the l0th and 11th

centuries. As a wife, the woman was protected by the setting up of a dowry or decimum. Admittedly, the purpose of this was to protect her against the risk of desertion, but in reality its function in the social and family life of the time was much more important. The decimum was the wife's right to receive a tenth of all her husband's property. The wife had the right to withhold consent, in all transactions the husband would make. **And more than just a right: the documents show that she enjoyed a real power of decision, equal to that of her husband.** In no case do the documents indicate any degree of difference in the legal status of husband and wife.

The wife shared in the management of her husband's personal property, but the opposite was not always true. Women seemed perfectly prepared to defend their own inheritance against husbands who tried to exceed their rights, and on occasion they showed a fine fighting spirit. A case in point is that of Maria Vivas, a Catalan woman of Barcelona. Having agreed with her husband Miro to sell a field she had inherited, for the needs of the household, she insisted on compensation. None being offered, she succeeded in dragging her husband to the scribe to have a contract duty drawn up assigning her a piece of land from Miro's personal inheritance. The unfortunate husband was obliged to agree, as the contract says, "for the sake of peace". **Either through the dowry or through being hot-tempered, the Catalan wife knew how to win herself, within the context of the family, a powerful economic position.**

【分析】

此文第一段的主题句在段首第一句，点出妇女在 10 世纪和 11 世纪的南欧社会中享有很高的地位。随后，这一段的倒数第二句指出妻子拥有作出决定的合法权力，这种权力与丈夫的权力平等。

第二段最后一句是这一段的主题句，告诉读者：加泰罗尼亚（Catalan）妇女在家里享有强有力的经济地位。

例题 2：

Road Technology Since the Romans

Important principles of road building were known to the Romans. How has technology developed since then?

1 Between 43 A.D. and 81 A.D. Roman Britain acquired a 6,000 kilometres network, of technically advanced, hard wearing and straight highways linking towns of importance. Today, Britain's motorway system is only half that length. **The basic Roman philosophy of building a road to cope with different types and volumes of vehicles and using local materials is still applied today.**

2 Roman roads were cambered with ditches on either side and built on embankments to give them a properly drained base. A surfacing layer of small stones was used over gravel or larger stones, although some Roman roads were covered with large paving flags, which is where the term "pavement" originates.

3 Once the Romans left Britain, its roads fell into ruin through lack of maintenance. They became run-down, dusty highways in the summer and quagmires in the winter. **It seems that the next milestone in the history of roads did not appear until the 18th and 19th centuries, with the advent of the Turnpike Trust.** This raised cash for necessary maintenance in local areas to cope with the increasing numbers of wheeled vehicles, coaches and carriages wishing to travel at faster speeds.

4 **In 1816 John McAdam observed that it was the native soil that supported the weight of traffic which, when dry, would carry any weight without sinking.** He advised that the native soil be made dry and a covering impenetrable to rain be placed over it. However, road maintenance was not given much priority due to the popularity of the railways, until the motor car superseded the horse and cart. Cars, however, accentuated the problem of dust, described by the medical journal *The Lancet* in 1907 as "the greatest modern plague".

5 **Like so many other scientific advances, the solution came by accident.** Tar mixed with stone had been used in footpaths in certain parts of Britain in 1832, and tarred gravel was applied to roads in Nottingham in 1869, but the biggest breakthrough came in 1901. A surveyor called E. Purnell Hooley was visiting Derby Iron Works near Derby when he noticed a dust-free length of road produced by a burst tar barrel. The resulting pool of tar had been covered with ironworks slag. Hooley experimented with blending hot slag and tar as a byproduct from the coal industry and in 1902 patented the process produced by a company known as Tar MacAdam Syndicate Ltd. The company's name was later changed to Tarmac.

6 Nowadays, blacktop materials are made up of bitumen from oil which is blended with rock, gravel or slag. **A number of varieties have evolved for different uses in road construction, including hot-rolled asphalt for surfacing major roads, dense bitumen macadam for lower layers of a road and open-textured macadam.** Modern surfaces are bituminous-bound, graded stone supplied as a premix. Binders themselves have undergone technical developments. They are customised, ranging from soft to very hard to suit the traffic flow.

7 To accommodate higher traffic levels, either the thickness of the road must be increased or the materials improved. Hence the introduction within the last 10 years of heavy duty macadam in the road base which is three times as stiff as the dense bitumen and aggregate mix.

8 **Alternatively, the structural design can be changed.** For example, on an experimental reconstruction section of the M6 at Bescot, West Midlands, the heavy duty "upside-down design" was introduced in the 1980s. Here, rolled asphalt overlays a thinner than normal road-base macadam, over a second rolled asphalt layer, all of which lie on a sub-base which is again thinner than normal. This structure is thought to perform well due to the lower rolled asphalt layer being more resistant to deformation and inhibiting cracking at the bottom of the road base.

9 **Another innovative idea is the use of geotextiles.** In research geotextiles are being placed between the sub-grade soil and a drainage layer beneath the sub-base. The subgrade material is often clay and in the absence of the geotextile could, over time, clog the sub-base and reduce its efficiency as a drainage layer. But geotextiles can also have structural uses, and could provide improved resistance to cracking arid rutting in roads.

【分析】

第 1 段：最后一句是主题句。

根据这个主题句，你可能概括出下列段落大意：Roman philosophy of building a road is

applied today。

第 2 段：没有主题句。

你可能概括出下列段落大意：how Roman roads were built。试与原作者的概括进行比较：Roman road technology。

第 3 段：第三句是主题句。

根据这个主题句，你可能概括出下列段落大意：The next milestone in the road history did not appear until the 18th and 19th centuries。试与原作者的概括进行比较：The first development after the Romans。

第 4 段：第一句是主题句。

根据这个主题句，你可能概括出下列段落大意：McAdam observed something about native soil。试与原作者的概括进行比较：A new observation。

第 5 段：第一句是主题句。

根据这个主题句，你可能概括出下列段落大意：The solution came accidentally。试与原作者的概括进行比较：A chance discovery。

第 6 段：第二句是主题句。

根据这个主题句，你可能概括出下列段落大意：A number of varieties of blacktop materials for different uses in road construction。试与原作者的概括进行比较：Varieties of blacktop materials。

第 7 段：没有主题句。这一段中的两句话形成了因果关系，阐述的意思是：因为要适应更高的交通水平，所以使用了经过改良的材料。

你可能概括出下列段落大意：The introduction of heavy duty macadam for accommodating higher traffic levels。试与原作者的概括进行比较：Stronger materials for heavier traffic。

第 8 段：第一句是主题句。

根据这个主题句，你可能概括出下列段落大意：The structural design can be changed。试与原作者的概括进行比较：Structural varieties。

第 9 段：第一句是主题句。

根据这个主题句，你可能概括出下列段落大意：The use of geotextiles。试与原作者的概括进行比较：A road material for the future。

2.4.2 专项训练

现在进行更多的强化练习。用略读技巧快速读完下列短文，注意各段落主题句的位置。如果有主题句，根据主题句选择表达段落大意的最佳答案；如果没有主题句，则读完后自己总结，然后选择最佳答案，最后根据答案作出分析。

Reading Passage 1: Faster Effective Reading

1 The comprehension passages on this course are designed to help you increase your reading speed. A higher reading rate, with no loss of comprehension, will help you in other subjects as well as English, and the general principles applied to any language. Naturally, you will not read every book at the same speed. You would expect to read a newspaper, for example, much more rapidly than a physics or economics textbook — but you can raise your average reading speed over the whole range of materials you wish to cover so that the percentage gained will be the same whatever kind of reading you are concerned with.

2 The following reading passages are all of an average level of difficulty for your stage of instruction. They are all approximately 500 words long. They are about topics of general interest which do not require a great deal of specialised knowledge. Thus they fall between the kind of reading you might find in your textbooks and the much less demanding kind you will find in a newspaper or light novel. If you read this kind of English, with understanding, at, say, 400 words per minute, you might skim through a newspaper at perhaps 650—700, while with a difficult textbook you might drop to 200 or 250.

3 Perhaps you would like to know what reading speeds are common among native English-speaking university students and how those speeds can be improved. Tests in Minnesota, U.S.A., for example, have shown that students without special training can read English of average difficulty, for example, Tolstoy's *War and Peace* in translation, at speeds of between 240 and 250 w.p.m. (words per minute) with about 70% comprehension. Minnesota claims that after 12 half-hour lessons, once a week, the reading speed can be increased, with no loss of comprehension, to around 500 w.p.m. It is further claimed that with intensive training over seventeen weeks, speeds of over 1,000 w.p.m. can be reached, but this would be quite exceptional.

4 If you get to the point where you can read books of average difficulty at between 400 and 500 w.p.m. with 70% or more comprehension, you will be doing quite well, though of course any further improvement of speed-with-comprehension will be a good thing.

5 In this and the following three passages we shall be looking at some of the obstacles to faster reading and what we can do to overcome them.

Think of the passage as a whole

6 When you practise reading with passages shorter than book length, like the passages in this course, do not try to take in each word separately, one after the other. It is much more difficult to grasp the broad theme of the passage this way, and you will also get stuck at individual words which may not be absolutely essential to a general understanding of the passage. It is a good idea to skim through the passage very quickly first (say 500 words in a minute or so) to get the general idea of each paragraph. Titles, paragraph headings and emphasised words (underlined or in italics) can be a great help in getting this skeleton outline of the passage. It is surprising how many people do not read titles, introductions or paragraph headings. Can you, without looking back, remember the title of this passage and the heading of this paragraph?

Spot the topic:

Which of the following choices — A, B or C — most adequately sums up the idea of each paragraph?

(1) Para. 1 (   )

A How to increase your reading speed.

B The advantages of a generally higher reading speed.

C The advantages to your English of a higher reading speed.

(2) Para. 2 (   )

A The interest of the reading passages in this course.

B Newspapers can be read more quickly than textbooks.

C The speed at which you might expect to read different types of English.

(3) Para. 3 (   )

A How native English speakers read faster than others.

B How speed reading courses affect students' reading speeds.

C How native English university students increase their reading speed to 1,000 w.p.m. on average.

(4) Para. 4 (   )

A A guide to the reading speed you could aim for.

B The point of reading books of average difficulty.

C Why further improvement is a good thing.

(5) Para. 6 (   )

A Advice on how to get the general idea of a piece of reading quickly.

B The use of the title.

C The disadvantage of a careful initial reading.

【参考答案】

(1) B   (2) C   (3) B   (4) A   (5) A

Reading Passage 2: Hints for Reading Practice

Dictionaries slow you down!

1 If you have chosen the right, fairly easy, sort of book for your general reading practice, you will not need to use a dictionary for such an exercise. If you really must know the dictionary meaning of all the words you meet (a doubtful necessity), jot them down on a piece of paper to look up later. Actually, the meanings of many words will be clear, from the sentences around them — what we call the "context". Here is an example. Do you know the word *sou'wester*? It has two meanings in English as the following sentences indicate:

a) In spite of the fact that the fishermen were wearing *sou'westers*, the storm was so heavy that they were wet through.

b) An east or northeast wind brings cold, dry weather to England, but a *sou'wester* usually brings rain.

2 You should have guessed very easily that in sentence a) the word *sou'wester* refers to some kind of waterproof clothing, presumably quite thick and heavy since it is worn by fishermen in storms. In sentence b) it is clearly a kind of wind, coming from a southwesterly direction. Incidentally, you would have had the greatest difficulty in finding this word in most dictionaries since it often appears a long way down among the secondary meanings of south. If you did not know that *sou'* meant "south" in the first place you could only have found the word by the merest chance.

Pay attention to paragraph structure

3 Most paragraphs have a "topic sentence" which expresses the central idea. The remaining sentences expand or support that idea. It has been estimated that between 60% and 90% of all expository* paragraphs in English have the topic sentence first. Always pay special attention to the first sentence of a paragraph — it is most likely to give you the main idea.

4 Sometimes, though, the first sentence in the paragraph does not have the feel of a "main idea" sentence. It does not seem to give us enough new information to justify a paragraph. The next most likely place to look for the topic sentence is the last sentence of the paragraph. Take this paragraph for example: "Some students prefer a strict teacher who tells them exactly what to do. Others prefer to be left to work on their own. Still others like a democratic discussion type of class. No one teaching method can be devised to satisfy all students at the same time."

5 Remember that the opening and closing paragraphs of a passage or chapter are particularly important. The opening paragraph suggests the general direction and content of the piece, while the closing paragraph often summarises the very essence of what has been said.

* expository: giving information

Spot the topic:

Which of the following choices — A, B or C — most adequately sums up the idea of each paragraph?

(1) Para. 1 (　　)

A A dictionary is always a useful book to have at hand.

B Context is a more useful indicator of meaning than a dictionary when you are speed reading.

C If you jot down words on a slip of paper, you can look them up in a dictionary afterwards.

(2) Para. 2 (　　)

A The word *sou'wester* has two meanings.

B The world *sou'wester* is not easy to find in the dictionary.

C An example of how contexts give meaning without recourse to the dictionary.

(3) Para. 3 (　　)

A The function and usual place of the paragraph structure.

B The function and usual place of the topic sentence.

C What the topic sentence does.

(4) Para. 4 ( )

A The topic sentence is not always at the beginning of the paragraph.

B An example of a non-final topic sentence in a paragraph.

C An example of how a topic sentence can come at the end of a paragraph.

(5) Para. 5 ( )

A The importance of opening and closing sentences in a paragraph.

B The importance of first and final paragraphs in a passage.

C The importance of the general direction and content of a piece of writing.

【参考答案】

(1) B (2) C (3) B (4) C (5) B

Reading Passage 3: Canning Food

1 Food which is kept too long decays because it is attacked by yeasts, moulds and bacteria. The canning process, however, seals the product in a container so that no infection can reach it, and then it is sterilised by heat. Heat sterilisation destroys all infections present in food inside the can. No chemical preservatives are necessary, and properly canned food does not deteriorate during storage.

2 The principle was discovered in 1809 by a Frenchman called Nicolas Appert. He corked food lightly in wide-necked glass bottles and immersed them in a bath of hot water to drive out the air, then he hammered the corks down to seal the jars hermetically. Appert's discovery was rewarded by the French government because better preserved food supplies were needed for Napoleon's troops on distant campaigns.

3 By 1814 an English manufacturer had replaced Appert's glass jars with metal containers and was supplying tinned vegetable soup and meat to the British navy. The next scientific improvement, in 1860, was the result of Louis Pasteur's work on sterilisation through the application of scientifically controlled heat.

4 Today vegetables, fish, fruit, meat and beer are canned in enormous quantities. Within three generations the eating habits of millions have been revolutionised. Foods that were previously seasonal may now be eaten at any time, and strange foods are available far from the countries where they are grown. The profitable crops many farmers now produce often depend on the proximity of a canning factory.

5 The first stage in the canning process is the preparation of the raw food. Diseased and waste portions are thrown away; meat and fish are cleaned and trimmed; fruit and vegetables are washed and graded for size. The jobs are principally done by machine.

6 The next stage, for vegetables only, is blanching. This is immersion in very hot or boiling water for a short time to remove air and soften the vegetable. This makes it easier to pack into cans for sterilisation. Some packing machines fill up to 400 cans a minute. Fruit, fish and meat are packed raw and cold into cans, and then all the air is removed. When the cans are sealed, the pressure inside each can is only about half the pressure of the outside air. This is "vacuum" packing.

7 During the sterilisation process which follows, the cans are subjected to steam or boiling water, with the temperature and duration varying according to the type of food. Cans of fruit, for example, take only 5—10 minutes in boiling water, while meat and fish are cooked at higher temperatures for longer periods. After sterilisation, the cans are cooled quickly to 32 °C to prevent the contents from becoming too soft.

8 The final stage before dispatch to the wholesale or retail grocer is labelling, and packing the tins into boxes. Nowadays, however, labelling is often printed on in advance by the can-maker and no paper labels are then required.

Spot the topic:

Which of the following choices — A, B or C — most adequately sums up the idea of each paragraph?

(1) Para. 1 (   )

A Food scientifically sealed in cans is safe from decay.

B Sterilisation — the key to the safe-keeping of food.

C The use of chemicals in preventing the decay of food.

(2) Paras. 2 and 3 (   )

A The history and early methods of preserving food.

B The French influence in food canning.

C The scientific principles of food canning.

(3) Para. 4 (   )

A The ways in which the canning industry affects our lives.

B The economic effects of the canning industry.

C The range and diverse advantages of canned food.

(4) Paras. 5—8 (   )

A The mechanical miracle of food canning.

B The step-by-step modern processes of canning food.

C The process of preparing, washing and grading food for canning.

(5) Paras. 5—8 (   )

Put the following key processes in the order in which they occur.

A blanching	**B** preparing the raw food	**C** labelling and packing
D sterilising	**E** filling and sealing cans	**F** cooling

【参考答案】

(1) A (2) A (3) C (4) B (5) B, A, E, D, F, C

Reading Passage 4: Dreams — What Do They Mean?

1 Dreams have always held a universal fascination. Some primitive societies believe that the soul leaves the body and visits the scene of the dream. Generally, however, dreams are accepted to be illusions, having much in common with day-dreams — the fantasies of our waking life. When dreaming, however, one tends to believe fully in the reality of the dream world, however inconsistent, illogical and odd it may be.

2 Although most dreams apparently happen spontaneously, dream activity may be provoked by external influences. "Suffocation" dreams are connected with the breathing difficulties of a heavy cold, for instance. Internal disorders such as indigestion can cause vivid dreams, and dreams of racing fire engines may be caused by the ringing of an alarm bell.

3 Experiments have been carried out to investigate the connection between deliberately inflicted pain and dreaming. For example, a sleeper pricked with a pin perhaps dreams of fighting a battle and receiving a severe sword wound. Although the dream is stimulated by the physical discomfort, the actual events of the dream depend on the associations of the discomfort in the mind of the sleeper.

4 A dreamer's eyes often move rapidly from side to side. Since people born blind do not dream visually and do not manifest this eye activity, it is thought that the dreamer may be scanning the scene depicted in his dream. A certain amount of dreaming seems to be a human requirement — if a sleeper is roused every time his eyes begin to move fast, effectively depriving him of his dreams, he will make more eye movements the following night.

5 People differ greatly in their claims to dreaming. Some say they dream every night, others only very occasionally. Individual differences probably exist, but some people immediately forget dreams and others have good recall.

6 Superstition and magical practices thrive on the supposed power of dreams to foretell the future. Instances of dreams which have later turned out to be prophetic have often been recorded, some by men of the highest intellectual integrity. Although it is better to keep an open mind on the subject, it is true that the alleged power of dreams to predict future events still remains unproved.

7 Everyone knows that a sleeping dog often behaves as though he were dreaming, but it is impossible to tell what his whines and twitches really mean. By analogy with human experience, however, it is reasonable to suppose that at least the higher animals are capable of dreaming.

8 Of the many theories of dreams, Freud's is probably the best known. According to Freud, we revert in our dreams to the modes of thought characteristic of early childhood. Our thinking becomes concrete, pictorial and non-logical, and expresses ideas and wishes we are no longer conscious of. Dreams are absurd and unaccountable because our conscious mind, not willing to acknowledge our subconscious ideas, disguises them. Some of Freud's interpretations are extremely fanciful, but there is almost certainly some truth in his view that dreams express the subconscious mind.

Spot the topic:

Which of the following choices — A, B or C — most adequately sums up the idea of each paragraph?

(1) Para. 1 (　　)

A Fantastic dreams.

B Attitudes to dreams.

C The dream world.

(2) Para. 2 (　　)

A Probable causes of dreams.

B The effects of dreams.

C The vividness of dreams.

(3) Para. 3 (　　)

A Science and dream sequences.

B The effects the mind has on dreams.

C The connection between pain and dreams.

(4) Para. 4 (　　)

A Eye movement in dreams — its possible significance.

B The difference between dreaming in the sighted and the blind.

C The apparent need for humans to dream.

(5) Para. 6 (　　)

A Beliefs about dreaming.

B Are dreams prophetic?

C Dreams foretell the future.

(6) Para. 8 (　　)

A Freud's dreams.

B Freud and the dreams of early childhood.

C The Freudian interpretations of dreaming.

【参考答案】

(1) B　(2) A　(3) C　(4) A　(5) B　(6) C

Reading Passage 5: Cats

1 The cat has probably been associated with human beings since it was first given a place by his fire in return for keeping the cave dwelling free of rats and mice. The relationship between the cat and human beings has not been constant, however. People's attitude has ranged through indifference and neglect to the extremes of persecution and worship.

2 To the early Egyptians, the cat was a goddess and temples were built in her honour. Probably the most revered of animal deities was Bast, the cat-headed goddess. There was even a city, Bubastis, named after her. Occasionally, Bast was depicted as lion-headed, but the majority of the statues of her show her as cat-headed, often surrounded by sacred cats or kittens.

3 The Egyptians had great faith in the power of a living cat to protect them from both natural and supernatural evils. They made small ornaments and charms representing cats and the various cat deities. These decorated their homes and were buried with them to ensure that the soul of the dead person was protected on its perilous journey through the hostile spirit world.

4 Pious Egyptians always mummified* their cats and had them buried with almost as much reverence as if they were human beings. At the end of last century, a cat cemetery was discovered near the site of the ancient city of Bubastis. Here literally hundreds of thousands of little cat mummies were found ranged neatly on shelves. Some were stolen, some destroyed, and antique dealers sold many to tourists. Thousands were left.

5 An Alexandrian speculator finally thought of a way of turning them into money. He offered them for sale as manure and, in 1890, he had a cargo of 180,000 of them shipped to Liverpool. They were sold by auction and the auctioneer actually used one instead of his hammer! They made less than £4 a ton, much less than the value of a single specimen today.

6 The ancient Jews believed that when a religious person who had reached a high degree of sanctity died, his soul entered the body of a cat and remained there until the cat itself died a natural death. Only then could it enter Paradise.

7 Exactly the same belief existed in Burma and Thailand until comparatively recently, and beautiful sacred cats were kept in great luxury in the temples. When a member of the royal house of Siam died, his favourite cat was buried alive with him but a small opening was always left for its escape. When the cat emerged, the priests knew that the Prince's soul had safely entered its feline host, and the cat was ceremonially escorted to the Temple. At the crowning of the young King of Siam in 1926, a white cat was carried by a court official in the procession to the Throne Room. The old King's soul was resting in this cat, and his faithful former courtiers knew that he would want to be present at the crowning of his successor.

* mummify: preserve by embalming with chemicals. Ancient Egyptian bodies of men or animals preserved in this way are called "mummies".

Spot the topic:

Which of the following choices — A, B or C — most adequately sums up the idea of each paragraph?

(1) Para. 1 ( )

A The usefulness of cats to human beings.

B The relationship between cats and human beings.

C Human beings' indifference to and neglect of cats.

(2) Para. 2 ( )

A Bast.

B Bast and Bubastis.

C Bast — the most important Egyptian animal deity.

(3) Para. 3 ( )

A Early Egyptian beliefs and practices concerning cats.

B Early Egyptian beliefs about living cats.

C Early Egyptian beliefs about the powers of a living cat and why they always treated their animals kindly.

(4) Para. 4 ( )

A Egyptian mummies — their strange history.

B An Egyptian cat cemetery was discovered.

C Egyptian cat mummies and their fate.

(5) Para. 7 ( )

A Certain beliefs and practices concerning cats.

B Thai or Siamese cats.

C Thai court ceremonies.

【参考答案】

(1) B (2) C (3) A (4) C (5) A

Reading Passage 6: Dried Food

1 Centuries ago, man discovered that removing moisture from food helps to preserve it, and that the easiest way to do this is to expose the food to sun and wind. In this way the North American Indians produce pemmican (dried meat ground into powder and made into cakes), the Scandinavians make stockfish and the Arabs dried dates and "apricot leather."

2 All foods contain water — cabbage and other leaf vegetables contain as much as 93% water, potatoes and other root vegetables 80%, lean meat 75% and fish anything from 80% to 60% depending on how fatty it is. If this water is removed, the activity of the bacteria which cause food to go bad is checked.

3 Fruit is sun-dried in Asia Minor, Greece, Spain and other Mediterranean countries, and also in California (the U.S.), South Africa and Australia. The methods vary, but in general, the fruit is spread out on trays in drying yards in the hot sun. In order to prevent darkening, pears, peaches and apricots are exposed to the fumes of burning sulphur before drying. Plums, for making prunes, and certain varieties of grapes for making raisins and currants, are dipped in an alkaline solution in order to crack the skins of the fruit slightly and remove their wax coating, so as to increase the rate of drying.

4 Nowadays most foods are dried mechanically. The conventional method of such dehydration is to put food in chambers through which hot air is blown at temperatures of about 110 °C at entry and about 43 °C at exit. This is the usual method for drying such things as vegetables, minced meat, and fish.

5 Liquids such as milk, coffee, tea, soups and eggs may be dried by pouring them over a heated horizontal steel cylinder or by spraying them into a chamber through which a current of hot air passes. In the first case, the dried material is scraped off the roller as a thin film which is then broken up into small, though still relatively coarse flakes. In the second process it falls to the bottom of the chamber as a fine powder. Where recognizable pieces of meat and vegetables are required, as in soup, the ingredients are dried separately and then mixed.

6 Dried foods take up less room and weigh less than the same food packed in cans, and they do not need to be stored in special conditions. For these reasons they are invaluable to climbers, explorers and soldiers in battle, who have little storage space. They are also popular with housewives because it takes so little time to cook them. Usually it is just a case of replacing the dried-out moisture with boiling water.

Spot the topic:

Which of the following choices — A, B or C — most adequately sums up the idea of each paragraph?

(1) Para. 1 (　　)

A Drying fruit.

B Different methods of preserving things.

C Preserving food by drying.

(2) Para. 2 (　　)

A The relationship between water content and food decay.

B The relative water content of different types of food.

C The water content of vegetables.

(3) Para. 3 (　　)

A The use of sulphur in preserving food.

B The sun-drying method of preserving fruit.

C The relative geographical distribution of food preservation techniques.

(4) Paras. 4 and 5 ( )

A Heat drying of liquids and minced meat.

B Hot-air chamber drying of food.

C The three principal methods of mechanical food drying.

(5) Para. 6 ( )

A The general convenience of dried foods.

B The reason for housewives to prefer dried foods.

C The advantages of canned and dried foods.

【参考答案】

(1) C (2) A (3) B (4) C (5) A

Reading Passage 7: Pasteurisation

1 The value of heat for the preservation of food has been known for thousands of years, but it was not realised until the nineteenth century that a very mild heat treatment far below the boiling point, made liquid foods such as milk keep much longer. The discovery followed the work of the French scientist Louis Pasteur on wine and beer.

2 The process, called after him "pasteurisation", is a carefully controlled mild heat treatment. It was found that the process served two purposes: it prevented the souring of milk, and it destroyed the dangerous disease germs which sometimes occur in this product. These germs include the bacteria which cause tuberculosis, undulant fever, typhoid and paratyphoid fevers, dysentery, diphtheria, scarlet fever and septic sore throat.

3 It has long been known to bacteria experts that the tubercle bacillus* is the germ in milk which most strongly resists heat treatment. To destroy this organism it is necessary to heat milk to about 60 °C for 15 minutes, and its destruction has always been taken as a way of testing the efficiency of pasteurisation. A heat treatment of this kind destroys about 99% of the common bacteria in milk, including nearly all those which cause milk to turn sour.

4 To ensure the certain destruction of tuberculosis and other disease germs in milk, it must be held at a fixed temperature for a fixed time. In Britain, for example, these conditions were defined by law in 1923 as 63 °C — 66 °C for 30 minutes. This became known as the "holder" process, since the raw milk had to be pumped into a large tank, heated to just over 63 °C, held in the tank for half an hour and then pumped out and cooled. This was a slow process and required a very cumbersome plant, so scientists worked for many years to produce a simpler, more convenient method, with less bulky equipment.

5 The latest method, officially approved in Britain in 1949, is known as the high-temperature-short-time, or H.T.S.T. method. It has now almost entirely replaced the "holder" process. In the H.T.S.T. system, the milk flows continuously through many sections of thin stainless steel pipes. During the process, the milk is held at 72 °C for at least 15 seconds, then, as it cools, the heat it loses is used, in part, to raise the temperature of the incoming milk in a device called a "heat-exchanger".

6 Efficient pasteurisation may reduce the bacteria in raw milk from, say, one million to only a few thousand per cubic centimetre. The bacteria left are chemically mostly of the inert type, that is, they either do not sour milk at all, or sour it only slowly. Very strict cleanliness is, however, essential and all pipes, containers and bottling machines in a pasteurising plant must be cleaned and sterilised daily. If the slightest trace of dirt remains, all the benefits of pasteurisation are wasted.

* tubercle bacillus: the name for the bacteria which cause tuberculosis — an often-fatal lung disease

Spot the topic:

Which of the following choices — A, B or C — most adequately sums up the idea of each paragraph?

(1) Para. 2 ( )

A The two effects of pasteurisation on milk.

B Pasteurisation and the souring of milk.

C Mild heat treatment of milk prevents ill-health.

(2) Para. 3 ( )

A The tubercle bacillus as a criterion for sterilisation.

B Pasteurisation and lactic streptococci.

C Time and temperature criteria for the souring of milk.

(3) Para. 4 ( )

A The "holder" process.

B The 1923 law against tuberculosis in Britain.

C The superiority of the "holder" process.

(4) Para. 5 ( )

A The "heat-exchanger".

B The H.T.S.T. method.

C The disadvantage of the high-temperature process.

(5) Para. 6 ( )

A The importance of cleanliness for effective pasteurisation.

B Pasteurisation kills all germs.

C Pipes, containers and bottling machines, their manufacture and maintenance.

【参考答案】

(1) A (2) A (3) A (4) B (5) A

Reading Passage 8: Rabies

1 Rabies is an ordinarily infectious disease of the central nervous system, caused by a virus* and, as a rule, spread chiefly by domestic dogs and wild flesh-eating animals. Human beings and all warm-blooded animals are susceptible to rabies. The people of ancient Egypt, Greece and Rome ascribed rabies to evil spirits because ordinarily gentle and friendly animals suddenly became vicious and violent without evident cause and, after a period of maniacal behaviour, became paralysed and died.

2 Experiments carried out in Europe in the early nineteenth century of injecting saliva* from a rabid dog into a normal dog proved that the disease was infectious. Preventive steps, such as the destruction of stray dogs, were taken and by 1826 the disease was permanently eliminated in Norway, Sweden and Denmark. Though urban centres on the continent of Europe were cleared several times during the nineteenth century, they soon became reinfected since rabies was uncontrolled among wild animals.

3 During the early stages of the disease, a rabid animal is most dangerous because it appears normal and friendly, but it will bite at the slightest provocation. The virus is present in the salivary glands and passes into the saliva so that the bite of the infected animal introduces the virus into a fresh wound. If no action is taken, the virus may become established in the central nervous system and finally attack the brain. The incubation period varies from ten days to eight months or more, and the disease develops more quickly the nearer to the brain the wound is. Most infected dogs become restless, nervous, and irritable and vicious, then depressed and paralysed. With this type of rabies, the dog's death is inevitable and usually occurs within three to five days after the onset of the symptoms.

4 In 1881 Pasteur discovered that the infective agent of rabies could be recovered from the brain of an animal that had died of rabies. He experimented on rabbits and developed a new variety of rabies which could safely be used for vaccination*. A series of injections of this new virus made dogs resistant to the common natural virus. For the first time in 1885 the substance was used in a desperate attempt to save a badly bitten boy. The theory was that if dogs could be protected in a two-week period, the longer incubation period of human beings would allow the development of a high degree of protection before the potential onset of the disease. The treatment proved successful and the boy remained well.

5 Anti-rabies vaccine is widely used nowadays in two ways. Dogs may be given three-year protection against the disease by one powerful injection, while persons who have been bitten by rabid animals are given a course of daily injections over a week or ten days. The mortality rate from all types of bites from rabid animals has dropped from 9% to 0.5%. In rare cases, the vaccine will not prevent rabies in human beings because the virus produces the disease before the person's body has time to build up enough resistance. Because of this, immediate vaccination is essential for anyone bitten by an animal observed acting strangely and the animal should be captured circumspectly, and examined professionally or destroyed.

* virus: disease-carrying organism much smaller than bacteria

saliva: moisture which foams in the mouths of humans and other animals

vaccination: protection from a disease by the injection of dead or weakened germs which cause that disease

Spot the topic:

Which of the following choices — A, B or C — most adequately sums up the idea of each paragraph?

(1) Para. 1 ( )

A General ignorance about rabies today.

B A scientific account of rabies compared with some historical misconceptions.

C The symptoms of a rabid dog.

(2) Para. 2 ( )

A Early scientific attempts to control rabies.

B The clearing of urban centres on the continent.

C Experiments on the saliva of rabid dogs.

(3) Para. 3 ( )

A A clinical description of rabies in animals.

B The incubation period of rabies.

C The effect of rabies on infected dogs.

(4) Para. 4 ( )

A Pasteur and the immunisation of dogs against the disease.

B A boy being once cured of rabies.

C Pasteur and the development of the rabies vaccine.

(5) Para. 5 ( )

A The final eradication of rabies.

B The rabies immunisation of dogs by vaccination.

C Vaccine types and the importance of early treatment for humans.

【参考答案】

(1) B (2) A (3) A (4) C (5) C

Reading Passage 9: Bringing up Children

1 Where one stage of child development has been left out, or not sufficiently experienced, the child may have to go back and capture the experience of it. A good family makes this possible, for example, by providing the opportunity for the child to play with a clockwork car or toy railway train up to any age if he still needs to do so. This principle, in fact, underlies all psychological treatment of children in difficulties with their development, and is the basis of work in child clinics.

2 The beginnings of discipline are in the nursery. Even the youngest baby is taught by gradual stages to wait for food, to sleep and wake at regular intervals and so on. If the child feels the world around him is a warm and friendly one, he slowly accepts its rhythm and accustoms himself to conforming to its demands. Learning to wait for things, particularly for food, is a very important element in upbringing, and is achieved successfully only if too great demands are not made before the child can understand them.

3 Every parent watches eagerly the child's acquisition of each new skill — the first spoken words, the first independent steps, or the beginning of reading and writing. It is often tempting to hurry the child beyond his natural learning rate, but this can set up dangerous feelings of failure and states of anxiety in the child. This might happen at any stage. A baby might be forced to use a toilet too early. A young child might be encouraged to learn to read before he knows the meaning of the words he reads. On the other hand, though, if a child is left alone too much, or without any learning opportunities, he loses his natural zest for life and his desire to find out new things for himself.

4 Learning together is a fruitful source of relationship between children and parents. By playing together, parents learn more about their children and children learn more from their parents. Toys and games which both parents and children can share are an important means of achieving this co-operation. Building-block toys, jigsaw* puzzles and crosswords* are good examples.

5 Parents vary greatly in their degree of strictness or indulgence towards their children. Some may be especially strict in money matters, others are severe over times of coming home at night, punctuality for meals or personal cleanliness. In general, the controls imposed represent the needs of the parents and the values of the community as much as the child's own happiness and well-being.

6 As regards the development of moral standards in the growing child, consistency is very important in parental teaching. To forbid a thing one day and excuse it the next is no foundation for morality. Also, parents should realise that "example is better than precept". If they are hypocritical and do not practise what they preach, their children may grow confused and emotionally insecure when they grow old enough to think for themselves, and realise they have been to some extent deceived. A sudden awareness of a marked difference between their parents' ethics and their morals can be a dangerous disillusion.

* jigsaw: a puzzle in which irregularly shaped, cut-out pieces must be fitted together to form a complete picture

crossword: a form of puzzle often found in newspapers in which a pattern of blank squares is filled in with words guessed from a set of clues containing hidden meanings

Spot the topic:

Which of the following choices — A, B or C — most adequately sums up the idea of each paragraph?

(1) Para. 2 (　　)

A The baby's life in the nursery.

B Learning to wait for food.

C The gradual process of learning discipline.

(2) Para. 3 (　　)

A The delicate balance between parental support and excessive interference.

B The parents' willingness to watch their children's development.

C The dangers of leaving a child alone too much.

(3) Para. 5 (　　)

A Parents must be strict with their children.

B Parental restrictions vary, and are not always enforced for the child's benefit alone.

C Parental rules should include punctuality for meals and personal cleanliness.

(4) Para. 6 (　　)

A In moral matters, parents should be strict and should also try to keep to the rules themselves.

B In moral matters, parents should be aware of the marked differences between adults and children.

C Simply forbidding things is not a good foundation for morality.

【参考答案】

(1) C　(2) A　(3) B　(4) A

3 学习构词法——甩掉词汇包袱事半功倍

3.1 英语中的词根和前后缀

虽然学了多年英语，但在英语阅读中总会碰到陌生的单词，这是困扰每个人（包括母语是英语者）的问题。全球语言监察机构（The Global Language Monitor）指出，截止到 2006 年 6 月已出现 100 万个英语单词。该机构资料库在 2005 年登记的英语新词共 20,000 个，较数年前增加了一倍。面对如此庞大的单词量，恐怕很多读者都会感到手足无措——什么时候才可以学完啊？

全部学完是不可能的事情，幸亏人类十分聪明，可以用数千个单词表达几乎一切事物。根据语言学家的统计分析，现代的英语报刊、杂志和一般的非专业书籍中，95% 以上的词汇属于英语词汇中最核心的词汇，数量为 3,000—5,000 个。因此，一篇文章中有一二十个超出这个范围的生词是不影响对整篇文章的理解的，况且文章作者通常会有意识地对专业词汇作出解释，并且读者通常可以通过上下文猜出生词的意思（有关这点将在下面的章节里讨论），此外读者也可以运用构词法的知识来猜测生词的大概意思。

本章主要探讨构词法。中国的基础英语教育理论要求学生掌握 3,000—5,000 个核心英语词汇，这也是中学英语和大学英语四级考试的要求。在这个基础上，如果读者有意识地借助构词法学习英语词汇，将会达到事半功倍的效果。

英语中最常用的词根和前后缀大约是 500 个左右，知道了它们的意思，就打下了猜测成千上万甚至更多生词的基础。英语的词根和前后缀主要有三大来源：拉丁语、希腊语和盎格鲁—撒克逊语（即古英语）。下面选出大约 90 个最常用的词缀和词干，希望读者能够掌握。在雅思阅读考试的文章中，这些词缀和词干也是十分常见的，掌握了它们，对减轻记忆词汇的压力，增强信心，提高阅读理解能力大有帮助。

3.1.1 前缀

Prefix	Meaning	Prefix	Meaning
a-, an-	not, without, lacking	dia-	through, across
ante-	before	epi-	upon, over, outer
bene-	well	hyper-	above, beyond
bi-	two	hypo-	under, beneath, down
by-	aside or apart from the common, secondary	in-, im-	in, into, on
circum-	around	in-, im-, il-, ir-	not
com-, con-, col-, cor-, co-	together, with	inter-	between
contra-, anti-	against	intro-, intra-	within
de-	down from, away	micro-	small

（续表）

Prefix	Meaning	Prefix	Meaning
mis-	wrong, unfavourable	semi-	half
mono-	one, single	sub-, suc-, suf-, sug-, sup-, sus-	under
multi-	many	super-	above, over
peri-	around	syn-, sym-, syl-	with, together
poly-	many	trans-	across
post-	after	tri-	three
pre-	before	ultra-	beyond, excessive, extreme
re-, retro-	backward, back, behind	uni-	one

3.1.2 词干

Stem	Meaning	Stem	Meaning
anthrop, anthropo	man	metr, meter	measure
arch	first, chief	mit, miss	send
aster, astro, stellar	star	morph	form
audi, audit	hear	mort	death
auto	self	onym, nomen	name
bio	life	ortho	straight, correct
capit	head	pathy	feeling, suffering
ced	go, move, yield	phil	love
chron	time	phon	sound
corp	body	pod, ped	foot
cycl	circle	polls	city
derm, -derm	skin	port	carry
dic, dict	say, speak	psych	mind
duc	lead	scop	see, look at
fact, feet	make, do	scoope	instrument for seeing or observing
fleet	bend	scrib, script	write
gain	marriage	sequ, secut	follow
geo	earth	spect	look at
graph, gram	write, writing	spit	breathe
hetero	different, other	soph	wise
homo	same	tele	far
hydr, hydro	water, liquid	theo, the	god
lith	stone	therm, thermo	heat
log, ology	speech, word, study	vene, vent	come
man, manu	hand	ver	true
mega	great	voc	call

3.1.3 后缀

Suffix	Meaning	Suffix	Meaning
-able, -ible, -ble	capable of, fit for	-ist	one who
-ate	make	-ise	to make
-er, -or	the one who	-oid	like, resembling
-fy	make do, build, produce	-ous, ious, ose	full of, of the nature of
-ic, -al	relating to, having the nature of	-tion, ation	condition, the act of
-ism, -ist	action or practice, state or condition		

3.2 构词法学习专项训练

根据上一节讲述的前后缀及词根，猜测并写出下列斜体词的意思或同义词：

1.

(1) *In retrospect*, we would have been wise to leave our money in the bank.

(2) He lost his *spectacles*.

(3) He drew *concentric circles*.

(4) The first thing Jim did when he got off the train was looking for a *porter*.

【参考答案】

(1) thinking back to a time in the past (2) glasses

(3) circles which have the same centre (4) someone whose job is to carry travellers' luggage

2.

(1) No matter what Fred said, Noam *contradicted* him.

(2) He *circumvented* the problem.

(3) He was interested in *anthropology*.

【参考答案】

(1) to disagree with something by saying that it is wrong or not true

(2) to avoid a problem

(3) the scientific study of people, their societies, cultures etc.

3.

(1) Some citizens say the election of William Blazer will lead to *anarchy*.

(2) That man is a *bigamist*.

(3) The reviewer criticised the poet's *amorphous* style.

(4) Dan says he is an *atheist*.

(5) There was a great *antipathy* between the brothers.

【参考答案】

(1) the absence of a controlling government (2) man who marries two women

(3) lacking in organisation and form (4) one who believes there is no god

(5) dislike

4.

(1) To apply to some universities, you must fill out the application form and include a short *autobiography*.

(2) The policeman used a *megaphone*.

(3) Dr. Swanson has written articles about *interstellar* travel.

(4) Janet is interested in *autographs* of famous people.

(5) An *asterisk* is a written symbol which looks like a star.

【参考答案】

(1) account of your life written by yourself (2) an instrument to make one's voice louder

(3) outer space (4) signatures (5) a mark like a star (*)

5.

(1) Mr. Adams is employed at a *hydroelectric* plant.

(2) The government is financing a study of the effects on man of living in a *megalopolis*.

(3) Children learning to ride bicycles probably already know how to ride a *tricycle*.

(4) Nautical means pertaining to seamen, ships, or navigation. According to the formation of the word nautical, explain how the word *astronaut* is formed.

(5) People who study population are often concerned about the world *mortality rate*. What is the opposite of *mortality rate*?

【参考答案】

(1) using water power to produce electricity

(2) (an) extremely large city

(3) a bicycle with three wheels

(4) an astronaut is a person who sails (travels) to the outer space

(5) birth rate

6.

(1) After spending so many days lost in the desert, he was suffering from severe *dehydration*.

(2) Before Cindy gets dressed in the morning, she looks at the *thermometer* hanging outside her room.

(3) Some doctors prescribe medication to slow down *hyperactive* children.

(4) I'm not sure if that information is correct, but I'll look in our records to *verify* it.

【参考答案】

(1) loss of water from the body

(2) an instrument that measures heat and indicates temperature

(3) overactive; too active; abnormally active

(4) to make sure it is true; to confirm

7.

(1) June's father's hobby is photography, so she bought him a top-quality *tripod* for his birthday.

(2) He will never learn how to improve his writing unless he stops being so *hypersensitive* to criticism.

(3) Dr. Robinson said that just the sight of a *hypodermic* needle is enough to frighten many of his patients.

(4) Although she finished her degree in dentistry in 1960, she wants to go back to school next year to specialise in *orthodontics*.

(5) The immigration authorities *deported* Mr. Jensen because he did not have a legal passport.

(6) The average *per capita* annual income in this country for people between the ages of sixteen and sixty-five has risen dramatically in the last ten years.

(7) Mr. Thompson made an appointment with a *dermatologist* because he noticed small red spots appeared on his legs.

(8) Scientists have developed a sensitive instrument to measure *geothermal* variation.

(9) Anthropologists say that bipedalism played an important role in the cultural evolution of the human species. Because early man was *bipedal*, his hands were free to make and use tools.

【参考答案】

(1) a three-legged stand used to hold a camera

(2) overly sensitive; too easily hurt

(3) a needle used to inject substances under skin

(4) a type of dentistry concerned with straightening teeth

(5) to make one person leave the country

(6) individual; for each person

(7) a doctor who treats skin diseases

(8) heat of the earth

(9) walking on two feet

4 弄清句子的结构关系——克服思维障碍，句子结构一通百通

现代英语和汉语在语言学上被看作是分析性语言（analytic language），句中词的语法功能没有显性特征，只有分析句子结构才能看清句法关系。两种语言均没有繁冗复杂的变位：汉语不存在词语内部的屈折变化（inflections），而英语在历经了大约1,500年的发展之后，词尾变化基本消失，只剩下了为数不多的词尾变化，基本上不影响句子意义的表达。因此英语发展成为一种讲究词序（word order）的语言，句子的意义要依赖词序安排，而词在句子中的位置变得越来越重要。事实上，由于母语是汉语，中国学生在学习英语词序和句子结构上有着得天独厚的优势。

4.1 明确句子结构的重要性

在快速阅读的过程中，读者不用拘泥于对每个词的理解，最重要的是要马上抓住句子的结构，理解整句的含义。要学会先快速区分主干（主语—谓语—宾语，即句子的核心）和从属的次要部分（修饰语、关系从句和状语从句等，这些成分只是起到进一步提供细节信息或修饰的作用）。抓住了主干，整句的主要意思就明白了，阅读速度自然也就快了。用一句话来总结，就是要分清主次，抓住主要，忽略次要。掌握了这种方法，中国学生们就能在国外的学习中应付教授布置的大量阅读任务，并且能在略读的基础上将阅读速度进一步提高。

请看下面的例题。

1. Read the following sentences and find out the subject and the main verb of each sentence.

One team that performed more than two hundred operations found that nearly half of the patients underwent a change of personality.

In one publicised case in England a young salesman with an apparent compulsion to gamble was arrested for larceny.

【参考答案】

第一句：subject: one team	main verb: found
第二句：subject: a young salesman	main verb: was arrested

2. The following sentences are all from *Time*. Read them and answer the questions that follow.

1) Mostly because of inflation, but also because *taxes* have been creeping upward, the actual *buying power* that *people* have been getting from the money in their paycheques has declined by nearly 4% over the past twelve months.

Match the subjects and verbs.

taxes — ________

buying power — ________

people — ________

【参考答案】

taxes — have been creeping upward

buying power — has declined

people — have been getting

2) One index of how financially pressed Americans *feel is* the popularity of grocery coupons, those little pieces of paper snipped from product labels or newspaper ads *that* housewives have long used to save nickels and dimes at the check-out counter.

What is the subject of "feel"?

What is the subject of "is"?

What noun phrase does "that" refer to?

A newspaper ads **B** product labels **C** pieces of paper **D** popularity

【参考答案】

Americans; one index; C

3) Magazine writers, or the authors of books about current affairs, often find themselves gratefully surprised by how much remains unexplored and untold about major events that the day press and television once swarmed all over, then abandoned.

Find the subjects in the left column that match the verbs in the right column.

A magazine writers	**i** find
B books	**ii** remains
C current affairs	**iii** swarmed
D how much	**iv** abandoned
E major events	
F the day press and television	

【参考答案】

A i　D ii　F iii　F iv

4) One of the major reasons photo collecting has flowered only recently *was* the realisation that a photograph, unlike a painting or a drawing, *can* be reproduced forever, as long as the negative exists.

What is the subject of "was"?

What is the subject of "can"?

A the realisation　**B** a photograph　**C** a painting　**D** a drawing

【参考答案】

one of the major reasons; B

4.2 英语句型基本结构

4.2.1 英语句型概述

要做到在快速阅读中分清主次，达到又快又准的目的，就要了解英语的基本结构。英语句子有短有长，有简有繁，结构多种多样，十分庞杂。但根据许多语法学家长期的研究，在句子结构上，现代英语只有五种基本句型。我们一开始就学习这五种基本句型，是要培养读者在阅读中关注句子结构的意识。所有的英语句子都可以归纳为这五种基本句型，掌握这五种基本句型是提高英语阅读能力的关键。

有许多人学了不少英语单词，但还是无法说出或写出正确、完整的句子，这主要是因为缺乏句子结构的有关知识，没有运用这些基本句型去造句。明白了这个道理，如果读者能下点功夫，进行系统的句型学习和不断的练习，就一定可以逐步掌握和灵活运用这些句型，在阅读时也能按照英语句法的表达思路，加强对文本的理解。

以下是英语的五种基本句型：

1. Subject + Transitive Verb + Object（主语 + 及物动词 + 宾语）
2. Subject + Transitive Verb + Object + Object Complement

   （主语 + 及物动词 + 宾语 + 宾语补足语）
3. Subject + Transitive Verb + Object + Object（主语 + 及物动词 + 宾语 + 宾语）
4. Subject + Linking Verb + Subject Complement [主语 + 系动词 + 主语补足语（表语）]

5. Subject + Intransitive Verb (+ Adverbial / Adjunct) [主语 + 不及物动词（+ 状语 / 修饰语）]

4.2.2 句子成分介绍

上面列出的五种基本句型都包含必不可少的句子成分 S（主语）和 V（动词，充当谓语）。

1. S (Subject) 主语：由名词、代词、数词等充当。

2. V (Verb) 谓语动词：由动词充当。由于各类动词的性质不同，在使用上有五种不同的模式，因而形成了五种基本句型，并产生了其他各有特点、不可缺少的成分，如：

1) SC (Subject Complement) 主语补足语：由名词、形容词等充当。

2) O (Object) 宾语：有单个的，也有两个的（称为直接宾语和间接宾语），由名词、代词等充当。

3) OC (Object Complement) 宾语补足语: 由名词、形容词或句子充当，修饰宾语，补充说明宾语的行为、特征或状态等。

此外，还有修饰性的附加成分，可以根据需要用于任何句型中：

1) Ad (Adverbial Adjunct) 状语修饰语：由副词、短语或句子充当，修饰动词或动词短语。

2) At (Attribute) 定语：由形容词、短语等充当，描述人或物的性质。

这些句子成分如同积木，可以用它们组合成各种各样的句子。

4.2.3 25 种扩展句型介绍

以上讲述的五种基本句型可衍生出 25 种扩展句型。

1. Subject	+	**Verb**	+	**Direct Object**				
He		cut		his finger.				
She		smiled		her thanks.				
2. Subject	+	**Verb**	+	**(not)**		**to**	+	**Infinitive, etc.**
I		have promised				to		help them.
He		pretended		not		to		see me.
3. Subject	+	**Verb**	+	**Noun / Pronoun**	+ **(not)**	**to**	+	**Infinitive**
He		likes		his wife		to		dress well.
He		wants		me	not	to		be late.
4. Subject	+	**Verb**	+	**Noun / Pronoun**	+	**(to be) Complement**		
They		believed		him		(to be) innocent.		
I		consider		it		(to be) a shame.		

5. **Subject**	+	**Verb**	+	**Noun / Pronoun**	+	**Infinitive, etc.**
I		made		him		do it.
They		felt		the house		shake.

6. **Subject**	+	**Verb**	+	**Noun / Pronoun**	+	**Present Participle**
He		kept		me		waiting.
I		feel		the house		shaking.

7. **Subject**	+	**Verb**	+	**Object**	+	**Adjective**
We		painted		the door		green.
He		pushed		the window		open.

8. **Subject**	+	**Verb**	+	**Object**	+	**Noun**
They		elected		him		president.
We		call		the dog		"Spot".

9. **Subject**	+	**Verb**	+	**Object**	+	**Past Participle**
You		must get		your hair		cut.
She		had		a new dress		made.

10. **Subject**	+	**Verb**	+	**Object**	+	**Adverb, Adverbial Phrase, etc.**
He		took		his hat		off.
He		showed		me		to the door.

11. **Subject**	+	**Verb**	+	**(that)**	+	**Clause**
I		hope		(that)		you will come.
He		explained		that		nothing could be done.

12. **Subject**	+	**Verb**	+	**Noun / Pronoun**	+	**(that)**	+	**Clause**
I		told		the man		(that) he was mistaken.		
I		remind		him		that he must be here early.		

13. **Subject**	+	**Verb**	+	**Conjunctive**	**to**	+	**Infinitive, etc.**
I		wonder		how	to		do it.
I		do not know		whether	to		go or stay.

14. **Subject**	+	**Verb**	+	**Noun / Pronoun**	+	**Conjunctive**	+	**to**	+	**Infinitive, etc.**
We		showed		him		how		to		do it.
My mother		told		me		which		to		take.

15. **Subject**	+	**Verb**	+	**Conjunctive**	+	**Clause**
I		wonder		why		he has not come.
I		do not mind		where		we go.

16. **Subject**	+	**Verb**	+	**Noun / Pronoun**	+	**Conjunctive**	+	**Clause**
They		asked		us		when		we should be back.

Can you	inform	me	when	the train leaves?

17. Subject + Verb + Gerund, etc.

Subject	Verb	Gerund, etc.
1) I	remember	doing it.
They	went on	talking.
2) He	likes	swimming (= to swim).
I	prefer	staying (= to stay) indoors alone.
3) Your work	needs	correcting (= to be corrected).
It	wants	doing (= to be done).

18. Subject + Verb + Direct Object + Preposition + Prepositional Object

Subject	Verb	Direct Object	Preposition	Prepositional Object
1) I	gave	the money	to	my friend.
I	owe	ten pounds	to	my tailor.
2) He	bought	a gold watch	for	his wife.
He	saved	some bread	for	me.
3) She	compared	this	with	that.
She	prevented	me	from	coming.

19. Subject + Verb + Indirect Object + Direct Object

Subject	Verb	Indirect Object	Direct Object
1) They	paid	me	the money.
I	read	him	the letter.
The students	greeted	their teacher	"Good morning".
2) She	made	herself	a cup of tea.
He	bought	me	one.
Subject +	**Verb +**	**1st Object +**	**2nd Object**
3) I	envy	you	your fine garden.
He	forgave	us	our sins.
That	will save	me	a great deal of trouble.

20. Subject + Verb + (for) + Complement

Subject	Verb	(for)	Complement
We	walked	(for)	five miles.
He	waited	(for)	two hours.
It	cost		ten pounds.

21. Subject + Verb

Subject	Verb
Fire	burns.
We all	breathe, eat, and drink.

22. Subject + Verb + Predicative

Subject	Verb	Predicative
This	is	a book.
It	feels	soft.
His dream	came	true.
The plan	proved	useless / of no use.

23. **Subject** +	**Verb** +	**Adverbial Adjunct**	
He	will come	as soon as he is ready.	
A chair	will not stand	on two legs.	

24. **Subject** +	**Verb** +	**Preposition** +	**Prepositional Object**
It	depends	on	the weather.
He	succeeded	in	solving the problem.
I	will arrange	for	transport.

25. **Subject** +	**Verb** +	**to** +	**Infinitive**
1) We	stopped	to	have a rest.
I	am waiting	to	hear your opinion.
2) He	lived	to	be ninety.
He	decided	to	join the team.
3) He	awoke	to	find the house on fire.
The good old days	have gone	never to	return.
4) They	seemed	not to	notice it.
She	happened	to	know where he is.
5) We	are	to	be married in May.
I	am	to	stand here for ever.

4.3 英语句型结构专项训练

下面的练习是基于上面介绍的内容而设计的。每个练习后面均附有答案，以便读者自我检测。

1. Write the following sentences with the word groups arranged in what appears to be the most suitable order for the meaning expressed. In some cases the preposition "to" or "for" may have to be added.

(1) his symptoms / his doctor / explained / the patient

(2) good morning / you must / him / say

(3) the actress / dared to ask / her age / the reporter

(4) she / a lie / I think / him / told

(5) the mini-skirt / his girlfriend / gave / he

(6) offer / I / a cigar / you / may

(7) some fish / she will bring / the dog / the cat / some bones / and

(8) the way he planned to decorate the room / described / his wife / he

(9) us / expressed / his doubts / the scientist

【参考答案】

(1) The patient explained his symptoms to his doctor.

(2) You must say good morning to him.

(3) The reporter dared to ask the actress her age.

(4) I think she told him a lie.

(5) He gave his girlfriend the mini-skirt.

(6) May I offer you a cigar?

(7) She will bring some fish for the cat and some bones for the dog. / She will bring the cat some fish and the dog some bones.

(8) He described to his wife the way he planned to decorate the room.

(9) The scientist expressed his doubts to us.

2. Arrange the phrases grouped together in their correct sentence order.

(1) (I wonder) (the driver of that car) (along the wrong side of the road) (he is doing) (thinks) (what) (now racing)

(2) (he fell) (a little drunk) (headlong) (coming home late last night) (into the ditch)

(3) (the small girl) (the furry caterpillar) (along the leaf) (in terror) (as) (slowly) (crawled) (screamed)

(4) (why) (tell) (this morning) (the cook) (me) (did) (that) (not)

(5) (some students) (in gloomy cafés) (very much) (with one another) (excitedly) (enjoy) (arguing)

(6) (he) (had arrived) (told) (at Victoria) (at exactly four minutes past four) (to London) (1944) (me) (on his first visit) (he) (on the 4th April) (that)

(7) (he) (during his holiday) (to his mother) (by registered post) (some embroidered linen handkerchiefs) (in Ireland) (sent)

(8) (her husband) (always) (very quietly) (the rest of the family) (still) (at six o'clock) (left) (upstairs) (were) (when he had to go to work) (soundly) (the house) (so as not to disturb) (who) (sleeping)

(9) (the Duchess) (choosing vegetables) (has) (in the market) (often) (early in the morning) (carefully) (been seen)

【参考答案】

(1) I wonder what the driver of that car now racing along the wrong side of the road thinks he is doing.

(2) Coming home late last night a little drunk, he fell headlong into the ditch.

(3) As the furry caterpillar slowly crawled along the leaf, the small girl screamed in terror.

(4) Why did the cook not tell me that this morning?

(5) Some students very much enjoy arguing with one another excitedly in gloomy cafés.

(6) He told me that on his first visit to London he had arrived at Victoria at exactly four minutes past four on the 4th April, 1944.

(7) During his holiday in Ireland he sent some embroidered linen handkerchiefs to his mother by registered post.

(8) When he had to go to work at six o'clock, her husband always left the house very quietly so as not to disturb the rest of the family who were still sleeping soundly upstairs.

(9) The Duchess has often been seen in the market early in the morning carefully choosing vegetables.

3. Rewrite these sentences with the negative or other relevant adverbial phrases at the beginning. Make any other changes if necessary.

(1) He had never in his life worked so hard.

(2) She didn't realise her good fortune until then.

(3) Fishermen have to be very patient. Their wives do, too.

(4) We rarely have such a stormy summer.

(5) Most politicians think about fulfilling their earlier promises only in an election year.

(6) He realised the danger he had been in only after he had read the newspaper the following morning.

【参考答案】

(1) Never in his life had he worked so hard.

(2) Not until then did she realise her good fortune.

(3) Fishermen have to be very patient. So do their wives.

(4) Rarely do we have such a stormy summer.

(5) Only in an election year do most politicians think about fulfilling their earlier promises.

(6) Only after he had read the newspaper the following morning did he realise the danger he had been in.

4. Rewrite the following sentences so as to make the meaning less ambiguous.

(1) He has ordered a dictionary to improve his spelling.

(2) The aspidistra near the window which keeps out the light annoys me.

(3) The guide was showing the prehistoric carvings to the tourists with their grotesque faces and staring eyes.

(4) He only speaks his own language.

(5) I bought some fish in the market place which smells atrocious.

(6) The flowers will be examined by the judges in clusters of three or four.

(7) He hardly eats anything.

(8) Several moons have been detected by astronomers circling round the planet Jupiter.

(9) It is always interesting to read about the new fashions in newspapers.

(10) The director said he barely earned enough to pay his chauffeur.

(11) He assured me that a ghostly horse had been seen without a head.

(12) Your prize can either be a washing machine or a frige.

【参考答案】

(1) He has ordered a dictionary as he wants to improve his spelling.

(2) The fact that the aspidistra near the window keeps out the light annoys me.

(3) The guide was showing the tourists the prehistoric carvings with their grotesque faces and staring eyes.

(4) He speaks only his own language.

(5) In the market place I bought some fish which smells atrocious.

(6) The judges will examine the flowers in clusters of three or four.

(7) He eats hardly anything.

(8) Astronomers have detected several moons circling round the planet Jupiter.

(9) It is always interesting to read in newspapers about the new fashions.

(10) The director said he earned barely enough to pay his chauffeur.

(11) He assured me that a ghostly horse without a head had been seen.

(12) Your prize can be either a washing machine or a frige.

5. Explain the significance of the word order in the following sentences in expressing a certain shade of meaning.

(1) The postman came yesterday at seven o'clock in the evening.

(2) He speaks politely occasionally.

(3) Only after he had consulted his solicitor would he answer their questions.

(4) She walked through the High Street quickly.

(5) The news will be published soon.

(6) Why did he give the job to you?

(7) He will come next week without fail.

(8) Never had he seen such chaos.

(9) I enjoy a cigarette sometimes.

【参考答案】

(1) The postman usually comes much earlier or later.

(2) Normally he does not speak politely.

(3) Emphasis is laid on his refusal to answer the questions before.

(4) Emphasis is laid on how fast she moved.

(5) Emphasis is laid on the fact that there will not be a long wait for this.

(6) And not to someone else?

(7) This will quite certainly happen.

(8) The chaos was quite unprecedented.

(9) But most of the time I am not interested in it.

4.4 英语动词结构专讲

4.4.1 动词结构概述

从以上章节可知，英文的语法结构并不复杂，所有的结构均已在中学学完。在一定基础上，再重新审视英文的全部语法结构，你就会觉得，原来英语就是这么简单。熟练运用这些句型就可以写出和说出符合英语表达习惯的句子，熟悉了这些句子就可以在阅读时克服思维障碍，一通百通。

纵观上面的英语句型，我们知道动词是句子的灵魂。因此，有必要进一步学习动词。下面介绍句子或从句中主动词后面的四种非限定性结构：

1. 带 to 或不带 to 的动词不定式：He wants to come. / He can come.

2. 动名词：He enjoys coming.

3. 分词：I watched the train coming.

4. 从句：He says (that) he will come.

动词与介词搭配和动词与副词搭配形成的动词短语后面必须跟动名词。例如：

He **is looking forward to** travelling.

He **has given up** travelling.

要仔细区别动词与介词 to 搭配而成的动词短语（例如：look forward to，take to）和带 to 的动词不定式（例如：want to，intend to，tend to）。

在某些动词后可跟不止一种结构，但在意义上没有变化。例如：

He suggested our sitting down.

He suggested (that) we (should) sit down.

4.4.2 常见动词结构一览

英语学习中的难点就体现在英语的动词结构上，在这方面没有规则可循，所有的个案均是语言习惯约定俗成的。若想掌握它们，只能在阅读中多观察，在写作和说话中多使用，直至最后熟悉并能自如地运用它们。

下面列出了几种比较常用的动词结构，仅供参考：

Verb	Infinitive	Gerund	Clause
abstain		from voting	
accuse		of cheating	
admit		(to) knowing	(that) one knows
advise	(me) to rest	me against going	
agree	to share	about sharing	(that) we should share
aim	to write	at achieving	
allow	to go		
apologise		for forgetting	
appear	to like		
approve		of smoking	
arrange	to meet		that we should meet
ask	to see		if / whether I can see
assist		in compiling	
assume			(that) he will come
attempt	to compose		
avoid		hurting	
be able	to understand		
beg	to be forgiven		

（续表）

Verb	Infinitive	Gerund	Clause
begin	to search	searching	
believe		in saving	(that) he lives
beware		of losing	
bid	(to) sit down		
blame		for spoiling	
boast		of winning	(that) they have won
bother	to learn	about learning	
bribe	to support		
can	read		
cause	to postpone		
cease	to struggle	struggling	
challenge	to fight		
claim	to own		(that) he owns
command	to advance		that they should advance
compel	to obey		
complain		about losing	that he has lost
confess		to stealing	(that) he has stolen
confirm		writing	(that) he had written
consist		of preparing	
contemplate		changing	
continue	to row	rowing	
contribute		to building	
convince			someone (that) he should stay
cope		with looking after	
counsel	to withdraw		that they should withdraw
cure		of stammering	
dare	(to) jump		
decide	to buy	on buying	(that) he will buy
declare			(that) he will stay

（续表）

Verb	Infinitive	Gerund	Clause
defer		applying	
deign	to speak		
delay		starting	
delight		in listening	
demand	to see		that he should see
deny		breaking	(that) he broke
describe	how to make	making	
despair		of teaching	
deter		from investing	
determine	to travel		(that) he would travel
detest		scrubbing	
direct	to proceed		
discourage		from smoking	
dislike	to drive	driving	
dissuade		from reading	
doubt			whether he should go
dread		losing	
dream		of living	(that) he would live
educate	to appreciate		
encourage	to drink	drinking	
endeavour	to create		
enjoy		dancing	
ensure			(that) it is ready
entail		planning	
entitle	to inherit		
entreat	to forgive		
envisage		winning	(that) we should win
escape		drowning	
estimate			that something will improve

（续表）

Verb	Infinitive	Gerund	Clause
evade		paying	
excel		in running	
excuse		(my) interrupting	
expect	to succeed		(that) he will succeed
fail	to realise		
fancy		winning	(that) he will be promoted
fear	to trust		(that) he must be ill
feel	(something) tremble	(something) trembling	(that) something will happen
feel like		resting	
finish		eating	
forbid	someone to go		
force	someone to yield		
forecast			(that) he will lose
forget	to pay	paying	(that) one must pay
go on	to say	speaking	
guarantee	to deliver		(that) we shall deliver
guess			what he will say
had better	wait		
happen	to remark		
hasten	to qualify		
hate	to admit	writing	
hear	(someone) scream	(someone) screaming	(that) something has happened
help	(someone) (to) carry		
cannot help		smiling	
hesitate	to criticise		
hope	to see		(that) I (may) see
imagine		living	(that) he is the director
incite	to rebel		
incur		spending	

（续表）

Verb	Infinitive	Gerund	Clause
induce	to contribute		
indulge		in day dreaming	
inform			(that) I should apply
inquire		about going	whether he should go
insist		on seeing	(that) I should see
inspire	to compose		
instruct	to attend		
intend	to move		
invite	to stay		
joke		about making a fortune	
keep (on)		talking	
know	how to knit		(that) the world is round
learn	(how) to drive		(that) he must obey
leave	to prepare	preparing	
leave off		working	
let	(someone) come		
like	to sing	singing	
(should) like	to come		
loathe		waiting	
long	to return		
look forward		to celebrating	
love	to dance	dancing	
make	(someone) pay		
manage	to carry		
may	borrow		
mean	to finish		
mind		helping	
miss		seeing	
must	improve		

（续表）

Verb	Infinitive	Gerund	Clause
need	to reorganise	reorganising	
notice	(someone) walk	walking	(that) he is walking
object		to meeting	
observe	(someone) enter	entering	that someone is entering
offer	to help		
omit	to sign	signing	
oppose		(to) supporting	
order	to advance		
ought	to study		
pause	to consider		
pay	to watch	for watching	
permit	to attend		
persevere		in practising	
persist		in interrupting	
persuade	to change		
plan	to build		
plead	to be forgiven		
pray	to recover		(that) he might recover
prefer	to ride	riding to driving	
prepare	to set out		
presume	to approach		(that) we may come
pretend	to understand		that he understands
prevent		him from / his entering	
proceed	to report		
profit		from investing	
prohibit		from entering	
promise	to reform		(that) they will reform
propose	to construct	constructing	(that) a road should be constructed
protest		against fighting	

（续表）

Verb	Infinitive	Gerund	Clause
punish		for trespassing	
read			(that) something has happened
realise			(that) it will fall
recall		meeting	(that) something happened
recollect		meeting	(that) something happened
recommend	to buy	buying	(that) you should buy
refrain		from applauding	
refuse	to conform		
regret	to report	having reported	(that) we must report
rely		on discovering	
remain		standing	
remark			(that) the weather is fine
remember	to take	taking	(that) I must take
remind	to send		(that) we should bring
report		seeing	(that) sales have increased
reply			(that) he disagrees
request	to leave		(that) he should leave
resist		spending	
resolve	to achieve		(that) he will achieve
risk		damaging	
say			(that) he is hungry
scorn	to yield		
see	(something) change	changing	(that) it has changed
seek	to understand		
seem	to enjoy		
shirk		helping	
show	how to make (them)	making	(that) something can be done
sit		thinking	
smell		(something) cooking	

（续表）

Verb	Infinitive	Gerund	Clause
spend (time)		arguing	
stand		watching	
start	to rain	raining	
state			(that) a meeting is to be held
stay	to help		
stop	to listen	listening	
stress			(that) they should bring
strive	to win		
struggle	to escape		
study	to pass		
succeed		in inventing	
suppose			(that) you are right
suspect		of cheating	(that) he has cheated
swear	to avenge		(that) he is innocent
teach	(how) to type		
tell	to fetch		
tempt	to spend		
tend	to exaggerate		
think		of changing	(that) he will change
train	to imitate		
trouble	to move		
try	to capture	using	
understand	how to solve		(that) I am to write
undertake	to return		
urge	to reconsider		
unite		in defending	
venture	to suggest		
visualise		wearing	
volunteer	to carry		

（续表）

Verb	Infinitive	Gerund	Clause
vow	to return		(that) he will return
wait	to see / and see		
want	to fly		
warn		(about) against driving	
watch	(someone) jump	jumping	
wish	to inspect		(that) I could do it
wonder	(how) to make		how I could / should make
would rather	remain		
yearn	to travel		

4.5 动词结构专项训练

以下练习是为熟悉动词结构而专门设计的。每组练习后都附有参考答案，方便读者检测。

1. On each of the line in the following sentences write as many words as you wish to complete the sentences given. Each word group supplied should contain a verbal form (gerund, infinitive, or finite verb in a clause) depending on the verb or adjective already provided. In some cases a preposition will precede the appropriate verbal form.

(1) Many old people are interested ________ and they enjoy ________ .

(2) The guide suggested ________ but we thought ________ .

(3) If that book is worth ________ I would like ________ . The last one that author produced was too obscure ________ .

(4) The matron does not allow visitors ________ , but some people insist ________ .

(5) Marie Curie succeeded ________ . Her husband helped her ________ .

(6) The bad weather prevented us ________ . We had been looking forward ________ .

(7) After Mrs. White had finished ________ , she felt like ________ .

(8) Fishermen don't mind ________ , but most other people would loathe ________ .

(9) The young motor cyclist was boasting ________ . If what he said was true, he should be punished ________ .

(10) The bus conductor accused ________ . He made her ________ .

(11) The education committee spent an hour ________ . It was then agreed to postpone ________ .

(12) The people in the bus queue were watching ________ . They were tired ________ .

(13) If you arrive late you had better ________ . Mr. Smith does not like ________ .

(14) The sales manager doubts ________ . He insists ________ .

(15) Our cat is sitting ________ . She objects to ________ .

(16) When the house decorator had finished ________ , he intended ________ .

(17) Most little boys prefer ________ . They never complain ________ .

(18) You had better not ________ . If you do, you risk ________ .

(19) The old lady said she remembered ________ , but she refused ________ .

(20) Persevere ________ and you will not fail ________ .

(21) In spring birds are busy ________ . By instinct they know ________ .

(22) The accused man denied ________ , but the police took him to headquarters ________ .

(23) It is so warm I should like ________ . But I expect ________ .

(24) I could not help ________ , but I soon regretted ________ .

(25) Would you rather ________ or have you definitely decided ________ ?

(26) He apologised profusely ________ , but I told him ________ .

(27) The heckler kept ________ . When he challenged ________ , he was asked ________ . He then apologised ________ .

(28) His parents did not forbid ________ , but they discouraged ________ . He finally promised ________ .

(29) When I visited London I missed ________ .

(30) My sister wanted ________ but I forgot ________ .

(31) You will be very ill if you stop ________ . It is very important ________ .

【参考答案】

(1) in gardening; pottering about out of doors

(2) visiting the museum; we would like to see the harbour

(3) reading; to borrow it; for me to understand

(4) to give the patients cigarettes; on bringing in packets

(5) in isolating radium; to achieve this

(6) from reaching the summit; to seeing the view

(7) cleaning the house; having a cup of tea
(8) standing in the rain; getting wet
(9) of / about overtaking everything on the road; for speeding
(10) the woman of failing to pay; get off the bus
(11) arguing; making a decision
(12) the men working; of waiting
(13) not come in; latecomers to disturb the lesson
(14) whether the price is competitive; on our reviewing it
(15) sulking; being given fish for breakfast
(16) whitewashing the ceiling; to paint the woodwork
(17) playing to learning; of having too much free time
(18) take photographs here; being arrested
(19) reading the forbidden book; to tell us what it was about
(20) in learning to drive; to pass the test eventually
(21) building their nests; how to construct them
(22) having robbed the bank; to question him
(23) to sleep out of doors; it will rain during the night
(24) losing my temper; showing my true feelings
(25) borrow my typewriter; to buy one of your own
(26) for disturbing me; not to worry
(27) interrupting; the speaker to admit he was lying; to leave; for disturbing the meeting with the truth
(28) him to become an artist; him from giving up his studies; to postpone his decision
(29) riding and driving through the countryside
(30) me to buy her a hand-embroidered blouse; to look for one
(31) taking these tablets; to take them regularly

2. From the four words or phrases listed in each of the following sentences, point out the correct one.

Modify each sentence in as many ways as are necessary to incorporate each of the other three words in a grammatical construction.

(1) He ________ to study mathematics.

A is　　**B** makes me　　**C** lets me　　**D** had better

(2) I ________ to meet him.

A avoided　　**B** postponed　　**C** happened　　**D** insisted

(3) Do you ________ to go home alone?

A mind　　**B** persist　　**C** object　　**D** dare

(4) He ________ to calculate how much it might cost.

A suggested　　**B** is used　　**C** promised　　**D** succeeded

(5) I ________ to have played with trains as a child.

A should like　　**B** remember　　**C** deny　　**D** missed

(6) He ________ to play chess.

A knows　　**B** spends time　　**C** would rather　　**D** is learning

(7) The retired boxer ________ to buy a public house.

A suggests　　**B** means　　**C** thinks　　**D** had better

(8) The harbour master ________ that the boat will arrive early.

A wants　　**B** thinks　　**C** will allow　　**D** prefers

(9) He ________ to eat a ham sandwich.

A feels like　　**B** has finished　　**C** enjoys　　**D** has decided

(10) He seldom ________ sending news to his brother abroad.

A fails　　**B** forgets　　**C** troubles　　**D** suggests

(11) I ________ that I am late.

A apologise　　**B** cannot help　　**C** regret　　**D** prefer

(12) I ________ to ski through the forest.

A am looking forward　　**B** am longing　　**C** enjoy　　**D** imagine myself

【参考答案】

(1) A

He makes me study / lets me study / had better study mathematics.

(2) C

I avoided meeting / postponed meeting / insisted on meeting him.

(3) D

Do you mind going / persist in going / object to going home alone?

(4) C

He suggested calculating / is used to calculating / succeeded in calculating how much it might cost.

(5) A

I remember playing / deny having played / missed playing with trains as a child.

(6) D

He knows how to play / spends time playing / would rather play chess.

(7) B

The retired boxer suggests buying / thinks he will buy / had better buy a public house.

(8) B

The harbour master wants the boat to arrive / will allow the boat to arrive / prefers the boat to arrive early.

(9) D

He feels like eating / has finished eating / enjoys eating a ham sardwich.

(10) D

He fails to send / forgets to send / troubles to send news to his brother abroad.

(11) C

I apologise for being / cannot help being / prefer to be late.

(12) B

I am looking forward to skiing / enjoy skiing / imagine myself skiing through the forest.

5 把握上下文线索——逻辑推断连猜带蒙

有效的阅读需要使用解决难题的不同技巧。由于英语的词汇量巨大，具有一词多义和一义多词的特征，且词法松散欠严谨，因此没有一个人在阅读中能懂得每个词的确切含义。但是，掌握并使用猜测词义的技巧，就能够理解一个句子、一个段落或一篇文章。除了第三章中谈到的利用构词法去猜测词义的技巧，根据上下文的线索猜测词义也是一种行之有效的方法。而要使用这种方法猜测词义，必须运用句子结构的相关知识（见第四章）和理解作者的写作意图。虽然提高猜词能力并无固定方法可循，但是在阅读中要谨记以下几点。

5.1 阅读中的注意事项和猜词方式

1. 充分利用句子或段落中其他词汇的意义和句子的整体意义，抓大放小，尽量不去猜测不影响理解的生词。

2. 利用句子中表示不同部分关系的语法结构和标点符号。

3. 在通读与略读时，大概领会词义即可，不必求精确的理解。

4. 通过对句子中词序和结构（参考第四章）的学习，学会辨认在哪种情况下哪个生词是不用懂的或是可以忽略的（参考第一章）。

一般说来，作者在行文中会考虑到读者的需求，对生词或难词的意思作出解释。通常读者会看到这样的解释方式：________ is a ________ which ________. 但是，很多时候读者不太容易看出某个词的意思，因为还有很多其他的下定义的方式。下面介绍各种不同的方式，熟悉了这些方式，猜测词义就容易多了。

1. 在同一句中可能给出生词的同义词。例如：His anger was as **huge** as his **massive** chest. 因为是对两种事物作类比，所以在句子中有两个意义相同的词，于是可以猜到 massive 的意义与 huge 的一样。当然，这样猜测是建立在懂得 as...as 这种比较结构的基础上的。

2. 有时候可以根据下一句猜出前一句中生词的意思，因为下一句给出了生词的定义。例如："The bottom part of my face is **numb**," he says evenly. "**It's got no feeling in it at all.**"

3. 在很多类型的文本中，一种常见的下定义的方法是给出生词的同位语。例如：The Americans would tell him he wasn't a **blue blood, a second- or third-generation circus performer**. 有时候同位语由 or 引出，如下面的例子：The **shaykhs** or **leaders of Bedouin tribes**, were usually chosen from specific families.

4. 有时候生词前的一句或几句就是它的定义。例如："He was rushed to the hospital, where **they wrapped bandages around his torn-up head, his right arm, and his whole chest**." He performed that night, however. "I looked like a **mummy**, " he laughed.

5. 有时候一个生词正好是文中的某个或某些词的反义词。例如：He was **strong and brave**; this man was no **namby-pamby**. strong and brave 的反义词是 weak and timid，而 weak and timid 就是 namby-pamby 的含义。

6. 常常可以通过上下文的因果关系猜出一个词的意思，因为它引出了文中描述的一些结果。例如：The **conflagration** was so fierce that within just a few seconds one could see towering **flames** where the house had stood, and the smoke which filled the sky could be seen for miles and miles.

7. 有时候可以通过同一句或同一个段落中稍后给出的细节去猜测词义。例如：The soldier was filled with intense **remorse** when he saw the terrible injuries suffered by people hit by the bomb his plane had dropped. He was ashamed to look at the bleeding and broken bodies as they were carried into the hospital. He cried and moaned when he saw that one was just a small child. 根据这段后面的细节描述，可以看出 remorse 显然就是"悔恨"或"自责"的意思。

8. 有时候生词正好与下文提到的某种东西属于同一类。例如：She decided to try to grow **garbanzo beans** that summer. Like **soybeans** and other legumes, they are a rich source of protein, and she was anxious to see whether they could be made into dishes her family would find tasty.

5.2 热身练习

你可能不知道下面这些单词的意思：famished, flipper, shred, trudge, lintel, gaudy, sallow, surreptitiously, goggle, pillion。看看它们在下面的句子中是如何使用的，然后说出或写出你认为它们是什么意思（不要查词典）。

(1) Have you got a piece of bread or something? I'm absolutely **famished**.

(2) — My God, he's swimming fast.

— Yes, he's got **flippers** on.

(3) She read my letter slowly to the end and then tore it to **shreds**.

(4) On the way, we drove past a column of depressed-looking soldiers, **trudging** along wearily through the mud and rain.

(5) The door was so low that I hit my head on the **lintel**.

(6) Sebastian hates fairs. The loud, vulgar music, the cheap **gaudy** colours, the noise, the whole atmosphere — everything makes him feel ill.

(7) Twenty years in an unhealthy tropical climate had given his face a permanently **sallow** complexion.

(8) I looked round the church: two of the children were playing cards under the seat, and another was **surreptitiously** eating a cream bun.

(9) What are you all **goggling** at me like that for? Have I got two heads or something?

(10) Mark got on the motorbike. I sat behind him on the **pillion**, and we roared off into the night.

【参考答案】

(1) very hungry; starving

(2) big rubber "feet" that you put on to make you swim faster

(3) small torn piece (of paper or cloth)

(4) walking heavily and wearily

(5) beam across the top of a door

(6) brightly-coloured in a vulgar, cheap-looking way

(7) an unhealthy yellowish colour

(8) secretly; trying to hide what he was doing

(9) look in amazement

(10) passenger seat on a motorbike

下面的报道选自英国的《每日镜报》。简洁的文体、极短的句子、平易近人的生活题材是这份报纸的特点。请猜一猜文中黑体字的意思，看看你的猜测与答案是否相同。

Baggy Pants

Everyone laughed when Albert went to work in his **baggy pants**. Everyone but Albert. He punched one of his workmates in the eye.

And that's when the joke really **fell flat**. For the incident led to a strike which **crippled** production at a carpet factory.

The trousers that caused all the trouble were in a **shapeless fawn**-coloured material. They **flapped** round Albert's legs as he walked into the Victoria Carpet Factory in Kidderminster, Worcestershire.

Other workers **winked** and **smirked**. There were **ribald** comments. Albert thought it was quite amusing at first. But after half an hour, the **wisecracks got him down**.

So he **planted one on** seventeen-year-old apprentice David Bishop. Then the foreman **intervened**. He didn't see the funny side of it. He **suspended David** for two days and Albert for three.

Other workers held an emergency meeting and decided that David had been treated unfairly. They asked for him to be **reinstated**. The management refused — and 100 men walked out.

David said at home in Kidderminster yesterday: "The trousers were just hopeless. You could have got two people in them. But it seems our fun went too far. Albert suddenly came across and hit me in the face. Later, the foreman sent me home. I have lost £3 in wages and that hurts me more than anything."

The strikers are expected back at work today. But no one is expecting a return of Albert's troublesome trousers.

【参考答案】

baggy pants: wide and shapeless trousers
fell flat: didn't amuse people
crippled: stopped or drastically reduced
shapeless: without shape
fawn: light yellowish-brown
flapped: moved loosely from side to side
winked: closed one eye in a significant way
smirked: smiled unkindly
ribald: mocking; unkindly humorous
wisecracks: jokes
got him down: upset him; depressed him
planted one on: hit
intervened: came between them; stopped the fight
suspended David: sent David away from work
reinstated: given permission to work again

5.3 猜测词义专项训练

做下面的练习，训练根据上下文的线索猜测词义的技巧。每个练习后均配有参考答案。

1. Read each sentence quickly and supply a word for each blank. There is no single correct answer. You are to use context clues to help you provide a word which is appropriate in terms of grammar and meaning.

(1) I removed the ________ from the shelf and began to read.

(2) Harvey is a thief; he would ________ the gold from his grandmother's teeth and not feel guilty.

(3) Our uncle was a ________ , an incurable wanderer who never could stay in one place.

(4) Unlike his brother, who is truly a handsome person, Hogartty is quite ________ .

(5) The Asian ________ , like other apes, is specially adapted for life in trees.

(6) But surely everyone knows that if you step on an egg, it will ________ .

(7) Tom got a new ________ for his birthday. It is a sports model, red, with white interior and bucket seats.

【参考答案】

(1) book (2) steal (3) tramper (4) ugly (5) gibbon (长臂猿) (6) break (7) car

2. Here is another way to do the above excercises. Choose the apporiate answers and read the explanations below.

(1) I removed the ________ from the shelf and began to read.

A book **B** magazine **C** paper **D** newspaper

(2) Harvey is a thief; he would ________ the gold from his grandmother's teeth and not feel guilty.

A steal **B** take **C** rob **D** make

(3) Our uncle was a ________ , an incurable wanderer who never could stay in one place.

A nomad **B** roamer **C** traveller **D** drifter

(4) Unlike his brother, who is truly a handsome person, Hogartty is quite ________ .

A ugly **B** homely **C** plain **D** gentle

(5) The Asian ________ , like other apes, is specially adapted for life in trees.

A gibbon **B** monkey **C** chimp **D** ape

(6) But surely everyone knows that if you step on an egg, it will ________ .

A break **B** burst **C** burn **D** leak

(7) Tom got a new ________ for his birthday. It is a sports model, red, with white interior and bucket seats.

A car **B** cap **C** suit **D** shoe

【解释】

(1) The number of things that can be taken from a shelf and read is so few that the word "book" probably jump into your mind at once. Here, the association between the object and the purpose for which it is used is so close that you have very little difficulty guessing the right word.

(2) Harvey is a thief. A thief steals. The semicolon (;) indicates that the sentence which follows contains an explanation of the first statement. Further, you know that the definition of "thief" is: a person who steals.

(3) The comma (,) following the blank indicates a phrase in apposition, that is, a word or group of words which can be used as a synonym of the unfamiliar word. The four words are all synonyms of "wanderer".

(4) Hogartty is the opposite of his brother, and since his brother is handsome, Hogartty must be

ugly. The word "unlike" signals the relationship between Hogartty and his brother.

(5) You probably didn't write "gibbon", which is the word the author used. Most native speakers wouldn't be familiar with this word, either. But since you know that the word is the name of a type of ape, you don't need to know anything else. This is an example of how context can teach you the meaning of unfamiliar words.

(6) You recognised the "cause and effect" relationship in this sentence. There is only one thing that can happen to an egg when it is stepped on.

(7) The description in the second sentence gives you all the information you need to guess the word "car".

下面的专项训练，读者可根据自己的情况有选择地来做。

1. In the following exercise, do NOT try to learn the bold words (粗体字). Concentrate on developing your ability to guess the meaning of unfamiliar words using context clues. Read each sentence carefully, and write a definition (定义), synonym (同义词), or description (描述) of the bold word on the line provided.

(1) ________ We watched as the cat came quietly through the grass toward the bird. When it was just a few feet from the victim, it gathered its legs under itself, and **pounced**.

(2) ________ What could John expect? He had left his wet swimming trunks in the dark closet for over a week. Of course they had begun to **mildew**.

(3) ________ In spite of the fact that the beautiful **egret** is in danger of dying out completely, many clothing manufacturers still offer handsome prices for their long, elegant tail feathers, which are used as decorations on ladies' hats.

(4) ________ When he learned that the club was planning to admit women, the colonel began to **inveigh against** all forms of liberalism; his shouting attack began with universal voting and ended with a protest against the volunteer army.

(5) ________ The snake **slithered** through the grass.

(6) ________ The man thought that the children were defenseless, so he walked boldly up to the oldest and demanded money. Imagine his surprise when they began to **pelt** him with rocks.

(7) ________ Experts in **kinesics**, in their study of body motion as related to speech, hope to discover new methods of communication.

(8) ________ Unlike her **gregarious** sister, Jane is a shy, unsociable person who does not like to go to parties or to make new friends.

(9) ________ After a day of hunting, Harold is **ravenous**. Yesterday, for example, he ate two bowls of soup,

salad, a large chicken, and a piece of chocolate cake before he was finally satisfied.

(10) ________ After the accident, the ship went down so fast that we weren't able to **salvage** any of our personal belongings.

【参考答案】

(1) jump
(2) mold; rot
(3) a type of bird
(4) talk loudly against; attack verbally; protest
(5) move like a snake; slide
(6) hit
(7) the study of body motion
(8) sociable; friendly
(9) extremely hungry
(10) to save

2. In the following exercise, do NOT try to learn the bold words. Concentrate on developing your ability to guess the meaning of unfamiliar words using context clues. Read each sentence carefully, and write a definition, synonym, or description of the bold word on the line provided.

(1) ________ The major points of your plan are clear to me, but the details are still **hazy**.

(2) ________ By **anticipating** the thief's next move, the police were able to arrive at the bank before the robbery occurred.

(3) ________ All of the palace's laundry, when gathered for washing, formed a **massive** bundle which required the combined efforts of all the servants to carry.

(4) ________ "Give me specific suggestions when you criticise my work," said the employee. "**Vague** comments do not help me improve."

(5) ________ The apple **appeased** my hunger temporarily, but I could still eat a big dinner.

(6) ________ After the attacks on civilians by army troops, a committee met to try to discover what could have **provoked** such action.

(7) ________ The king **manifested** his pleasure with a hearty laugh.

(8) ________ The nation's highway death **toll** has increased every year since the invention of the automobile.

(9) ________ The workers' lives were **wretched**; they worked from morning to night in all kinds of weather, earning only enough money to buy simple food and cheap clothes.

(10) ________ In a series of bold moves, government attorneys attacked the **mammoth** auto industry, saying that the size of the business endangered the financial freedom of the individual buyer.

【参考答案】

(1) not clear

(2) guess in advance; think of ahead of time; foresee

(3) large; heavy; clumsy

(4) not specific; not clear; imprecise

(5) satisfy

(6) cause

(7) show; demonstrate

(8) total amount; count; extent of loss

(9) poor; miserable

(10) large

3. In the following exercise, do NOT try to learn the bold words. Concentrate on developing your ability to guess the meaning of unfamiliar words using context clues. Read each sentence carefully, and write a definition, synonym, or description of the bold word on the line provided.

(1) ________ It is difficult to list all of my father's **attributes** because he has so many different talents and abilities.

(2) ________ Mary, the president of the family council, **conferred** upon Robert the title of vice president, because she thought he would do a good job.

(3) ________ Mother was tall, fat, and middle-aged. The principal of the school was an older woman, almost as **plump** as Mother, and much shorter.

(4) ________ When Mark was in one of his **pedantic** moods, he assumed the manner of a distinguished professor and lectured for hours, on minute, boring topics.

(5) ________ Many members of the old wealthy families in society held themselves **aloof** from Gatsby, refusing even to acknowledge his existence.

(6) ________ I became angrier and angrier as Don talked, but I **refrained** from saying anything.

(7) ________ Mr. Doodle is always busy in an **ineffectual** way; he spends hours running around, accomplishing nothing.

(8) ________ Ian was proud of the neat rows of **marigolds** in his flower beds which he tended with great care.

(9) ________ Most dentists' offices are **drab** places, but Emilio's new office is a bright, cheerful place.

(10) ______ The inner and outer events of a plant are interdependent; but this isn't saying that the **skin**, **cortex**, **membrane**, or whatever you want to call the boundary of the individual is meaningless.

【参考答案】

(1) qualities; talents; abilities

(2) grant; give to

(3) fat; chubby

(4) bookish; boring; giving attention to small, unimportant, scholarly details

(5) above; apart from

(6) hold back; control oneself

(7) not effective; not producing the intended effect

(8) a (type of) flower

(9) uninteresting; dull; cheerless; lacking in colour or brightness

(10) outside cover of a body or organ; boundary

6 注意指代关系——理解文本的有机联系

为了写出简洁明了的文章，一个常用的方法就是使用诸如 this, that, it 等代词，把各个结构独立的句子连结起来。这些代词可以指代前面已经提到过的内容，或者在后面要提到的内容。读者如果不理解这些指代关系会直接影响对文本的理解，甚至导致严重的误解。因此，认识和理解指代关系是进行阅读技巧训练的重点之一，在此过程中也可加强对文本各部分之间关系的理解，从而进一步加深对全文的理解。

6.1 指代关系基础训练

基础训练 1

在下面的短文中，所有的粗体字指代的都是文中前面或后面提到的事物。仔细阅读短文，完成后面的练习。

The idea of evolution (**which** is a gradual change) was not a new **one**. The Greeks had thought of **it**, so had Erasmus Darwin, the grandfather of Charles, and also the Frenchman, Lamarck. **It** is one thing to have an idea; we all can guess and sometimes make a lucky guess. **It** is quite another thing to produce a proof of the correctness of that idea. Darwin thought he had **that** proof in **his** notebooks. **He** saw that all animals had to struggle to survive. **Those** which were best at surviving **their** environment passed on the good qualities which had helped **them** to **their** descendants. **This** was called "the survival of the fittest". For example, in a cold climate, **those** who have the warmest fur will live. Darwin believed that **this** necessity for an animal to deal with **its** environment explained the immense variety of creatures.

分析下面的代词指代的是前面还是后面提到的事物，并在表中填入其所指代的具体事物，前四个代词已作为例子给出。

Example:

	Before	**After**	**What it refers to**
which	√		evolution
one	√		idea
it	√		evolution
it		√	to have an idea

	Before	After	What it refers to
It			
that			
his			
He			
Those			
their			
them			
their			
This			
those			
this			
its			

【参考答案】

	Before	After	What it refers to
It		√	to produce a proof of the correctness of that idea
that	√		proof of the correctness of that idea
his	√		Darwin's
He	√		Darwin
Those		√	(animals) which were best at surviving their environment
their	√		those (animals')
them	√		those (animals)
their	√		those (animals')
This		√	"the survival of the fittest"
those		√	(animals) who have the warmest fur
this		√	necessity for an animal to deal with its environment
its	√		an animal's

基础训练 2

阅读下列短文，完成短文后面的练习。

Dr. Evelyn Weston looks beyond the accident figures and outlines the conditions that predispose us to injuries and casualties of one kind or another.

Accidents are caused; **they** don't just happen. **The reason** may be easy to see: an overloaded tray, a shelf out of reach, a patch of ice on the road. But more often than not there is a chain of events leading up to the calamity — frustration, tiredness or just bad temper — that show what the accident really is, a sort of attack on oneself.

Road accidents, for example, happen frequently after a family row, and we all know people who are accident-prone, so often at odds with themselves and the world that they seem to cause accidents for themselves and others.

Yet **this** should not make us think that accidents happen to other people. By definition, an accident is something you cannot predict or avoid, and the idea which used to be current, that the majority of road accidents are caused by a minority of criminally careless drivers, is not supported by insurance statistics. **These** show that most accidents involve ordinary motorists in a moment of carelessness or thoughtlessness.

It is not always clear, either, what sort of conditions make people more likely to have an accident. For instance, the law requires all factories to take safety precautions and most companies have safety committees to make sure the regulations are observed; but still, every day in Britain, some fifty thousand men and women are absent from work due to an accident. These accidents are largely the result of human error or misjudgement — noise and fatigue, boredom or worry are possible factors which contribute to **this**. Doctors who work in factories have found that those who have a high anxiety level run three times the normal risk of accidents at work.

1. Line 1: "they" refers to ________________

   "the reason" refers to ________________

2. Line 8: "this" refers to the statement that ________________

3. Line 11: "these" refers to ________________

4. Line 16: "this" refers to ________________

【参考答案】

1. accidents; an overloaded tray, a shelf out of reach, a patch of ice on the road
2. Road accidents happen frequently after a family row, and we all know people who are accident-prone, so often at odds with themselves and the world that they seem to cause

accidents for themselves and others.

3. insurance statistics

4. the result of human error or misjudgment

基础训练 3

阅读下列短文，完成短文后面的练习。

If no more cases of smallpox are reported by the end of the year the World Health Organisation can declare the world free of this deadly disease

The world's last known case of smallpox (outside an outbreak in a Birmingham laboratory) was reported in Somalia, in the Horn of Africa, in October 1977. The victim was a young cook called Ali Maow Maalin. His case becomes a landmark in medical history — for smallpox is the first communicable disease ever to be eradicated.

The remarkable campaign to free the world from smallpox has been led by the World Health Organisation. The Horn of Africa, embracing the Ogaden region of Ethiopia and Somalia was one of the last smallpox-ridden areas of the world when the WHO-sponsored Smallpox Eradication Programme (SEP) got under way in 1971.

Many of the twenty-five million inhabitants, mostly farmers and nomads living in a wilderness of desert, bush and mountains, already had smallpox. The problem of tracing the disease in such formidable country was made even more difficult by the continuous warfare in the country.

The programme concentrated on an imaginative policy of "search and containment". Vaccination was used to reduce the widespread incidence of the disease; but the success of the campaign depended on the work of volunteers. These were men, paid by the day, who walked hundreds of miles in search of "rumours" — information about possible smallpox cases. Often these rumours turned out to be cases of measles, chicken pox or syphilis — but nothing could be left to chance. As the campaign progressed the disease was gradually brought under control. By September 1976 the SEP made its first report that no new cases had been reported.

But that first optimism was short-lived. A three-year-old girl called Amina Salat, from a dusty village in the Ogaden in the southeast of Ethiopia, had given smallpox to a young nomad visitor. Leaving the village, he had walked across the border into Somalia. There he infected 3,000 people, and among them had been the cook Ali. It was a further fourteen months before the elusive target zero was reached. Even now the search continues in "high risk" areas and in parts of the country unchecked for some time. The flow of rumours has now diminished to a trickle — but each must still be checked by a qualified person.

Victory is in sight, but two years must pass since the "last case" before an international committee can declare that the world is entirely free from smallpox.

讲解：

先看下面这两句话：

1. His case becomes a **landmark** in medical history — for smallpox is the first communicable disease ever to be **eradicated**. (Para. 1)

2. The **remarkable** campaign **to free the world from smallpox** has been led by the World Health Organisation. (Para. 2)

在这样的说明文中，理解文本中不同部分之间的关系是十分重要的。以上两个句子的关系是由第二句重复第一句的部分意思而体现出来的。请看对上面这两个句子的分析：Sentence 1 says that the case of Ali is a **landmark** — something to be noticed or **remarked**, and the same idea is taken up in sentence 2 with the word **remarkable**. In the same way, the idea of **eradicate** is repeated in **to free the world from smallpox**.

练习：

See if you can find how the links are made in these sentences.

1. (1) Many of the twenty-five million inhabitants, mostly farmers and nomads living in a wilderness of desert, bush and mountains, already had smallpox. (Para. 3)
   (2) The problem of tracing the disease in **such formidable country** was made even more difficult by the continuous warfare in the country. (Para. 3)
   "such formidable country" refers to ________________

2. (1) The programme concentrated on an imaginative policy of "**search and containment**". (Para. 4)
   (2) **Vaccination** was used to reduce the widespread incidence of the disease ... (Para. 4)
   (3) **These were men**, paid by the day, **who walked hundreds of miles** in search of "rumours" ... (Para. 4)
   Is "vaccination" an example of search or containment?
   Is "these were men ... who walked hundreds of miles" an example of search or containment?

3. (1) By September 1976 the SEP made its first report that no new cases had been reported. (Para. 4)
   (2) But **that first optimism** was short-lived. (Para. 5)
   "that first optimism" refers back to ________________

【参考答案】

1. a wilderness of desert, bush and mountains
2. Yes, "vaccination" is an example of containment.
   Yes, it is an example of search.
3. the SEP's first report that no new cases had been reported

基础训练 4

阅读下列短文，完成短文后面的练习。

The case for censoring television violence

by Conor Cruise O'Brien

Broadcasters are against censorship. That much was clear at a recent symposium on the subject of censorship at the Edinburgh International Television Festival.

It was not clear, however, what exactly broadcasters meant by censorship, or what a censor-free condition would be like. Some spoke as if they regarded the editing of anyone's work by anyone else as censorship. Others indicated that to refrain from saying or writing something others might object to is a form of self-censorship: it was implied that self-censorship was always a response to pressure from above — never to fashion or a desire for approval.

Because they are against censorship, one would expect broadcasters to be especially vigilant about the danger of commercial exploitation of socially harmful forces, such as the appeal of violence. But there are few signs of this — instead there are signs of a determination to play down serious evidence tending to show, for example, that exposure of children to television violence is likely to have a brutalising effect.

Evidence of this is provided in a recent book by H. S. Eysenck and D. K. B. Nias, *Sex, Violence and the Media*, which refers to the use of films by the American army to reduce the viewers' reaction to pain and suffering in others, so that in the end they will inflict pain and death without question.

The authors go on to set out in Chapter 7 mentioning that laboratory experiments show that exposure to "ordinary" or commercial televised violence can have a similar effect. With remarkable consistency, the groups of children and adults exposed to broadcast violence behaved more aggressively than the control groups.

讲解：

先看下面这句话：

That much was clear at a recent symposium on the subject of censorship of the Edinburgh International Television Festival.

这篇短文的各个句子是按照逻辑排列组合起来的，表达了一个完整的意思。其中一种连结句子的方式是通过使用 this, that, so, similar 这些词指称文中先前提过的事物。在上面的这句话中，that much 指的是 Broadcasters are against censorship. 这句话。

练习：

1. **Some** spoke as if they regarded the editing of anyone's work by anyone else as censorship. **Others** indicated that to refrain from saying or writhing something others might object to is a form of self-censorship ... (Para. 2)

"some" refers to ____________________

"others" refers to ____________________

2. Because they are against censorship, one would expect broadcasters to be especially vigilant about the danger of commercial exploitation of socially harmful forces, **such as** the appeal of violence. (Para. 3)

"such as" refers to ____________________

3. But there are few signs of **this** ... (Para. 3)

"this" refers to ____________________

4. Evidence of **this** is provided in a recent book by H. S. Eysenck and D. K. B. Nias, *Sex, Violence and the Media*, which refers to the use of films by the American army to reduce the viewers' reaction to pain and suffering in others, so that in the end they will inflict pain and death without question. (Para. 4)

"this" refers to ____________________

5. ... laboratory experiments show that exposure to "ordinary" or commercial televised violence can have a **similar** effect. (Para. 5)

"similar" refers to ____________________

【参考答案】

1. some broadcasters; other broadcasters
2. the danger of commercial exploitation of socially harmful forces
3. the whole sentence that goes before
4. the whole sentence that goes before in the paragraph above
5. the effect of the example that goes before in the paragraph above

基础训练 5

阅读下列短文，完成短文后面的练习。

Pain — It's All in the Mind

Pain is easier to endure if you know you can end it. Speakers at a session on pain at the British Association's psychology section have new evidence to support this idea for two common experiences of pain: in childbirth and at the dentist's. On the other side of the coin, their inability to control pain may explain why some people with chronic pain have psychological problems as well.

Dr. J. Robinson, a psychologist at University College in Cardiff, found out about the phenomenon of self-controlled pain almost by accident. He was studying the effects of analgesics used to control pain during childbirth and as part of the experiment made it possible for women having their child to press a button which gave an automatic injection — instead of having all injections made by the doctor. Afterwards these women did not say that they had less pain than other women in childbirth, but they did use considerably less of the drug.

J. Atkins, a dental surgeon, has observed a similar phenomenon. As part of their efforts to make dentistry painless, Atkins and researchers at Aston University in Birmingham offered patients a switch they could flip to turn off the dentist's drill whenever they chose. But, after trying the switch on 50 patients Atkins gave up, none of the patients had ever flipped the switch.

Perhaps the extra endurance was because the Aston team also use other methods to make dentistry painless. Apparently few other dentists are so considerate. The end result is, according to the Birmingham survey, is that British people avoid going to the dentist, with the consequence that almost 30% of people in England and Wales have lost all their teeth, and more than seven out of ten have lost at least six teeth. Less than half of the public pay regular visits to the dentist. To find out why, Atkins and psychologist W. G. Cumberbatch interviewed a sample of patients attending a dental hospital. The most common reason people gave for not having dental check-ups were fear and pain.

By using a little care and taking time to explain what will happen, Atkins feels, dentists could overcome these fears. There are techniques for giving injections without pain, and a "calm unhurried approach" to drilling can make that painless, too.

Sadly, few dentists seem to take much trouble with their patients. "I am not nervous when I go to the dentist, and I do not have any pronounced sympathy for those who are," said one dentist. "I tend to take the point of view that they are being unreasonable at my expense."

1. Speakers at a session on pain at the British Association's psychology section have new evidence to support this idea for **two common experiences of pain**. (Para. 1)

"two common experiences of pain" refers to ______________________________

2. On the other side of the coin, **their** inability to control pain may explain why some people with chronic pain have psychological problems as well. (Para. 1)

"their" refers to ______________________________

3. Afterwards **these women** did not say that they had less pain than other women in childbirth, but they **did use** considerably less of the drug. (Para. 2)

"these women" refers to ______________________________

Why did the writer of the passage put "did use" instead of "used" here?

4. Apparently few other dentists are **so** considerate. (Para. 4)

"so" refers to ________________________________

5. Atkins feels, dentists could overcome **these fears**. (Para. 5)

"these fears" refers to ________________________________

6. "I tend to take the point of view that **they** are being unreasonable at my expense." (Para. 6)

"they" refers to ________________________________

【参考答案】

1. experiences of pain in childbirth and at the dentist's
2. some people's
3. women having their child to press a button which gave an automatic injection
   The writer wanted to emphasise the effect of using considerably less of the drug.
4. so considerate as the Aston team
5. fear and pain
6. those who are nervous

基础训练 6

阅读下列文章，完成后面的练习。

Snowball and Napoleon

In January there came bitterly hard weather. The earth was like iron, and nothing could be done in the fields. Many meetings were held in the big barn, and the pigs occupied themselves with planning out the work of the coming season. It had come to be accepted that the pigs, who were manifestly cleverer than the other animals, should decide all questions of farm policy, though **their**[1] decisions had to be ratified by a majority vote. **This arrangement**[2] would have worked well enough if it had not been for the disputes between Snowball and Napoleon. These two disagreed at every point where disagreement was possible. If one of them suggested sowing a bigger acreage with barley, the other was certain to demand a bigger acreage of oats, and if one of them said that such and such a field was just right for cabbages, the other would declare that **it**[3] was useless for anything except roots. **Each**[4] had his own following, and there were some violent debates. At the meetings Snowball often won over the majority by his brilliant speeches, but Napoleon was better at **canvassing support**[5] for himself in between times. He was especially successful with the sheep. Of late the sheep had taken to bleating "Four legs good, two legs bad" **both in and out of season**[6], and they often interrupted the meeting with **this**[7]. It was noticed that they were especially liable to break into "Four legs good, two legs bad" at the crucial moments in Snowball's speeches. Snowball had made a close study of some back numbers of the

Farmer and Stockbreeder[8] which he had found in the farmhouse, and was full of plans for innovations and improvements. He talked learnedly about field-drains, silage, and basic slag, and had worked out a complicated scheme for all the animals to drop their dung directly in the fields, at a different spot every day, to save the labour of cartage. Napoleon produced no schemes of his own, but said quietly that **Snowball's**[9] would come to nothing, and seemed to be biding his time. But of all their controversies, none was so bitter as the one that took place over the windmill.

In the long pasture, not far from the farm buildings, there was a small knoll which was the highest point on the farm. After surveying the ground, Snowball declared that **this**[10] was just the place for a windmill, which could be made to operate a dynamo and supply the farm with electrical power. **This**[11] would light the stalls and warm them in winter, and would also **run**[12] a circular saw, a chaff-cutter, a mangel-slicer, and an electric milking machine. The animals had never heard of anything of this kind before (for the farm was an old-fashioned one and had only the most primitive machinery), and they listened in astonishment while Snowball conjured up pictures of fantastic machines which would do their work for them while they grazed at their ease in the fields or improved their minds with reading and conversation.

Within a few weeks Snowball's plans for the windmill were fully worked out. The mechanical details came mostly from three books which had belonged to Mr. Jones — *One Thousand Useful Things to Do About the House*, *Every Man His Own Bricklayer*, and *Electricity for Beginners*. Snowball used as his study a shed which had once been used for incubators and had a smooth wooden floor, suitable for drawing on. He was closeted there for hours at a time. With his books held open by a stone, and with a piece of chalk gripped between the knuckles of his trotter, he would move rapidly to and fro, drawing in line after line and uttering little whimpers of excitement. Gradually the plans grew into a complicated mass of cranks and cog-wheels, covering more than half the floor, which the other animals found completely unintelligible but very impressive. All of them came to look at Snowball's drawings at least once a day. Even the hens and ducks came, and, were at pains not to tread on the chalk marks. Only Napoleon held aloof. He had declared himself against the windmill from the start. One day, however, he arrived unexpectedly to examine the plans. He walked heavily round the shed, looked closely at every detail of the plans and snuffed at them once or twice, then stood for a little while contemplating them out of the corner of his eye; then suddenly he lifted his leg, urinated over the plans, and walked out without uttering a word.

The whole farm was deeply divided on the subject of the windmill. Snowball did not deny that to build it would be a difficult business. Stone would have to be quarried and built up into walls, then the sails would have to be made and after that there would be need for dynamos and cables. (How these were to be procured, Snowball did not say.) But he maintained that **it**[13] could all be done in a year. And thereafter, he declared, so much labour would be saved that the animals would only need to work three days a week. Napoleon, on the other hand, argued that the great need of the moment was to increase food production, and that if they wasted time on the windmill they would all starve to death. The animals formed themselves into two factions under the slogans, "Vote for Snowball and the three-day week" and "Vote for Napoleon and the full manger". Benjamin was the only animal who did not side with either faction. He refused to believe either that food would become more plentiful or that the windmill would save work. Windmill or no windmill, he said, life would go on as it had always gone on — that is, badly.

(1) What does the word "their" refer to? ______

(2) What was "this arrangement"? ______

(3) What does "it" refer to? ______

(4) What does "each" mean ? ______

(5) What do you think is meant by "canvassing support"? ______

(6) Explain "both in and out of season". ______

(7) What is "this"? ______

(8) What do you think the *Farmer and Stockbreeder* was? ______

(9) What is meant by "Snowball's" ? ______

(10) What does "this" refer to? ______

(11) What does "this" refer to ? ______

(12) What is the subject of the verb "run"? ______

(13) What is the meaning of "it"? ______

【参考答案】

(1) The pigs'.

(2) The fact that the pigs acted as leaders.

(3) The field in question.

(4) Each of the two pigs, Snowball and Napoleon.

(5) Persuading the other animals to support him.

(6) At the right moment and at the wrong moment.

(7) The slogan "Four legs good, two legs bad".

(8) A farmer's magazine.

(9) Snowball's plans.

(10) The small knoll.

(11) Electric power.

(12) Electric power.

(13) Building the windmill.

6.2 指代关系强化训练

6.2.1 代词部分

1. In the following sentences, pronouns are used carelessly and in such a way as to cause ambiguity. Rewrite the sentences so that their meanings are quite clear. In some cases you will have to decide for yourself the meanings intended.

(1) A man carrying a red flag preceded the train along the quayside street. It was crowded with holiday-makers.

(2) He has rented a caravan near a farm. He says he can buy most of his food from it.

(3) I put a pie to warm in the oven, which was already very hot. After ten minutes I was able to eat it.

(4) The clock on the mantelpiece, which has to be wound up twice a day, is very old.

(5) BBC interviewers often question people in the streets. They are sometimes indignant.

(6) The rose bowl in the centre of the table, which she had just filled with fresh water, had come from Italy.

【参考答案】

(1) A man carrying a red flag preceded the train along the quayside street which was crowded with holiday-makers.

Or: The train crowded with holiday-makers was preceded along the quayside street by a man carrying a red flag.

(2) He says he can buy most of his food from the farm near which he has rented a caravan.

(3) The oven was already very hot, so after ten minutes I was able to eat the pie which I had put in it to warm.

(4) The clock which stands on the mantelpiece has to be wound up twice a day as it is very old.

(5) The people questioned by BBC interviewers in the streets are sometimes indignant.

(6) In the centre of the table stood an Italian rose bowl which she had just filled with fresh water.

2. The following sentences, which are considerably longer than the preceding ones, also contain ambiguities. Various kinds of changes, including the substitution of nouns for pronouns or of the passive for the active voice, and also the omission of a few words, may be necessary. The rewritten sentences should be quite clear and not miss any meaning of the sentences being corrected.

(1) On a fine Summer Bank Holiday, seaside places are so crammed with people and cars that they can hardly find space to sit down which is why those people who hate crowds keep away from them.

(2) Many British farmers rear turkeys for the Christmas festivities. They usually get good prices for them,

though sometimes, when there is a surplus of them, they fall considerably, and some even remain unsold. In this case, much of their trouble and the food which they have had to buy are wasted.

(3) The children watched the ripples spreading over the lake surface. They were caused by the stones they were throwing. They lifted momentarily the floating dead leaves, which gave the impression of a miniature ocean. They were like tiny waves rocking minute and fragile boats.

(4) The intonation with which one expresses what he wants to say may alter your meaning completely. One is sometimes unaware that one seems abrupt which may offend people. This is not because of the words he is using but because the rise and fall of your voice convey its own special meaning. One is advised to accustom his ear to detecting the varying shades of meaning that you can give to any one phrase merely by a change in intonation.

(5) Owing to the shortage of milk supplies, which is essential for children, it must be imported, which is regrettable as it will necessitate the organisation of a special transport service, which will be very difficult, as it can be obtained in sufficient quantities only from countries a considerable way off.

【参考答案】

(1) People who hate crowds keep away from those seaside places which, on a fine Summer Bank Holiday, are so crammed with people and cars that there is almost no space to sit down.

(2) Many British farmers rear turkeys for the Christmas festivities and usually get good prices for the birds. Sometimes, however, a surplus may cause prices to fall considerably and some turkeys even remain unsold. In this case, much of the trouble taken and food bought are wasted.

(3) The children were throwing stones and watching the ripples which were caused spreading over the lake surface. By lifting momentarily the dead leaves, like tiny waves rocking minute and fragile boats, the ripples gave the impression of a miniature ocean.

(4) Meaning may be completely altered by the intonation with which ideas are expressed. An unconscious abruptness which may offend people can result not from the words used but from the fact that the rise and fall of the voice convey its own special meaning. It is advisable to accustom the ear to detecting the varying shades of meaning that can be given to any one phrase merely by a change in intonation.

(5) Milk, which is essential for children, is in short supply and so unfortunately must be imported. As it can be obtained in sufficient quantities only from countries a considerable way off, there will be difficulty in organising the necessary special transport service.

3. Rewrite the following sentences, supplying a suitable antecedent for the relative pronoun.

(1) They have rounded up the ponies in the forest and are counting them, which happens only once a year.

(2) The ship ran around in the fog, which could have been disastrous.

(3) A body has been discovered near the sea, which the police are investigating.

(4) William fought the Battle of Hastings in 1066, which everybody remembers.

【参考答案】

(1) They have rounded up the ponies in the forest and are counting them, an operation which happens only once a year.

(2) The ship ran around in the fog, a mishap which could have been disastrous.

(3) A body has been found near the sea, a discovery which the police are investigating.

(4) William fought the Battle of Hastings in 1066, a battle which everybody remembers.

4. From the alternatives given in the following sentences, choose and underline the form which can be correctly used in written English.

(1) In these roughly-cobbled streets, one / he / you long(s) to examine the

beautifully-carved facades of the houses to one's / his / your left and right,

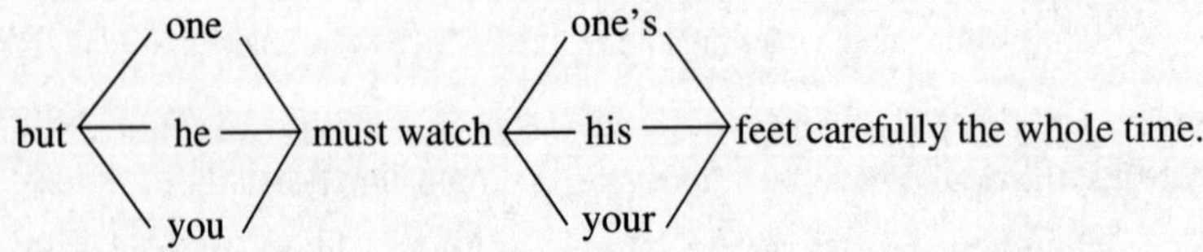

(2) The missing journalist, who / whom the newspapers had denounced

as a spy and who / whom had left the country with official secrets, was discovered quietly fishing

from the end of Southend Pier.

(3) The children all say that their mother needs a holiday more

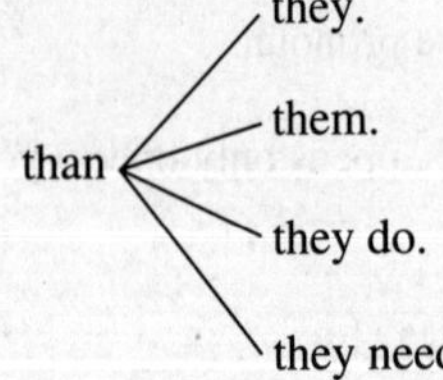

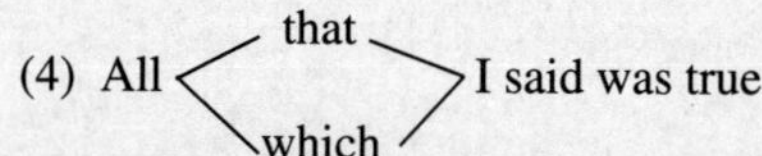

(4) All that / which I said was true.

(5) The Mayor of Biggleswig, who / whom / that the police arrested yesterday by mistake, is threatening to sue the latter for assault.

(6) One says / It is said that a momentous battle was once fought here.

(7) They are driving the pig back into its / it's sty.

(8) He is one of those irritating people who has / have to force his / their opinions on other people.

(9) They have not lived in this neighbourhood as long as us. / we have. / we.

(10) The cowboy whose / of whom horse the cattle thieves had stolen was stranded on the vast empty prairie.

【参考答案】

(1) one / you; one's / your; one / you; one's / your　(2) whom; who　(3) they do
(4) that　(5) whom　(6) It is said　(7) its　(8) have; their　(9) we have
(10) whose

5. From the alternatives given in the following sentences, choose and underline the form which can be correctly used in written English.

(1) The character of Hamlet which / that can be interpreted in many ways has fascinated actors of most nationalities.

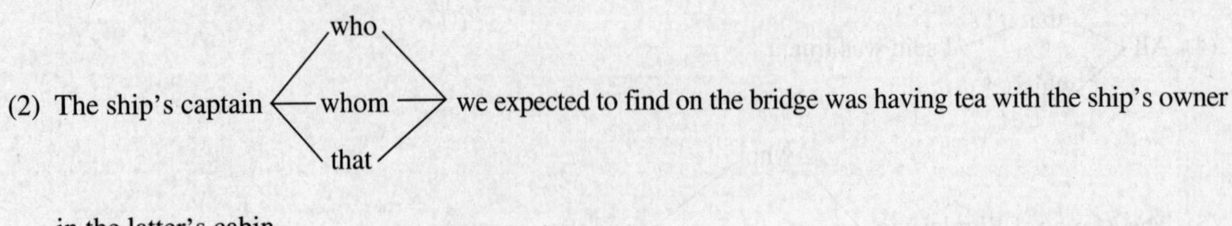

(3) I would like to have a word with the student who / that / whom drew that picture of me on the blackboard.

(4) Where did you put the recipe which / that Aunt Matilda gave me?

(5) Shropshire which / that A. E. Houseman commemorates in his poems is a wild and beautiful county.

(6) That is the most which / that I can do for you.

(7) The car which / that they are travelling in can be used as a camper.

(8) The wild flowers of the countryside which / that few people heed are as lovely as any which / that grow in the garden.

(9) His grandmother who / whom / that he often sends money to lives otherwise on a small pension.

(10) This is the mouse which / that lived in the house which / that Jack built.

(11) The girl who / whom / that they have chosen as the Carnival Queen has since received ten offers of marriage.

of which the author

(12) This satirical theatrical revue — the author of which — insists on remaining anonymous makes fun of the contemporary drama.

whose author

【参考答案】

(1) which / that (2) whom (3) who / that (4) which / that (5) which / that

(6) that (7) which (8) which / that; that (9) whom

(10) that / which; that / which (11) whom / that

(12) of which the author / whose author

6.2.2 形容词部分

1. Write down the adjective forms of the words given below. Do not give participles.

traitor ______	courage ______	fire ______	appear ______
reverse ______	parliament ______	government ______	consult ______
revolution ______	humour ______	intermission ______	impulse ______
monotony ______	enthusiasm ______	adventure ______	planet ______
science ______	sympathise ______	elude ______	circle ______
apology ______	energy ______	apathy ______	decoration ______
experiment ______	title ______	muscle ______	angle ______
mountain ______	water ______	winter ______	book ______
oblige ______	geometry ______	accept ______	invent ______
ingenuity ______	infant ______	idiot ______	absorb ______
dictator ______			

【参考答案】

traitorous; courageous; fiery; apparent; reversible; parliamentary; governmental; consultative; revolutionary; humorous; intermittent; impulsive; monotonous; enthusiastic; adventurous; planetary; scientific; sympathetic; elusive; circular; apologetic; energetic; apathetic; decorative; experimental; titular; muscular; angular; mountainous; watery; wintry; bookish; obligatory;

geometrical; acceptable; inventive; ingenious; infantile; idiotic; absorbent; dictatorial

2. Write down phrases to show the difference in meaning between the adjectives in the following groups.

earthy ______ earthly ______ earthen ______ hearty ______ heartful ______

brass ______ brassy ______ brazen ______ childish ______ childlike ______

young ______ youthful ______ graceful ______ gracious ______

old ______ elderly ______ olden ______ human ______ humane ______

wood ______ wooden ______ wooded ______ gold ______ golden ______

sunny ______ solar ______ glass ______ glassy ______ glazed ______

【参考答案】

the earthy smell of potatoes; earthly possessions (contrasted with spiritual); earthen pots; a hearty appetite; heartful sympathy; brass candlesticks; a brassy clang; brazen impudence; childish fits of temper; childlike innocence; young children; a youthful figure; a graceful dancer; a gracious smile; old books; an elderly solicitor; in olden times; human needs; the humane treatment of animals; a wood fire; a wooden floor; a wooded hill-slope; gold coins; golden hair; sunny weather; the solar system; glass vases; a glassy stare; a glazed door

3. Use each of the following words in two phrases, in the first case as a noun, in the second as an adjective. The form of the word is the same, but its meaning may be different.

light ______ ______ fit ______ ______

cold ______ ______ chief ______ ______

principal ______ ______ common ______ ______

square ______ ______ top ______ ______

fat ______ ______ stout ______ ______

【参考答案】

a bright light; a light punishment

a fit of coughing; to get fit again after illness

a cold in the head; cold weather

a tribal chief; the chief industries

a college principal; the principal subjects

a walk across the common; common interests

a large square; a square handkerchief

the top of the hill; a top man

rich fat; a fat pig

a glass of stout; a stout stick

4. By using it in a phrase, show how each of the following nouns can do the work of an adjective.

prize ______ correspondence ______ Brussels ______

garden ______ stamp ______ evening ______

bargain ______ toy ______ china ______

tape ______

【参考答案】

prize cattle; a correspondence course; Brussels lace; a garden path;

a stamp collection; evening dress; a bargain basement; a toy train;

a china cup; a tape measure

5. One adjective corresponding to each of the following words is different in form from the words given. Write down the related adjective. In some cases the meaning is slightly modified and in these instances point out the difference.

surface ______ moon ______ night ______ island ______

mind ______ nose ______ eye ______ ear ______

hand ______ back ______ tooth ______ mouth ______

time ______ wall ______ sea ______ thought ______

law ______

【参考答案】

superficial (shallow); lunar; nocturnal; insular (narrow-minded);

mental; nasal; ocular; aural; manual; dorsal; dental; oral (spoken);

temporal (temporary = for a short time); mural; marine; thoughtful (pensive); legal

6. Each of the following words has at least two adjectives (excluding participles) with different meanings corresponding to it. Write down the adjectives and their meanings.

	Adjective 1	Meaning	Adjective 2	Meaning
tolerate				
trust				
confide				
select				
appreciate				
night				
power				
nerve				
gas				
pity				
event				
effect				
depend				
comprehend				
flower				
luxury				
brother				
father				
mother				
continue				
force				
nebula				
star				
hard				
law				
picture				

【参考答案】

	Adjective 1	Meaning	Adjective 2	Meaning
tolerate	tolerant	open-minded	tolerable	bearable
trust	trustworthy	reliable	trustful	without suspicion
confide	confident	sure	confidential	secret
select	selective	subject to choice	select	distinguished
appreciate	appreciative	admiring	appreciable	considerable

（续表）

	Adjective 1	Meaning	Adjective 2	Meaning
night	nightly	every night	nocturnal	by night
power	powerful	strong	powerless	unable to act
nerve	nervous	from the nerves	nervy	easily agitated
gas	gassy	effervescent	gaseous	consisting of gas
pity	pitiful / piteous	causing pity	pitiable	worthy of pity
event	eventual	final	eventful	with many things happening
effect	effectual	removing all difficulties	effective	producing a result
depend	dependable	reliable	dependent	needing support from someone
comprehend	comprehensive	inclusive	comprehensible	can be understood
flower	flowery	over-decorated (language)	floral	of flowers
luxury	luxurious	richly comfortable	luxuriant	plentiful
brother	brotherly	as felt by brothers	fraternal	linked by common ties
father	fatherly	kindly and protective	paternal	having the characteristics of a father
mother	motherly	kind and sympathetic	maternal	of a mother
continue	continual	recurring over a period	continuous	unbroken over a period
force	forceful	masterful and energetic	forcible	by force
nebula	nebulous	unsubstantial	nebular	of a large star group
star	starry	shining like stars	stellar	of stars
hand	handy	accessible	manual	operated by hand
law	lawful	allowed by law	legal	connected with the law
picture	picturesque	having the prettiness of a picture	pictorial	having the characteristics of a picture

7. Before each of the hyphens shown, supply an adverb which will modify the given participle. The adverbs should all be positive in implication.

a ________ -read newspaper a ________ -esteemed statesman a ________ -planned campaign

a ________ -organised society a ________ -lit room a ________ -criticised report a ________ -made suit　　a ________ -needed reform　　a ________ -coloured poster

a ________ -awaited change

Present participles are less commonly modified. Here are a few examples:

a hard-working student, rapidly-rising costs, fast-moving traffic

【参考答案】

widely; highly; carefully; highly; brightly; strongly; well; much; brightly; long

8. Explain the difference in meaning made in the following sentences by the use of the present participle or the corresponding past participle.

(1) Tribesmen gathering / gathered from all parts of the country were being organised in combat groups.

(2) Watched / Watching intently, the prisoner stood motionless in the dock.

(3) The man following / followed was obviously in a hurry.

(4) Fruit ripening / ripened in the sun could be seen in every orchard.

(5) The cows sheltering / sheltered from the rain under the trees continued peacefully to chew the cud.

(6) The men discussing / discussed in the public house did not seem to be popular.

(7) The race just starting / started is one of the preliminary heats.

(8) The holy man worshipping / worshipped at the shrine was gaunt and fiery-eyed.

(9) The writer now criticising / criticised in the review is well known for his sarcasm.

【参考答案】

(1) gathering: this was still happening
gathered: they were already assembled

(2) watched: the prisoner was being watched
watching: he was watching

(3) following: the man walking close behind
followed: the man walking in front

(4) ripening: getting ripe
ripened: already ripe

(5) sheltering: they had come there for shelter
sheltered: the trees protected them

(6) discussing: the men talking
discussed: the men being talked about

(7) starting: it is starting now
started: it is already being run

(8) worshipping: the man is showing reverence
worshipped: others are reverencing him

(9) criticising: the writer is criticising
criticised: the writer is being criticised

9. Complete the following sentences with comparisons.

(1) Teenagers are not ________ conservative ________ their elders.

(2) English people are usually ________ reserved ________ Italians.

(3) A lorry is ________ powerful ________ a car.

(4) Housework is ________ tiring ________ office work.

(5) Eve is said to have been ________ ________ woman on earth.

(6) Lead is ________ ________ aluminum.

(7) Wasps are not ________ ________ ________ bees.

(8) Swans are ________ ________ ________ ducks.

(9) A gold sovereign is ________ ________ ________ a pound note.

(10) It takes nearly ________ ________ to reach London Airport by coach from the terminal ________ it does to fly from the Airport to Paris.

(11) Many people consider Einstein ________ ________ ________ twentieth century scientist.

【参考答案】

(1) so; as (2) more; than (3) more; than (4) more; than
(5) the; first (6) heavier; than (7) so; useful; as (8) more; graceful; than
(9) worth; more; than (10) as; long; as (11) the; most; influential

10. Rewrite the following sentences in such a way as to make the sentences grammatically and logically correct.

(1) When depressed, a new hat makes my mother feel happier.

(2) Loaded with a Christmas tree, parcels and a bulging shopping bag, a taxi was a welcome sight.

(3) Speaking as a married man, my five-year-old son is far more advanced than I was at his age.

(4) Carried away by his enthusiasm, every obstacle in his path disappeared.

(5) Having been deserted by his guide, there seemed little hope that the explorer would find his way through the jungle.

(6) Racing along the quiet road at sixty miles an hour, an old man suddenly started to cross in front of him.

【参考答案】

(1) When my mother is depressed, a new hat will make her feel happier.
(2) As he was loaded with a Christmas tree, parcels and a bulging shopping bag, a taxi was a welcome sight.
(3) In my opinion as a married man, my five-year-old son is far more advanced than I was at his age.
(4) He was so completely carried away by his enthusiasm that every obstacle in his path disappeared.
(5) There seemed little hope that the explorer, who had been deserted by his guide, would find his way through the jungle.
(6) He was racing along the quiet road at sixty miles an hour when an old man suddenly started to cross in front of him.

7 关注连接词——弄清句与句之间的逻辑关系，树立整体观念

7.1 阅读中需要注意的连接词

文章不是一组互不联系的、独立的句子集合，而是由相互关联的句子组成的网状整体，各个句子表述的含义息息相关，连贯地表达出一个总体信息或思想。除了可以从指代关系（详见本书第六章）看出文本中词义的关系，还可以从连接词看出文中句法的关系。连接词能帮助读者在寻读（见本书第一章）时更好地理解文中论点、事实和思想的发展，甚至还有修辞上的意义（如强化、解释等），从而帮助读者更好地使用寻读这一阅读技巧。

在阅读中要认识和注意表示关系的连接词。请看下面的例子：

- The school has grown **from** a small building holding 200 students **to** a large institute which educates 4,000 students a year.

from ... to 表示阶段变化的起点和终点。

- Many critics have proclaimed Doris Lessing as **not only** the best writer of the postwar generation, **but also** a penetrating analyst of human affairs.

not only ... but also 的意思基本等同于 both ... and，但侧重点放在 but also 上。

- **In order to** graduate on time, you will need to take five courses each semester.

in order to 和 if 一样，表示在另一事件能够发生之前，某个事件必须存在。

- **As a result of** three books, a television documentary, and a special exposition at the Library of Congress, the mystery has aroused considerable public interest.

as a result of 表示因果关系。跟在 as a result of 后面的是原因（即 three books, television documentary 和 special exposition）； the arousal of considerable public interest 是结果。

- **Because of** the impact of these ideas, **which** had been introduced originally to Europe by soldiers returning from the East, the West was greatly changed.

because of 也表示因果关系。the West was greatly changed 是这些 ideas 的结果；which 指代 these ideas。

表示句子关系的连接词还有：

1. 表原因（cause）：because, as, since, due to, owing to, and
2. 表结果（consequence / result）：so, therefore, as a result, so ... that, such ... that, in order that, consequently, as a result

3. 表时间 / 时间顺序（time / time sequence）：first, next, then, after that, finally, before, after, as soon as, hardly ... when, no sooner ... than, when, once, until, till, as long as

4. 表让步（concession）：although, though, even though, even if, in spite of, despite, nevertheless

5. 表相反、对比（opposition / contrast）：but, however, while, whereas, in contrast, on the other hand, yet

6. 表目的（purpose）：in order to, so as to, to, so that, in case

7. 表附加（addition）：not only ... but also, moreover, furthermore, in addition to, as well as, besides

8. 表并列（juxtaposition）：and, and then, but, for, nor, or, so, yet, either ... or, neither ... nor, not only ... but ..., also, as well, too

下面先做一些练习，以便认识连接词的用法和作用。每个练习后附有答案，以供读者自我检测。

7.2 连接词专项训练

7.2.1 基础语句训练

1. Connect each pair of the sentences with the words in the box. Use only one word from the box to connect these two sentences. Where two answers are possible, choose the more likely one.

and	but	so	then	before	after	because

Example:

I got out of the car. / I walked into the house.

I got out of the car and walked into the house.

(1) The weather was lovely. / We stayed in the garden.

____

(2) We went to bed. / I locked all the doors.

____

(3) The little boy was wet and cold. / He wasn't hurt.

____

(4) We turned off the lights. / We left the room.

____

(5) I had a bath. / We played football.

____

(6) I sat in the kitchen. / I read a book.

____

(7) She worked hard. / She failed all her exams.

____

(8) I do some exercises. / I go to work in the morning.

____

(9) They took me to hospital. / The crash happened.

____

(10) We had no money. / The banks were closed.

____

(11) We paid our hotel bill. / We left.

____

(12) I had to walk to work. / The car wouldn't start.

____

(13) It was very cold. / We didn't go out.

____

【参考答案】

(1) The weather was lovely, so we stayed in the garden.

(2) Before we went to bed, I locked all the doors.

(3) The little boy was wet and cold, but he wasn't hurt.

(4) We turned off the lights and then left the room / before we left the room.

(5) I had a bath after we played football.

(6) I sat in the kitchen and read a book.

(7) She worked hard, but failed all her exams.

(8) I do some exercises before I go to work in the morning.

(9) They took me to hospital after the crash happened.

(10) We had no money because / and the banks were closed.

(11) We paid our hotel bill and then left.

(12) I had to walk to work because the car wouldn't start.

(13) It was very cold so we didn't go out.

2. Link the two sentences to make one sentence, using the words given. Don't change the order of the two original sentences. Use a comma if the conjunction comes at the beginning of your sentence.

Examples:

She was very tired. / She went to bed. (as)

As she was very tired, she went to bed.

I can't use my car. / It's broken down. (because)

I can't use my car because it's broken down.

(1) He hasn't done any work. / I don't think he'll pass the exam. (since)

____

(2) The bus crashed. / The driver fell asleep. (because)

____

(3) It was raining. / We decided not to go out. (as)

____

(4) The climate is changing. / The earth is getting warmer. (because)

____

(5) Monday is a public holiday. / We're going to spend the weekend in the mountains. (since)

____

(6) Romeo committed suicide. / He thought Juliet was dead. (because)

____

(7) You haven't seen the cathedral yet. / I'll take you there on Sunday. (as)

____

(8) The concert was cancelled. / The singer was ill. (because)

____

【参考答案】

(1) Since he hasn't done any work, I don't think he'll pass the exam.

(2) The bus crashed because the driver fell asleep.

(3) As it was raining, we decided not to go out.

(4) The climate is changing because the earth is getting warmer.

(5) Since Monday is a public holiday, we're going to spend the weekend in the mountains.

(6) Romeo committed suicide because he thought Juliet was dead.

(7) As you haven't seen the cathedral yet, I'll take you there on Sunday.

(8) The concert was cancelled because the singer was ill.

3. Rewrite each pair of the sentences as one sentence using "both ... and", "both", or "neither ... nor".

Examples:

Maria comes from Colombia. Felipe also comes from Colombia.

Both Maria and Felipe come from Colombia. / Maria and Felipe both come from Colombia.

The police couldn't catch him. The army couldn't catch him.

Neither the police nor the army could catch him.

(1) Greg likes surfing. Liz likes surfing.

____

(2) The house wasn't attractive. The garden wasn't attractive.

____

(3) The food was terrible. The service was terrible, too.

____

(4) Angela played the piano. Lucy also played the piano.

____

(5) Jessica wasn't at home. Chloe wasn't at home.

____

(6) His family didn't know about his accident. His friends didn't know about his accident.

____

(7) Eagles hunt small animals. Wolves hunt small animals.

____

(8) The film is very funny. The book is also very funny.

____

(9) The beach isn't far away. The shops aren't far away.

____

(10) Japan has a lot of earthquakes. New Zealand has a lot of earthquakes.

____

【参考答案】

(1) Both Greg and Liz like surfing. / Greg and Liz both like surfing.

(2) Neither the house nor the garden was attractive.

(3) Both the food and the service were terrible. / The food and the service were both terrible.

(4) Both Angela and Lucy played the piano. / Angela and Lucy both played the piano.

(5) Neither Jessica nor Chloe was at home.

(6) Neither his family nor his friends knew about his accident.

(7) Both eagles and wolves hunt small animals. / Eagles and wolves both hunt small animals.

(8) Both the film and the book are very funny. / The film and the book are both very funny.

(9) Neither the beach nor the shops are far away.

(10) Both Japan and New Zealand have a lot of earthquakes. / Japan and New Zealand both have a lot of earthquakes.

4. Complete the sentences using the conjunctions in the box below.

while / whereas	although	in contrast	on the other hand	but	yet

Example:

Mick likes playing tennis, *but* only if he wins!

(1) Dogs are loving and loyal, ________ cats are very independent.

(2) Hugo claims to be a strict vegetarian and ________ he regularly eats chicken!

(3) Cars produce a great deal of pollution. Bicycles, ________, are totally environmentally friendly.

(4) Checkers is a relatively easy game to master, ________ learning to play chess takes a very long time.

(5) Ms. Ross will be able to see you tomorrow ________ not before 11:00 am.

(6) Some people regard television as no more than "chewing gum for the eyes", ________ many others appreciate its educative value.

(7) ________ Jo likes living in the country, she does miss the convenience of living in town.

【参考答案】

(1) while / whereas　(2) yet　(3) in contrast / on the other hand
(4) while / whereas　(5) but　(6) while / whereas　(7) Although

5. Correct any illogical linking devices in the following sentences.

Example:

Because he'd never tried it before he was very good at it.

Although he'd never tried it before, he was very good at it.

(1) Don't forget to phone us finally you get there.

____

(2) Despite being an accomplished musician, Freda is also a first-rate painter.

____

(3) As well as the bad weather, the race meeting has been cancelled.

____

(4) I hope to get some work done while the holidays.

____

(5) So that you're always borrowing a pen, I've decided to buy you one.

____

(6) Cars are expensive to maintain, whereas bicycles cost very little.

____

(7) I put the vases on top of the piano since they wouldn't get broken.

____

(8) While a little sunshine can be good for you, too much can be very harmful.

____

(9) The job is a little tedious, but however it offers lots of fringe benefits.

____

(10) Credit may be arranged so as to spread payment over twelve months.

____

(11) Tony has decided to take a year off owing to travel around the world.

____

【参考答案】

(1) finally → as soon as / once
(2) Despite → As well as / In addition to
(3) As well as → Owing to / Due to
(4) while → during
(5) So that → Since /As
(6) No mistake.
(7) since → so that
(8) No mistake.
(9) Delete "however".
(10) No mistake.
(11) owing to → in order to / so as to / to

6. Complete the following sentences with suitable linking devices (addition, concession, contrast). An asterisk (*) indicates at least two possible answers.

Example:

Jenny speaks *<u>*both / not only*</u> Russian <u>*and / but also*</u> excellent Chinese.

(1) ________ does Jenny speak Russian, ________ excellent Chinese.

(2) Jenny speaks Russian.* ________ she speaks excellent Chinese.

(3) * ________ Russian, Jenny speaks excellent Chinese.

(4) They looked at us * ________ we came from another planet!

(5) * ________ the doctor told him to rest for a week, he was back at work after two days.

(6) ________ we'd caught the earlier train we wouldn't have got there on time. So, stop worrying!

(7) I know she's a sensible girl and ________ I can't help worrying about her.

(8) They played golf all morning * ________ the torrential rain.

(9) We thought it was going to be a great match. ________ it turned out to be rather dull.

(10) They've got no chance of winning the game; ________ they're training every day.

(11) Some people like boxing, * ________ others absolutely detest it.

【参考答案】

(1) Not only, but also
(2) Moreover / Furthermore
(3) In addition to / As well as / Besides
(4) as if / as though
(5) Although / Even though / Though
(6) Even if
(7) yet
(8) in spite of / despite
(9) However
(10) nevertheless
(11) while / whereas

7. Complete the following sentences with suitable linking devices (cause and result, purpose and time). An asterisk (*) indicates at least two possible answers.

Example:

It was necessary to use a microscope *<u>*in order to / so as to / to*</u> detect the existence of organisms in the drinking water.

(1) They got to the shop at 6:00 am * ________ they would be able to get the best bargains in the sale.

(2) You'd better take your chequebook with you ________ it costs more than you expect.

(3) The apple crop this year has been terrible * ________ the unseasonal frosts we had in May.

(4) * ________ there was a train strike, we had to spend an extra two days on Otranto.

(5) The man was ________ rude ________ the manager had to ask him to leave the restaurant.

(6) Vince didn't get to bed until 5:00 am ________ he's feeling exhausted this morning.

(7) Erica's new boss turned out to be ________ a tyrant ________ she resigned after a week!

(8) The new model is slightly larger and * ________ more expensive.

(9) * ________ you arrive in Bombay, give us a call to let us know everything's OK.

(10) We won't be able to forward the goods * ________ we receive your cheque.

(11) ________ I had the chance to reverse into the parking space someone else drove straight into it.

(12) * ________ had I dropped off to sleep ________ next door's dog started howling at the moon.

(13) ________ he ate all the sandwiches; * ________ he drank all the wine; ________ he collapsed on the sofa!

(14) ________ Steve was upstairs having a shower, the burglars were downstairs helping themselves to his stereo, computer and TV.

【参考答案】

(1) so that / in order that
(2) in case
(3) due to / owing to / as a result of / because of
(4) As / Since / Because
(5) so; that
(6) so
(7) such; that
(8) consequently / therefore / as a result
(9) As soon as / When / Once
(10) until / till
(11) Before
(12) Hardly / No sooner; when / than
(13) First; then / next / after that; finally
(14) While

7.2.2 短文训练

下面做整篇短文的练习，即在整篇文章中体会连接词的用法和作用。做这种练习要有整体的观念，除了要注意上下文的影响与关联，还要注意意思上的联系。

1. In the following text, a number of conjunctions are printed in bold. Replace them by other conjunctions, or rewrite the sentences, making sure the meaning remains the same.

Botany Bay

"Australia became prosperous **because of**[1] the wickedness of England," someone said. What was meant by this?

Simply that in the beginning Australia was a place to which convicts were sent. It was expensive to keep them in prison **so**[2] the government was anxious to be rid of them. Before 1783 they had shipped convicts to the American colonies. **But**[3] the United States of America after 1783 did not want any more of these unruly immigrants. For a year or two they were kept in disused rotting ships on the Thames, **until**[4] the suggestion was made that Australia, 12,000 miles away, would be an excellent country to harbour them. Captain Cook had sailed round the Coast and discovered a place he called Botany Bay **because**[5] the flowers there were so wonderful, and this was chosen for a convict settlement.

A certain Captain Phillip was given charge of the first group to go there in 1788. **After**[6] five months' sailing they arrived at Botany Bay, **but**[7] Captain Phillip decided it was not suitable and went farther on and landed at what is now called Sydney Harbour. The term Botany Bay was **nevertheless**[8] used for this colony.

The government had shown little imagination in beginning this venture. Captain Phillip begged for more supplies. He needed seeds, farm implements and food. **Instead**[9] he was sent more convicts. **After**[10] four years of unrewarding labour Captain Phillip retired because of ill-health.

【参考答案】

(1) because of → due to / owing to

(2) so → therefore

(3) But → However

(4) until → till

(5) because → since / as

(6) Before they arrived at Botany Bay, they had sailed for five months ...

(7) but → however

(8) nevertheless → nonetheless

(9) Instead → But / However

(10) Before he retired because of ill-health, Captain Phillip had worked unrewardingly for four years.

2. Look at the above text "Botany Bay" and classify the conjunctions in bold according to their functions.

(1) Cause: ______________________

(2) Consequence: ______________________

(3) Time sequence: ______________________

(4) Concession: ______________________

(5) Opposition: ______________________

【参考答案】

(1) because of, because　　(2) so　　(3) until, after

(4) nevertheless　　(5) but, instead

3. Complete the following text and select the most appropriate conjunctions from the lists given below.

A colour consultant from Toronto explained to the Inter-Society Colour Council meeting in New York an ingenious scheme which a client company had conceived for increasing the sale of potato peelers. He began by pointing out a puzzling fact. (1) _______ potato peelers "never wear out", enough are sold in two years in his country to put one in every home. What happens to them? He gave this answer: "Investigation reveals that they get thrown away with the potato peelings." One of his colleagues, he added, had then come up with a dazzling plan for helping along this throw-away process. He proposed that their company paint their peelers "as much like a potato peeling as possible".

(2) _______ a potato-coloured peeler wouldn't have much eye-appeal on the sales counter. They decided to solve that by displaying the peeler on a colourful card. Once the housewife got the peeler home and removed the bright card, the chances that she would lose the peeler were excellent ...

In some cases the consumers have no choice but to be waste makers (3) _______ the way products are sold to them. Many paste pots come with brushes built into the cover, and the brushes fail by a half-inch to reach the bottom (4)_______ millions of "empty" paste jars are thrown away with a few spoonfuls of paste still in them. (5)_______, millions of "used" tubes of lipstick are thrown away with a half-inch of lipstick remaining in the tube.

(1) **A** Because　　**B** Although　　**C** For example　　**D** Since

(2) **A** In addition　　**B** On the contrary　　**C** In this way　　**D** However

(3) **A** in spite of　　**B** because of　　**C** as　　**D** in addition to

(4) **A** similarly　　**B** for example　　**C** however　　**D** thus

(5) **A** Likewise　　**B** On the contrary　　**C** Yet　　**D** For instance

【参考答案】

(1) D　　(2) D　　(3) B　　(4) D　　(5) A

4. Read the following passage and fill in the blanks with the appropriate words in the box. All these words have to be used but some of them may be used twice.

therefore	thus	yet	first	but	then

Numerical infinity had been causing trouble from the time of Zeno and his paradoxes. If we recall the race between Achilles and the Tortoise, we might put one of the puzzling aspects of this contest as follows: for every place Achilles has been at, there is a place that the tortoise has occupied. The two runners have (1) ________ at any time assumed all equal number of stations. (2) ________ obviously Achilles covers more ground. This seems to run counter the common sense notion that the whole is greater than the part. (3) ________ when we deal with infinite collections this is no longer so. (4) ________, to take a simple example, the series of positive numbers, which is an infinite collection, has in it odd and even number. Take away all the odd numbers, and you might think that what is left is half of what you begin with. (5) ________ there remain as many even numbers as there were numbers altogether at the start. This somewhat startling conclusion is quite easily demonstrated. (6) ________, we write down the series of natural numbers, and (7) ________, alongside it, a series resulting from it by doubling each member in turn. For every number in the first series there is a corresponding entry in the second. There is, as mathematicians put it, a one-one correspondence between them. The two series (8) ________ have the same number in terms. In the case of infinite collections, (9) ________, a part contains as many terms as the whole. This is the property that Cantor used to define an infinite collection.

(From Bertrand Russell: *The Wisdom of the West*)

【参考答案】

(1) therefore (2) Yet (3) But (4) First (5) Yet
(6) Then (7) then (8) thus (9) therefore

8 重述和推断——熟悉结构与词语转换，提高推断能力

英语考试最基本的目的是考查考生对语言的掌握程度；这是属于语言之内的东西；除此之外，还要考查语言之外的东西，如提取信息的能力、推断能力和逻辑判断能力。传统考试偏重于前者，雅思考试则偏重于后者。然而，任何语言测试都强调考生必须具备较扎实的英语基础知识，熟悉各种句型和结构的转换，还要熟练掌握中学所学的3,000个左右的单词，因为这些都是学习英语的基础。雅思就是按照这个基本要求出题的，所以考生的备考重点应该放在巩固英语基础上。语言基础打好了，才能谈及能力的提高。

本章从备考的角度介绍如何通过掌握结构与转换词语来提高推断能力。本章练习的技巧有助于考生应对任何英语考试（尤其是雅思阅读考试）的判断题，因为判断题综合性强，既会考到语言之内的东西，也会考到语言之外的东西。

8.1 什么是重述和推断

重述（restatement）——题目选项以不同的表达方式改写原文，但句子的意思不变或改写后与原文的某个观点一致（语言之内的东西）。

推断（inference）——题目的整体信息不能全部在原文中找到，但根据原文中的其他信息，可以用逻辑推理的方法推断出结论（语言之外的东西）。

知道了这两点，判断 True / False / Not Given 或 Yes / No / Not Given 这一类题就容易了。判断的标准由此而产生：

1) 以不同的表达方式改写原文，但句子的意思不变，也就是重述，或改写后与原文的某个观点一致，这时应判断为 True / Yes。这里主要考语言之内的东西。

2) 题目的整体信息不能全部在原文中找到，但根据原文中的其他信息，结论可以用逻辑推理的方法推断出来，这时应判断为 True / Yes。这里主要考语言之外的东西。

3) 题目的意思与原文相反或与原文的某个观点不一致，应判断为 False / No。这里主要考语言之内的东西。

4) 题目的整体信息不能全部在原文中找到，而根据原文中的其他信息，结论又不能用逻辑推理的方法推断出来，应判断为 Not Given。这里主要考语言之外的东西。

下面通过练习作进一步的分析。

8.2 单句判断练习

Example:

Heavy smokers and drinkers run a fifteen-times greater risk of developing cancer of the mouth and throat than nonsmokers and nondrinkers.

A Cancer of the mouth and throat is more likely to occur in heavy smokers and drinkers than in nonsmokers and nondrinkers.

B People who never drink and smoke will not get mouth or throat cancer.

C Heavy drinkers like running much more than nondrinkers.

D People who don't smoke and drink have less chance of getting cancer of the mouth and throat than those who smoke and drink heavily.

E People would probably be healthier if they did not drink and smoke too much.

【分析】

A **This is a restatement of the original sentence.** If heavy smokers and drinkers run a greater risk of developing cancer than those who do not drink or smoke, then cancer is more likely to occur in heavy smokers and drinkers.

B **It is not the same as the original sentence.** We only know that people who never smoke and drink are less likely to develop mouth or throat cancer.

C The word "run" in the original sentence is part of the phrase "to run a risk" which means "to be in danger". The sentence does not tell us anything about heavy drinkers who enjoy the sport of running. **The information is not given.**

D **This is a restatement of the original sentence.** If people who drink and smoke heavily have a greater chance of getting mouth and throat cancer than those who don't, then it must be true that those who don't smoke and drink heavily have less chance of developing this kind of cancer.

E **This is an inference** which can be drawn from the information given. If people who smoke and drink heavily run a high risk of developing cancer, then we can infer that people probably would be healthier if they didn't smoke and drink too much.

练习：

1. 对下面每句后的 A, B, C, D, E 五项作出判断，找出与原句表意相同的选项，即原句的重述或推断。练习后配有答案，便于读者自我检测。

(1) Nine out of ten doctors responding to a survey said they recommended our product to their patients if they

recommended anything.

A Nine out of ten doctors recommended the product.

B Of the doctors who responded to a survey, nine out of ten doctors recommended the product.

C If they recommended anything, nine out of ten doctors responding to a survey recommended the product.

D Most doctors recommended the product.

E We don't know how many doctors recommended the product.

(2) This organisation may succeed marvelously at what it wants to do, but what it wants to do may not be all that important.

A The organisation is marvelous.

B The organisation may succeed.

C Although the organisation may reach its goals, the goals might not be important.

D What the organisation wants is marvelous.

E The author questions the goals of the organisation.

(3) This book contains a totally new outlook which combines the wisdom of the past with scientific knowledge to solve the problems of the present.

A Problems of the past and present are solved in this book.

B In this book, current knowledge and past wisdom are combined to solve current problems.

C Only by using knowledge of the past and present can we solve problems.

D None of today's problems can be solved without scientific knowledge.

E This book is different because it combines the wisdom of the past with scientific knowledge.

(4) Like other timeless symbols, flags have accompanied mankind for thousands of years, gaining ever wider meaning, yet losing none of their inherent and original force.

A In spite of losing some of their original force, flags are a timeless symbol which has accompanied mankind for thousands of years.

B Flags have existed for thousands of years.

C Timeless symbols typically gain wider meaning while not losing their inherent force.

D Thousands of years ago, flags accompanied mankind but through time they have lost their force.

E Because flags are considered a timeless symbol, they have gained continually wider meaning without losing their inherent original force.

(5) When there is an absence of reliable information about drugs, the risks involved in using them are greatly increased.

A There is no reliable information about drugs.

B Using drugs is more dangerous when we don't know what effects and dangers are involved.

C The risks involved in using drugs have increased.

D People should try to find out about drugs before using them.

E There are no risks involved in using drugs if we have reliable information about them.

(6) The project of which this book is the result was first suggested in the summer of 1962, in the course of some leisurely conversations at the foot of and (occasionally) on top of the Alps of western Austria.

A This book was written in 1962.

B This book was written in Austria.

C This book is a collection of conversations held in 1962.

D This book is the end result of a project.

E This book is about western Austria.

(7) Los Angeles's safety record with school buses is generally a good one, but of course this record is only as good as the school bus drivers themselves.

A In spite of a generally good safety record for their school buses, Los Angeles's school bus drivers are not very good.

B If school bus drivers are not very good, the city's school bus safety record will not be very good either.

C If cities wish to maintain good safety records with school buses, they should hire good school bus drivers.

D With better school buses, drivers will be able to maintain better safety records.

E Los Angeles's safety record with school buses has improved because better bus drivers have been hired.

(8) Taxes being so high, the descendents of the wealthy class of the nineteenth century are being forced to rent out their estates to paying guests.

A In the nineteenth century, the wealthy class rented out its estates.

B Because of high taxes, families which were rich one hundred years ago now rent out their estates.

C Guests pay high taxes when they rent old estates.

D Some families which were once wealthy are having trouble paying their taxes.

E High taxes have changed the lives of some of the old wealthy families.

(9) According to the definition of Chinese traditional medicine, acupuncture is the treatment of disease — not just the alleviation of pain — by inserting very fine needles into the body at specific points called loci.

A The author believes some people do not know that acupuncture can be used to treat illness.

B Finely pointed needles called loci are used in acupuncture.

C In Chinese traditional medicine, acupuncture is known to treat disease and alleviate pain.

D Those using acupuncture treat disease by placing needles into the body at specific points.

E Only those who practise traditional Chinese medicine use acupuncture.

(10) It would be difficult to overpraise this book.

A This is a difficult book.

B This book deserves much praise.

C It is difficult not to overpraise this book.

D It is difficult to praise this book.

E The author of this sentence thinks this is an excellent book.

【参考答案】

(1) C, E　(2) B, C, E　(3) B, E　(4) B, C　(5) B, D
(6) D　(7) B, C　(8) B, D, E　(9) A, C, D　(10) B, E

2. 继续对下面每句后的 A, B, C, D, E 五项作出判断，找出与原句表意相同的选项，即原句的重述或推断。练习后配有答案，便于读者自我检测。

(1) A favourite definition of joking has long been the ability to find similarity between dissimilar things — that is, hidden similarities.

A Joking is the ability to find similarity in dissimilar things.

B It takes a long time to develop the ability to tell good jokes.

C This definition of joking is a new one in literary theory.

D Many people define joking as the ability to find similarity in dissimilar things.

E The author agrees with this definition.

(2) Since the Romantic period, most modern theory has dealt with the peculiar act of the poet rather than his product or its effect on the audience.

A Most modern theory does not deal with the poem itself or its effect on the audience.

B Most modern theory of poetry deals with the act of the poet.

C Since the Romantic period, literary theory has dealt with the effect of poetry on the reader.

D The author believes that literary theory should only deal with the peculiar act of the poet.

E Modern theory is considered to begin at the Romantic period.

(3) Although housewives still make up the majority of volunteer groups, male participation is reported on the rise nationwide as traditional distinctions between men's work and women's work begin to fade.

A As traditional social roles change, more men are becoming members of volunteer groups.

B Most members of volunteer groups are women.

C In the past, volunteer work was done mainly by women.

D Male participation in volunteer groups is increasing in all cities.

E The author believes there is a relationship between the changing social roles and the increasing willingness of men to do work previously done by females.

(4) The overall picture of this very early settled Peruvian population is that of a simple, peaceful people living in a small cultivable oasis by the sea, fishing, raising a few food crops, living in small, simple, nonmasonry houses and making the objects necessary for their economic and household life, with slight attention to art.

A This early Peruvian population had all the basic necessities of life available to it.

B We can assume that art only exists in very advanced societies.

C This society moved many times during the year.

D Because the people worked so hard they had no time for art.

E The author believes this society provides nothing of interest for historians.

(5) Only a small number of scholars can be named who have entered deeply into the problems of jokes.

A Only a few scholars have studied jokes.

B The area of jokes is so complex that only a small number of people have been able to study it.

C Few scholars have studied the problem of jokes deeply.

D The author cannot remember the names of scholars who have studied jokes.

E It is not possible to name all those who have studied jokes deeply.

(6) There is a question about the extent to which any one of us can be free of a prejudiced view in the area of religion.

A Probably everyone is prejudiced in his views on religion.

B Any one of us can be free of prejudice in the area of religion.

C To some extent we can never be free of prejudice in the area of religion.

D A prejudiced view in the area of religion is undesirable.

E Because we can't be free of prejudice in the area of religion, we should not practise a religion.

(7) Although the November election may significantly change the face of the county Board of Commissioners, the group will still have to confront the same old problems.

A The November election may give the Board of Commissioners a new building.

B The Board of Commissioners consists of several members.

C The November election may change the membership of the Board of Commissioners.

D Although board members may change, the problems will remain the same.

E The author does not believe that this election will change the difficulties facing the commissioners.

(8) If this book begins with a familiar theme — the Indian experience of the last 120 years — the author will bring to it great power and deep understanding.

A This book was written 120 years ago.

B The Indian experience of the last 120 years is a familiar experience, and nothing new can be written about it.

C The book may lack understanding of the Indian experience.

D The book may begin with a familiar theme.

E The author of this sentence likes the book.

(9) People should and do choose their elected representatives partly on the basis of how well they believe these representatives, once in office, can convince them to do or support whatever needs to be done.

A It is the author's belief that people should choose representatives whom they believe will convince them to take action.

B People choose representatives on the basis of whether or not they believe the representatives can be convinced to do what needs to be done.

C Although people should choose representatives whom they believe will convince them to take action, often they do not.

D People choose representatives whom they believe will convince them to take action.

E Representatives are elected only on the basis of their ability to take action.

【参考答案】

(1) D (2) A，B (3) A，B，C，E (4) A (5) C
(6) A，C (7) B，C，D，E (8) D (9) A，D

8.3 段落中句子的判断练习

Example:

Often people who hold higher positions in a given group overestimate their performance, while people in the lowest levels of the group underestimate theirs. While this may not always be true, it does indicate that often the actual position in the group has much to do with the feeling of personal confidence a person may have. Thus, if a member holds a high position in a group or if he feels that he has an important part to play in the group, he will probably have more confidence in his own performance.

A If a person has confidence in his own performance, he will achieve a high position in a group.

B If we let someone know he is an important part of a group, he will probably become more self-confident.

C People who hold low positions in a group often overestimate their performance.

D People in positions of power in a group may feel they do better work than they really do.

E People with higher positions in a group do better work than other group members.

【分析】

A **This cannot be inferred from the paragraph.** We know that people who hold higher positions have more self-confidence than those who don't. However, we don't know that people with more confidence will achieve higher status. Confidence may come only after one achieves a higher position.

B **This is an inference** which can be drawn from the last sentence in the paragraph. We know that if someone feels he has an important part to play in a group, he will probably have more self-confidence. We can infer that if we let someone know (and therefore make him feel) that he has an important part to play, he will probably become more self-confident.

C **This is false.** The first sentence states that the people in the lowest levels of a group underestimate, not overestimate, their performance.

D **This is a restatement of the first sentence.** People who hold higher positions tend to overestimate their performance — they may feel they do better work than they really do.

E **We do not know this from the paragraph.** We know that people who hold higher positions often think they do better work than others in a group. (They "overestimate their performance".) We do not know whether they actually do better work or not.

练习：

1. 对下面每段后的 A, B, C, D, E 五项作出判断，找出与原段文字表意相同的选项，即原句的重述或推断。练习后面配有答案，便于读者自我检测。

(1) Like any theory of importance, that of social or cultural anthropology was the work of many minds and took on many forms. Some, the best known of its proponents, worked on broad areas and attempted to describe and account for the development of human civilisation in its totality. Others restricted their efforts to specific aspects of the culture, taking up the evolution of art, or the state, or religion.

A Social anthropology concerns itself with broad areas while cultural anthropology concerns itself with specific aspects of culture.

B Cultural anthropologists, also known as social anthropologists, may work in either broad or restricted areas.

C Cultural anthropology is a new field of study.

D Any important area of study requires the work of many minds and is therefore likely to have different approaches.

E The best known people in cultural anthropology attempted to describe the development of human civilisation.

(2) I saw by the clock of the city jail that it was past eleven, so I decided to go to the newspaper immediately. Outside the editor's door I stopped to make sure my pages were in the right order; I smoothed them out carefully, stuck them back in my pocket, and knocked. I could hear my heart thumping as I walked in.

A The teller of this story has just left the city jail.

B He has been carrying his papers in his pocket.

C We know that the storyteller is a newspaper writer by profession.

D We might infer that the storyteller is going to show his paper to the editor.

E The meeting is important for the storyteller.

(3) In recent years there have been many reports of a growing impatience with psychiatry, with its seeming foreverness, its high cost, its debatable results, and its vague, esoteric terms. To many people it is like a blind man in a dark room looking for a black cat that isn't there. The magazines and mental health associations say psychiatric treatment is a good thing, but what it is or what it accomplishes has not been made clear.

A Even mental health associations haven't been able to demonstrate the value of psychiatry.

B The author believes that psychiatry is of no value.

C People are beginning to doubt the value of psychiatry.

D In recent years psychiatry has begun to serve the needs of blind people.

E Only magazines and mental health associations believe that psychiatry is a good thing.

(4) The Incas had never acquired the art of writing, but they had developed a complicated system of knotted cords called quipus. These were made of the wool of the alpaca or llama, dyed in various colours, the significance of which was known to the officials. The cords were knotted in such a way as to represent the decimal system. Thus an

important message relating to the progress of crops, the amount of taxes collected, or the advance of an enemy could be speedily sent by trained runners along the post roads.

A Because they could not write, the Incas are considered a simplistic, poorly developed society.

B Through a system of knotted cords, the Incas sent important messages from one community to another.

C Because runners were sent with the cords, we can safely assume that the Incas did not have domesticated animals.

D Both the colour of the cords and the way they were knotted formed part of the message of the quipus.

E The quipus were used for important messages.

(5) There was a time when scholars held that early man lived in a kind of beneficent anarchy, in which each person was granted his rights by his fellows and there was no governing or being governed. Various early writers looked back to this Golden Age but the point of view that man was originally a child of nature is best known to us in the writings of Rousseau, Locke, and Hobbes. These men described the concept of social contract, which they said had put an end to the state of nature in which earliest man is supposed to have lived.

A For Rousseau, Locke, and Hobbes, the concept of social contract put an end to the time of beneficent anarchy in which early man lived.

B According to the author, scholars today do not hold that early man lived in a state of anarchy.

C Only Rousseau, Locke, and Hobbes wrote about early man as a child of nature.

D The early writers referred to in this passage lived through the Golden Age of early man.

E We can infer that the author of this passage feels that concepts of government have always been present in human history.

【参考答案】

(1) B, D, E (2) B, D, E (3) A, C (4) B, D, E (5) A, B, E

2. 对下面每句后的 A, B, C, D, E 五项作出判断，找出与原段文字表意相同的选项，即原句的重述或推断。练习后面配有答案，便于读者自我检测。

(1) It was the weekend before the exam. We were at the Walker's house and it was pouring rain. Jack came in late, drenched to the skin. He explained that a car had broken down on the road and he had stopped to help push it onto the shoulder and out of the traffic. I remember thinking then how typical that was of Jack. So helpful, so accommodating.

A Jack came in late because it was raining.

B Jack came in late because his car had broken down.

C The narrator thinks Jack is typical.

D The narrator bases his opinion of Jack on this one experience.

E Jack often helps other people.

(2) The illustrations in books make it easier for us to believe in the people and events described. The more

senses satisfied, the easier is belief. Visual observation tends to be the most convincing evidence. Children, being less capable of translating abstractions into actualities, need illustration more than adults. Most of us, when we read, tend to create only vague and ghostlike forms in response to the words. The illustrator, when he reads, must see. The great illustrator sees accurately.

A Illustrations help us to believe events described in words.

B When most people read, they do not picture events as accurately as can a great illustrator.

C Children are less able than adults to visualise events described in books.

D The author believes illustrators are especially able to imagine visual details described with words.

E The author believes all illustrators see accurately.

(3) Surveys reveal that most adults consider themselves "well informed about the affairs of the nation and the world". Yet a regularly taken Roper poll that asks, "From where do you obtain most of your information about the world?" has found the percentage of people who reply "television" has been increasing steadily over the past decade. The latest questionnaire found that well over 60% of the respondents chose television over other media as their major source of information. These two facts are difficult to reconcile since even a casual study of television news reveals it is only a headline service and not a source of information enabling one to shape a world view.

A Most adults obtain most of their information about world affairs from the newspaper.

B The author of this passage does not believe that television provides enough information to make people well informed.

C The number of people answering the questionnaire has increased.

D Sixty per cent of the people questioned get all their news from television.

E Most adults are well informed about the affairs of the nation and the world.

(4) The dusty book room whose windows never opened, through whose panes the summer sun sent a dim light where gold specks danced and shimmered, opened magic windows for me through which I looked out on other worlds and times than those in which I lived. The narrow shelves rose halfway up the walls, their tops piled with untidy layers that almost touched the ceiling. The piles on the floor had to be climbed over, columns of books flanked the window, failing at a touch.

A The room is dusty and shadowy, filled with books from floor to ceiling.

B The sun never enters the room.

C The author spent time in this room as a child.

D The author did not like the room.

E Through the windows in the room, the author saw worlds other than those in which he lived.

(5) By voting against mass transportation, voters have chosen to continue on a road to ruin. Our interstate highways, those much praised golden avenues have been built to whisk expensive parking lots. That expense is not only economic, it is social. These highways have created great walls separating neighbourhood from neighbourhood, disrupting the complex social connections that help make a city livable.

A Interstate highways have created social problems.

B Highways create complex social connections.

C By separating neighbourhoods, highways have made cities more livable.

D The author supports the idea of mass transportation.

E The author agrees with a recent vote by the citizens.

【参考答案】

(1) E (2) A, B, C, D (3) B (4) A (5) A, D

8.4 篇章中句子的判断练习

篇章中句子的判断练习难度较大，要先确定题目是根据文章中哪一部分内容设计的，然后再对照原文进行判断。

要想在原文中很快地找到原句，就要利用前面介绍过的略读技巧。步骤如下：

首先，仔细阅读题目，记住关键词；然后用略读技巧快速搜寻定位，定位后理解原文的意思；最后进行判断。

1. 阅读下面的短文，判断文章后面的句子是否与原文原句的信息一致。本练习中原文中的原句已用粗体标出。

Reading Passage 1: The Olympic Games

In ancient Greece athletic festivals were very important and had strong religious associations. The Olympian athletic festival, held every four years in honour of Zeus, eventually lost its local character, became first a national event, and then, after the rules against foreign competitors had been waived, international. **No one knows exactly how far back the Olympic Games go, but some official records date from 776 B.C.**

The Games took place in August on the plain by Mount Olympus. Many thousands of spectators gathered from all parts of Greece, but no married woman was admitted even as a spectator. **Slaves, women and dishonoured persons were not allowed to compete.** The exact sequence of events is uncertain, but events included boys' gymnastics, horse-racing, field events such as discus and javelin throwing, and the very important foot races. There was also boxing and wrestling and special tests of varied ability such as the pentathlon, the winner of which excelled in running, jumping, discus and javelin throwing and wrestling. The evening of the third day was devoted to sacrificial offerings to the heroes of the day, and the fourth day, that of the full moon, was set aside as a holy day.

On the sixth and last day, all the victors were crowned with holy garlands of wild olive from a sacred wood. So great was the honour that the winner of the foot race gave his name to the year of his victory. Although Olympic winners received no prize money, they were, in fact, richly rewarded by their state authorities. **The public honour also made the strict discipline of the ten-month training period worthwhile. In spite of the lengthy training, however, runners were known to drop dead from strain at the winning post.** How their results compared with modern standards, we unfortunately have no means of telling.

After an uninterrupted history of almost 1,200 years, the Games were abolished in 394 A.D., the Christian era, because of their pagan origin. It was over 1,500 years before there was another such international athletics gathering. The Greek institution was revived in 1896 and the first small meeting took place in Athens. After the 1908 London Olympics, success was re-established and nations sent their best representatives. In times of peace, the Games have taken place ever since at four-yearly intervals. In Munich in 1972, competitors from more than 120 countries were watched by huge crowds.

Nowadays, the Games are held in different countries in turn. The host country provides vast facilities, including a stadium, swimming pools and living accommodation, but competing countries pay their own athletes' expenses. **Athletic contests are still the main feature, but now many more sports are represented.** The ancient pentathlon, for example, has been modified into a more comprehensive test, and the marathon races, initiated in 1896, are now a celebrated event.

The Olympics start with the arrival in the stadium of a torch, lighted on Mount Olympus by the sun's rays. It is carried by a succession of runners to the stadium. **The torch symbolises the continuation of the ancient Greek athletic ideals, and it burns throughout the Games until the closing ceremony.** The well-known Olympic flag, however, is a modern conception: the five interlocking rings symbolise the uniting of all five continents participating in the Games.

Say whether or not the statement is similar in meaning to the sentence in bold in the passage.

(1) We can ascertain when the Olympic Games first took place because official records date from 776 B.C. (Para. 1)

(2) Originally the only permitted competitors were those whose position in society was respected. (Para. 2)

(3) Because the ten-month period of training was so strenuous, competitors who did not achieve success felt that their efforts were wasted. (Para. 3)

(4) The intensive training gave all runners the strength to withstand even the strain of the great races. (Para. 3)

(5) As there is a greater variety of sports nowadays, athletic events have lost their importance. (Para. 5)

(6) Today, the Olympic torch burns throughout the Games to honour the ancient Greek athletic ideals. (Para. 6)

【参考答案】

(1) No　(2) Yes　(3) No　(4) No　(5) No　(6) Yes

Reading Passage 2: Making Leather

Hides and skins are the raw material of the leather manufacturer or tanner. When man first used animal skins is not known. Skins, even when preserved by tanning, do not last as long as stone, pottery, metals and bone, and our knowledge about the early use of skins is vague. **However, the numerous flint scrapers and bone or ivory sewing needles in our museums show that tens of thousands of years ago, in the early Stone Age, skins were prepared and used long before textiles.** Nowadays, hides and skins are essential raw materials and important articles of commerce.

Any animal skin can be made into leather, but the skins chiefly used come from cattle, sheep, goats, pigs and horses. To a lesser extent the skins from dogs, deer, reptiles, marine animals, fish and birds are also used. Snakes, lizards, seals, whales, and sharks all contribute to leather manufacture.

"Hide" is the trade word for the skins of the larger animals such as full-grown cattle and horses; and "skin" for the smaller animals, and immature large animals such as ponies and calves. **Some skins are made into leather after the hair or wool has been removed; but the skins of the fur-bearing animals and sometimes of sheep, lambs and ponies are processed, or "dressed", with the hair or wool still in place.**

Most cattle hides come from South America, the U.S. and Australia, with smaller quantities from East and West Africa, Central America and the Sudan. Sheepskins come from Australia and New Zealand, and the best goat skins come from India, Pakistan, Ethiopia, Arabia and Nigeria.

There is usually a long interval between the flaying, or stripping, of the skin from the animal and putting it into the tannery for processing. **If the flayed skins were left wet, they would go bad, just like meat;** they must therefore be preserved in some way. The commonest method is salting. **This involves sprinkling the skins with salt on their inner side; or immersing the skins completely in strong salt solution for some hours, after which they are drained and sprinkled with solid salt.**

Another method of drying is to stretch the skins out on the ground, or on frames and to dry them in the sun, or even better in the shade. Beetles and other insects eat skins and must be kept away by the use of some chemical such as D.D.T. **The dried skins are called "crust" leather and are sent in this form to the tanneries for the very complicated process of tanning.** After tanning, only the "corium" or middle layer of the skin is left to provide leather as we know it. It is to the closely knit fibre structure of the corium that leather owes its virtues of flexibility, strength and elasticity, its resistance to rubbing and its unique power of allowing water vapour and air to pass through it while resisting penetration by liquid water itself.

Say whether or not the statement is similar in meaning to the sentence in bold from the passage.

(1) Indications of the early use of skins by man are the tools used to prepare and sew them. (Para. 1)

(2) Some skins can be made into leather before or after the hair or wool has been removed. (Para. 3)

(3) Unless skins are left moist, like meat, they decay. (Para. 5)

(4) Each skin must go through 4 processes: a) salt is sprinkled on the inside; b) it is immersed in a salt

solution; c) it is drained; d) it is resprinkled with dry salt. (Para. 5)

(5) It is preferable to dry skins quickly in the sun rather than in the shade. (Para. 6)

(6) After the skins have dried into "crust" leather, there is very little else to do. (Para. 6)

【参考答案】

(1) Yes (2) Yes (3) No (4) No (5) No (6) No

Reading Passage 3: Electric Fish

The idea of a fish being able to generate electricity strong enough to light lamp bulbs — or even to run a small electric motor — is almost unbelievable, but several kinds of fish are able to do this. **Even more strangely, this curious power has been acquired in different ways by fish belonging to very different families.**

Perhaps the best known are the electric rays, or torpedoes, of which several kinds live in warm seas. **They possess on each side of the head, behind the eyes, a large organ consisting of a number of hexagonal shaped cells rather like a honeycomb.** The cells are filled with a jelly-like substance, and contain a series of flat electric plates. One side, the negative side, of each plate, is supplied with very fine nerves, connected with a main nerve coming from a special part of the brain. **Current passes from the upper, positive side of the organ downwards to the negative, lower side.** Generally it is necessary to touch the fish in two places, completing the circuit, in order to receive a shock.

The strength of this shock depends on the size of the fish, but newly born ones only about 5 centimetres across can be made to light the bulb of a pocket flashlight for a few moments, while a fully grown torpedo gives a shock capable of knocking a man down, and, if suitable wires are connected, will operate a small electric motor for several minutes.

Another famous example is the electric eel. This fish gives an even more powerful shock. **The system is different from that of the torpedo in that the electric plates run longitudinally** and are supplied with nerves from the spinal cord. Consequently, the current passes along the fish from head to tail. **The electric organs of these fish are really altered muscles and like all muscles are apt to tire, so they are not able to produce electricity for very long.** People in some parts of South America who value the electric eel as food, take advantage of this fact by driving horses into the water against which the fish discharge their electricity. The horses are less affected than a man would be, and when the electric eels have exhausted themselves, they can be caught without danger.

The electric catfish of the Nile and of other African fresh waters has a different system again by which current passes over the whole body from the tail to the head. The shock given by this arrangement is not so powerful as the other two, but is nonetheless unpleasant. The electric catfish is a slow, lazy fish, fond of gloomy places and grows to about one metre long; it is eaten by the Arabs in some areas.

The power of producing electricity may serve these fish both for defence and attack. If a large enemy attacks, the shock will drive it away; but it appears that the catfish and the electric eel use their current most often against smaller fish, stunning them so that they can easily be overpowered.

Say whether or not the statement is similar in meaning to the sentence in bold in the passage.

(1) It is hardly strange that this power has been acquired by different families of fish in different ways. (Para. 1)

(2) They possess behind the head, instead of eyes, a large hexagonal rather like a honeycomb. (Para. 2)

(3) Current travels in a downward direction from the upper side of the organ, which is positive, to the lower, or negative side. (Para. 2)

(4) A newly born one can be trained to provide light from a pocket flashlight while its fully grown partner knocks their victim down. (Para. 3)

(5) In that fish, the torpedo, the electric plates run lengthways. (Para. 4)

(6) Because the electric organs of these fish are altered muscles, they tire as muscles do, so they cannot produce electricity for very long periods of time. (Para. 4)

(7) The electric catfish shows an even further variation in its system of producing electricity, which involves the whole surface of the body. (Para. 5)

(8) Electric power may serve a dual purpose for these fish. (Para. 6)

【参考答案】

(1) No (2) No (3) Yes (4) No (5) No (6) Yes (7) Yes (8) Yes

Reading Passage 4: The United Nations

In one very long sentence, the introduction to the U.N. Charter expresses the ideals and the common aims of all the peoples whose governments joined together to form the U.N.

"We the peoples of the U.N. determined to save succeeding generations from the scourge of war, which twice in our lifetime has brought untold suffering to mankind, and to reaffirm faith in fundamental rights, in the dignity and worth of the human person, in the equal rights of men and women and of nations large and small, and **to establish conditions under which justice and respect for the obligations arising from treaties and other sources of international law can be maintained,** and to promote social progress and better standards of life in larger freedom, and for these ends, to practise tolerance and live together in peace with one another as good neighbours, and to unite our strength to maintain international peace and security, and **to ensure, by the acceptance of principles and the institution of methods, that armed force shall not be used, save in the common interest,** and **to employ international machinery for the promotion of economic and social advancement of all peoples,** have resolved to combine our efforts to accomplish these aims."

The name "United Nations" is accredited to U.S. President Franklin D. Roosevelt, and the first group of representatives of member states met and signed a declaration of common intent on New Year's Day in 1942. Representatives of five powers worked together to draw up proposals, completed at Dumbarton Oaks in 1944. These proposals, modified after deliberation at the conference on International Organisation in San Francisco which began in April 1945, were finally agreed on and signed as the U.N. Charter by 50 countries on 26 June, 1945. **Poland, not represented at the conference, signed the Charter later and was added to the list of original members.** It was not until that autumn, however, after the Charter had been ratified by China, France, the U.S.S.R., the U.K. and the U.S. and by a majority of the other participants that the U.N. officially came into existence. The date was 24 October, now universally celebrated as United Nations Day.

The essential functions of the U.N. are to maintain international peace and security, to develop friendly relations among nations, to cooperate internationally in solving international economic, social, cultural and human problems, promoting respect for human rights and fundamental freedoms and to be a centre for coordinating the actions of nations in attaining these common ends.

No country takes precedence over another in the U.N. Each member's rights and obligations are the same. All must contribute to the peaceful settlement of international disputes, and members have pledged to refrain from the threat or use of force against other states. **Though the U.N. has no right to intervene in any state's internal affairs, it tries to ensure that non-member states act according to its principles of international peace and security.** U.N. members must offer every assistance in an approved U.N. action and in no way assist states against which the U.N. is taking preventive or enforcement action.

Say whether or not the statement is similar in meaning to the sentence in bold in the passage. (Because the sentence from the introduction is so long, numbers 1, 2 and 3 are only extracts from it.)

(1) ... to create a situation which supports justice and the fulfillment of international agreements ... (Para. 2)

(2) ... by accepting principles and instituting methods, to prevent the use of arms at all times to save the common interest. (Para. 2)

(3) ... to create organs which function on a cooperative basis to encourage the economic and social progress of every nation. (Para. 2)

(4) In spite of not assisting at the Charter signing ceremony, Poland is nevertheless on the list of original members. (Para. 3)

(5) Having no right to interfere in any state's home affairs limits the U.N.'s power in international peace and security. (Para. 5)

【参考答案】

(1) Yes (2) No (3) Yes (4) Yes (5) No

Reading Passage 5: Modern Surgery

The need for a surgical operation, especially an emergency operation, almost always comes as a severe shock to the patient and his family. Despite modern advances, most people still have an irrational fear of hospitals and anaesthetics. Patients do not often believe they really need surgery — cutting into a part of the body as opposed to treatment with drugs.

In the early years of this century there was little specialisation in surgery. A good surgeon was capable of performing almost every operation that had been devised up to that time. Today the situation is different. **Operations that are now being carried out were not even dreamed of fifty years ago.** The heart can be safely opened and its valves repaired. Clogged blood vessels can be cleaned out and broken ones mended or replaced. **A lung, the whole stomach, or even part of the brain can be removed and still permit the patient to live a comfortable and satisfactory life.** However, not every surgeon wants to, or is qualified to carry out every type of modern operation.

The scope of surgery has increased remarkably in this century. Its safety has increased, too. Deaths from most operations are about 20% of what they were in 1910 and surgery has been extended in many directions, for example, to certain types of birth defects in newborn babies, and, at the other end of the scale, to life-saving operations for the octogenarian. The hospital stay after surgery has been shortened to as little as a week for most major operations. Most patients are out of bed on the day after an operation and may be back at work in two or three weeks.

Many developments in modern surgery are almost incredible. They include the replacement of damaged blood vessels with simulated ones made of plastic; the replacement of heart valves with plastic substitutes; the transplanting of tissues such as the lens of the eye; the invention of the artificial kidney to clean the blood of poisons at regular intervals and the development of heart and lung machines to keep patients alive during very long operations. All these things open a hopeful vista for the future of surgery.

One of the most revolutionary areas of modern surgery is that of organ transplants. **Until a few years ago, no person, except an identical twin, was able to accept into his body the tissues of another person without reacting against them and eventually killing them.** Recently, however, it has been discovered that with the use of X-rays and special drugs, it is possible to graft tissues from one person to another which will survive for periods of a year or more. **Kidneys have been successfully transplanted between non-identical twins. Heart and lung transplants have been reasonably successful in animals, though rejection problems in humans have yet to be solved.**

"Spare parts" surgery, the simple routine replacement of all worn-out organs by new ones, is still a dream of the distant future. As yet, surgery is not ready for such miracles. In the meantime, you can be happy if your doctor says to you, "Yes, I think it is possible to operate on you for this condition."

Say whether or not the statement is similar in meaning to the sentence in bold in the passage.

(1) Operations are now being carried out that no one even considered fifty years ago. (Para. 2)

(2) Repair and replacement of a lung, the whole stomach, or even part of the brain, allow patients to lead comfortable and satisfactory lives. (Para. 2)

(3) A large number of modern advances in surgery are difficult to believe. (Para. 4)

(4) Until fairly recently, no one except an identical twin could accept another person's tissues into his body without being killed by these tissues. (Para. 5)

(5) The replacement of the heart and the lungs in animals has been completely successful, though the problem with humans is that they reject the idea of organ transplants. (Para. 5)

【参考答案】

(1) Yes (2) No (3) Yes (4) No (5) No

Reading Passage 6: Vitamins

In the early days of sea travel, seamen on long voyages lived exclusively on salted meat and biscuits. Many of them died of scurvy, a disease of the blood which causes swollen gums, livid white spots on the flesh and general exhaustion. On one occasion, in 1535, an English ship arrived in Newfoundland with its crew desperately ill. **The men's lives were saved by Iroquois Indians who gave them vegetable leaves to eat. Gradually it came to be realised that scurvy was caused by some lack in the sailors' diet and Captain Cook, on his long voyages of discovery to Australia and New Zealand, established the fact that scurvy could be warded off by the provision of fresh fruit for the sailors.**

Nowadays it is understood that a diet which contains nothing harmful may yet result in serious disease if certain important elements are missing. These elements are called "vitamins". Quite a number of such substances are known and they are given letters to identify them, A, B, C, D, and so on. Different diseases are associated with deficiencies of particular vitamins. Even a slight lack of vitamin C, for example, the vitamin most plentiful in fresh fruit and vegetables, is thought to increase significantly our susceptibility to colds and influenza.

The vitamins necessary for a healthy body are normally supplied by a good mixed diet, including a variety of fruit and green vegetables. It is only when people try to live on a very restricted diet, say during extended periods of religious fasting, or when trying to lose weight, that it is necessary to make special provision to supply the missing vitamins.

Another example of the dangers of a restricted diet may be seen in the disease known as "beriberi", which used to afflict large numbers of Eastern peoples who lived mainly on rice. In the early years of this century, a Dutch scientist called Eijkman was trying to discover the cause of beriberi. At first he thought it was transmitted by a germ.

He was working in a Japanese hospital, where the patients were fed on rice which had the outer husk (rougher outer layer) removed from the grain. It was thought this would be easier for weak, sick people to digest.

Eijkman thought his germ theory was confirmed when he noticed the chickens in the hospital yard, which were fed on scraps from the patients' plates, were also showing signs of the disease. He then tried to isolate the germ he thought was causing the disease, but his experiments were interrupted by a hospital official, who decreed that the huskless polished rice, even though left over by the patients, was too good for chickens. It should be recooked and the chickens fed on cheap, coarse rice with the outer covering still on the grain.

Eijkman noticed that the chickens began to recover on the new diet. He began to consider the possibility that eating unmilled rice somehow prevented or cured beriberi — even that a lack of some ingredient in the husk might be the cause of the disease. Indeed this was the case. **The element needed to prevent beriberi was shortly afterwards isolated from rice husks and is now known as vitamin B.** The milled rice, though more expensive, was in fact perpetuating the disease the hospital was trying to cure. Nowadays, this terrible disease is much less common thanks to our knowledge of vitamins.

Say whether or not the statement is similar in meaning to the sentence in bold in the passage.

(1) Iroquois Indians saved the men's lives by giving them vegetable leaves to eat. (Para. 1)

(2) Dietary deficiencies were discovered to result in scurvy, which was further established by Captain Cook's successful attempt to counter the disease with supplies of fresh fruit. (Para. 1)

(3) Even an apparently harmless diet may be very unhealthy if it is not comprehensive enough. (Para. 2)

(4) Even a good mixed diet, with a variety of fruit and green vegetables, requires to be supplemented with the necessary vitamins. (Para. 3)

(5) The germ theory of Eijkman was confirmed when chickens, fed on scraps from sick patients, became ill also. (Para. 5)

(6) The ingredient required to ward off beriberi was extracted from rice husks and is called vitamin B. (Para. 6)

【参考答案】

(1) Yes (2) Yes (3) Yes (4) No (5) No (6) Yes

2. 阅读下面的短文，判断文章后面的句子是否与原文中的信息一致。原文中的原句需要考生自己找出来，然后再对照判断。

Reading Passage 1: Chimpanzees

Chimps apparently live in troops of between 20 and 50 animals. Within these troops they form small groups of varying composition; the most basic group consists of females or females plus offspring. Adult females spending much time together often turn out to be mother and daughter, or sisters. Mother and offspring live together consistently, at least for the first four or five years of life, longer than in any other primate except human being. During this time the young learn from their mother and from other chimps all the complicated acquired behaviours of chimpanzee adult life. Life for the young chimpanzee is relaxed and tolerant, and an infant will spend much of its time playing with other infants, with its mother and with its brothers and sisters. After this five-year initial period, contacts with the mother are still maintained, particularly by daughters. Even sons return from time to time from their wanderings to greet their mothers affectionately.

In the forest chimps are predominantly fruit-eaters (upon occasion they are cannibalistic), but in open woodland they may add more protein to their diet. Males sometimes kill colobus monkeys or bush-pigs; often males will gang up in a group to achieve their ends. Meat is a very choice item in chimpanzee diet and is eaten slowly and deliberately with a mouthful of leaves between each bite. It is sometimes shared out with other chimps who will beg for pieces. This food-sharing is very unusual among non-human primates; mostly it is every primate for himself. When the season is right chimps in woodlands also eat termites, and they do this by "fishing" for them. When beginning a bout of termiting, an animal will carefully select stems or piece of grass, trim them to the appropriate length, collect enough of them, and set out on the hunt for insects. It may pass over several termite hills if they are not ready and go on until it finds a mound ripe for fishing. Using a finger, a hole is scraped and the prepared twig inserted. Withdrawn covered with termites, it is passed carefully over the lower lip until every delicious morsel is removed, and the operation repeated. Clearly, in doing so, chimps are taking natural objects, modifying them to a standard pattern and using them for an objective which involves planning and forethought. They are, in fact, making tools. This has surprised many people, for previously man was considered to be the only tool-maker. In the chimpanzee, however, the intellectual abilities necessary for purposeful tool-making are already developed at an infrahuman level. Other examples of chimp tool-use in natural surroundings have also been seen. For instance, chewed leaves are used as sponges to soak up water from holes in trees. They are also used to wipe dung or mud from the body. Stones arid branches are used too in agonistic displays or when an animal is excited. They may be thrown under- or over-arm, often with considerable force and accuracy. Similar behaviour has been observed in other apes. Stones are used to open nuts, too.

There are still further peculiarities of ape behaviour which are quite fascinating. Jane van Lawick-Goodall once observed a chimpanzee sitting, apparently transfixed, watching a beautiful African sunset. Can chimps have aesthetic tastes? Examples of ape art in zoos would suggest that this is certainly the case. In London Zoo chimps have learnt how to paint, always with a detectable individualistic style. They can match the compositional abilities of a three-year-old human child, before the first diagrammatic representation of the face. Painting is to a high degree "autotelic", that is to say, self-rewarding. Ape painters hate being interrupted, even for food! Jane van Lawick-Goodall has also seen what she calls a "rain-dance", an energetic and rhythmic series of movements performed by males, watched by excited females, when there is a tropical rainstorm.

Decide whether or not the statement is similar in meaning to the coherent sentence in the passage.

(1) The simplest social group of chimpanzees consists of mother, father and children.

(2) Members of chimp families seem to be rather affectionate to each other.

(3) A baby chimp spends most of its time learning and playing.

(4) The kind of food chimps eat depends partly on their environment.

(5) Meat is very rare in a chimpanzee diet.

(6) Food-sharing is unusual among chimpanzees.

(7) Sometimes they eat fish.

(8) Chimpanzees have been observed to paint diagrammatic representations of the human face.

【参考答案】

(1) No (2) Yes (3) Yes (4) Yes (5) No (6) No (7) No (8) No

Reading Passage 2: Physical Fitness

The human body is made up mainly of bone, muscle, and fat. Some 639 different muscles account for about 45% of the body weight. Each of these muscles has four distinct and measurable qualities which are of interest to us:

(1) it can produce force which can be measured as strength of muscle;

(2) it can store energy which permits it to work for extended periods of time independent of circulation — this is generally referred to as muscular endurance;

(3) it can shorten at varying rates. This is called speed of contraction;

(4) it can be stretched and will recoil. This is called the elasticity of muscle.

The combination of these four qualities of muscle is referred to as muscular power.

If muscles are to function efficiently, they must be continually supplied with energy fuel. This is accomplished by the blood which carries the energy fuel from lungs and digestive system to the muscles. The blood is forced through the blood vessels by the heart. The combined capacity to supply energy fuels to the working muscles is called organic power.

The capacity and efficiency with which your body can function depends on the degree of development of both your muscular and organic power through regular exercise. However, the level to which you can develop these powers is influenced by such factors as the type of body you have, the food you eat, presence or absence of disease, rest and sleep. You are physically fit only when you have adequately developed your muscular and organic power to perform with the highest possible efficiency.

Heredity and health determine the top limits to which your physical capacity can be developed. This is known as your "potential physical capacity". This potential capacity varies from individual to individual. Most of us, for example, could train for a lifetime and never come close to running a four-minute mile simply because we weren't "built" for it. The top level at which you can perform physically right now is called your "acquired capacity" because it has been acquired or developed through physical activity in your daily routines.

Your body, like a car, functions most efficiently well below its acquired capacity. A car, for example, driven at its top speed of, say, 110 miles per hour uses more petrol per mile than when it is driven around 50—60 miles per hour, which is well below its capacity.

Your body functions in the same way, in which the ratio of work performed to energy expended is better when it functions well below acquired capacity. You can avoid wastage of energy by acquiring a level of physical capacity well above the level required to perform your normal daily tasks. This can be accomplished by supplementing your daily physical activity with a balanced exercise programme performed regularly. Your capacity increases as you progressively increase the load on your muscular and organic systems. Exercise will increase physical endurance and stamina thus providing a greater reserve of energy for leisure-time activities.

Decide whether or not the statement is similar in meaning to the sentence in the passage.

(1) The human body is made entirely of bone, muscle and fat.

(2) The body contains some 639 different muscles.

(3) Some of these muscles are strong, some have endurance, some can work fast, and some are elastic.

(4) Different muscles can shorten by different amounts.

(5) All muscles can stretch.

(6) The blood carries energy from the lungs to the digestive system and from there to the muscles.

(7) Organic power is the ability of the heart, lungs and digestive system, all together, to supply energy to the muscles through the blood.

(8) Exercise can develop both organic and muscular power.

(9) Not everybody can get up to the same level of physical performance.

(10) Most of us couldn't run a mile in four minutes because we're not fit enough.

(11) A car uses more energy, proportionately, when it goes at 50—60 miles per hour than when it goes at top speed.

(12) You should develop more fitness than you need just for your work.

【参考答案】

(1) No (2) Yes (3) No (4) No (5) Yes (6) No
(7) Yes (8) Yes (9) Yes (10) No (11) No (12) Yes

9 事实和论点——提高理解与辨别事实和论点的能力

9.1 如何理解与辨别事实和论点

雅思阅读考试的能力测试之一就是考查考生理解与辨别事实和论点的能力。其他语言考试也有类似的要求，不过没有像雅思考试如此地强调。雅思阅读考试把这种测试贯穿在几种题型中，如判断题、分类题、搭配题和选择题等。考生提高这种能力首先是对应试有帮助，更重要的是为以后的学习（如研究生阶段的学习）打下基础。

从考试的角度看，阅读考试不仅考查语言之内的东西（如词汇和句子结构等），还会考查语言之外的东西（如风俗和文化等）。在社会生活中，有的话语能够使人判断出说话人的态度，而有的则不能。因此，考生首先要具备理解与辨别事实和论点的能力。话语中含有说话人的意见、观点或论点时，一定会反映出他(她)的主观态度；而话语中只是谈论客观事实时，就没有反映出他（她）的态度。

怎样判断一句话是含有说话人的意见、观点或论点，还是纯粹地陈述客观事实呢？其实很简单：语言中的褒义词、贬义词和“应该”、“必须”等词是用来表达说话人的喜好、厌恶、支持或反对等态度的，这些词就能直接反映出说话人的态度；如果一句话只摆事实或列举数字（例如：Water is composed of two parts hydrogen and one part oxygen.）就反映不出说话人的态度。

下面我们通过不同的练习来提高这种判断和辨别的能力。

9.2 辨别事实和论点专项训练

专项训练 1

完成下列句子练习。

Read the following statements and decide whether they are facts or opinions.

(1) Edgar Allan Poe is the greatest writer of horror stories in the world.

(2) Poe had to leave the University of Virginia because he couldn't pay his debts.

(3) Edgar Allan Poe should not have drunk so much.

(4) Lovecraft has often been compared to Edgar Allan Poe.

(5) When Lovecraft died, he was practically unknown.

(6) Lovecraft died in conditions of shameful neglect.

(7) Lovecraft's stories are far more horrible than those of Edgar Allan Poe.

(8) Edgar Allan Poe's stories reflect his powerful imagination and his love for analysis.

(9) Baudelaire wrote that Edgar Allan Poe "pursued imagination and subjected it to the most stringent analysis".

(10) It is because of Baudelaire that Edgar Allan Poe became famous in France.

【参考答案】

(1) opinion	(2) fact	(3) opinion	(4) fact	(5) fact
(6) opinion	(7) opinion	(8) opinion	(9) opinion	(10) fact

专项训练 2

完成下列短文练习。

In the following passage a journalist explains why people join the Peoples Temple. Read the passage through, then consider the underlined statements — sentences or phrases — and decide whether they are facts or opinions. Whenever you think they are opinions, write down in the second column which words mostly influenced your decision.

Why People Join

(He has) no more pressing need than the one to find somebody to whom he can surrender, as quickly as possible, that gift of freedom which he, the unfortunate creature, was born with. (Dostoyevsky. The Brothers Karamazov*)*

(1) The landscape of their minds was as grotesque as the corpse-littered village they left behind. They had started as seekers after meaning, direction, comfort and love. (2) The Peoples Temple, which provided a number of social services to the poor, had filled their lives with purpose. But in the jungle of Guyana, it had all turned into fear and hatred.

Why did they join an organisation like the Peoples Temple? And why did they stay in it? (3) Few if any of the thousands of cult groups in the U.S. are as violent as the Guyana group was in its last days, but many of them share a number of unusual characteristics. Social scientists who have studied these groups agree that most cult members are in some sort of emotional trouble before they join ...

(4) Once recruits start going to meetings, they are frequently subjected to various drills and disciplines that weary them both physically and emotionally, producing a sort of trance.

Cut off from family and friends, the new member gets repeated infusions of the cult's doctrines. The lonely, depressed, frightened and disoriented recruit often experiences what amounts to a religious conversion. (5) Former members of such cults frequently say that something in them "snaps", report Flo Conway and Jim Siegelman, authors of *Snapping*, a new book on what they call "America's epidemic of sudden personality change".

At this point, the cultist's life is no longer his own. Personalities change from the lively and complex patterns of normality to those of an automation reciting what he has been taught. The usual problems of living have been replaced by a nearly childish existence in which the cult and its leaders supply all rules and all answers. (6) Erich Fromm, in his classic treatise on the rise of Nazism called this process the "escape from freedom".

Just as the cult members give themselves up to the group, the leader, too, takes his entire identity from his followers.

Both leader and followers thus see an overwhelming necessity to keep the group alive and intact. (7) Dissenters are often punished severely. Loyalty is intensified by claims that the outside world is evil and threatening. Return to normal life becomes more and more difficult, even terrifying.

"The gravest threat imaginable to such a group is for someone to try to take members out of the 'family'," says U.C.L.A. Psychologist David Wellisch. (8) Leo Ryan's mission to Guyana may have been just such a threat, the spark that triggered the tragedy.

With Jones' own behaviour growing more paranoid and the sudden presence of the Congressman and tile press, some experts believe there was almost a psychological inevitability to the disaster. "Following that type of fragmentation, there was only one thing left," says Dr. Stanley Cath, a Boston psychiatrist. "They could return to the world of reality, but they would have had to face their own inadequacies, the world they had already discarded, the families they had already discarded. (9) So for them, death was preferable because death had already been proclaimed rebirth."

Sentence No.	Fact or opinion	Words turning the statement into an opinion
(1)		
(2)		
(3)		
(4)		
(5)		
(6)		
(7)		
(8)		
(9)		

【参考答案】

Sentence No.	Fact or opinion	Words turning the statement into an opinion
(1)	opinion	as grotesque as
(2)	fact	
(3)	opinion	unusual
(4)	fact	
(5)	fact	
(6)	opinion	... called ... the "escape from freedom"
(7)	fact	
(8)	opinion	... may have been just such a threat, the spark ...
(9)	opinion	So for them, death was preferable ...

专项训练 3

完成下列短文练习。

Do Apes Ape?

Recent studies by two famous scientists show that chimpanzees and other apes can learn by imitation.

A The notion that the great apes — chimpanzees and gibbons — can imitate one another might seem unsurprising to anyone who has watched these animals playing at the zoo. But in scientific circles, the question of whether apes really do "ape" has become controversial.

B Consider a young chimpanzee watching his mother crack open a coula nut, as has been observed in the Taï Forest of West Africa. In most cases, the youth will eventually take up the practice himself. Was this because he imitated his mother? Sceptics think perhaps not. They argue that the mother's attention to the nuts encouraged the youngsters to focus on them as well. Once his attention had been drawn to the food, the young chimpanzee learned how to open the nut by trial and error, not by imitating his mother.

C Such a distinction has important implications for any discussion of chimpanzee cultures. Some scientists define a cultural trait as one that is passed down not by genetic inheritance but instead when the younger generation copies adult behaviour. If cracking open a coula nut is something that chimpanzees can simply figure out how to do on their own once they hold a hammer stone, then it can't be considered part of their culture. Furthermore, if these animals learn exclusively by trial and error, then chimpanzees must, in a sense, reinvent the wheel each time they tackle a new skill. No cumulative culture can ever develop.

D The clearest way to establish how chimpanzees learn is through laboratory experiments. One of us (Whiten), in collaboration with Deborah M. Custance of Goldsmith's College, University of London, constructed artificial fruits to serve as analogues of those the animals must deal with in the wild. In a typical experiment, one group of chimpanzees watched a complex technique for opening one of the fruits, while a second group observed a very different method; we then recorded the extent to which the chimpanzees had been influenced by the method they observed. We also conducted similar experiments with three-year-old children as subjects. Our results demonstrate that six-year-old chimpanzees show imitative behaviour that is markedly like that seen in the children, although the fidelity of their copying tends to be poorer.

E In a different kind of experiment, one of us (Boesch), along with some co-workers, gave chimpanzees in the Zurich Zoo in Switzerland hammers and nuts similar to those available in the wild. We then monitored the repertoire of behaviour displayed by the captive chimpanzees. As it turned out, the chimpanzees in the zoo exhibited a greater range of activities than the more limited and focused set of actions we had seen in the wild. We interpreted this to mean that a wild chimpanzee's cultural environment channeled the behaviour of youngsters, steering them in the direction of the most useful skills. In the zoo, without the benefit of existing traditions, the chimpanzees experimented with a host of less useful actions.

F Interestingly, some of the results from the experiments involving the artificial fruits converge with this idea. In one study, chimpanzees copied an entire sequence of actions they had witnessed, but did so only after several viewings and after trying some alternatives. In other words, they tended to imitate what they had observed others doing at the expense of their own trial-and-error discoveries.

G In our view, these findings taken together suggest that apes do ape and that this ability forms one strand in cultural transmission. Indeed, it is difficult to imagine how chimpanzees could develop certain geographic variations in activities such as ant-dipping and parasite-handling without copying established traditions. They must be imitating other members of their group.

H We should note, however, that — just as is the case with humans — certain cultural traits are no doubt passed on by a combination of imitation and simpler kinds of social learning, such as having one's attention drawn to useful tools. Either way, learning from elders is crucial to growing up as a competent wild chimpanzee.

(From *Scientific American*)

Questions (1)—(5)

Label the following sentences as A for "argument" or F for "fact".

(1) Young apes watch their parents as they feed.

(2) Young chimpanzees learn how to open nuts by trial and error only.

(3) A cultural trait must be gained through genetic inheritance.

(4) Chimpanzees need to watch behaviour repeatedly before they can try to copy it.

(5) Chimpanzee skills include ant-dipping and parasite handling.

【参考答案】

(1) F (2) A (3) A (4) F (5) F

Questions (6)—(11)

Which THREE of the following arguments are stated by the writer of the passage?

(6) Not everyone agrees that chimpanzees copy each other's behaviour.

(7) Chimpanzee behaviour depends on the type of tool that they use.

(8) Chimpanzee behaviour is best understood by observing them in their natural habitat.

(9) Children are better imitators than chimpanzees.

(10) Captive chimpanzees have a clearer idea of how to open nuts than those in the wild.

(11) Chimpanzees' observation of parent behaviour is vital to their development.

【参考答案】

(6), (9), (11)

雅思阅读考试

实践篇

10 雅思A类和G类阅读技巧和测试要求

10.1 雅思阅读考试的宗旨和测试手段

雅思考试旨在考查考生在中学阶段英语学习的基础上能否有效地用英语来进行交流，也就是考查考生实际运用语言的能力。因此，要考好雅思的阅读考试，就有必要了解该考试注重测试考生的什么能力，以及该考试是通过什么方式（即题型）来测试考生的这些能力的。

下面列出的是雅思 A 类（学术类）和 G 类（培训类）考试阅读技巧的测试要求。

1. What reading skills are tested in IELTS Academic Reading?

This is a test of reading comprehension in a general academic context. The texts used and the skills tested are intended to reflect the target language needs of undergraduate and postgraduate students, without bias for or against students of any particular discipline. Candidates may have to:

- identify the writer's overall purpose, target audience, sources, etc.;
- identify and follow key arguments in a text;
- identify opinions and attitudes as opposed to facts;
- locate specific information;
- read for detailed information;
- extract relevant information;
- distinguish the main idea from supporting detail;
- recognise key points for a summary;
- group pieces of information in a text in accordance with salient criteria;
- extract information from a prose text to put into a diagrammatic representation;
- make inferences;
- use correct spelling and correct grammar in their answers.

2. What reading skills are tested in IELTS General Training Reading?

In IELTS General Training Reading candidates are expected to be able to deal with texts from a range of social and educational, training and work contexts which are general rather than discipline specific. Technical terms are avoided and low frequency lexical items may be glossed. It is a test of reading and not of general knowledge. Candidates may have to:

- identify the writer's overall purpose, target audience, sources, etc.;
- identify and follow key arguments in a text;
- identify opinions and attitudes as opposed to facts;
- locate specific information;
- read for detailed information;
- extract relevant information;
- distinguish the main idea from supporting detail;
- reorganise key points for a summary;
- group pieces of information in a text in accordance with salient criteria;
- extract information from a prose text to put into a diagrammatic representation;
- make inferences;
- use correct spelling and correct grammar in their answers;
- use skimming and scanning skills to locate information in a text.

从上面列出的测试要求可以看出，雅思考试对A类和G类考生的要求基本上是一致的。以剑桥学者为主的考官们的观点十分明确：雅思阅读考试就是要考查阅读技巧的掌握与运用。在一定的英语基础上，无论是高中生、本科生还是研究生，掌握了阅读技巧就能提高阅读的能力和速度，从而在考试中取得更好的成绩。实际上，学习语言是为了使用，而不是为了证书。准备考雅思的学子首先要透彻地了解这点，否则就会准备不足、事倍功半。

本书第一大部分“阅读技巧学习篇”就是围绕这些阅读技巧展开讨论的。要应付雅思阅读考试，先要学习阅读技巧。掌握了这些技巧，不但对所有的阅读考试有帮助，而且对考生今后在国外的留学和生活也会大有裨益。

10.2 雅思A类和G类阅读测试指导

每种测试都有自己的宗旨，测试就是要实现这个宗旨，因此应试者研究分析不同的测试，就是要从试题的题型出发，再研究破解这些题型的方法，最后实践这些方法并证明它们是有效的。这样，考生就可以做到有的放矢，发挥出最大的潜力，取得突破。下面看看雅思考官们是采用何种手段来测试这些能力的。

1. A类阅读测试指导（资料源自雅思官方网站）

The Academic Reading Module takes 60 minutes. There are 40 questions. There are three reading passages with a total of 2,000 to 2,750 words.

Texts are taken from magazines, journals, books, and newspapers. Texts have been written for a non-specialist audience. All the topics are of general interest. They deal with issues which are interesting, recognisably appropriate and accessible to candidates entering postgraduate or undergraduate courses.

At least one text contains detailed logical argument. One text may contain non-verbal materials such as diagrams, graphs or illustrations.

If texts contain technical terms, then a simple glossary is provided.

Texts and tasks become increasingly difficult through the paper.

Some of the questions may appear before a passage, some may come after, depending on the nature of the questions.

A variety of questions are used, chosen from the following types:

1) Multiple Choice;

2) Short Answer Questions;

3) Sentence Completion;

4) Notes / Summary / Diagram / Flow Chart / Table Completion;

5) Choosing from a "Heading Bank" for Identified Paragraphs / Sections of the Text;

6) Identification of Writer's Views / Claims — Yes, No or Not Given;

7) Identification of Information in the Text — Yes, No or Not Given / True, False or Not Given;

8) Classification;

9) Matching Lists / Phrases.

Instructions are clear and easy to follow. Examples of any unfamiliar question types are given.

Texts and questions appear on a Question Paper which candidates can write on but not remove from the exam room.

All answers must be entered on an Answer Sheet during the 60 minute test. **No extra time is allowed to transfer answers.**

One mark is awarded for each of the 40 items in the test. A Band Score conversion table is produced for each version of the Academic Reading Module which translates scores out of 40 onto the IELTS 9-band scale. Scores are reported as a whole band or a half band. Candidates should note that care should be taken when writing their answers on the Answer Sheet as poor spelling and grammar are penalised.

2．G 类阅读测试指导（资料源自雅思官方网站）

The General Training Reading Module takes 60 minutes. There are 40 questions. There are three sections of increasing difficulty with a total of 2,000 to 2,750 words.

Texts are taken from notices, advertisements, official documents, booklets, newspapers, instruction manuals, leaflets, timetables, books and magazines.

The first section, social survival, contains texts relevant to basic linguistic survival in English with tasks mainly about retrieving and providing general factual information.

Training survival, the second section, focuses on the training context, for example, on the training programme itself or on welfare needs. This section involves a text or texts of more complex language with some precise or elaborated expression.

The third section, general reading, involves reading more extended prose with a more complex structure but with the emphasis on descriptive and instructive rather than argumentative texts, in a general context relevant to the wide range of candidates involved.

Some of the questions may appear before a passage, some may come after, depending on the nature of the questions.

A variety of questions are used, chosen from the following types:

1) Multiple Choice;

2) Short Answer Questions;

3) Sentence Completion;

4) Notes / Summary / Diagram / Flow Chart / Table Completion;

5) Choosing from a "Heading Bank" for Identified Paragraphs / Sections of the Text;

6) Identification of Writer's Views / Claims — Yes, No or Not Given;

7) Identification of Information in the Text — Yes, No or Not Given / True, False or Not Given;

8) Classification;

9) Matching Lists / Phrases.

Instructions are easy and clear to follow. Examples of any unfamiliar question types are given.

Texts and questions appear on a Question Paper which candidates can write on but not remove from the exam room.

All answers must be entered on an Answer Sheet during the 60 minute test. **No extra time is allowed to transfer answers.**

One mark is awarded for each of the 40 items in the test. A Band Score conversion table is produced for each version of the General Training Reading Module which translates scores out of 40 onto the IELTS 9-band scale. Scores are reported as a whole band or a half band. Candidates should note that care should be taken when writing their answers on the Answer Sheet as poor spelling and grammar are penalised.

从以上文字可见，虽然 A 类和 G 类的阅读试题在来源、内容和深度方面均有所不同，但题型是一样的。题型一样就意味着测试手段相同，手段相同则需要采取的阅读技巧就一致。

11 雅思阅读文本信息性质分析和阅读题型归类

11.1 雅思阅读文本信息性质分析

任何说明文的阅读文本都含有两大类信息：具体的细节信息和笼统的总体信息。雅思阅读文本都可以归入说明文阅读文本类型，同时也都含有这两大类信息。雅思阅读考试旨在考查考生的各种阅读能力，其中也包括提取信息的能力，因此考生首先要学会如何提取信息，然后才谈得上运用其他能力。基于这一点，下面就将雅思阅读题型进行归类。

11.2 雅思阅读题型归类

阅读文本中的这两大类信息，即具体的细节信息和笼统的总体信息，在雅思阅读文本中又可以根据信息的覆盖面分成三类：单个信息（覆盖面小，但孤立存在）、组团信息（覆盖面中等，但扎堆存在，信息之间息息相关，形成相对孤立的组团）和整篇信息（覆盖面大，由各段或者各组团信息连环组成）。

1. 雅思阅读九类题型中可归入提取单个信息的题型

1) Multiple Choice (部分)

2) Short answer Questions (大部分)

3) Sentence Completion

4) Notes / Table Completion

6) Identification of Writer's Views / Claims — Yes, No or Not Given (部分)

7) Identification of Information in the Text — Yes, No or Not Given / True, False or Not Given

8) Classification

9) Matching Lists / Phrases

2. 雅思阅读九类题型中可归入提取组团信息的题型

1) Multiple Choice (部分)

2) Short Answer Questions (少部分)

4) Summary (部分) / Diagram / Flow Chart (部分) Completion

5) Choosing from a “Heading Bank” for Identified Paragraphs / Sections of the Text

6) Identification of Writer’s Views / Claims — Yes, No or Not Given (部分)

8) Classification

9) Matching Lists / Phrases

3．雅思阅读九类题型中可归入提取整篇信息的题型

4) Summary Completion (部分)

12 雅思阅读九类题型分类破解——提取单个信息的题型

具体信息内容分析

雅思阅读考试中提取单个信息的题型特点是信息覆盖面小，但孤立存在。要破解这类题型，首先要了解单个存在的信息包含什么具体内容。这类信息主要包含数字、名称、事件和对事物的描述、对物体用途或目的的说明、颜色和大小、所有关系等。

1. 以阿拉伯数字为主的数字。具体体现形式为日期、时刻、时段、人口、数量、空间（面积和体积）、尺度（长度、宽度、高度和深度）、重量、预算、门牌号码及其他号码等。

2. 名称。具体体现形式为人名、地名、组织机构名、江河湖泊名、国家名、政体名、种（部）族名、语言名及项目名等。

3. 事件。具体体现形式为发生了什么，也包括怎样发生和为什么发生。至于什么时候发生、谁做了什么和在哪里发生，可归到前两类中。

4. 其他类型。具体体现形式为对事物的描述。说明物体的用途或目的、颜色和大小、所有关系、方式和过程、健康或状况等。

对具体信息的提问方式

其次要知道这些信息是以什么方式提问的。简而言之，这些信息都是以初中阶段所学的特殊疑问句的方式提问的。

1. 问数字的有：when，what time / date / year ...，which day / month / year ...，how long ...，how much / many ...，how long / high ...，what size / height ...，what's the population / budget / height / number ...，how often ... 等。

2. 问名称的有：who (whom)，where，which country / boy ...，what is he called，what's his name 等。

3. 问事件的有：what happened ...，what did somebody do，what is somebody doing ...，how did it happen，why did it happen ... 等。

4. 问其他类型的有：what ... is like，what colour / size ...，whose，how did you spend your time while you were on holiday ... 等。

从另一个角度看，特殊疑问词可归类如下：

1. Who is / has / had / will / would ...?

   Who(m) did you meet?

2. What is / has / have / will ...?
   What book / books ...?
   What boy / boys ...?
   What is ... like?
   What does ... look like?
   What's he / this called?
   What nationality ...
   What does she do?
   What time / date / year ...?
   What's this for / did you do that for?
   What kind(s) / sort(s) of ...?
   What colour / size / height / age / length / breadth / width / depth ...?
   What's the height ...?
3. When is / has / have / will ...?
4. Which have / will ...?
   Which book / books / boy / boys / girl / girls ...?
   Which of them / of the two ...?
   Which day / month / year ...?
   Which way ...?
5. Why is / has / had / would / will ...?
   Why don't / doesn't / not ...?
6. Where is / has / have / had / would / will ...?
   Where ... from?
7. Whose (umbrella) ...?
   Whose son / daughter / children ...?
8. How is / has / had / would / will ...?
   How much / many ...?
   How big / deep / far / long / old / sharp / wide ...?
   How often ...?
   How long ...?
   How / What about ...?

知道了这些，就有了破解提取单个信息题型的方法。不但简答题是直接用这些特殊疑问词来提问的，而且其他的题型也是简答题的变种，因为提取的信息性质相同，故也可以用相同的方法来破解。本章将通过分类练习对上述题型进行详细的说明。

12.1 简答题

12.1.1 题型分析破解

解决以简答题（Short Answer Questions）（大部分）为首的提取单个信息的题型的方法：

1. 仔细阅读问题。
1) 明确需要寻找的内容。
2) 确定回答的形式（如要填单词的词性）。
3) 牢记问题中的关键词，如名词、动词、数词、形容词和副词等。
2. 快速移动眼球，定位关键词首次出现的地方。
3. 阅读文本，选出正确答案。

这种方法其实是提取细节信息的寻读技巧的具体运用。（有关寻读技巧的内容请参见本书第一章的内容。）提取细节信息的各种题型均可按此简单的“三步曲”进行破解，各种题型的细节差异会分别在以下章节中详细分析。

12.1.2 练习及解析

阅读下面的文章，用上面介绍的方法回答文章后面的问题。

The Spectacular Eruption of Mount St. Helens

A The eruption in May 1980 of Mount St. Helens, Washington State, U.S.A., astounded the world with its violence. A gigantic explosion tore much of the volcano's summit to fragments; the energy released was equal to that of 500 of the nuclear bombs that destroyed Hiroshima, Japan in 1945.

B The event occurred along the boundary of two of the moving plates that make up the earth's crust. They meet at the junction of the North American continent and the Pacific Ocean. One edge of the continental North American plate over-rides the oceanic Juan de Fuca micro-plate, producing the volcanic Cascade range that includes Mounts Baker, Rainier and Hood, and Lassen Peak as well as Mount St. Helens.

C Until Mount St. Helens began to stir, only Mount Baker and Lassen Peak had shown signs of life during the 20th century. According to geological evidence found by the United States Geological Survey, there had been two major eruptions of Mount St. Helens in the recent (geologically speaking) past: around 1900 B.C., and about 1500 A.D. Since the arrival of Europeans in the region, it had experienced a single period of spasmodic activity, between 1831 and 1857. Then, for more than a century, Mount St. Helens lay dormant.

D By 1979, the Geological Survey, alerted by signs of renewed activity, had been monitoring the volcano for 18 months, warned the local population against being deceived by the mountain's outward calm, and forecast that an eruption would take place before the end of the century. The inhabitants of the area did not have to wait that long. On March 27, 1980, a few clouds of smoke formed above the summit, and slight tremors were felt. On the 28th, larger and darker clouds, consisting of gas and ashes, emerged and climbed as high as 20,000 feet. In April, a slight lull ensued, but the volcanologists remained pessimistic. Then, in early May, the northern flank of the mountain bulged, and the summit rose by 500 feet.

E Steps were taken to evacuate the population. Most — campers, hikers, timber-cutters — left the slopes of the mountain. Eighty-four-year-old Harry Truman, a holiday lodge owner who had lived there for more than 50 years, refused to be evacuated, in spite of official and private urging. Many members of the public, including an entire class of school children, wrote to him, begging him to leave. He never did.

F On May 18, at 8:32 in the morning, Mount St. Helens blew its top, literally. Suddenly, it was 1,300 feet shorter than it had been before its growth had begun. Over half a cubic mile of rock had disintegrated. At the same moment, an earthquake with an intensity of 5 on the Richter scale was recorded. It triggered an avalanche of snow and ice, mixed with hot rock — the entire north face of the mountain had fallen away. A wave of scorching volcanic gas and rock fragments shot horizontally from the volcano's riven flank, at an inescapable 200 miles per hour. As the sliding ice and snow melted, it touched off devastating torrents of mud and debris, which destroyed all life in their path. Pulverised rock climbed as a dust cloud into the atmosphere. Finally, viscous lava, accompanied by burning clouds of ash and gas, welled out of the volcano's new crater, and from lesser vents and cracks in its flanks.

G Afterwards, scientists were able to analyse the sequence of events. First, magma — molten rock — at temperatures above 2,000 °F had surged into the volcano from the earth's mantle. The build-up was accompanied by an accumulation of gas, which increased as the mass of magma grew. It was the pressure inside the mountain that made it swell. Next, the rise in gas pressure caused a violent decompression, which ejected the shattered summit like a cork from a shaken soda bottle. With the summit gone, the molten rock within was released in a jet of gas and fragmented magma, and lava welled from the crater.

H The effects of the Mount St. Helens eruption were catastrophic. Almost all the trees of the surrounding forest, mainly Douglas firs, were flattened, and their branches and bark ripped off by the shock wave of the explosion. Ash and mud spread over nearly 200 square miles of country. All the towns and settlements in the area were smothered in an even coating of ash. Volcanic ash silted up the Columbia River 35 miles away, reducing the depth of its navigable channel from 210 feet to 14 feet, and trapping sea-going ships. The debris that accumulated at the foot of the volcano reached a depth, in places, of 200 feet.

I The eruption of Mount St. Helens was one of the most closely observed and analysed eruptions in history. Because geologists had been expecting the event, they were able to amass vast amounts of technical data when it happened. Study of atmospheric particles formed as a result of the explosion showed that droplets of sulphuric acid, acting as a screen between the sun and the earth's surface, caused a distinct drop in temperature. There is no doubt that the activity of Mount St. Helens and other volcanoes since 1980 has influenced our climate. Even so, it has been calculated that the quantity of dust ejected by Mount St. Helens — a quarter of a cubic mile — was negligible in comparison with that thrown out by earlier eruptions, such as that of Mount Katmai in Alaska in 1912 (three cubic miles). The volcano is still active. Lava domes have formed inside the new crater, and have periodically burst. The threat of Mount St. Helens lives on.

This reading passage has 9 paragraphs labelled **A—I**.

(1) Which paragraph describes the evacuation of the mountain?

(2) Which paragraph describes the moment of the explosion of Mount St. Helens?

【参考答案】

(1) E (2) F

分析：这两题同属一个系列，即找出某个信息或某个事件出现在哪个段落中。这种问题在简答题的所有题型中属于最容易的，与英语知识多少无关，只需要记住关键词，用寻读技巧快速搜寻就可以。如在第（1）题中，记住 evacuation 这个词，不用知道它的意思（知道最好），在原文中搜寻，很快就可以发现它的动词形式 evacuate 和 be evacuated 出现在 E 段中，因此就可断定答案是 E。

第（2）题还可以用一点小智慧，把 moment（这是中学词汇）变成 at + 阿拉伯数字的形式来表达时刻，一下子就在 F 段发现了 at 8:32 这个时间。再看看上下文，就发现问句中的关键词在这里重现，包括 Mount St. Helens 和 explosion（在原文中是 blew its top），因此就可断定答案是 F。因为一个事件只可能在某个时刻发生，如果文章中还有另外的时间，那么肯定不会是相同的事件。掌握了解题方法，问题也就轻松快速地解决了。

(3) What are the dates of the TWO major eruptions of Mount St. Helens before 1980?

【参考答案】

1900 B.C.; 1500 A.D.

分析：这道题是要求考生找到两个日期，其实就是找阿拉伯数字，解题过程也就是一个快速搜寻的过程。可抓住问题中的 before 1980 这个关键词，在第一段就碰到 1945 年这个在 1980 年前的日期。但由于只有一个日期，而上下文又没有问题中的关键词重现，因此马上否决。再往下搜寻发现，C 段中有四个 1980 年前的日期，再发现前面两个日期所在的句子中重现了问题中的关键词，因此可确定答案就是前两个日期——1900 B.C. 和 1500 A.D.。这道题属于简答题的另一个类别——搜寻阿拉伯数字与名称。这种类别占据了单个信息题型的大部分，而且都有明显的标志，在搜寻过程中会很容易发现。

(4) How do scientists know that the volcano exploded around the two dates above?

Use **NO MORE THAN THREE WORDS** to answer this question.

【参考答案】

geological evidence

分析：这道题属于用文字回答的简答题。这种题最难，下面会在另一个练习中专门讨论此类简答题。

这道题由于有第（3）题作参考并不难做。题目问的是科学家怎样知道火山是在以上两个日期前后爆发的，根据第（3）题找到的两个日期的位置，答案就在这个句子的上下文中。这里要重点强调的是，一定要读懂问题。很多考生都不注意读问题，这样就导致定了位却找不到答案。这道题是问 how——怎么样，解答的方法有两种，一是找副词（多数副词以 -ly 结尾），二是找介词短语（如 by ..., in ..., from ..., through ..., according to ... 等）。那么再看第（3）题两个日期所在的句子：According to geological evidence found by the United States Geological Survey, there had been two major eruptions of Mount St. Helens in the recent (geologically speaking) past: around 1900 B.C., and about 1500 A.D. 马上就可以发现 according to geological evidence 就是个介词短语，也就是答案。由于这道题规定答案不得超过三个词，因此要省去 according to，剩下的 geological evidence 就是答案。

有关如何省略的问题，将在后面的章节中详细讨论。

12.1.3 纯文字回答类的简答题

1. 答题技巧

这种题需用寻读技巧搜寻定位。如果没有明显的关键词，如阿拉伯数字、大写字母或特殊的标点符号（如引号等），那么要点就是要记住问题中所有的关键词。一旦在搜寻过程中发现大多数关键词反复出现在一个句子中，这时考生就可以定位了。有三种情况：一是问题中的关键词在原文某处全部重现，且没有变化，这种情况最好定位；二是问题中的关键词在原文某处部分重现，部分变成了相应的同义词或改变了结构，这种情况下还是比较好定位的，况且基础扎实的考生一般都能看出变化；三是问题中的关键词在原文某处完全不重现，全部变为同义词或同义结构。这种情况多会出现在问题很短，关键词又不多的时候。这种情况下，定位较难，全凭考生自身的英语基础看出变化才能定位。建议如果一下子无法定位，先暂时放弃，接着做下面的题。千万不能死缠烂打，这样做不仅会使自己乱了方寸，还浪费时间。放一放，说不定在继续做题的过程中就会找到答案，因为简答题的题型基本是按文章叙述的顺序出题的。

下面使用寻读技巧解答简答题。

2. 练习及解析

Painful Poultry

1 It's common practice in the poultry industry to amputate the beaks of chickens to prevent them pecking each other. Techniques of "debeaking" vary, but in the U.K. it is performed on chicks when they are a few days old, and usually involves amputating one third of the upper part of the beak with a heated blade. The poultry industry has always assumed that chickens quickly recover, but evidence presented at the International Ornithological Congress in New Zealand suggests otherwise. Dr. Michael Gentle, of the Institute of Animal Physiology and Genetics Research in Edinburgh, has shown that chickens can feel chronic pain for weeks, and sometimes even months, after the operation.

2 Chickens have pain receptors in their beaks, and so slicing their beaks off with a hot knife must hurt them. What Dr. Gentle has found is that the pain may be delayed, as is the case with human burn victims. "The chickens are not in pain initially, but 24 hours later they show clear pain-related behaviour." After the beak is amputated, the remaining stump may take two to four weeks to heal. But even then, pain may continue: the damaged nerves still grow, and may be "abnormally and spontaneously active" (believed to be the cause of stump pain in human amputees). Even two months later, the stump is unusually sensitive to touch and temperature changes.

3 Many aspects of a chicken's behaviour also suggest that it experiences the long-term pain, and perhaps even the depression, typically felt by human amputees. In the first few weeks after debeaking, a chicken spends more time resting than usual. And even six weeks later, when the stump has healed over, a chicken avoids using its beak.

4 The habit of pecking each other doesn't necessarily start off as aggressive behaviour — it may simply be a substitute for pecking at litter — but it can quickly escalate once one bird is injured, and sometimes leads to the death of weaker birds.

5 Is debeaking really the solution, though? A very preliminary survey in Scotland, of two commercial laying breeds, found debeaking had no effect on the extent of feather and comb damage, or on body weights or the number of birds that died. A much more effective approach would be to remove the conditions — such as overcrowding and bright light, for example, that are known to contribute to feather-pecking and cannibalism. Where chickens really have to be kept in such conditions, a more sensible solution than debeaking, says Dr. Gentle, would be to breed strains of chickens that don't peck each other.

Questions:

(1) What has been the poultry industry's assumption about the debeaking process, in relation to chicks?

____

(2) According to the reading passage, how long might chickens feel pain for after the operation?

____

(3) Dr. Gentle compares the chickens with humans twice. Write the two categories of humans he compares them with.

____

(4) What two pieces of evidence does Dr. Gentle give to show that chickens suffer from long-term pain and even depression?

____

【参考答案】

(1) Chickens quickly recover.

分析：先要读懂问题，确定答案的词性。第一题主要提问的是主语部分——What has been the poultry industry's assumption? 回答时要先确定主语部分要用什么词性的词。名词、数词、代词、动名词、动词不定式都可充当主语，但由于"家禽养殖业假定的事实 "需要多个词才讲得清，而以上列出的这几类都是单个的词汇，不足以表达清楚，因此马上否决，转而考虑短语或从句。动名词短语、动词不定式短语或名词从句都可以充当主语。然后，记住问题中的关键词，在文章中搜寻，很快就可以发现原文在第一段第三句 The poultry industry has always assumed that chickens quickly recover... 中，assumed 是 assumption 的动词形式，跟在它后面的宾语从句是名词从句，那么这就是答案了，把这个从句全部抄下来就行。但简答题要省略一些文字（省略技巧另辟章节讨论），那么把 that 省掉，剩下的 chickens quickly recover 就是答案。

(2) months

分析：确定答案的形式也是至关重要的。注意，问题不只是问 how long ...，而是问 how long might ...，问的是可能性。用寻读的技巧不难找到原文在第一段最后一句：... chickens can feel chronic pain for weeks, and sometimes even months, after the operation ... 通常，考生可能会把 weeks, and sometimes even months 全部照抄下来，实际上只需回答 months 即可，因为 months 是最大的可能性，已包含了 weeks 的较小可能性。

(3) (human) burn victims; (human) amputees

分析：这道题非常容易，动动脑筋就能破解。整篇文章描写的是鸡的情况，而题目要求找出两种有关人的信息，用寻读技巧就能轻松解答。全文只有第二段有 human burn victims 和 human amputees。第三段也有 human amputees，但与第二段中提到的第二种人是一样的，那么答案就是 (human) burn victims 和 (human) amputees。

(4) Chickens / They spend more time resting (than usual).

Chickens / They avoid using their beaks.

分析：用寻读技巧可很快发现关键词在第三段第一句，但文中并没有直接给出答案，因此这里要看上下文。上文的各个段落分别谈论的是几个中心内容，因而，只需看下文 ... a chicken spends more time resting than usual ... a chicken avoids using its beak ...，这就是答案了。但不能照抄，因为问题中的 chicken 改为复数 chickens 了，因此答案应为 Chickens / They spend more time resting (than usual) 和 Chickens / They avoid using their beaks。这里再次强调仔细阅读题目的重要性，雅思阅读测试题的答案一般是从原文中直接提取的，但有时题目中有些细节会稍有改动（例如关键词的单复数等），这时就不可盲目照抄，要进行相应的改动。

12.1.4 专项训练

下面做两个练习，专项训练 1 是 A 类题，专项训练 2 是 G 类题。这两题反映了简答题的三种情况：一是寻找的信息出现在某个段落；二是要求寻找与数字和名称有关的信息；三是用纯文字回答问题。

专项训练 1

Changing Our Understanding of Health

The concept of health holds different meanings for different people and groups. These meanings of health have also changed over time. This change is no more evident than in Western society today, when notions of health and health promotion are being challenged and expanded in new ways.

For much of recent Western history, health has been viewed in the physical sense only. That is, good health has been connected to the smooth mechanical operation of the body, while ill health has been attributed to a breakdown in this machine. Health in this sense has been defined as the absence of disease or illness and is seen in medical terms. According to this view, creating health for people means providing medical care to treat or prevent disease and illness. During this period, there was an emphasis on providing clean water, improved sanitation and housing.

In the late 1940s, the World Health Organisation challenged this physically and medically oriented view of health. They stated that “health is a complete state of physical, mental and social well-being and is not merely the absence of disease” (WHO, 1946). Health and the person were seen more holistically (mind / body / spirit) and not just in physical terms.

The 1970s was a time of focusing on the prevention of disease and illness by emphasising the importance of the lifestyle and behaviour of individual. Specific behaviour which was seen to increase risk of disease, such as smoking, lack of fitness and unhealthy eating habits, were targeted. Creating health meant providing not only medical health care, but health promotion programmes and policies which would help people maintain healthy behaviour and lifestyles. While this individualistic healthy lifestyles approach to health worked for some (the wealthy members of society) people experiencing poverty, unemployment, underemployment or little control over the conditions of their daily lives benefited little from this approach. This was largely because both the healthy lifestyles approach and the medical approach to health largely ignored the social and environmental conditions affecting the health of people.

During the 1980s and 1990s there has been a growing swing away from seeing lifestyle risks as the root cause of poor health. While lifestyle factors still remain important, health is being viewed also in terms of the social, economic and environmental contexts in which people live. This broad approach to health is called the socio-ecological view of health. The broad socio-ecological view of health was endorsed at the first International Conference of Health Promotion held in 1986, Ottawa, Canada, where people from 38 countries agreed and declared that:

> The fundamental conditions and resources for health are peace, shelter, education, food, a viable income, a stable eco-system, sustainable resources, social justice and equity. Improvement in health requires a secure foundation in these basic requirements.

It is clear from this statement that the creation of health is about much more than encouraging healthy individual behaviour and lifestyles and providing appropriate medical care. Therefore, the creation of health must include addressing issues such as poverty, pollution, urbanisation, natural resource depletion, social alienation and poor working conditions. The social, economic and environmental contexts which contribute to the creation of health do not operate separately or independently of each other. Rather, they are interacting and interdependent, and it is the complex interrelationships between them which determine the conditions that promote health. A broad socio-ecological view of health suggests that the promotion of health must include a strong social, economic and environmental focus.

At the Ottawa Conference in 1986, a charter was developed which outlined new directions for health promotion based on the socio-ecological view of health. This charter, known as the Ottawa Charter for Health Promotion, remains as the backbone of health action today. In exploring the scope of health promotion it states that:

> Good health is a major resource for social, economic and personal development and an important dimension of quality of life. Political, economic, social, cultural, environmental, behavioural and biological factors can all favour health or be harmful to it.

The Ottawa Charter brings practical meaning and action to this broad notion of health promotion. It presents fundamental strategies and approaches in achieving health for all. The overall philosophy of health promotion which guides these fundamental strategies and approaches is one of "enabling people to increase control over and to improve their health".

Use **NO MORE THAN THREE WORDS** from the passage to answer the following questions.

(1) In which year did the World Health Organisation define health in terms of mental, physical and social well-being?

(2) Which members of society benefited most from the healthy lifestyles approach to health?

(3) Name the three broad areas which relate to people's health, according to the socio-ecological view of health.

(4) During which decade were lifestyle risks seen as the major contributors to poor health?

【参考答案】

(1) 1946. (2) The wealthy members.

(3) Social, economic, environmental. (4) The 1970s.

专项训练 2

下面的练习是雅思 G 类阅读材料，材料内容稍浅，考查考生涉及社会生存的阅读技能，但题型相同，解题方法就一样。更多同类练习请参看本书第一章第二节的内容。

SCHOOL EXCURSIONS

A Ancient and Modern Museum This is a museum with a difference. Along with the usual historical exhibits, this museum features an up-to-date display of hands-on information technology.	***B Shortlands Wildlife Park*** This is not the usual "animal goal". Here exotic animals wander free in large compounds, separated in such a way that they can't harm one another.
C Botanical Gardens Besides the many exotic plants one expects to see in a botanical garden, these gardens feature an array of native birds and other wildlife.	***D Wax World*** If you're interested in seeing how people used to live and dress, Wax World is the place for you. Featuring over 100 wax models of famous people, this venue is well-suited to anyone interested in changing trends in clothing.
E The Central Art Gallery The art gallery has six chambers each exhibiting paintings from different periods, from the Middle Ages to the present. The walking tour, recorded on tape, is designed for visitors interested in art history and criticism.	***F Technology Park*** In the planetarium you can observe features of the night sky, and learn about such historical events as the origin of the crab nebula. This excursion also includes a visit to the Satellite Mapping Centre.
G Parliament Students are met at the entrance by ushers who show them around the Houses. The tour includes the Hansard Library, the grand lounge, government and opposition offices and public gallery.	***H St. Cedric's Cathedral*** With the Bishops' Throne as its central feature, this building is a classic example of the excesses of architecture. This excursion is a must for any student interested in sculpture and stained glass as art forms.

（续表）

I The Light Fantastic	*J Trolland's Caves*
Find out about the fascinating process of candle making. This factory also holds the additional attraction of illustrating the diverse uses that candles and other wax products can have — from the projection of film, to their use in the art of sculpture and decoration.	These caves, situated below the hills to the north of the city, are entered via the Widmore River. The caves are home to colonies of glow worms that shine like stars on the ceilings and walls of the caves, casting an eerie light on the many stalagmites and stalactites.

Answer questions (1)—(7) below by writing the appropriate letters **A—J** in the brackets after each question.

Example:

Which excursion would you choose if you are interested in famous people? (*D*)

(1) Which excursion would you choose if you wanted to know about the different uses of wax? ( )

(2) Where could students learn something about the animals of the country they are studying in? ( )

(3) On which excursion is it possible to learn something about the stars? ( )

(4) Which excursion would be suitable for students of fashion and design? ( )

(5) Which excursion would attract people interested in computers? ( )

(6) On which excursion would you expect to listen to an art critic? ( )

(7) On which excursion would you need to travel by boat? ( )

【参考答案】

(1) D　(2) C　(3) F　(4) D　(5) A　(6) E　(7) J

12.2 完成句子题

12.2.1 题型分析破解

完成句子题（Sentence Completion）也是考查考生提取单个信息的能力。

这一题型的形式与简答题不同，但其实是简答题的变形。每个空都可以改编成一道简答题，根据上下文，就可判断每个空应该填什么词性的词。譬如上文是介词，这个空必然要填名词性的词；上文是 to，这个空就要填名词性的词或动词不定式；上文是及物动词，这个空就要填名词性的词、动词不定式或宾语从句等；上文是 that 或关系代词或关系副词，这个空就要填从句；上文是副词，这个空就要填动词、形容词或副词；

上文是系动词，这个空就要填形容词或名词短语；上文是冠词，这个空就要填名词性的词；上文是名词，这个空就要填后置定语；下文是后置定语，这个空就要填名词。

如本书第四章所讲，英语是讲究词序的分析性语言，每句中各种位置放什么词性的词是固定不变的，因此掌握好英语的句子结构至关重要。

这种题型的解题步骤与简答题一样。

12.2.2 练习及解析

1. 下面就以下练习作进一步的分析。

Come to a Full Stop — the Perils of Punctuation

Punctuation makes the written language intelligible. It does the job, on the page, of the changes of pitch, pace and rhythm which make it possible to understand speech. Unsurprisingly, therefore, a requirement for some knowledge of how to punctuate makes an early appearance in an English curriculum.

The trouble is, that necessary though punctuation is, the task of teaching it to adults and children is considerably more challenging than it might appear. To believe, for example, that it is possible to instruct children about writing in sentences by telling them about full stops and capital letters is to court frustration and failure. **The notion of the sentence as a statement — a free-standing chunk of information — is something that children come to gradually.** Nor, interestingly, do they come first to short sentences and then proceed to longer ones. For a child, the piece of information which "free-stands" in the head may be a whole description or section of narrative. She may be reading three-word sentences in her reading book; but her own writing will be in chunks of up to a page.

Gradually, as written work grows longer and more complicated, so the perception of the shorter sentence increases. **Good teachers will, in their teaching of early writing, watch for the child's ability to compose in sentences and then point out how the use of punctuation will define them more clearly.**

So where, in all this, comes the mechanical definition of a sentence — that it needs a verb for example? The pragmatic answer, I suspect, is that it comes nowhere at all. Adult writers do not, on the whole, look back at their sentences to make sure they contain verbs. We all, surely, feel our sentences intuitively. Most of the time, to be sure, they will contain verbs. Occasionally, though, they may not — and where's the harm? What is certain is that you cannot possibly use the grammatical rule as a tool with which to teach a seven-year-old child about sentence-writing. The child can be nudged and helped towards writing in sentences, but on the whole she will not do it until she is ready.

The point is that punctuation is an aid which the writer brings into play to illuminate an already-formed idea. Before you can learn the punctuation, you have to know what you want to punctuate. A child's readiness to take teaching about punctuation can best be judged by her ability to use the constructions for which the punctuation is needed. Thus you teach capital letters, full stops, question marks and exclamation marks to a child who is already writing sentences, questions and exclamations. Similarly, you teach direct speech punctuation to a child who is already writing dialogue. The development of the child's writing will always be a step ahead of the punctuation, and to reverse the process in response, say, to the short-term demands of a curriculum, is to put later progress at risk.

This, incidentally, makes assessment notoriously difficult. How do you compare the writing of a child who writes in correctly punctuated simple sentences with that of the child who writes good, but unpunctuated, dialogue?

Finally, **what about the most misused device in the English language — the apostrophe?** The problem which teachers have here is that we are living in the midst of change. The conventions we were all taught are not really difficult, but they do call for a fairly sophisticated level of conceptual understanding. There are traps, too, lurking within such distinctions as that between "it's" and "its", and even the most competent of writers is likely to be floored occasionally by words which end with "s" and are not plurals. How confidently would you render, "the strings of the double bass", in apostrophised form, for example?

Choose **ONE OR TWO WORDS** from the text to fill in each gap in the statements.

(1) Children slowly acquire the ______________ that information exists in individual chunks, or sentences.

(2) A good way for teachers to help their students is by showing them how punctuation clarifies meaning at a time when the child shows the ______________ write sentences.

(3) The apostrophe causes many difficulties and is frequently ______________.

【参考答案】

(1) notion

分析：这道题的空格中要填一个名词，其实是一个 what 问题。做这种题要充分运用英语句法结构知识。原文中的句子结构如下：

定语　同位语　　　　定语从句

The notion ... — ... — is something that children come to gradually.

题目其实是把原句的结构转换了一下，用原定语从句中的 children 作主语，把 gradually 改成了 slowly，come to 改成了 acquire。原句中 come to 后面跟的是由关系代词 that 引起的定语从句，而 that 等于先行词 something，而 something 跟在系动词后，是主语 notion 的补足语，具体说明主语是什么。从这个意义上来说，something 等于 notion，那么 acquire 后面的空格就应该填 notion，而不是 notion 后面的 sentence 或 statement。

(2) ability to

分析：这道题同样也是对原句结构和部分单词进行了改写。先确定 the 后面应该跟一个名词，而名词后的 write 应该是动词不定式作定语，用来修饰这个名词。原句中的 compose 的意思与 write 相同。原文中 compose 是在短语 ability to compose 中的，所以这个空应填 ability to。

(3) misused

分析：解答这题请注意原句 ... the most misused device ... the apostrophe 的结构。misused device 是过去分词作定语，用来修饰后面的名词。由于过去分词含有完成与被动的意思，所以“过去分词 + 名词”的结构可转化为“a / the + 名词 + is / has been + 过去分词”。那么 misused device 就可转化为 the device is / has been misused，而 apostrophe 在句子中是 device 的同位语，用 apostrophe 替代了 device，所以空格中应填 misused。弄懂了句子的结构，即使不懂 apostrophe 的意思，也可以填对。

2. 下面用寻读技巧和步骤继续练习。

The discovery that language can be a barrier to communication is quickly made by all who travel, study, govern or sell. Whether the activity is tourism, research, government, policing, business, or data dissemination, the lack of a common language can severely impede progress or can halt it altogether. “Common language” here usually means a foreign language, but the same point applies in principle to any encounter within unfamiliar dialects or styles within a single language. “They don’t talk the same language” has a major metaphorical meaning alongside its literal one.

Although communication problems of this kind must happen thousands of times each day, very few become public knowledge. Publicity comes only when a failure to communicate has major consequences, such as strikes, lost orders, legal problems, or fatal accidents — even, at times, war. One reported instance of communication failure took place in 1970, when several Americans ate a species of poisonous mushroom. No remedy was known, and two of the people died within days. A radio report of the case was heard by a chemist who knew of a treatment that had been successfully used in 1959 and published in 1963. Why had the American doctors not heard of it seven years later? Presumably because the report of the treatment had been published only in journals written in European languages other than English.

Several comparable cases have been reported. But isolated examples do not give an impression of the size of the problem — something that can come only from studies of the use or avoidance of foreign language materials and contacts in different communicative situations. In the English-speaking scientific world, for example, surveys of books and documents consulted in libraries and other information agencies have shown that very little foreign language material is ever consulted. Library requests in the field of science and technology showed that only 13% were for foreign language periodicals. Studies of the sources cited in publications lead to a similar conclusion: the use of foreign language sources is often found to be as low as 10%.

The language barrier presents itself in stark form to firms who wish to market their products in other countries. British industry, in particular, has in recent decades often been criticised for its linguistic insularity — for its assumption that foreign buyers will be happy to communicate in English, and that awareness of other languages is not therefore a priority. In the 1960s, over two-thirds of British firms dealing with non-English-speaking customers were using English for outgoing correspondence; many had their sales literature only in English; and as many as 40% employed no one was able to communicate in the customers’ languages. A similar problem was identified in other English-speaking countries, notably the U.S., Australia and New Zealand. And non-English-speaking countries were by no means exempt — although the widespread use of English as an alternative language made them less open to the charge of insularity.

The criticism and publicity given to this problem since the 1960s seems to have greatly improved the situation. Industrial training schemes have promoted an increase in linguistic and cultural awareness. Many firms now have their own translation services; to take just one example in Britain, Rowntree Mackintosh now publish their documents in six languages (English, French, German, Dutch, Italian and Xhosa). Some firms run part-time language courses in the languages of the countries with which they are most involved; some produce their own technical glossaries, to ensure consistency when material is being translated. It is now much more readily appreciated that marketing efforts can be delayed, damaged, or disrupted by a failure to take account of the linguistic needs of the customer.

The changes in awareness have been most marked in English-speaking countries, where the realisation has gradually dawned that by no means everyone in the world knows English well enough to negotiate in it. This is especially a problem when English is not an official language of public administration, as in most parts of the Far East, Russia, Eastern Europe, the Arab world, Latin America and French-speaking Africa. Even in case where foreign customers can speak English quite well, it is often forgotten that they may not be able to understand it to the required level — bearing in mind the regional and social variation which permeates speech and which can cause major problems of listening comprehension. In securing understanding, how "we" speak to "them" is just as important, it appears, as how "they" speak to "us".

Complete each of the following statements with words taken from the reading passage. Write **NO MORE THAN THREE WORDS** for each answer.

(1) Language problems may come to the attention of the public when they have ____________ , such as fatal accidents or social problems.

(2) Evidence of the extent of the language barrier has been gained from ____________ of materials used by scientists such as books and periodicals.

(3) An example of British linguistic insularity is the use of English for materials such as ____________ .

(4) An example of a part of the world where people may have difficulty in negotiating English is ____________ .

【参考答案】

(1) major consequences (2) survey (3) sales literature

(4) Far East / Russia / Eastern Europe / the Arab world / Latin America / French-speaking Africa

3. 继续做下面的题，注意先确定空格中要填什么词性的词。

The Effects of Light on Plant and Animal Species

Light is important to organisms for two different reasons. Firstly it is used as a cue for the timing of daily and seasonal rhythms in both plants and animals, and secondly it is used to assist growth in plants.

Breeding in most organisms occurs during a part of the year only, and so a reliable cue is needed to trigger breeding behaviour. Day length is an excellent cue, because it provides a perfectly predictable pattern of change within the year. In the temperate zone in spring, temperatures fluctuate greatly from day to day, but day length increases steadily by a predictable amount. The seasonal impact of day length on physiological responses is called "photoperiodism", and the amount of experimental evidence for this phenomenon is considerable. For example, some species of birds' breeding can be induced even in midwinter simply by increasing day length artificially. Other examples of photoperiodism occur in plants. A short-day plant flowers when the day is less than a certain critical length. A long-day plant flowers after a certain critical day length is exceeded. In both cases the critical day length differs from species to species. Plants which flower after a period of vegetative growth, regardless of photoperiod, are known as day-neutral plants.

Breeding seasons in animals such as birds have evolved to occupy the part of the year in which offspring have the greatest chances of survival. Before the breeding season begins, food reserves must be built up to support the energy cost of reproduction, and to provide for young birds both when they are in the nest and after fledging. Thus many temperate-zone birds use the increasing day lengths in spring as a cue to begin the nesting cycle, because this is a point when adequate food resources will be assured.

The adaptive significance of photoperiodism in plants is also clear. Short-day plants that flower in spring in the temperate zone are adapted to maximising seedling growth during the growing season. Long-day plants are adapted for situations that require fertilisation by insects, or a long period of seed ripening. Short-day plants that flower in the autumn in the temperate zone are able to build up food reserves over the growing season and over winter as seeds. Day-neutral plants have an evolutionary advantage when the connection between the favourable period for reproduction and day length is much less certain. For example, desert annuals germinate, flower and seed whenever suitable rainfall occurs, regardless of the day length.

The breeding season of some plants can be delayed to extraordinary lengths. Bamboos are perennial grasses that remain in a vegetative state for many years and then suddenly flower, fruit and die. Every bamboo of the species *Chusquea abietifolia* on the island of Jamaica flowered, set seed and died during 1884. The next generation of bamboo flowered and died between 1916 and 1918, which suggests a vegetative cycle of about 31 years. The climatic trigger for this flowering cycle is not yet known, but the adaptive significance is clean. The simultaneous production of masses of bamboo seeds (in some cases lying 12 to 15 centimetres deep on the ground) is more than all the seed-eating animals can cope with at the time, so that some seeds escape being eaten and grow up to form the next generation.

The second reason light is important to organisms is that it is essential for photosynthesis. This is the process by which plants use energy from the sun to convert carbon from soil or water into organic material for growth. The rate of photosynthesis in a plant can be measured by calculating the rate of its uptake of carbon. There is a wide range of photosynthetic responses of plants to variations in light intensity. Some plants reach maximal photosynthesis at one-quarter full sunlight, and others, like sugarcane, never reach a maximum, but continue to increase photosynthesis rate as light intensity rises.

Plants in general can be divided into two groups: shade-tolerant species and shade-intolerant species. This classification is commonly used in forestry and horticulture. Shade-tolerant plants have lower photosynthetic rates and hence have lower growth rates than those of shade-intolerant species. Plant species become adapted to living in a certain kind of habitat, and in the process evolve a series of characteristics that prevent them from occupying other habitats. Grime (1966) suggests that light may be one of the major components directing these adaptations. For example, eastern hemlock seedlings are shade-tolerant. They can survive in the forest understorey under very low light levels because they have a low photosynthetic rate.

Complete the sentences. Choose **NO MORE THAN THREE WORDS** from the passage for each answer.

(1) Day length is a useful cue for breeding in areas where ________ are unpredictable.

(2) Plants which do not respond to light levels are referred to as ________ .

(3) Birds in temperate climates associate longer days with nesting and the availability of ________ .

(4) Plants that flower when days are long often depend on ________ to help them reproduce.

(5) Desert annuals respond to ________ as a signal for reproduction.

(6) There is no limit to the photosynthetic rate in plants such as ________ .

(7) Tolerance to shade is one criterion for the ________ of plants in forestry and horticulture.

【参考答案】

(1) temperatures

(2) day-neutral / day-neutral plants

(3) food / food resources / adequate food / adequate food resources

(4) insects / fertilisation by insects

(5) rainfall / suitable rainfall

(6) sugarcane

(7) classification

12.3 完成表格题

12.3.1 题型分析破解

完成表格题（Table Completion）也是简答题的变形，因为提取的信息性质（单个孤立信息）相同，也可以用应对简答题的方法破解。

由于这种题型是以表格形式出现的，因此首先要提高理解和分析图表的能力，也就是说，考生不但要具备读“文”的能力，也要具备读“图”的能力，这也是现代教育和雅思考试要求学生掌握的图文转换技能。

下面先具体分析表格的变化形式，共有如下三种：

1)

问题	问题	问题
...	...	1. ______
...	2. ______	...
3. ______	...	...

表格第一栏的短语可以转换为简答题，实际上表格题就是简答题的变形。每一个空格应填写的内容其实就是上面问题的答案，空格所在行中出现的词语就是用于定位的关键词。

2)

问题	问题	问题
...	...	1. ... ______
...	2. ... ______	...
3. ... ______	...	...

这种表格空格处应填写的内容并不能直接回答上面的问题，而是要将空格里的短语补充完整。这种题型可看作是完成表格题和完成句子题两种题型的混合。

3)

问题	问题	问题
...	...	1. … ______
...	2. ______	…
3. … ______	...	4. ______

这种表格是前两种表格题的混合形式，部分空格处应填写的内容可直接回答上面的问题；其余空格处应填写的内容不能直接回答上面的问题，而是要将空格里的短语补充完整。

表格中的题目基本上按原文信息出现的顺序设计。

12.3.2 练习及解析

现在通过下面的这几篇文章对此类题型进行分析。

Creating Artificial Reefs

In the coaster waters of the U.S., a nation's leftovers have been discarded. Derelict ships, concrete blocks, scrapped cars, army tanks, tyres filled with concrete and redundant planes litter the seafloor. However, this is not waste disposal, but part of a coordinated, state-run programme. To recently arrived fish, plants and other sea organisms, these artificial reefs are an ideal home, offering food and shelter.

Sea-dumping incites widespread condemnation. Little surprise when oceans are seen as "convenient" dumping grounds for the rubbish we have created but would rather forget. However, scientific evidence suggests that if we dump the right things, sea life can actually be enhanced. And more recently, purpose-built structures of steel or concrete have been employed — some the size of small apartment blocks — principally to increase fish harvests.

The choice of design and materials for an artificial reef depends on where it is going to be placed. In areas of strong currents, for example, a solid concrete structure will be more appropriate than ballasted tyres. It also depends on what species are to be attracted. It is pointless creating high-rise structures for fish that prefer flat or low-relief habitat. But the most important consideration is the purpose of the reef.

In the U.S., where there is a national reef plan using cleaned up rigs and tanks, artificial reefs have mainly been used to attract fish for recreational fishing or sport-diving. But there are many other ways in which they can be used to manage the marine habitat. For as well as protecting existing habitat, providing purpose-built accommodation for commercial species (such as lobsters and octupi) and acting as sea defences, they can be an effective way of improving fish harvests.

Japan, for example, has created vast areas of artificial habitat — rather than isolated reefs — to increase its fish stocks. In fact, the cultural and historical importance of seafood in Japan is reflected by the fact that it is a world leader in reef technology; what's more, those who construct and deploy reefs have sole rights to the harvest.

In Europe, artificial reefs have been mainly employed to protect habitat. Particularly so in the Mediterranean where reefs have been sunk as physical obstacles to stop illegal trawling, which is destroying sea grass beds and the marine life that depends on them. "If you want to protect areas of the seabed, you need something that will stop trawlers dead in their tracks," says Dr. Antony Jensen of the Southampton Oceanography Centre.

Italy boasts considerable artificial reef activity. It deployed its first scientifically planned reef, using concrete cubes assembled in pyramid forms in 1974 to enhance fisheries and stop trawling. And Spain has built needy 50 reefs in its waters, mainly to discourage trawling and enhance the productivity of fisheries. Meanwhile, Britain established its first quarried rock artificial reef in 1984 off the Scottish coast, to assess its potential for attracting commercial species.

But while the scientific study of these structures is a little over a quarter of a century old, artificial reefs made out of readily available materials such as bamboo and coconuts have been used by fishermen for centuries. And the benefits have been enormous. By placing reefs close to home, fishermen can save time and fuel. But unless they are carefully managed, these areas can save time and fished. In the Philippines, for example, where artificial reef programmes have been instigated in response to declining fish populations, catches are often allowed to exceed the maximum potential new production of the artificial reef because there is no proper management control.

There is no doubt that artificial reefs have lots to offer. And while purpose-built structures are effective, the real challenge now is to develop environmentally safe ways of using recycled waste to increase marine diversity. This will require more scientific research. For example, the leachates from one of the most commonly used reef materials, tyres, could potentially be harmful to the creatures and plants that they are supposed to attract. Yet few extensive studies have been undertaken into the long-term effects of disposing of tyres at sea. And at the moment, there is little consensus about what is environmentally acceptable to dump at sea, especially when it comes to oil and gas rigs. Clearly, the challenge is to develop environmentally acceptable ways of disposing of our rubbish while enhancing marine life, too. What we must never be allowed to do is to have an excuse for dumping anything we like at sea.

Complete the table below. Choose **NO MORE THAN THREE WORDS** from the passage for each answer.

Area / Country	**Type of Reef**	**Purpose**
the U.S.	made using old (1)	to attract fish for leisure activities
Japan	forms larger area of artificial habitat	to improve (4)
Europe	lies deep down to form (2)	to act as a sea defence
Italy	consists of pyramid shapes made of (3)	to prevent trawling
Britain	made of rock	to encourage (5) fish species

【参考答案】

(1) rigs and / or tanks (2) physical obstacles (3) concrete cubes (4) fish stocks (5) commercial

分析：这篇文章的表格属于第二种类型的表格。空格中的内容并不能直接回答标题行中的问题，而是要填出空格里的短语。这种表格可看作是完成表格题和完成句子题两种题型的混合，做法与完成句子题一样。注意，第三个空格前的短语是 made of，而不是 made from，因此答案处要填表示原材料的 concrete cubes，而不是 concrete。

The Rollfilm Revolution

The introduction of the dry plate process brought with it many advantages. Not only was it much more convenient, so that the photographer no longer needed to prepare his material in advance, but its much greater sensitivity made possible a new generation of cameras. Instantaneous exposures had been possible before, but only with some difficulty and with special equipment and conditions. Now, exposures short enough to permit the camera to be held in the hand were easily achieved. As well as fitting shutters and viewfinders to their conventional stand cameras, manufacturers began to construct smaller cameras intended specifically for hand use.

One of the first designs to be published was Thomas Bolas's "Detective" camera of 1881. Externally a plain box, quite unlike the folding bellows camera typical of the period, it could be used unobtrusively. The name caught on, and for the next decade or so almost all hand cameras were called "Detectives". Many of the new designs in the 1880s were for magazine cameras, in which a number of dry plates could be pre-loaded and changed one after another following exposure. Although much more convenient than stand cameras, still used by most serious workers, magazine plate cameras were heavy, and required access to a darkroom for loading and processing the plates. This was all changed by a young American bank clerk turned photographic manufacturer, George Eastman from Rochester, New York.

Eastman began to manufacture gelatine dry plates in 1880, being one of the first to do so in America. He soon looked for ways of simplifying photography, believing that many people were put off by the complication and messiness. His first step was to develop, with the camera manufacturer William H. Walker, a holder for a long roll of paper negative "film". This could be fitted to a standard plate camera and up to forty-eight exposures made before reloading. The combined weight of the paper roll and the holder was far less than the same number of glass plates in their light-tight wooden holders. Although roll-holders had been made as early as the 1850s, none had been very successful because of the limitations of the photographic materials then available. Eastman's rollable paper-film was sensitive and gave negatives of good quality; the Eastman-Walker roll-holder was a great success.

The next step was to combine the roll-holder with a small hand camera. Eastman's first design was patented with an employee F. Cossitt in 1886. It was not a success. Only fifty Eastman detective cameras were made, they were sold as a lot to a dealer in 1887; the cost was too high and the design too complicated. Eastman set about developing a new model, which was launched in June 1888. It was a small box, containing a roll of paper-based stripping film sufficient for 100 circular exposures 6 centimetres in diameter. Its operation was simple: sat the shutter by pulling a wire string; aimed the camera using the V line impression in the camera top; pressed the "release" button to activate the exposure; and turn a special key wind on the film. A hundred exposures had to be made, so it was important to record each picture in the memorandum book provided, since there was no exposure counter. Eastman gave his camera the invented name "Kodak", which was easily pronounceable in most languages, and had two K's which Eastman felt was a firm, uncompromising kind of letter.

The importance of Eastman's new roll-film camera was not that it was the first. There had been several earlier cameras, notably the Stirn "America", first demonstrated in the spring of 1887 and on sale from early 1888. This also used a roll of negative paper, and had such refinements as a reflecting viewfinder and an ingenious exposure marker. The real significance of the first Kodak camera was that it was backed up by a developing and printing service. Hitherto, virtually all photographers developed and printed their own pictures. This required the facilities of a darkroom and the time and inclination to handle the necessary chemicals, to make the prints and so on. Eastman recognised that not everyone had the resources or the desire to do this. When a customer had made a hundred exposures in the Kodak camera, he sent it to Eastman's factory in Rochester (or later in Harrow in England) where the film was unloaded, processed and printed, the camera reloaded and returned to the owner. "You Press the Button, We Do the Rest" ran Eastman's classic marketing slogan; photography had been brought to everyone. Everyone, that is, who could afford $25 or five guineas for the camera and $10 or two guineas for the developing and printing. A guinea ($5) was a week's wages for many at the time. So this simple camera cost the equivalent of hundreds of dollars today.

In 1889, an improved model with a new shutter design was introduced, and it was called the "No. 2 Kodak camera". The paper-based stripping film was complicated to manipulate, since the processed negative image had to be stripped from the paper base for printing. At the end of 1889, Eastman launched a new roll film on a celluloid base. Clear, tough, transparent and flexible, the new film not only made the roll-film camera fully practical, but provided the raw material for the introduction of cinematography a few years later. Other, larger models were introduced, including several folding versions, one of which took pictures 21.6 cm × 16.5 cm in size. Other manufacturers in America and Europe introduced cameras to take the Kodak roll-films, and other firms began to offer developing and printing services for the benefit of the new breed of photographers.

By September 1889, over 5,000 Kodak cameras had been sold in the U.S., and the company was daily printing 6,000—7,000 negatives. Holidays and special events created enormous surges in demand for processing: 900 Kodak users returned their cameras for processing and reloading in the week after the New York centennial celebration.

Complete the table below. Choose **NO MORE THAN THREE WORDS** from the passage for each answer.

Year	Developments	Name of person / people
1880	manufacture of gelatine dry plates	(1) ______
1881	release of "Detective" camera	Thomas Bolas
(2) ______	the roll-holder combined with (3) ______	Eastman and F. Cossitt
1889	introduction of model with (4) ______	Eastman

【参考答案】

(1) (George) Eastman (2) 1886 (3) (a) (small) hand camera (4) (a) (new) shutter design

分析：这篇文章的表格属于第三种类型的表格。这种表格是第一种和第二种类型的混合，部分空格中的内容可直接回答标题行中的问题；其余空格中的内容不能直接回答标题行中的问题，而是要将空格里的短语补充完整。本题前两个空格属于第一种类型，后两个空格属于第二种类型。

A Remarkable Beetle

Some of the most remarkable beetles are the dung beetles, which spend almost their whole lives eating and breeding in dung*.

More than 4,000 species of these remarkable creatures have evolved and adapted to the world's different climates and the dung of many animals. Australia's native dung beetles are scrub and woodland dwellers, specialising in coarse marsupial droppings and avoiding the soft cattle dung in which bush flies and buffalo flies breed.

In the early 1960s, George Bornemissza, then a scientist at the Australian Government's premier research organisation, the Commonwealth Scientific and Industrial Research Organisation (CSIRO), suggested that dung beetles should be introduced to Australia to control dung-breeding flies. Between 1868 and 1932, the CSIRO imported insects from about 50 different species of dung beetles, from Asia, Europe and Africa, aiming to match them to different climatic zones in Australia. Of the 26 species that are known to have become successfully integrated into the local environment, only one, an African species released in northern Australia, has reached its natural boundary.

Introducing dung beetles into a pasture is a simple process: approximately 1,500 beetles are released, a handful at a time, into fresh cow pats* in the cow pasture. The beetles immediately disappear beneath the pats digging and tunnelling and, if they successfully adapt to their new environment, soon become a permanent, self-sustaining part of the local ecology. In time they multiply and within three or four years the benefits to the pasture are obvious.

Dung beetles work from the inside of the pat so they are sheltered from predators such as birds and foxes. Most species burrow into the soil and bury dung in tunnels directly underneath the pats, which are hollowed out from within. Some large species originating from France excavate tunnels to a depth of approximately 30 centimetres below the dung pat. These beetles make sausage-shaped brood chambers along the tunnels. The shallowest tunnels belong to a much smaller Spanish species that buries dung in chambers that hang like fruit from the branches of a pear tree. South African beetles dig narrow tunnels of approximately 20 centimetres below the surface of the pat. Some surface-dwelling beetles, including a South African species, cut perfectly-shaped balls from the pat, which are rolled away and attached to the bases of plants.

For maximum dung burial in spring, summer and autumn, farmers require a variety of species with overlapping periods of activity. In the cooler environments of the state of Victoria, the large French species (2.5 centimetres long) is matched with smaller (half this size), temperate-climate Spanish species. The former are slow to recover from the winter cold and produce only one or two generations of offspring from late spring until autumn. The latter, which multiply rapidly in early spring, produce two to five generations annually. The South African ball-rolling species, being a subtropical beetle, prefers the climate of northern and coastal New South Wales where it commonly works with the South African tunnelling species. In warmer climates, many species are active for longer periods of the year.

Dung beetles were initially introduced in the late 1960s with a view to controlling buffalo flies by removing the dung within a day or two and so preventing flies from breeding. However, other benefits have become evident. Once the beetle larvae have finished pupation, the residue is a first-rate source of fertiliser. The tunnels abandoned by the beetles provide excellent aeration and water channels for root systems. In addition, when the new generation of beetles has left the nest the abandoned burrows are an attractive habitat for soil-enriching earthworms. The digested dung in these burrows is an excellent food supply for the earthworms, which decompose it further to provide essential soil nutrients. If it were not for the dung beetle, chemical fertiliser and dung would be washed by rain into streams and rivers before it could be absorbed into the hard earth, polluting water courses and causing blooms of blue-green algae. Without the beetles to dispose of the dung, cow pats would litter pastures making grass inedible to cattle and depriving the soil of sunlight. Australia's 30 million cattle each produces 10—12 cow pats a day. This amounts to 1.7 billion tonnes a year, enough to smother about 110,000 square kilometres of pasture, half the area of Victoria.

Dung beetles have become an integral part of the successful management of dairy farms in Australia over the past few decades. A number of species are available from the CSIRO or through a small number of private breeders, most of whom were entomologists with the CSIRO's dung beetle unit who have taken their specialised knowledge of the insect and opened small businesses in direct competition with their former employer.

* dung: the droppings or excreta of animals

cow pats: droppings of cows

Complete the table below. Choose **NO NORE THAN THREE WORDS OR A NUMBER** from the passage for each answer.

Species	**Size**	**Preferred climate**	**Complementary species**	**Start of active period**	**Number of generations per year**
French	2.5 cm	cool	Spanish	late spring	1—2
Spanish	1.25 cm	(1)	×	(2)	(3)
South African ball roller	×	(4)	(5)	×	×

【参考答案】

(1) temperate (2) early spring (3) 2—5 / two to five

(4) sub-tropical (5) South African tunnelling / tunneller (species)

12.4 笔记填充题

12.4.1 题型分析破解

笔记填充题（Notes Completion）也是简答题的变形，因为提取的信息性质（单个孤立信息）相同，也可以用相同的方法破解。

此类题型分为两大类：1. 就文章的某个部分设计笔记；2. 就全篇文章设计笔记。此类题型本来属于组团信息和整篇信息（见第 13 章和第 14 章），但由于这些笔记中一般有足够多的关键词，其形式其实是简答题和完成句子题的结合与变化，因此破解的方法和步骤一样。

12.4.2 练习及解析

1. 接下来结合下面的文章进行具体分析。

People and Organisations: the Selection Issue

A In 1991, according to the Department of Trade and Industry, a record 48,000 British companies went out of business. When businesses fail, the post-mortem analysis is traditionally undertaken by accountants and market strategists. Unarguably organisations do fail because of undercapitalisation, poor financial management, adverse market conditions, etc. Yet, conversely, organisations with sound financial backing, good product ideas and market acumen often underperform and fail to meet shareholders' expectations. The complexity, degree and sustainment of organisational performance requires an explanation which goes beyond the balance sheet and the "paper conversion" of financial inputs into profit making outputs. A more complete explanation of "what went wrong" necessarily must consider the essence of what an organisation actually is and that one of the financial inputs, the most important and often the most expensive, is people.

B An organisation is only as good as the people it employs. Selecting the right person for the job involves more than identifying the essential or desirable range of skills, educational and professional qualifications necessary to perform the job and then recruiting the candidate who is most likely to possess these skills or at least is perceived to have the ability and predisposition to acquire them. This is a purely person-skills match approach to selection.

C Work invariably takes place in the presence and / or under the direction of others, in a particular organisational setting. The individual has to "fit" in with the work environment, with other employees, with the organisational climate, style of work, organisation and culture of the organisation. Different organisations have different cultures. Working as an engineer at British Aerospace will not necessarily be a similar experience to working in the same capacity at GEC or Plessey.

D Poor selection decisions are expensive. For example, the costs of training a policeman are about £20,000 (approx. US$30,000). The costs of employing an unsuitable technician on an oil rig or in a nuclear plant could, in an emergency, result in millions of pounds of damage or loss of life. The disharmony of a poor person-environment fit (PE-fit) is likely to result in low job satisfaction, lack of organisational commitment and employee stress, which affect organisational outcomes i.e. productivity, high labour turnover and absenteeism, and individual outcomes i.e. physical, psychological and mental well-being.

E However, despite the importance of the recruitment decision and the range of sophisticated and more objective selection techniques available, including the use of psychometric tests, assessment centres etc., many organisations are still prepared to make this decision on the basis of a single 30 to 45 minute unstructured interview. Indeed, research has demonstrated that a selection decision is often made within the first four minutes of the interview. In the remaining time, the interviewer then attends exclusively to information that reinforces the initial "accept" or "reject" decision. Research into the validity of selection methods has consistently demonstrated that the unstructured interview, where the interviewer asks any questions he or she likes, is a poor predictor of future job performance and fares little better than more controversial methods like graphology and astrology. In times of high unemployment, recruitment becomes a "buyer's market" and this was the case in Britain during the 1980s.

F The future, we are told, is likely to be different. Detailed surveys of social and economic trends in the European Community show that Europe's population is falling and getting older. The birth rate in the Community is now only three-quarters of the level needed to ensure replacement of the existing population. By the year 2020, it is predicted that more than one in four Europeans will be aged 60 or more and barely one in five will be under 20. In a five-year period between 1983 and 1988, the Community's female workforce grew by almost six million. As a result, 51% of all women aged 14 to 64 are now economically active in the labour market compared with 78% of men.

G The changing demographics will not only affect selection ratios. They will also make it increasingly important for organisations wishing to maintain their competitive edge to be more responsive and accommodating to the changing needs of their workforce if they are to retain and develop their human resources. More flexible working hours, the opportunity to work from home or job share, the provision of childcare facilities etc., will play a major role in attracting and retaining staff in the future.

Complete the notes below with words taken from the passage above. Use **ONE OR TWO WORDS** for each answer.

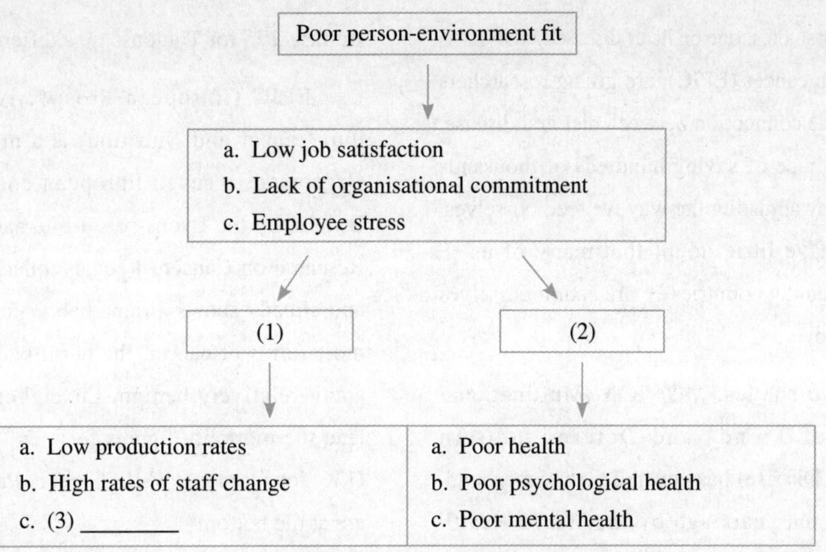

【参考答案】

(1) Organisational outcomes (2) Individual outcomes (3) Absenteeism

分析：用寻读技巧快速地搜索原文，可发现所有的关键词都出现在D段最后一句，因此可以定位了。充分运用已掌握的句法结构知识，即使看不懂个别单词，也能答对题目。对这道题的结构分析如下：

The disharmony of a poor person-environment fit (PE-fit) is likely to result in

a. low job satisfaction,

b. lack of organisational commitment, and

c. employee stress,

which affect

(1) organisational outcomes, i.e. __________

a. productivity, b. high labour turnover, and c. absenteeism,

and (2) individual outcomes, i.e.

a. physical, b. psychological, and c. mental well-being.

经过这样的分析，答案就一目了然了。

2. 下面这篇文章的笔记是根据整篇文章设计出来的，复杂了很多。但图是根据文章画出来的，文章也可以根据图写出来，因此提高图文转换的能力是关键。下面结合具体的题目进行分析。

A Great Way to Live Longer

Two major studies, one on heart disease (MONICA) and the other on cancer (EPIC), are giving researchers a new look at the connection between diet and disease. They offer the hope of saving hundreds of thousands of lives a year by adjusting the way we feed ourselves. The studies leave little doubt that many of us — especially in wealthy countries — are eating ourselves into an early grove.

Of the two studies, MONICA (Multinational Monitoring of Trends and Determinants in Cardiovascular Disease) has covered the most ground. It was started ten years ago by the World Health Organisation (WHO), and the £33-million project is the most ambitious study ever undertaken on heart and vascular disease. Using standardised data collection techniques, WHO's correspondents gathered statistics on more than ten million men and women in more than 39 population centres, ranging from Siberia to California, Australia to Israel. The study rapidly disclosed some startling facts.

MONICA showed that in Finland, for example, men die of coronary disease 11 times more often than they do in Japan, while in Glasgow women die of heart disease 12 times more often than those in north-eastern Spain or southern France.

Compass points. As the results flowed in, a clear pattern emerged: in Europe, the further north you live, the more likely you are to die from a heart attack. Two cities typical of this north-south gradient are Belfast and Toulouse, in southwestern France. In the most recent period studied, the heart-disease death rate for men aged 45 to 54 is 237 per 100,000 population in Belfast, but only 56 in Toulouse. For the age group 55 to 64, the contrast is even more striking: 761 for Belfast, 175 for Toulouse — a difference of 4.3 to l.

EPIC (European Prospective Investigation into Cancer and Nutrition) is a more recent study. Organised in seven European countries including Britain, by the Lyons-based International Agency for Research on Cancer, it began collecting data in 1993, and already shows a remarkably similar outcome: for most forms of cancer, the north is dangerous and the south relatively benign. Luxembourg and Belgium lead the mortality figures for men (Denmark and the U.K. for women), while Greece, Portugal and Spain are at the bottom.

Split results. Why should residence in the developed north, with all its wealth and public services, make death by cardiovascular disease or cancer more likely than in the generally poorer south? The question seems to be all the more puzzling because MONICA found no significant differences in smoking, high-blood pressure or cholesterol — the three classic indicators of heart trouble — to explain the regional disparities. The further the investigations progress, the more one factor presents itself as the likely answer: diet.

Clearly, southern Europeans know something about eating that their northern brethren do not. The most confounding information is in the MONICA data from France, the country with the Western world's highest life expectancy.

The French outlive Americans, for example, by more than four years, suffer less than half as much from coronary heart disease and yet smoke more, drink more and have blood pressure and cholesterol counts just as high — while enjoying the diet that has made French cuisine a byword for high living. Those startling facts are the basis of "the French paradox".

Dr. Serge Renaud, epidemiologist and director of nutritional studies at France's National Institute of Health and Medical Research, had been studying the relation between nourishment and heart disease for more than 30 years in serene anonymity.

Then the MONICA figures revealed the differences between France and more other industrialised nations: Scotland, Finland, the United States and Australia were at the top of the scale for premature deaths from heart disease, while France was nearly at the bottom, edged out only by rice-and-fish-eating Japan. Renaud was suddenly besieged with queries. Could he shed some light on the puzzle?

He could indeed. His five-year study of some 600 Lyons-area cardiac patients, completed in Spring 1993, proved to be a show-piece for the influence of diet on health. Safe and sound, Renaud put half of his volunteers on the medically recommended diet for heart-attack victims, and the other half on a diet he developed himself, reducing red-meat consumption and calling for greater amounts of bread, fresh and dried vegetables, fruits, fish and white meat. His diet also replaced butter with a margarine-style spread developed in his laboratory. Renaud's greater emphasis on fruits, grains, vegetables and his margarine cut the chances of death from a second heart attack by 76%.

Complete the notes below with words taken from the passage above. Use **ONE OR TWO WORDS** for each answer.

Rationale for MONICA and EPIC studies.
Is there a link between (1) ____________ and (2) ____________ ?

TWO MAJOR STUDIES STARTED	MONICA	EPIC
	10 years ago by WHO.	(3) ________
(4) ____________	Using 10 million men and women in 39 locations.	In seven European countries.
(5) ____________	In Europe numbers of deaths from heart disease increases from south to north.	There are more deaths from (6) ________ in the north of Europe than in the south.

NORTH / SOUTH FACTS

1) North is more (7) ________ than south. 2) Smoking, blood pressure and cholesterol rates were the same in the north and in the south. 3) (8) ________ is different in the north and in the south.

CONCLUSIONS

Eating more vegetables, fruits, fish and white meat has a positive effect upon health.

【参考答案】

(1) diet	(2) disease	(3) (in) 1993	(4) data-collection / collecting data
(5) results	(6) cancer	(7) developed	(8) Diet / Eating

分析：这篇笔记其实是对全文的总结，但由于有足够多的关键词，也可使用寻读技巧来解题。首先要做的是对整篇笔记有一个整体认识，缩小搜索范围。最上面的方框其实是一个介绍，考生可以判断出它是根据第一段设计出来的，空格（1）和（2）的答案在第一段中找；MONICA 方框下的信息出现在第二至四段；EPIC 方框下的（3）和（6）的答案在第五段中找；空格（7）和（8）的答案在第六段中找；空格（4）其实是个问题，并与 Using 10 million men and women in 39 locations 和 In seven European countries 两个方框平行，因此在原文中必然有与后两者意思相同的句子，用寻读技巧在描述 MONICA 的段落和描述 EPIC 的段落中很快就能发现要找的原句，然后比较原句与题目中的句子，具有相同意义和词性的词就是答案；空格（5）的解题方法与空格（4）的一样，照此做法就能找到答案。

12.5 选择题

12.5.1 题型分析破解

选择题（Multiple Choice）在形式上分为三类：

1. ... ?

   A ...

   B ...

   C ...

   D ...

该类题型是简答题的变形，答案不用考生自己写出来，只要从给出的选项中选出正确答案即可。

2. ..., ... ________.

A ...

B ...

C ...

D ...

该类题型是完成句子题的变形，答案也不用考生自己写出来，只要从给出的选项中选出正确答案即可。

3. 类型 1 和 2 的混合型，即简答题的变形 + 完成句子题的变形。

选择题在信息提取的性质上分为三类：

1) 全部为单个细节信息提取；

2) 全部为段落总体信息提取；

3) 单个细节信息和段落总体信息提取相结合。

任何阅读文本都存在单个细节信息和段落总体信息这两种信息，提取这两种信息的能力是所有阅读试题都要测试的。而传统的阅读考试题型单一，基本就只是选择题，因此掌握了雅思选择题型的破解技巧，也就解决了传统阅读考试中的大部分问题。这些解题技巧也适用于大学英语四、六级，专业英语四、八级以及新托福考试中的阅读测试。

本部分集中讨论提取单个细节信息的选择题，提取总体信息的选择题将在另一章中进行分析。

12.5.2 练习及解析

下面结合具体习题进行分析。

1. 下面这篇文章的选择题属于第二种题型，属于对单个细节信息的提取。用寻读技巧完成文章后面的练习。

The Spectacular Eruption of Mount St. Helens

A The eruption in May 1980 of Mount St. Helens, Washington State, U.S.A., astounded the world with its violence. A gigantic explosion tore much of the volcano's summit to fragments; the energy released was equal to that of 500 of the nuclear bombs that destroyed Hiroshima, Japan in 1945.

B The event occurred along the boundary of two of the moving plates that make up the earth's crust. They meet at the junction of the North American continent and the Pacific Ocean. One edge of the continental North American plate over-rides the oceanic Juan de Fuca micro-plate, producing the volcanic Cascade range that includes Mounts Baker, Rainier and Hood, and Lassen Peak as well as Mount

St. Helens.

C Until Mount St. Helens began to stir, only Mount Baker and Lassen Peak had shown signs of life during the 20th century. According to geological evidence found by the United States Geological Survey, there had been two major eruptions of Mount St. Helens in the recent (geologically speaking) past: around 1900 B.C., and about 1500 A.D. Since the arrival of Europeans in the region, it had experienced a single period of spasmodic activity, between 1831 and 1857. Then, for more than a century, Mount St. Helens lay dormant.

D By 1979, the Geological Survey, alerted by signs of renewed activity, had been monitoring the volcano for 18 months, warned the local population against being deceived by the mountain's outward calm, and forecast that an eruption would take place before the end of the century. The inhabitants of the area did not have to wait that long. On March 27, 1980, a few clouds of smoke formed above the summit, and slight tremors were felt. On the 28th, larger and darker clouds, consisting of gas and ashes, emerged and climbed as high as 20,000 feet. In April a slight lull ensued, but the volcanologists remained pessimistic. Then, in early May, the northern flank of the mountain bulged, and the summit rose by 500 feet.

E Steps were taken to evacuate the population. Most — campers, hikers, timber-cutters — left the slopes of the mountain. Eighty-four-year-old Harry Truman, a holiday lodge owner who had lived there for more than 50 years, refused to be evacuated, in spite of official and private urging. Many members of the public, including an entire class of school children, wrote to him, begging him to leave. He never did.

F On May 8, at 8:32 in the morning, Mount St. Helens blew its top, literally. Suddenly, it was 1,300 feet shorter than it had been before its growth had begun. Over half a cubic mile of rock had disintegrated. At the same moment, an earthquake with an intensity of 5 on the Richter scale was recorded. It triggered an avalanche of snow and ice, mixed with hot rock — the entire north face of the mountain had fallen away. A wave of scorching volcanic gas and rock fragments shot horizontally from the volcano's riven flank, at an inescapable 200 miles per hour. As the sliding ice and snow melted, it touched off devastating torrents of mud and debris, which destroyed all life in their path. Pulverised rock climbed as a dust cloud into the atmosphere. Finally, viscous lava, accompanied by burning clouds of ash and gas, welled out of the volcano's new crater, and from lesser vents and cracks in its flanks.

G Afterwards, scientists were able to analyse the sequence of events. First, magma — molten rock — at temperatures above 2,000 ℉ had surged into the volcano from the earth's mantle. The build-up was accompanied by an accumulation of gas, which increased as the mass of magma grew. It was the pressure inside the mountain that made it swell. Next, the rise in gas pressure caused a violent decompression, which ejected the shattered summit like a cork from a shaken soda bottle. With the summit gone, the molten rock within was released in a jet of gas and fragmented magma, and lava welled from the crater.

H The effects of the Mount St. Helens eruption were catastrophic. Almost all the trees of the surrounding forest, mainly Douglas firs, were flattened, and their branches and bark ripped off by the shock wave of the explosion. Ash and mud spread over nearly 200 square miles of country. All the towns and settlements in the area were smothered in an even coating of ash. Volcanic ash silted up the Columbia River 35 miles away, reducing the depth of its navigable channel from 210 feet to 14 feet, and trapping sea-going ships.

The debris that accumulated at the foot of the volcano reached a depth, in places, of 200 feet.

I The eruption of Mount St. Helens was one of the most closely observed and analysed eruptions in history. Because geologists had been expecting the event, they were able to amass vast amounts of technical data when it happened. Study of atmospheric particles formed as a result of the explosion showed that droplets of sulphuric acid, acting as a screen between the sun and the earth's surface, caused a distinct drop in temperature. There is no doubt that the activity of Mount St. Helens and other volcanoes since 1980 has influenced our climate. Even so, it has been calculated that the quantity of dust ejected by Mount St. Helens — a quarter of a cubic mile — was negligible in comparison with that thrown out by earlier eruptions, such as that of Mount Katmai in Alaska in 1912 (three cubic miles). The volcano is still active. Lava domes have formed inside the new crater, and have periodically burst. The threat of Mount St. Helens lives on.

Choose the correct answer for the following question.

According to the text, the eruption of Mount St. Helens and other volcanoes has influenced our climate by ________ .

A increasing the amount of rainfall

B heating atmosphere

C cooling the air temperature

D causing atmospheric storms

【参考答案】

C

分析：读完题干的句子，就知道了要寻找的目标就是火山的爆发通过什么影响气候。可用关键词进行快速搜索，将其定位在I段中间的There is no doubt ... 一句，因为全部关键词都在这一段中出现。但此句只提到火山爆发影响气候的事实，并没有告诉考生火山爆发是通过什么来影响气候的，因此考生要通过上下文来进行判断。上文中出现 ... caused a distinct drop in temperature，这就是答案，四个备选答案中与这个短语同义的只有选项C。

建议考生在做这类题时，先不要看备选答案，因为其中有三项是文中没有提到的信息，是干扰项，先看备选项容易被误导。考生要先用题干句子中的关键词定位，在原文中找到原句后，再根据原文信息从四个选项中选出正确的答案。

2. 看下面这篇文章。文后的选择题属于哪种题型？要求考生找什么类型的信息？

Impact of Global Warming on Climate

1 There are hidden factors which scientists call "feedback mechanisms". No one knows quite well how they will interact with the changing climate. Here's one example: plants and animals adapt to climate change over centuries. At the current estimate of half a degree centigrade of warming per decade, vegetation may not keep up. Climatologist James Hansen of the U.S. space agency NASA predicts climate zones will shift toward the poles by 50 to 75 kilometres a year — faster than trees can naturally migrate. Species that find themselves in an unfamiliar environment will die. The 1,000-kilometre-wide strip of coniferous forest running through Canada, Russia and Scandinavia could be cut by half, setting in motion a chain reaction. Millions of dying and diseased trees would soon lead to massive forest fires, releasing tons of CO_2 and further boosting global warming.

2 There are dozens of other possible "feedback mechanisms". Higher temperatures will fuel condensation and increase cloudiness, which may actually damp down global warming. Others, like the "albedo" effect, will do the opposite. The "albedo" effect is the amount of solar energy reflected by the earth's surface. As northern ice and snow melts and the darker sea and land pokes through, more heat will be absorbed, adding inexorably to the global temperature increase.

3 Scientists continue to tinker away with their computer models, but the bare-bones facts are clear. Even if we were to magically stop all greenhouse-gas emissions tomorrow the impact on global climate would continue for decades. Delay, any delay, will simply make the problem worse. The fact is that some of us are doing quite well the way things are. In the developed world prosperity has been built on 150 years of cheap fossil fuels. Oil fires cars and powers industry, coal generates electricity and indirectly runs TVs, dishwashers and VCRs. Gas heats water and warms homes and factories.

4 Material progress has been linked to energy consumption. Today 75% of all the world's energy is consumed by a quarter of the world's population. The average rich-world resident adds about 3.2 tons of CO_2 yearly to the atmosphere, more than four times the level added by each Third World citizen, India, China and Brazil, which make up nearly half the world's population, accounted for barely 15% of global warming during the 1980s, according to the U.S. Environmental Protection Agency. The U.S., with just 7% of the global population, is responsible for 22%.

Choose the correct alternatives and put the appropriate letter in the space provided.

Example:

Feedback mechanisms are __B__.

A statistics

B concealed causes

C known results

D scientific methods

【分析】

这种选择题属于第二种题型，属于对单个细节信息和段落总体信息的提取。

(1) In Paragraph 1 the writer is ________.

A rejecting a scientific belief

B giving an example

C reaching a conclusion

D defending a theory

(2) If greenhouse-gas emissions were stopped immediately, the world's climate would ________.

A soon regain its balance

B continue to be affected but without serious consequences

C continue to be affected for many years to come

D be affected for another 10 years

(3) According to the writer, cheap fossil fuels have ________.

A formed the basis of the developed world's success

B contributed to the developed world's success

C aided the developed world's building trade

D caused 150 years of global warming

(4) A person from a developing country adds ________ of CO_2 yearly to the atmosphere.

A more than 3 tons

B about 12.8 tons

C 4 tons

D less than a ton

【参考答案】

(1) B　(2) C　(3) A　(4) D

分析：第一题属于段落总体信息提取这一类型，具体的应对方法将在后文中详谈。

先在第二题题干中找到关键词：greenhouse-gas emissions，stopped immediately 和 world's climate，然后快速地在文中搜索，发现它们在第三段第二句中。再根据这句话的意思作出选择。不少考生可能会错选 D，可能是因为他们没注意原文中的 decades 是复数，意思是“几十年”。

第三题题干中的关键词是 cheap fossil fuels，在文中快速搜寻，发现它们在第三段第五句中，再根据这句话的意思作出选择。不少考生可能会错选 B，可能是因为他们没有理解原句中的 ... has been built on ... 的意思是“建立在……的基础上”，而 contributed 表达的只是“作出一部分贡献”，并不能形成 basis。

第四题题干中的关键词是 person 和 developing country，在文中快速搜寻，发现它们在第四段第三句中，只不过题目中用 a person from a developing country 代替了原句中的 each Third World citizen，然后考生就根据原句的意思作出选择。不少考生可能会错选 B，可能是因为他们把原文的意思理解反了。

3. 分析下面这篇文章的选择题属于哪种题型，要找什么类型的信息，并完成后面的练习。

The Truth about the Environment

For many environmentalists, the world seems to be getting worse. They have developed a hit-list of our main fears: that natural resources are running out; that the population is ever growing, leaving less and less to eat; that species are becoming extinct in vast numbers, and that the planet's air and water are becoming even more polluted.

But a quick look at the facts shows a different picture. First, energy and other natural resources have become more abundant, not less so, since the book *The Limits to Growth* was published in 1972 by a group of scientists. Second, more food is now produced per head of the world's population than at any time in history. Fewer people are starving. Third, although species are indeed becoming extinct, only about 0.7% of them are expected to disappear in the next 50 years, not 25%—50%, as has so often been predicted. And finally, most forms of environmental pollution either appear to have been exaggerated, or are transient — associated with the early phases of industrialisation and therefore best cured not by restricting economic growth, but by accelerating it. One form of pollution — the release of greenhouse gases that causes global warming — does appear to be a phenomenon that is going to extend well into our future, but its total impact is unlikely to pose a devastating problem. A bigger problem may well turn out to be an inappropriate response to it.

Yet opinion polls suggest that many people nurture the belief that environmental standards are declining and four factors seem to cause this disjunction between perception and reality.

One is the lopsidedness built into scientific research. Scientific funding goes mainly to areas with many problems. That may be wise policy, but it will also create an impression that many more potential problems exist than is the case.

Secondly, environmental groups need to be noticed by the mass media. They also need to keep the money rolling in. Understandably, perhaps, they sometimes overstate their arguments. In 1997, for example, the World Wide Fund for Nature issued a press release entitled Two Thirds of the World's Forests Lost Forever. The truth turns out to be nearly 20%.

Though these groups are run overwhelmingly by selfless folk, they nevertheless share many of the characteristics of other lobby groups. That would matter less if people applied the same degree of scepticism to environmental lobbying as they do to lobby groups in other fields. A trade organisation arguing for, say, weaker pollution controls is instantly seen as self-interested. Yet a green organisation opposing such a weakening is seen as altruistic, even if an impartial view of the controls in question might suggest they are doing more harm than good.

A third source of confusion is the attitude of the media. People are clearly more curious about bad news than good. Newspapers and broadcasters are there to provide what the public wants. That, however, can lead to significant distortions of perception. An example was America's encounter with El Niño in 1997 and 1998. This climatic phenomenon was accused of wrecking tourism, causing allergies, melting the ski-slopes and causing 22 deaths. However, according to an article in the *Bulletin of the American Meteorological Society*, the damage it did was estimated at US$4 billion but the benefits amounted to some US$19 billion. These came from higher winter temperatures (which saved an estimated 850 lives, reduced heating costs and diminished spring floods caused by meltwaters).

The fourth factor is poor individual perception. People worry that the endless rise in the amount of stuff everyone throws away will cause the world to run out of places to dispose of waste. Yet, even if America's trash output continues to rise as it has done in the past, and even if the American population doubles by 2100, all the rubbish America produces through the entire 21st century will still take up only one 12,000th of the area of the entire United States.

So what of global warming? As we know, carbon dioxide emissions are causing the planet to warm. The best estimates are that the temperatures will rise by 2 °C—3 °C in this century, causing considerable problems, at a total cost of US$5,000 billion.

Despite the intuition that something drastic needs to be done about such a costly problem, economic analyses clearly show it will be far more expensive to cut carbon dioxide emissions radically than to pay the costs of adaptation to the increased temperatures. A model by one of the main authors of the United Nations Climate Change Panel shows how an expected temperature increase of 2.1 degrees in 2100 would only be diminished to an increase of 1.9 degrees. Or to put it another way, the temperature increase that the planet would have experienced in 2094 would be postponed to 2100.

So this does not prevent global warming, but merely buys the world six years. Yet the cost of reducing carbon dioxide emissions, for the United States alone, will be higher than the cost of solving the world's single, most pressing health problem: providing universal access to clean drinking water and sanitation. Such measures would avoid 2 million deaths every year, and prevent half a billion people from becoming seriously ill.

It is crucial that we look at the facts if we want to make the best possible decisions for the future. It may be costly to be overly optimistic — but more costly still to be too pessimistic.

Choose the correct answer for each of the following questions.

(1) What aspect of scientific research does the writer express concern about in Paragraph 4?

A The need to produce results.

B The lack of financial support.

C The selection of areas to research.

D The desire to solve every research problem.

(2) The writer quotes from the World Wide Fund for Nature to illustrate how ________.

A influential the mass media can be

B effective environmental groups can be

C the mass media can help groups raise funds

D environmental groups can exaggerate their claims

(3) What is the writer's main point about lobby groups in Paragraph 6?

A Some are more active than others.

B Some are better organised than others.

C Some receive more criticism than others.

D Some support more important issues than others.

(4) The writer suggests that newspapers print items that are intended to ________.

A educate readers

B meet their readers' expectations

C encourage feedback from readers

D mislead readers

(5) What does the writer say about America's waste problem?

A It will increase in line with population growth.

B It is not as important as we have been led to believe.

C It has been reduced through public awareness of the issues.

D It is only significant in certain areas of the country.

【参考答案】

(1) C (2) D (3) C (4) B (5) B

这篇文章的选择题属于第三种题型，是对单个细节信息的提取。

12.6 判断作者观点、态度和文本信息题

12.6.1 题型分析破解

1. 题型介绍及分析

判断作者观点、态度和文本信息题（Identification of Writer's Views / Attitudes and Information in the Text）亦在考查考生提取单个信息的能力，其解题步骤与简答题一样，都是要快速搜寻定位。不同的是，与简答题相比，这种题型的难度明显加大了，增加了针对句型结构与词语的转换和推断能力的测试。测试的深度和广度也加大了，能较全面地测试学生的语言基础、提取信息的能力、推断能力和逻辑判断能力，因此这种题型在雅思阅读测试中成为了必考题型。

这类题型要求考生具备较为扎实的英语基础知识：熟悉各种句型和结构的转换，并熟练掌握中学所学的 3,000 个左右的单词，因为这些都是考生需要掌握的最基本的英语知识。雅思考试就是基于这个下限出题的，所以考生的备考重点应该放在巩固英语基础上。

本书的主要目的是要帮助考生熟悉雅思阅读考试，提高阅读技巧和能力，不仅帮助他们考得更好，还要让他们能在国外的学习中运用这些技巧完成大量阅读任务。出于这个目的，本节将逐一就以下各点进行分析：

1) 出题形式：基于原文某句或某个孤立细节设计题目。如下图：

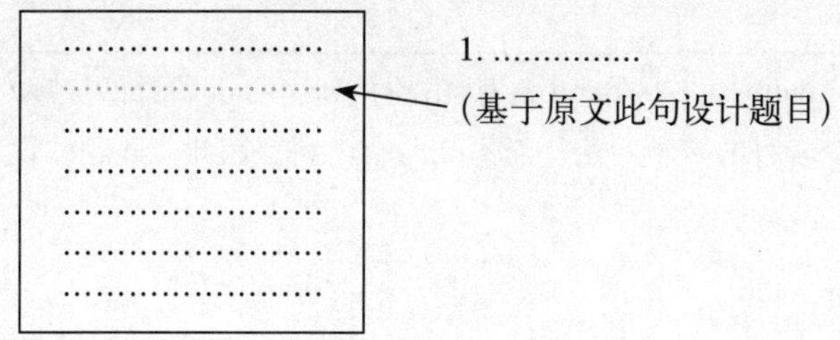

2) 信息的性质：要考生判断题目是 True / False / Not Given 或 Yes / No / Not Given。题目是根据原文中的某个信息而设计的，因此信息的性质属于单个的细节信息。

3) 题目测试范围：

(1) 考生用寻读技巧快速搜寻定位，并提取单个信息。

(2) 题目是根据原文某处内容改写的，经过了句子结构与词语的转换，要求考生进行判断。

(3) 题目要求考生根据原文中某处信息作出推断和逻辑推理，然后进行判断。

4) 出题规律：考点多变，完全没有规律。任何所谓的“规律”都是对考生的误导，偏离了雅思考试的宗旨，助长了侥幸心理，应该摒弃。

由于要考查考生掌握语言的熟练程度和提取单个信息的能力，原文的每个句子或每个句子的每个成分都可以通过转换而成为考点。譬如，一个结构为“主语 + 谓语动词 + 宾语 + 宾语补足语 + 状语从句”的句子，句中的每一个成分都可能被转换而成为考点；也可能整句结构或分句结构被转换而成为考点，如主动语态变为被动语态，状语从句变为分词短语，定语从句变为其他定语性质的短语或句子。其他从句（如主语从句、表语从句、宾语从句）也可相应地变为其他表达形式，甚至一个并列连词或冠词也可成为考点。题目还可能考查考生根据上下文进行因果关系判断的能力；有时在选项中甚至可以无中生有，加上原文中没有直接出现的信息让考生进行推理和判断。由于有这么多的变化，因此这类题型是不可能有一个固定的出题方式的，也不可能存在规律性；可以说，题目是根据语言变化的规律、要考查的能力和原文的实际情况等综合因素而“随意”出的。因此，考生需要具备扎实的英语语言基础、清醒的头脑和敏锐的目光。

2. 例题分析

请看下面的例子：

1) Like any theory of importance, that of social or cultural anthropology was the work of many minds and took on many forms. Some, the best known of its proponents, worked on broad areas and attempted to describe and account for the development of human civilisation in its totality. Others restricted their efforts to specific aspects of

the culture, taking up the evolution of art, or the state, or religion.

选项 (1) Social anthropology concerns itself with broad areas while cultural anthropology concerns itself with specific aspects of culture.

【分析】

这是针对原文第一句 ... social or cultural anthropology ... 中的并列连词 or 设计的选项，以考查考生能否辨别出这是一个学科的两种叫法，而不是两个学科。因此，此题的说法与原文不符。

选项 (2) Cultural anthropologists, also known as social anthropologists, may work in either broad or restricted areas.

【分析】

这个选项是对原文要点的扼要概述，因此是符合原文意思的选项。

选项 (3) Cultural anthropology is a new field of study.

【分析】

这个选项属于“无中生有”：new 是原文中没有出现的信息，需要考生根据文章的意思自己进行推理和判断。

选项 (4) Any important area of study requires the work of many minds and is therefore likely to have different approaches.

【分析】

这个选项是对原文第一句的改写。原文说：Like any theory of importance, that of social or cultural anthropology was ... 既然社会或文化人类学如任何重要理论一样具备某些特性，那么那些重要理论也自然具有相同的特性。题目中还加了 therefore 一词提示考生要作因果关系的判断。

选项 (5) The best known people in cultural anthropology attempted to describe the development of human civilisation.

【分析】

这个选项是对原文第二句的重述，只是用 the best known people 替换了 some。此题要求考生看出原文中的 the best known of its proponents 是 some 的同位语。

2) Like other timeless symbols, flags have accompanied mankind for thousands of years, gaining ever wider meaning, yet losing none of their inherent and original force.

选项 (1) In spite of losing some of their original force, flags are a timeless symbol which have accompanied mankind for thousands of years.

【分析】

这个选项与原文的信息不一致。选项说旗帜丧失了一些原有的功能，与原文的意思正好相反。

选项 (2) Flags have existed for thousands of years.

【分析】

这个选项是对主句的重述：既然旗帜伴随了人类好几千年那么换言之就是旗帜已存在了几千年。

选项 (3) Timeless symbols typically gain wider meaning while not losing their inherent force.

【分析】

这个选项要考生推断：既然旗帜与其他永恒的象征一样，那么反过来，其他永恒的象征也与旗帜一样具有这些特点。

选项 (4) Thousands of years ago flags accompanied mankind but through time they have lost their force.

【分析】

这个选项与选项 (1) 一样，意思与原文表意正好相反。

选项 (5) Because flags are considered a timeless symbol, they have gained continually wider meaning without losing their inherent original force.

【分析】

这个选项中加了 because，就是要考生作因果关系的判断。经判断得知，题目中的逻辑有误，表现为因果顺序颠倒。

3. 判断标准

以上的例子说明，这类题型考点多变，完全没有规律可循。要进行正确的判断，就必须要确认判断的标准。判断标准如下：

1）用不同的表达方式改写原文，但句子的意思不变，也就是重述或改写后的句子表达的观点与原文的观点一致，这时的判断结果为 True 或 Yes。这里主要是考语言的基本功，如上面第 1）题中的选项（2）和选项（5），以及第 2）题中的选项（2）。

2）题目的整体信息在原文中不能全部找到，但根据原文中的其他信息，可以推断出结论，这时的判断结果为 True 或 Yes。这里主要是考逻辑推断能力，如上面第 1）题中的选项（4）和第 2）题中的选项（3）。

3）题目的意思与原文相反或与原文的某个观点不一致，这时的判断结果为 False 或 No。这里主要是考语言的基本功，如上面第 1）题中的选项（1）和第 2）题中的选项（1）及选项（4）。

4）题目的整体信息在原文中不能全部找到，而根据原文中的其他信息又不能推断出结论，这时的判断结果为 Not Given。这里主要是考逻辑推断能力，如上面第 1）题中的选项（3）。

4. 实际操作步骤

首先读题目，找到并记住关键词，然后用寻读技巧快速搜寻定位；定位后理解原文，最后根据上面介绍的判断标准进行判断。

12.6.2 例题及分析

下面结合实际的题目进行详细分析。

1. 下面这篇文章属于 G 类题目。前面谈到过，虽然 A 类和 G 类的阅读题在来源、内容和深度方面均有所不同，但题型是一样的。这就意味着解题方法相同，解题方法相同，用到的阅读技巧也就相同。

下面的文章是机场指南的节选，要求考生判断文中的信息与题目是否一致。

Arriving at London Airports

Just follow these simple steps for a trouble-free arrival.

Follow the ARRIVALS sign if you are ending your journey in London or transferring to a U.K. domestic flight.

This will take you to the Immigration Hall where you must present your passport and any necessary visa / health documentation.

At HEATHROW airport, proceed downstairs to claim your baggage from the carousel indicating your flight number. At GATEWICK airport, proceed downstairs in the North Terminal to claim your baggage from the carousel indicating your flight number. Free trolleys are available for your bags. To clear customs, take the Red Channel if you have goods to declare or the Green Chanel if you have no goods to declare. You will then be in the Arrivals Hall. From here you can obtain transport into central London; transfer between GATEWICK and HEATHROW airports and transfer to U.K. domestic flights.

Decide if the following statements are TRUE, FALSE, or if the information you need is NOT GIVEN according to the passage, and write T for true, F for false, or NG for not given in the space provided.

The first one has been done for you as an example.

Example:

If you want to visit London you should follow the ARRIVALS sign. (*T*)

(1) If you want to transfer to an international flight, you should follow the transfer sign. ( )

【参考答案】

NG

分析：原文没提到有关国际航班转机的这个信息，只提到 Follow the ARRIVALS sign if you are ... transferring to a U.K. domestic flight。题目中的信息在原文中找不到又不能根据逻辑关系推断出来，因此答案是 NG。

(2) You can collect your baggage from any carousel. ( )

【参考答案】

F

分析：原文第四段前两句说的是 At HEATHROW airport ... claim your baggage from the carousel indicating your flight number. At GATEWICK airport ... claim your baggage from the carousel indicating your flight number. 也就是说，行李要在指定的行李

传送带取，而不是在任何的行李传送带取。题目的信息与原文不一致，因此判断为F。

(3) When you reach the Arrivals Hall you have completed airport formalities. ( )

【参考答案】

T

分析：原文最后一段说 ... in the Arrivals Hall. From here you can obtain transport ... transfer ... and transfer to ... 意思是乘客到了大厅，就可以离开机场了，大厅是乘客离开机场的地点。因此，一旦乘客到达大厅，就可以推断出他肯定已经完成了登机的手续，否则是到不了大厅的。题目的信息在原文中找不到，但结论可以根据逻辑关系推断出来，因此答案是T。

2. 下面这篇文章也是要考生判断文中的信息是否与题目一致或能否在文中找到。进一步分析这篇文章，熟悉并掌握判断标准。

Planes That Fall to Pieces

On April 28, 1988, the roof came off a Boeing 737 of Aloha Airlines while it was flying over Hawaii. In the explosive decompression that followed, a flight attendant was sucked out to her death and seven passengers were seriously injured, but miraculously the aircraft managed to land, 18 minutes later, without disintegrating.

It was a dramatic introduction to the phenomenon of the geriatric jet. Until then, few air travellers worried about the age of aircraft. It was generally assumed that international regulatory authorities insisted on rigorous maintenance and inspection procedures specifically designed to detect and prevent structural fatigue and corrosion.

Aloha Airlines aircraft number N73711 changed all that. It was discovered that rivets holding two sections of the fuselage together had blown and the bonding had failed. The cause: corrosion and metal fatigue. The plane was 19 years old and had completed 89,680 take-off and landing cycles. Its design life was 75,000 cycles. Nor was its age in any way unusual. Boeing produced figures this year showing that 558 of its aircraft were still in service beyond their "economic design life objective" of 20 years.

Ensuring aircraft are safe to fly depends on a crucial troika: the national regulatory authority, which grants airworthiness certificates; the aircraft manufacturer, which issues technical instructions for the maintenance, inspection and replacement of parts; and the airline, which is supposed to carry out the manufacturers' instructions.

In the case of N73711, Aloha Airlines' maintenance procedures were seriously deficient. Its aircraft were overworked on short, island-hopping flights and were exposed to a corrosive salt atmosphere, yet its corrosion control programme was inadequate. Boeing, which had discovered the problems at Aloha, had failed to alert the FAA. With a worldwide shortage of new aircraft and an ever-ageing fleet, it was realised belatedly that growing numbers of elderly aircraft were going to pose problems hitherto unforeseen — like the need to check 70,000 rivets, rivet by rivet, on other geriatric jets.

"We no longer believe you can rely on inspections forever as aircraft approach their life-limit goal," says Tom Swift, a British-born metallurgist at the FAA. "We think it is important to establish a point at which you must start replacing parts."

A particular recent concern is the phenomenon of "multi-site damage", when airline cracks develop behind a row of rivets and create a fault that can rip apart like serrated paper. MSD was identified as the cause of the crash of the Japanese Airlines Boeing 747 in 1985, when 520 people lost their lives.

In Britain, the CAA has a good record for upholding high standards of aircraft maintenance, insisting on fatigue testing of every fuselage and pioneering the concept of structural audits to find fault at an early stage. Nevertheless, Ronald Ashford, the director of safety, admits that there were shortcomings. "In future there will be much more rigorous inspection programmes and a greater tendency to require replacement of large areas of frames and skins."

Decide whether the statements are, according to the text, TRUE, FALSE or the information is NOT GIVEN and write T for true, F for false, and NG for not given, in the space provided.

(1) In the Aloha Airlines accident the roof blew off because of explosive decompression in the plane. (　)

【参考答案】

F

分析：原文第一段第一句和第二句的前半句说的是 the roof came off，跟着就是 decompression，这里形成了前后逻辑关系。因此，题目实际上考查了考生对因果关系的分析和理解能力，但有意地颠倒了因与果，所以此题答案是 F。

做这道题时即使不懂 decompression 这个词，但只要看懂了后面的定语从句 that followed，就可以搞清前后关系了，就这点来说，掌握句法结构知识比扩大单词量要重要得多。

(2) According to the writer it is remarkable that the aeroplane did not break apart before landing. (　)

【参考答案】

T

分析：原文第一段第二句后半句说的是飞机着陆了并且没有解体，这是非常令人惊讶的。而题目说的是飞机在着陆前没有解体——既然飞机着陆时没有解体，那么就可以推断飞机着陆前肯定没有解体，因此答案是 T。

(3) The cause of the Aloha Airlines accident was never discovered. ( )

【参考答案】

F

分析：原文第三段第二句和第三句说 It was discovered that ... The cause: ... 也就是说原因被找到了，而题目说原因从未被找到，正好与原文意思相反，因此答案是 F。

(4) Many old aircraft still in use beyond their 20-year-limit have passed Boeing fitness tests. ( )

【参考答案】

NG

分析：原文第三段最后一句说的是波音公司的统计数字表明，558 架超过 20 年设计使用年限的飞机仍在使用，而没有提到它们是否通过了波音的 fitness tests。该题属于找不到出处又推断不出来的信息，因此答案是 NG。

(5) The safety of aircraft depends on, among other things, the airline following the instructions given by the aircraft manufacturer. ( )

【参考答案】

T

分析：原文第四段说的是要保证飞机安全飞行要靠三个条件：the national regulatory authority, ...; the aircraft manufacturer, ...; and the airline, ... 出题者可以直接把三个条件写出来，但为了不至于说得太明显，只提了 the airline 一个条件。短语 among other things 使其巧妙地包括了其他两个条件，因此这是对原文的重述，答案是 T。

3. 读下面这篇文章，判断文中作者的观点与题目是否一致或能否在文中找到。

A Sprinkling of Herbs

The medicinal plants (or botanicals) that were the basis of nineteenth century drugs have today been largely superseded by synthetic chemicals. Some botanicals, such as digitalis, used in the treatment of heart conditions, remain in wide use, but they are heavily outnumbered by formulations that, while they may be modelled after older herbal concoctions, differ from them in both their molecular form and their method of preparation.

Not everyone, however, has welcomed this change. Many modern drugs, especially those for chronic disorders, have both variable success rates and a high incidence of unpleasant, even dangerous, side-effects. And man-made drugs tend to be more expensive. Unlike time-honoured plant preparations, they are new when they are introduced, so can be patented. Drug companies charge high prices in order to recoup their research and development costs and reap their profits. The reaction in same western countries, where conventional medicine has tended to dismiss botanicals, has been a renewed interest in plants with therapeutic properties.

There is evidence that garlic can (in sufficient concentration and properly coated to ensure that enzymes in the stomach do not digest it before it is absorbed significantly) lower cholesterol; that valerian root helps people to sleep; that a tincture made from the above-ground parts of the purple-coneflower plant does as much as its synthetic competitors to relieve cold and influenza symptoms; and that migraine sufferers derive as much benefit from dried feverfew leaves as from standard headache drugs. And the botanicals have minimal side-effects. Why, then, have botanicals had to struggle to gain the respect of much — some would say most — of the medical establishment?

One reason is that in many countries medical schools teach very little about drugs, whether synthetic or botanical. Similarly, the professional journals that tend to carry the most weight with doctors (because of their large international circulations) rarely report on plant-based therapies. An unusual break in the silence was a recent study reported in a journal that confirmed the efficacy of cranberry juice for bladder infections, long claimed by its advocates outside the medical profession. But for every such favourable report there are other negative ones. Another study drew its readers' attention to an epidemic of irreversible kidney failure among women in Belgium who had used a slimming formula containing a toxic Chinese herb.

Herbalists can counter negative reports with corresponding stories of the mischief done by synthetic drugs. In America during the 1930s, for example, a drug, dinitrophenol, was popular for slimming — until it was found that many of its users developed cataracts. More recently, Oraflex, an arthritis drug (called Opren in Europe), was taken off the market after a spate of deaths following its introduction in 1982. It is, in fact, precisely such episodes that make some health officials mistrustful of all drugs, and thus reluctant to give herbal medicines the benefit of the doubt on safety.

Among these experts is Robert Temple, who runs the Office of Drug Evaluation and Research at America's Food and Drug Administration. At a recent conference in Washington, D.C., where it was argued that many herbal preparations have been used since antiquity and so can be assumed to be harmless, Dr. Temple disagreed. If nothing else makes the premise questionable, he noted, it is that the toxicity of tobacco went unrecognised for centuries. Besides, he added, people are living longer than they used to, and thus are at greater risk than in the past from any medicine — natural or synthetic — that seems safe in the short run but that has not been sufficiently studied to detect delayed adverse effects.

The World Health Organisation, a regulatory arm of the United Nations has, by contrast, proposed to permit ready access to virtually every botanical with a track record unless modern scientific data exists that casts doubt on its safety. Given that three-quarters of the world's population are believed to use botanicals, the approach seems reasonable, perhaps even wise.

On the other hand, a passive policy has drawbacks. Almost inevitably, it would discourage investment in research aimed at pushing knowledge about "natural" remedies — their efficacy, as well as their safety — beyond the limited information now available. There is a lot left to learn.

Do the following statements agree with the views of the writer in the passage?

In the space after each statement, write:

YES if the statement agrees with the writer;

NO if the statement does not agree with the writer;

NOT GIVEN if there is no information about this in the passage.

(1) Standard synthetic drugs for migraine are more effective than the botanical drug for migraine. ( )

【参考答案】

NO

分析：原文第三段中的句子 ... migraine sufferers derive as much benefit from dried feverfew leaves as from standard headache drugs，说的是两种药具有相同的效力。题目的意思与原文意思不一致，因此答案是 NO。

(2) The medical world has been right not to respect botanicals. ( )

【参考答案】

NO

分析：原文第三段最后一句用了一个反问句：Why, then, have botanicals had to struggle to gain the respect of much — some would say most — of the medical establishment? 结合前面所谈的草药的种种好处，反映出作者认为医药界一直以来不重视草药的态度是不对的，因此题目的观点与作者的观点相反，答案是 NO。

(3) Medical journals should publish more reports on the use of botanicals. ( )

【参考答案】

YES

分析：原文第四段讲了草药不被重视的原因，其中之一是：Similarly, the professional journals that tend to carry the most weight with doctors (because of their large international circulations) rarely report on plant-based therapies. 这就是说专业期刊很少报道基于植物的治疗方法，而作者认为医学期刊应该多发表关于草药使用的报道，因此题目与作者的观点一致，答案是 YES。

(4) The 1930s was a peak period for the development of synthetic drugs. (   )

【参考答案】

NOT GIVEN

分析：原文第五段第二句 In America during the 1930s, for example, a drug, dinitrophenol, was popular for slimming — until it was found that many of its users developed cataracts. 只介绍了美国 20 世纪 30 年代一种受欢迎的减肥药的副作用，而没有谈到 20 世纪 30 年代是合成药物发展的高峰期，因此该信息既无法在原文中找到又不能根据逻辑关系推断出来，答案是 NOT GIVEN。

(5) People should not be allowed access to botanical drugs. (   )

【参考答案】

NO

分析：原文第七段第一句 The World Health Organisation, a regulatory arm of the United Nations has, by contrast, proposed to permit ready access to virtually every botanical with a track record unless modern scientific data exists that casts doubt on its safety. 说明，世界卫生组织建议，允许使用几乎任何有跟踪记录的草药。结合下一句 ... the approach seems reasonable, perhaps even wise，我们看到作者是赞同这种做法的，因此题目与原文意思相反，答案是 NO。

4. 读下面这篇文章，判断文章作者的主张或断言（claims）与题目是否一致或能否在原文中找到。

A Remarkable Beetle

Some of the most remarkable beetles are the dung beetles, which spend almost their whole lives eating and breeding in dung*.

More than 4,000 species of these remarkable creatures have evolved and adapted to the world's different climates and the dung of many animals. Australia's native dung beetles are scrub and woodland dwellers, specialising in coarse marsupial droppings and avoiding the soft cattle dung in which bush flies and buffalo flies breed.

In the early 1960s George Bornemissza, then a scientist at the Australian Government's premier research organisation, the Commonwealth Scientific and Industrial Research Organisation (CSIRO), suggested that dung beetles should be introduced to Australia to control dung-breeding flies. Between 1968 and 1982, the CSIRO imported insects from about 50 different species of dung beetles, from Asia, Europe and Africa, aiming to match them to different climatic zones in Australia. Of the 26 species that are known to have become successfully integrated into the local environment, only one, an African species released in northern Australia, has reached its natural boundary.

Introducing dung beetles into a pasture is a simple process: approximately 1,500 beetles are released, a handful at a time; into fresh cow pats* in the cow pasture. The beetles immediately disappear beneath the pats digging and tunnelling and, if they successfully adapt to their new environment, soon become a permanent, self-sustaining part of the local ecology. In time they multiply and within three or four years the benefits to the pasture are obvious.

Dung beetles work from the inside of the pat so they are sheltered from predators such as birds and foxes. Most species burrow into the soil and bury dung in tunnels directly underneath the pats, which are hollowed out from within. Some large species originating from France excavate tunnels to a depth of approximately 30 centimetres below the dung pat. These beetles make sausage-shaped brood chambers along the tunnels. The shallowest tunnels belong to a much smaller Spanish species that buries dung in chambers that hang like fruit from the branches of a pear tree. South African beetles dig narrow tunnels of approximately 20 centimetres below the surface of the pat. Some surface-dwelling beetles, including a South African species, cut perfectly-shaped balls from the pat, which are rolled away and attached to the bases of plants.

For maximum dung burial in spring, summer and autumn, farmers require a variety of species with overlapping periods of activity. In the cooler environments of the state of Victoria, the large French species (2.5 centimetres long) is matched with smaller (half this size), temperate-climate Spanish species. The former are slow to recover from the winter cold and produce only one or two generations of offspring from late spring until autumn. The latter, which multiply rapidly in early spring, produce two to five generations annually. The South African ball-rolling species, being a subtropical beetle, prefers the climate of northern and coastal New South Wales where it commonly works with the South African tunnelling species. In warmer climates, many species are active for longer periods of the year.

Dung beetles were initially introduced in the late 1960s with a view to controlling buffalo flies by removing the dung within a day or two and so preventing flies from breeding. However, other benefits have become evident. Once the beetle larvae have finished pupation, the residue is a first-rate source of fertiliser. The tunnels abandoned by the beetles provide excellent aeration and water channels for root systems. In addition, when the new generation of beetles has left the nest the abandoned burrows are an attractive habitat for soil-enriching earthworms. The digested dung in these burrows is an excellent food supply for the earthworms, which decompose it further to provide essential soil nutrients. If it were not for the dung beetle, chemical fertiliser and dung would be washed by rain into streams and rivers before it could be absorbed into the hard earth, polluting water courses and causing blooms of blue-green algae. Without the beetles to dispose of the dung, cow pats would litter pastures making grass inedible to cattle and depriving the soil of sunlight. Australia's 30 million cattle each produces 10—12 cow pats a day. This amounts to 1.7 billion tonnes a year, enough to smother about 110,000 sq km of pasture, half the area of Victoria.

Dung beetles have become an integral part of the successful management of dairy farms in Australia over the past few decades. A number of species are available from the CSIRO or through a small number of private breeders, most of whom were entomologists with the CSIRO's dung beetle unit who have taken their specialised knowledge of the insect and opened small businesses in direct competition with their former employer.

* dung: the droppings or excreta of animals

cow pats: droppings of cows

Do the following statements reflect the claims of the writer in the passage?

In the space after each statement, write:

YES	if the statement reflects the claims of the writer;
NO	if the statement contradicts the claims of the writer;
NOT GIVEN	if it is impossible to say what the writer thinks about this.

(1) Bush flies are easier to control than buffalo flies. ( )

【参考答案】

NOT GIVEN

分析：原文第二段第二句 ... and avoiding the soft cattle dung in which bush flies and buffalo flies breed 和第三段第一句 ... suggested that dung beetles should be introduced to Australia to control dung-breeding flies. 均没提到题目中的论断，也不能凭逻辑推断出这个结论，因此答案为 NOT GIVEN。

(2) Four thousand species of dung beetle were initially brought to Australia by the CSIRO. ( )

【参考答案】

NO

分析：原文第三段第二句 Between 1968 and 1982, the CSIRO imported insects from about 50 different species of dung beetle ... 提到 CSIRO 引进了 50 种蜣螂，并非 4,000 种，题目的信息与原文不一致，因此答案是 NO。

(3) Dung beetles were brought to Australia by the CSIRO over a fourteen-year period. ( )

【参考答案】

YES

分析：原文第三段第二句 Between 1968 and 1982, the CSIRO imported insects ... 给出的时间跨度与题目的一致，因此答案是 YES。

(4) At least twenty-six of the introduced species have become established in Australia. ( )

【参考答案】

YES

分析：原文第三段最后一句 Of the 26 species that are known to have become successfully integrated into the local environment ... 给出的数字和意思与题目相符，因此答案是 YES。

(5) The dung beetles cause an immediate improvement to the quality of a cow pasture. ( )

【参考答案】

NO

分析：原文第四段最后一句 In time they multiply and within three or four years the benefits to the pasture are obvious. 说的是经过一段时间的繁殖后，也就是在三四年之后才会见到明显的好处，这与题目的 an immediate improvement 的论断不一致，因此答案是 NO。

5. 下面这篇文章需要考生针对文章作者的态度进行判断：题目的论断反映了作者正面（肯定）或负面（否定）的态度，或者没有反映作者的任何态度。

这种判断题涉及另一层面的测试。除了考查语言基本功，还考查了理解与辨别事实和论点的能力。有的陈述可以反映说话人的态度，有的陈述不能反映说话人的态度。因此，首先要具备理解与辨别事实和论点的能力：若陈述中含有说话人的意见、观点或论点，那么该陈述一定会反映出他（她）的态度；若陈述中只是纯粹地讲事实，那么就不能由此判断他（她）的态度。

怎样判断一句话是含有说话人的意见、观点或论点，还是纯粹地陈述事实呢？其实很简单。语言中的褒义词、贬义词和“应该”、“必须”等词是用来表达说话人的喜好、厌恶、支持或反对等态度的，这些词就直接反映了说话人正面或反面的态度；如果一句话只摆事实或列举数字，那么这句话就不能反映说话人的态度。

其他题型也可以测试考生理解与辨别事实和论点的能力，本书将在另外的章节结合具体题型详细讨论这个问题。

下面结合以下文章进行具体分析。

Education for the Rural Disadvantaged

1 The vast majority of people in the developing countries live in rural areas, on farms, in villages or in rural market towns. In some countries, such as Rwanda, Burkina Faso and Malawi, more than 90% of the total population lives in the rural areas.

2 The projections are that the rural populations of the less-developed countries will increase substantially in the decades to come. The U.N. predicts these will increase from 1.9 billion in 1970 to 2.6 billion by 1990. Thailand's rural population alone will increase from 30.6 million in 1970 to 570 million by the year 2000. Furthermore, because of high birth rates and declining infant mortality rates, more than half of the rural population of developing countries is under 20 years of age. This raises serious implications for education.

3 The main purpose of education is to provide everybody (not only those in urban areas) with relevant knowledge skills, attitudes and ideas which will enable them to lead more fulfilling, productive and satisfying lives. To assert that everyone has a "right" to education has little practical meaning unless this "right" is translated into terms of some "minimum package" of attitudes, knowledge and skills for all people in a given society. To do otherwise is to create a privileged class at the expense of everyone else. Vague objectives such as "giving every child a good basic education (often defined as four to six or more years of formal schooling)" are meaningless when huge sections of the population are getting little or no education at all.

4 People in rural areas suffer from inadequate educational facilities and opportunities. In most rural areas in developing countries, the out-of-school group constitutes a vast majority of the whole population from, say, 10 to 20 years old. For all practical purposes, they are beyond the reach of formal education. But no section of the community should be shortchanged by its educational system.

5 Where there are rural primary schools they benefit far fewer rural young people than educational statistics often imply. Primary schools, instead of being the great equalisers of educational opportunity they were meant to be, are the great discriminators. In the rural areas they equip only a small minority of the young for effective and satisfying adulthood. The great majority of rural youngsters are destined to live out the all-too-familiar grind of ignorance and poverty.

6 This vicious circle has to be broken; the goal must be to provide everybody with basic knowledge and skills. Rather than attempt to enroll every child for a seven- or eight-year cycle of primary schooling, which is not financially feasible anyway for many countries for many years to come, the strategy should be a shorter four- to five-year primary cycle to provide every child with the minimum educational needs — literacy, numeracy, health education and those technical and entrepreneurial skills needed to make a decent living. This primary education should be geared for the large majority who will not continue their studies beyond this stage, who will enter straight into productive life.

Decide whether the author of the passage has a positive or negative attitude to the statements below, or whether it is impossible to tell what attitude is. Write P if the author has a positive attitude, N if negative, or IT if it is impossible to tell, in the space provided.

The first one has been done as an example.

Example:

Most rural 10—20 year olds are beyond the reach of formal education. (*N*)

(1) Over half the rural population in developing countries is under 20. ( )

【参考答案】

IT

分析：这道题一看就知道是纯粹在讲事实。如果不放心，用寻读技巧很快找到原文第二段倒数第二句 ... more than half of the rural population of developing countries is under 20 years of age。原文意思与题目一致且不带有任何主观色彩，因此答案为IT。

(2) The aim of education is to equip everybody for effective and satisfying adulthood. ( )

【参考答案】

P

分析：这道题表明了作者的观点，结合原文第三段第一句 The main purpose of education is to provide everybody (not only those in urban areas) with relevant knowledge skills, attitudes and ideas which will enable them to lead more fulfilling, productive and satisfying lives，题目的论断与原文作者的观点一致，而且题目使用了褒义词 effective 和 satisfying，原文使用了褒义词 fulfilling，productive 和 satisfying，反映了作者的正面态度，因此答案为P。

(3) Education can create a privileged class. ( )

【参考答案】

N

分析：这道题中使用了带有消极意义的词 privileged，见原文第三段第三句 To do otherwise is to create a privileged class at the expense of everyone else. 这里不仅使用

了 privileged，还用了短语 at the expense of everyone else，充分反映了作者对此种做法的否定态度，因此答案为 N。

(4) Every rural child should be enrolled in a seven- or eight-year cycle of primary schooling. ( )

(5) Every rural child should be enrolled in a four- or five-year cycle of primary schooling. ( )

【参考答案】

(4) N (5) P

分析：第（4）题和第（5）题中均使用了 should，由此可见两个句子都表明了一种态度。两句信息几乎相同，只有 seven- or eight-year 和 four- or five-year 不同，因此需要找到对应的原文再进行判断。原文第六段第二句 Rather than attempt to enroll every child for a seven- or eight-year cycle of primary schooling, which is not financially feasible anyway for many countries for many years to come, the strategy should be a shorter four- to five-year primary cycle to provide every child with the minimum educational needs — literacy, numeracy, health education and those technical and entrepreneurial skills needed to make a decent living. 表明作者反对 a seven- or eight-year cycle of primary schooling，因此第（4）题答案为 N，这句话还表明作者赞成 a four- or five-year cycle of primary schooling，因此第（5）题答案为 P。

(6) Many rural children start work immediately after primary school. ( )

【参考答案】

IT

分析：这道题一看就知道是在纯粹讲事实，再看原文第六段最后一句 ... the large majority who will not continue their studies beyond this stage, who will enter straight into productive life. 这句话与题目一样，是在纯粹讲事实且不带有任何主观色彩，因此答案为 IT。

12.6.3 专项训练

1. 读下面这篇文章，判断题目是否与作者的观点一致。做题时先用寻读技巧定位，理解原句或上下文，然后根据已经学过的标准进行判断。做完后核对答案，再分析为什么做对了或做错了。

Tourism

A Tourism, holiday-making and travel are these days more significant social phenomena than most commentators have considered. On the face of it there could not be a more trivial subject for a book. And indeed since social scientists have had considerable difficulty explaining weightier topics, such as work or politics, it might be thought that they would have great difficulties in accounting for more trivial phenomena such as holiday-making. However, there are interesting parallels with the study of deviance. This involves the investigation of bizarre and idiosyncratic social practices which happen to be defined as deviant in some societies but not necessarily in others. The assumption is that the investigation of deviance can reveal interesting and significant aspects of "normal" societies. It could be said that a similar analysis can be applied to tourism.

B Tourism is a leisure activity which presupposes its opposite, namely regulated and organised work. It is one manifestation of how work and leisure are organised as separate and regulated spheres of social practice in modern societies. Indeed acting as a tourist is one of the defining characteristics of being "modern" and the popular concept of tourism is that it is organised within particular places and occurs for regularised periods of time. Tourist relationships arise from a movement of people to, and their stay in, various destinations. This necessarily involves some movement, that is the journey and a period of stay in a new place or places. The journey and the stay are by definition outside the normal places of residence and work and are of a short term and temporary nature and there is a clear intention to return "home" within a relatively short period of time.

C A substantial proportion of the population of modern societies engages in such tourist practices; new socialised forms of provision have developed in order to cope with the mass character of the gazes of tourists as opposed to the individual character of travel. Places are chosen to be visited and be gazed upon because there is an anticipation, especially through daydreaming and fantasy, of intense pleasures, either on a different scale or involving different senses from those customarily encountered. Such anticipation is constructed and sustained through a variety of non-tourist practices such as films, TV, literature, magazines, records and videos which construct and reinforce this daydreaming.

D Tourists tend to visit features of landscape and townscape which separate them off from everyday experience. Such aspects are viewed because they are taken to be in some sense out of the ordinary. The viewing of these tourist sights often involves different forms of social patterning, with a much greater sensitivity to visual elements of landscape or townscape than is normally found in everyday life. People linger over these sights in a way that they would not normally do in their home environment and the vision is objectified or captured through photographs, postcards, films and so on which enable the memory to be endlessly reproduced and recaptured.

E One of the earliest dissertations on the subject of tourism is Boorstin's analysis of the "pseudo event" where he argues that contemporary Americans cannot experience "reality" directly but thrive on "pseudo events". Isolated from the host environment and the local people, the mass tourist travels in guided groups and finds pleasure in inauthentic contrived attractions, gullibly enjoying the pseudo events and disregarding the real world outside. Over time the images generated of different tourist sights come to constitute a closed self-perpetuating system of illusions which provide the tourist with the basis for selecting and evaluating potential places to visit. Such visits are made, says Boorstin, within the "environmental bubble of the familiar American-style hotel which insulates the tourist from the strangeness of the host environment".

F To service the burgeoning tourist industry, an array of professionals has developed who attempt to reproduce ever new objects for the tourist to look at. These objects or places are located in a complex and changing hierarchy. This depends upon the interplay between, on the one hand, competition between interests involved in the provision of such objects and, on the other hand, changing class, gender, and generational distinctions of taste within the potential population of visitors. It has been said that to be a tourist is one of the characteristics of the "modern experience". Not to go away is like not possessing a car or a nice house. Travel is a marker of status in modern societies and is also thought to be necessary for good health. The role of the professional, therefore, is to cater for the needs and tastes of the tourists in accordance with their class and overall expectations.

Do the following statements agree with the views of the writer in the passage? In the space given after each statement, write:

YES if the statement agrees with the writer;

NO if the statement contradicts the writer;

NOT GIVEN if it is impossible to say what the writer thinks about this.

Example:

People who can't afford to travel watch films and TV. (*NOT GIVEN*)

(1) Tourism is a trivial subject. ( )

(2) An analysis of deviance can act as a model for the analysis of tourism. ( )

(3) Tourists usually choose to travel overseas. ( )

(4) Tourists focus more on places they visit than those at home. ( )

(5) Tour operators try to cheat tourists. ( )

【参考答案】

(1) NO (2) YES (3) NOT GIVEN (4) YES (5) NOT GIVEN

2. 读下面的文章，判断题目中的信息是否与原文的信息一致。做题时先用寻读技巧定位，理解原句或上下文，然后根据已经学过的标准进行判断。做完后核对答案，再分析为什么做对了或做错了。

Johnson's Dictionary

For the century before *Johnson's Dictionary* was published in 1775, there had been concern about the state of the English language. There was no standard way of speaking or writing and no agreement as to the best way of bringing some order to the chaos of English spelling. Dr. Johnson provided the solution.

There had, of course, been dictionaries in the past, the first of these being a little book of some 120 pages, compiled by a certain Robert Cawdray, published in 1604 under the title *A Table Alphabetical of Hard Usual English Words*. Like the various dictionaries that came after it during the seventeenth century, Cawdray's tended to concentrate on "scholarly" words; one function of the dictionary was to enable its student to convey an impression of fine learning.

Beyond the practical need to make order out of chaos, the rise of dictionaries is associated with the rise of the English middle class, who were anxious to define and circumscribe the various words to conquer — lexical as well as social and commercial. It is highly appropriate that Dr. Samuel Johnson, the very model of an eighteenth-century literary man, as famous in his own time as in ours, should have published his Dictionary at the very beginning of the heyday of the middle class.

Johnson was a poet and critic who raised common sense to the heights of genius. His approach to the problems that had worried writers throughout the late seventeenth and early eighteenth centuries was intensely practical. Up until his time, the task of producing a dictionary on such a large scale had seemed impossible without the establishment of an academy to make decisions about right and wrong usage. Johnson decided he did not need an academy to settle arguments about language; he would write a dictionary himself, and he would do it single-handed. Johnson signed the contract for the Dictionary with the bookseller Robert Dosley at a breakfast held at the Golden Anchor Inn near Holborn Bar on 18 June, 1764. He was to be paid £1,575 in instalments, and from this he took money to rent 17 Gough Square, in which he set up his "dictionary workshop".

James Boswell, his biographer described the garret where Johnson worked as "fitted up like a counting house" with a long desk running down the middle at which the copying clerks would work standing up. Johnson himself was stationed on a rickety chair at an "old crazy deal table" surrounded by a chaos of borrowed books. He was also helped by six assistants, two of whom died whilst the Dictionary was still in preparation.

The work was immense: filling about eighty large notebooks (and without a library to hand), Johnson wrote the definitions of over 40,000 words, and illustrated their many meanings with some 114,000 quotations drawn from English writings on every subject, from the Elizabethans to his own time. He did not expect to achieve complete originality. Working to a deadline, he had to draw on the best of all previous dictionaries, and to make his work one of heroic synthesis. In fact, it was very much more. Unlike his predecessors, Johnson treated English very practically, as a living language, with many different shades of meaning. He adopted his definitions on the principle of English common law — according to precedent. After its publication, his Dictionary was not seriously rivalled for over a century.

After many vicissitudes the Dictionary was finally published on 15 April, 1775. It was instantly recognised as a landmark throughout Europe. "This very noble work," wrote the leading Italian lexicographer, "will be a perpetual monument of fame to the author, an honour to his own country in particular, and a general benefit to the republic of letters throughout Europe. The fact that Johnson had taken on the academies of Europe and matched them (everyone knew that forty French academics had taken forty years to produce the first French national dictionary) was cause for much English celebration."

Johnson had worked for nine years, "with little assistance of the learned, and without any patronage of the great; not in the soft obscurities of retirement, or under the shelter of academic bowers, but amidst inconvenience and distraction, in sickness and in sorrow". For all its faults and eccentricities his two-volume work is a masterpiece and a landmark, in his own words, "setting the orthography, displaying the analogy regulating the structures, and ascertaining the significations of English words". It is the cornerstone of Standard English, an achievement which, in James Boswell's words, "conferred stability on the language of his country".

The Dictionary, together with his other writings, made Johnson famous and so well esteemed that his friends were able to prevail upon King George III to offer him a pension. From then on, he was to become the Johnson of folklore.

Do the following statements agree with the information given in the passage?

In the space given after each statement, write:

TRUE if the statement agrees with the information;

FALSE if the statement contradicts the information;

NOT GIVEN if there is no information on this.

(1) The growing importance of the middle class led to an increased demand for dictionaries. ( )

(2) Johnson has become more well-known since his death. ( )

(3) Johnson had been planning to write a dictionary for several years. ( )

(4) Johnson set up an academy to help with the writing of his Dictionary. ( )

(5) Johnson only received payment for his Dictionary on its completion. ( )

(6) Not all of the assistants survived to see the publication of the Dictionary. ( )

【参考答案】

(1) TRUE (2) FALSE (3) NOT GIVEN

(4) FALSE (5) FALSE (6) TRUE

3. 读下面的文章，判断题目中的信息是否与原文的信息一致。做题时先用寻读技巧定位，理解原句或上下文，然后根据已经学过的标准进行判断。做完后核对答案，再分析为什么做对了或做错了。

The Effects of Light on Plant and Animal Species

Light is important to organisms for two different reasons. Firstly it is used as a cue for the timing of daily and seasonal rhythms in both plants and animals, and secondly it is used to assist growth in plants.

Breeding in most organisms occurs during a part of the year only, and so a reliable cue is needed to trigger breeding behaviour. Day length is an excellent cue, because it provides a perfectly predictable pattern of change within the year. In the temperate zone in spring, temperatures fluctuate greatly from day to day, but day length increases steadily by a predictable amount. The seasonal impact of day length on physiological responses is called *photoperiodism*, and the amount of experimental evidence for this phenomenon is considerable. For example, some species of birds' breeding can be induced even in midwinter simply by increasing day length artificially. Other examples of photoperiodism occur in plants. A short-day plant flowers when the day is less than a certain critical length. A long-day plant flowers after a certain critical day length is exceeded. In both cases the critical day length differs from species to species. Plants which flower after a period of vegetative growth, regardless of photoperiod, are known as day-neutral plants.

Breeding seasons in animals such as birds have evolved to occupy the part of the year in which offspring have the greatest chances of survival. Before the breeding season begins, food reserves must be built up to support the energy cost of reproduction, and to provide for young birds both when they are in the nest and after fledging. Thus many temperate-zone birds use the increasing day lengths in spring as a cue to begin the nesting cycle, because this is a point when adequate food resources will be assured.

The adaptive significance of photoperiodism in plants is also clear. Short-day plants that flower in spring in the temperate zone are adapted to maximising seedling growth during the growing season. Long-day plants are adapted for situations that require fertilisation by insects, or a long period of seed ripening. Short-day plants that flower in the autumn in the temperate zone are able to build up food reserves over the growing season and over winter as seeds. Day-neutral plants have an evolutionary advantage when the connection between the favourable period for reproduction and day length is much less certain. For example, desert annuals germinate, flower and seed whenever suitable rainfall occurs, regardless of the day length.

The breeding season of some plants can be delayed to extraordinary lengths. Bamboos are perennial grasses that remain in a vegetative state for many years and then suddenly flower, fruit and die. Every bamboo of the species *Chusquea abietifolia* on the island of Jamaica flowered, set seed and died during 1884. The next generation of bamboo flowered and died between 1916 and 1918, which suggests a vegetative cycle of about 31 years. The climatic trigger for this flowering cycle is not yet known, but the adaptive significance is clear. The simultaneous production of masses of bamboo seeds (in some cases lying 12 to 15 centimetres deep on the ground) is more than all the seed-eating animals can cope with at the time, so that some seeds escape being eaten and grow up to form the next generation.

The second reason light is important to organisms is that it is essential for photosynthesis. This is the process by which plants use energy from the sun to convert carbon from soil or water into organic material for growth. The rate of photosynthesis in a plant can be measured by calculating the rate of its uptake of carbon. There is a wide range of photosynthetic responses of plants to variations in light intensity. Some plants reach maximal photosynthesis at one-quarter full sunlight, and others, like sugarcane, never reach a maximum, but continue to increase photosynthesis rate as light intensity rises.

Plants in general can be divided into two groups: shade-tolerant species and shade-intolerant species. This classification is commonly used in forestry and horticulture. Shade-tolerant plants have lower photosynthetic rates and hence have lower growth rates than those of shade-intolerant species. Plant species become adapted to living in a certain kind of habitat, and in the process evolve a series of characteristics that prevent them from occupying other habitats. Grime suggests that light may be one of the major components directing these adaptations. For example, eastern hemlock seedlings are shade-tolerant. They can survive in the forest understorey under very low light levels because they have a low photosynthetic rate.

Do the following statements agree with the information given in the passage?

In the space given after each statement, write:

TRUE if the statement agrees with the information;

FALSE if the statement contradicts the information;

NOT GIVEN if there is no information on this.

(1) There is plenty of scientific evidence to support photoperiodism. ( )

(2) Some types of bird can be encouraged to breed out of season. ( )

(3) Photoperiodism is restricted to certain geographic areas. ( )

(4) Desert annuals are examples of long-day plants. ( )

(5) Bamboos flower several times during their life cycle. ( )

(6) Scientists have yet to determine the cue for Chusquea abietifolia's seasonal rhythm. ( )

(7) Eastern hemlock is a fast-growing plant. ( )

【参考答案】

(1) TRUE (2) TRUE (3) NOT GIVEN (4) FALSE
(5) FALSE (6) TRUE (7) FALSE

12.7 分类题和标题／短语搭配题

12.7.1 题型分析破解

分类题和标题／短语搭配题（Classification; Matching Lists / Phrases）这两种题型基本也是考查考生提取单个信息的能力，部分涉及组团信息的问题将在另外的章节中详细讨论（见第 13 章）。

这两种题型放在同一节里谈，主要是因为它们之间的界线模糊，很难清晰地界定。分类题在某种意义上属于标题搭配题，而后者在某种意义上也属于前者的范畴。

这两种题型的解题步骤与简答题有相同之处，二者都要看上下文，快速搜寻定位；不同之处是，简答题需要考生直接从原文中找出答案，而这两种题型要考生判断信息的归属和匹配。

解答这两种题型有一定的难度，因为需要归类和匹配的内容往往经过了改写，并且归类和匹配的依据繁多，如文章中出现的因果、因素、理由、事件和观点等都有可能成为考题的内容。考生在碰到不同性质或形式的归类和匹配题时，往往会误以为遇到了新题型而自乱阵脚。因此，考生要看清题目，提高审题能力、适应变化的能力和理解能力，在考场上时刻保持头脑清醒。

12.7.2 练习及解析

1. 这篇文章的题型属于分类题。

In Research of the Holy Grail

It has been called the Holy Grail of modern biology. Costing more than £2 billion, it is the most ambitious scientific project since the Apollo programme that landed a man on the moon. And it will take longer to accomplish than the lunar missions, for it will not be complete until early next century. Even before it is finished, according to those involved, this project should open up new understanding of, and new treatments for, many of the ailments that afflict humanity. As a result of the Human Genome Project, there will be new hope of liberation from the shadows of cancer, heart disease, autoimmune diseases such as rheumatoid arthritis, and some psychiatric illnesses.

The objective of the Human Genome Project is simple to state, but audacious in scope: to map and analyse every single gene within the double helix of humanity's DNA*. The project will reveal a new human anatomy — not the bones, muscles and sinews, but the complete genetic blueprint for a human being. Those working on the Human Genome Project claim that the new genetical anatomy will transform medicine and reduce human suffering in the twenty-first century. But others see the future through a darker glass, and fear that the project may open the door to a world peopled by Frankenstein's monsters and disfigured by a new eugenics*.

The genetic inheritance a baby receives from its parents at the moment of conception fixes much of its later development, determining characteristics as varied as whether it will have blue eyes or suffer from a life-threatening illness such as cystic fibrosis. The human genome is the compendium of all these inherited genetic instructions. Written out along the double helix of DNA are the chemical letters of the genetic text. It is an extremely long text, for the human genome contains more than 3 billions letters. On the printed page it would fill about 7,000 volumes. Yet, within little more than a decade, the position of every letter and its relation to its neighbours will have been tracked down, analysed and recorded.

Considering how many letters there are in the human genome, nature is an excellent proof-reader. But sometimes there are mistakes. An error in a single "word" — a gene — can give rise to the crippling condition of cystic fibrosis, the commonest genetic disorder among Caucasians. Errors in the genetic recipe for haemoglobin, the protein that give blood its characteristic red colour and which carries oxygen from the lungs to the rest of the body, give rise to the most common single-gene disorder in the world: thalassanemia. More than 4,000 such single-gene defects are known to afflict humanity. The majority of them are fatal; the majority of the victims are children.

None of the single-gene disorders is a disease in the conventional sense, for which it would be possible to administer a curative drug: the defect is pre-programmed into every cell of the sufferer's body. But there is hope of progress. In 1986, American researchers identified the genetic defect underlying one type of muscular dystrophy. In 1989, a team of American and Canadian biologists announced that they had found the site of the gene which, when defective, gives rise to cystic fibrosis. Indeed, not only had they located the gene, they had analysed the sequence of letters within it and had identified the mistake responsible for the condition. At the least, these scientific advances may offer a way of screening parents who might be at risk of transmitting a single-gene defect to any children that they conceive. Foetuses can be tested while in the womb, and if found free of the genetic defect, the parents will be relieved of worry and stress, knowing that they will be delivered of a baby free from the disorder.

In the mid-1980s, the idea gained currency within the scientific world that the techniques which were successfully deciphering disorder-related genes could be applied to a larger project: if science can learn the genetic spelling of cystic fibrosis, why not attempt to find out how to spell "human"? Momentum quickly built up behind the Human Genome Project and its objective of "sequencing" the entire genome — writing out all the letters in their correct order.

But the consequences of the Human Genome Project go far beyond a narrow focus on disease. Some of its supporters have made claims of great extravagance — that the Project will bring us to understand, at the most fundamental level, what it is to be human. Yet many people are concerned that such an emphasis on humanity's genetic constitution may distort our sense of values, and lead us to forget that human life is more than just the expression of a genetic programme written in the chemistry of DNA.

If properly applied, the new knowledge generated by the Human Genome Project may free humanity from the terrible scourge of diverse diseases. But if the new knowledge is not used wisely, it also holds the threat of creating new forms of discrimination and new methods of oppression. Many characteristics, such as height and intelligence, result not from the action of genes alone, but from subtle interactions between genes and the environment. What would be the implications if humanity were to understand with precision, the genetic constitution which, given the same environment, will predispose one person towards a higher intelligence than another individual whose genes were differently shuffled?

Once before in this century, the relentless curiosity of scientific researchers brought to light forces of nature in the power of the atom, the mastery of which has shaped the destiny of nations and overshadowed all our live. The Human Genome Project holds the promise that, ultimately, we may be able to alter our genetic inheritance if we so choose. But there is the central moral problem: how can we ensure that when we choose, we choose correctly? That such a potential is a promise and not a threat? We need only look at the past to understand the danger.

* DNA: deoxyribonucleic acid, molecules responsible for the transference of genetic characteristics
eugenics: the science of improving the qualities of the human race, especially the careful selection of parents

Classify the following statements as representing

A the writer's fears about the Human Genome Project;

B other people's fears about the Project reported by the writer;

C the writer's reporting of facts about the Project;

D the writer's reporting of the long-term hopes for the Project.

解题技巧：首先，快速阅读上述四项分类，了解各项分类的具体含义，然后开始做题。做题时先看懂题目，再用寻读技巧快速定位，读原文中的原句或上下文，最后根据句子内容进行归类。

Write the appropriate letters A, B, C, or D in the space given after each statement.

(1) The Project will provide a new understanding of major diseases. ( )

【参考答案】

D

分析：原文第一段最后一句 As a result of the Human Genome Project, there will be new hope of liberation from the shadows of cancer, heart disease, autoimmune diseases such as rheumatoid arthritis, and some psychiatric illnesses. 与题目意思相符，可归类为 D。

(2) All the components which make up DNA are to be recorded and studied. ( )

【参考答案】

C

分析：原文第二段第一句 The objective of the Human Genome Project is simple to state, but audacious in scope: to map and analyse every single gene within the double helix of humanity's DNA. 与题目的意思相符，可归类为 C。

(3) Genetic monsters may be created. ( )

【参考答案】

B

分析：原文第二段最后一句 But others see the future through a darker glass, and fear that the project may open the door to a world peopled by Frankenstein's monsters and disfigured by a new eugenics. 与题目的意思相符，可归类为 B。这道题一定要参考原文才能分辨这是作者的观点还是其他人的观点。

(4) The correct order and inter-relation of all genetic data in all DNA will be mapped. ( )

【参考答案】

C

分析：原文第三段最后一句 Yet, within little more than a decade, the position of every letter and its relation to its neighbours will have been tracked down, analysed and recorded. 与题目的意思相符，可归类为 C。

(5) Parents will no longer worry about giving birth to defective offspring. ( )

【参考答案】

D

分析：原文第五段最后两句 At the least, these scientific advances may offer a way of screening parents who might be at risk of transmitting a single-gene defect to any children that they conceive. Foetuses can be tested while in the womb, and if found free of the genetic defect, the parents will be relieved of worry and stress, knowing that they will be delivered of a baby free from the disorder. 与题目的意思相符，可归类为 D。

(6) Being "human" may be defined solely in terms of describable physical data. ( )

【参考答案】

B

分析：原文第六段第一句 ... the idea gained currency within the scientific world that the techniques which were successfully deciphering disorder-related genes could be applied to a larger project: if science can learn the genetic spelling of cystic fibrosis, why not attempt to find out how to spell "human"? 与题目的意思相符，可归类为 B。这道题一定要参看原文才能辨别是作者的观点还是其他人的观点。

(7) People may be discriminated against in new ways. ( )

【参考答案】

A

分析：原文倒数第二段第二句 But if the new knowledge is not used wisely, it also holds the threat of creating new forms of discrimination and new methods of oppression. 与题目的意思相符，可归类为 A。这道题一定要参看原文才能辨别是作者的观点还是其他人的观点。

(8) From past experience humans may not use this new knowledge wisely. ( )

【参考答案】

A

分析：原文最后一段第一句 Once before in this century, the relentless curiosity of scientific researchers brought to light forces of nature in the power of the atom, the mastery of which has shaped the destiny of nations and overshadowed all our live. 与题目的意思相符，可归类为 A。这道题一定要参看原文才能辨别是作者的观点还是其他人的观点。

2. 下面这篇文章的练习属于标题搭配题。完成练习后，请仔细研究参考答案后的分析。

The Pursuit of Happiness

New research uncovers some anti-intuitive insights into how many people are happy — and why.

Compared with misery, happiness is relatively unexplored terrain for social scientists. Between 1967 and 1994, 46,380 articles indexed in *Psychological Abstracts* mentioned depression, 36,851 anxiety, and 5,099 anger. Only 2,389 spoke of happiness, 2,340 life satisfaction, and 405 joy.

Recently we and other researchers have begun a systematic study of happiness. During the past two decades, dozens of investigators throughout the world have asked several hundred thousand representatively sampled people to reflect on their happiness and satisfaction with life — or what psychologists call "subjective well-being". In the U.S. the National Opinion Research Center at the University of Chicago has surveyed a representative sample of roughly 1,500 people a year since 1957; the Institute for Social Research at the University of Michigan has carried out similar studies on a less regular basis, as has the Gallup Organization. Government-funded efforts have also probed the moods of European countries.

We have uncovered some surprising findings. People are happier than one might expect, and happiness does not appear to depend significantly on external circumstances. Although viewing life as a tragedy has a long and honorable history, the responses of random samples of people around the world about their happiness paints a much rosier picture. In the University of Chicago surveys, three in ten Americans say they are very happy, for example. Only one in ten chooses the most negative description "not too happy". The majority describe themselves as "pretty happy".

How can social scientists measure something as hard to pin down as happiness? Most researchers simply ask people to report their feelings of happiness or unhappiness and to assess how satisfying their lives are. Such self-reported well-being is moderately consistent over years of retesting. Furthermore, those who say they are happy and satisfied seem happy to their close friends and family members and to a psychologist-interviewer. Their daily mood ratings reveal more positive emotions, and they smile more than those who call themselves unhappy. Self-reported happiness also predicts other indicators of well-being. Compared with the depressed, happy people are less self-focused, less hostile and abusive, and less susceptible to disease.

We have found that the even distribution of happiness cuts across almost all demographic classifications of age, economic class, race and educational level. In addition, almost all strategies for assessing subjective well-being — including those that sample people's experience by polling them at random times with beepers — turn up similar findings.

Interviews with representative samples of people of all ages, for example, reveal that no time of life is notably happier or unhappier. Similarly, men and women are equally likely to declare themselves "very happy" and "satisfied" with life, according to a statistical digest of 146 studies by Marilyn J. Hating, William Stock and Morris A. Okun, all then at Arizona State University.

Wealth is also a poor predictor of happiness. People have not become happier over time as their cultures have become more affluent. Even though Americans earn twice as much in today's dollars as they did in 1957, the proportion of those telling surveyors from the National Opinion Research Center that they are "very happy" has declined from 35%—29%.

Even very rich people — those surveyed among *Forbes* magazine's 100 wealthiest Americans — are only slightly happier than the average American. Those whose income has increased over a 10-year period are not happier than those whose income is stagnant. Indeed, in most nations the correlation between income and happiness is negligible — only in the poorest countries is income a good measure of emotional well-being.

Are people in rich countries happier, by and large, than people in not so rich countries? It appears in general that they are, but the margin may be slim. In Portugal, for example, only one in 10 people reports being very happy, whereas in the much more prosperous Netherlands the proportion of very happy is four in ten. Yet there are curious reversals in this correlation between national wealth and well-being — the Irish during the 1980s consistently reported greater life satisfaction than the wealthier West Germans. Furthermore, other factors, such as civil rights, literacy and duration of democratic government, all of which also promote reported life satisfaction, tend to go hand in hand with national wealth. As a result, it is impossible to tell whether the happiness of people in wealthier nations is based on money or is a by-product of other felicities.

Although happiness is not easy to predict from material circumstances, it seems consistent for those who have it. In one National Institute on Aging study of 5,000 adults, the happiest people in 1973 were still relatively happy a decade later, despite changes in work, residence and family status.

According to the passage, which of the findings below is quoted by Investigative Body (**A—G**)? Write your answers in the space given after each statement.

Note: There are more Investigative Bodies than findings, so you do not have to use all of them.

Investigative Bodies

A The National Opinion Research Centre, University Chicago

B Arizona State University

C The Institute for Social Research, University of Michigan

D *Forbes* magazine

E The National Institute on Aging

F The Gallup Organisation

G The Government

(1) Happiness is not gender related. ( )

(2) Over fifty per cent of people consider themselves to be "happy". ( )

(3) Happiness levels are marginally higher for those in the top income brackets. ( )

(4) "Happy" people remain happy throughout their lives. ( )

【参考答案】

(1) B (2) A (3) D (4) E

分析：这篇文章的题目相对容易。建议先用寻读技巧搜寻这些首字母大写的机构名称在原文中何处出现，然后阅读上下文，注意文章有没有谈到该机构的调查结果。如果有，就看这个结果与第（1）题至第（4）题中的哪道题在意思上相符，最后进行搭配。

首先发现第四段最后三句谈到 University of Chicago 的调查结果，最后一句 The majority describe themselves as "pretty happy". 与第(2)题的意思相符，因此匹配 A。

然后发现第七段最后一句谈到 Arizona State University 的调查结果 ... men and women are equally likely to declare themselves "very happy" and "satisfied" with life ... 与第（1）题的意思相符，因此匹配 B。不过，考生需要认识 gender 这个词，否则无法进行搭配。

接着发现第九段第一句谈到 *Forbes* magazine 的调查结果 Even very rich people — those surveyed among *Forbes* magazine's 100 wealthiest Americans — are only slightly happier than the average American. 与第（3）题的意思相符，因此匹配 D。不过，考生需要知道 marginally 是 slightly 的同义词，否则匹配会遇到困难。

最后看到最末一段的两句谈到 The National Institute on Aging 的调查结果 In one National Institute on Aging study of 5,000 adults, the happiest people in 1973 were still relatively happy a decade later, despite changes in work, residence and family status. 与第（4）题的意思相符，因此匹配 E。

3. 阅读下面这篇文章并完成后面的练习。题型与上一篇文章相同。做完后核对答案，分析为什么做对了或做错了。

Right- and Left-handedness in Humans

Why do humans, virtually alone among all animal species, display a distinct left- or right-handedness? Not even our closest relatives among the apes possess such decided lateral asymmetry, as psychologists call it. Yet about 90% of every human population that has ever lived appears to have been right-handed. Professor Bryan Turner at Deakin University has studied the research literature on left-handedness and found that handedness goes with sidedness. So nine out of ten people are right-handed and eight are right-footed. He noted that this distinctive asymmetry in the human population is itself systematic. "Humans think in categories: black and white, up and down, left and right. It's a system of signs that enables us to categorise phenomena that are essentially ambiguous."

Research has shown that there is a genetic or inherited element to handedness. But while left-handedness tends to run in families, neither left nor right handers will automatically produce offspring with the same handedness; in fact about 6% of children with two right-handed parents will be left-handed. However, among two left-handed parents, perhaps 40% of the children will also be left-handed. With one right and one left-handed parent, 15%—20% of the offspring will be left-handed. Even among identical twins who have exactly the same genes, one in six pairs will differ in their handedness.

What then makes people left-handed if it is not simply genetic? Other factors must be at work and researchers have turned to the brain for clues. In the 1860s the French surgeon and anthropologist, Dr. Paul Broca, made the remarkable finding that patients who had lost their powers of speech as a result of a stroke (a blood clot in the brain) had paralysis of the right half of their body. He noted that since the left hemisphere of the brain controls the right half of the body, and vice versa, the brain damage must have been in the brain's left hemisphere. Psychologists now believe that among right-handed people, probably 95% have their language centre in the left hemisphere, while 5% have right-sided language. Left-handers, however, do not show the reverse pattern but instead a majority also have their language in the left hemisphere. Some 30% have right hemisphere language.

Dr. Brinkman, a brain researcher at the Australian National University in Canberra, has suggested that evolution of speech went with right-handed preference. According to Brinkman, as the brain evolved, one side became specialised for fine control of movement (necessary for producing speech) and along with this evolution came right-hand preference. According to Brinkman, most left-handers have left hemisphere dominance but also some capacity in the right hemisphere. She has observed that if a left-handed person is brain-damaged in the left hemisphere, the recovery of speech is quite often better and this is explained by the fact that left-handers have a more bilateral speech function.

In her studies of macaque monkeys, Brinkman has noticed that primates (monkeys) seem to learn a hand preference from their mother in the first year of life but this could be one hand or the other. In humans, however, the specialisation in function of the two hemispheres results in anatomical differences: areas that are involved with the production of speech are usually larger on the left side than on the right. Since monkeys have not acquired the art of speech, one would not expect to see such a variation but Brinkman claims to have discovered a trend in monkeys towards the asymmetry that is evident in the human brain.

Two American researchers, Geschwind and Galaburda, studied the brains of human embryos and discovered that the left-right asymmetry exists before birth. But as the brain develops, a number of things can affect it. Every brain is initially female in its organisation and it only becomes a male brain when the male foetus begins to secrete hormones. Geschwind and Galaburda knew that different parts of the brain mature at different rates; the right hemisphere develops first, then the left. Moreover, a girl's brain develops somewhat faster than that of a boy. So, if something happens to the brain's development during pregnancy, it is more likely to be affected in a male and the hemisphere more likely to be involved is the left. The brain may become less lateralised and this in turn could result in left-handedness and the development of certain superior skills that have their origins in the left hemisphere such as logic, rationality and abstraction. It should be no surprise then that among mathematicians and architects, left-handers tend to be more common and there are more left-handed males than females.

The results of this research may be some consolation to left-handers who have for centuries lived in a world designed to suit right-handed people. However, what is alarming, according to Mr. Charles Moore, a writer and journalist, is the way the word "right" reinforces its own virtue. Subliminally he says, language tells people to think that anything on the right can be trusted while anything on the left is dangerous or even sinister. We speak of left-handed compliments and according to Moore, "it is no coincidence that left-handed children, forced to use their right hand, often develop a stammer as they are robbed of their freedom of speech". However, as more research is undertaken on the causes of left-handedness, attitudes towards left-handed people are gradually changing for the better. Indeed when the champion tennis player Ivan Lendl was asked what the single thing was that he would choose in order to improve his game, he said he would like to become a left-hander.

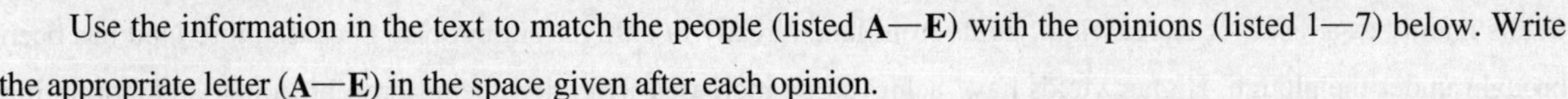

Use the information in the text to match the people (listed **A—E**) with the opinions (listed 1—7) below. Write the appropriate letter (**A—E**) in the space given after each opinion.

Example:

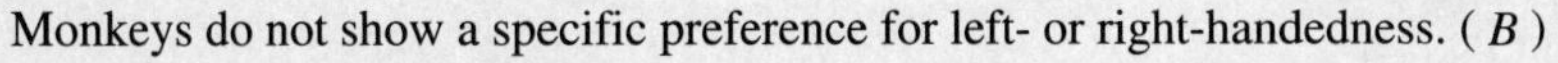

Monkeys do not show a specific preference for left- or right-handedness. (*B*)

A Dr. Broca
B Dr. Brinkman
C Geschwind and Galaburda
D Charles Moore
E Professor Turner

(1) Human beings started to show a preference for right-handedness when they first developed language. (　)

(2) Society is prejudiced against left-handed people. (　)

(3) Boys are more likely to be left-handed. (　)

(4) After a stroke, left-handed people recover their speech more quickly than right-handed people. (　)

(5) People who suffer strokes on the left side of the brain usually lose their power of speech. (　)

(6) The two sides of the brain develop different functions before birth. (　)

(7) Asymmetry is a common feature of the human body. (　)

【参考答案】

(1) B　(2) D　(3) C　(4) B　(5) A　(6) C　(7) E

4. 阅读下面这篇文章并完成后面的练习。题型与第二篇文章有所不同。做完后核对答案，分析为什么做对了或做错了，并总结出最佳解题方法。

Section A

The role of governments in environmental management is difficult but inescapable. Sometimes, the state tries to manage the resources it owns, and does so badly. Often, however, governments act in an even more harmful way. They actually subsidise the exploitation and consumption of natural resources. A whole range of policies, from farm-price support to protection for coal-mining, do environmental damage and (often) make no economic sense. Scrapping them offers a two-fold bonus: a cleaner environment and a more efficient economy. Growth and environmentalism can actually go hand in hand, if politicians have the courage to confront the vested interest that subsidies create.

Section B

No activity affects more of the earth's surface than farming. It shapes a third of the planet's land area, not counting Antarctica, and the proportion is rising. World food output per head has risen by 4% between the 1970s and

1980s mainly as a result of increases in yields from land already in cultivation, but also because more land has been brought under the plough. Higher yields have achieved by increased irrigation, better crop breeding, and a doubling in the use of pesticides and chemical fertilisers in the 1970s and 1980s.

Section C

All these activities may have damaging environmental impacts, for example, land clearing for agriculture is the largest single cause of deforestation; chemical fertilisers and pesticides may contaminate water supplies; more intensive farming and the abandonment of fallow periods tend to exacerbate soil erosion; and the spread of monoculture and use of high-yielding varieties of crops have been accompanied by the disappearance of old varieties of food plants which might have provided some insurance against pests or diseases in future. Soil erosion threatens the productivity of land in both rich and poor countries. The United States, where the most careful measurements have been done, discovered in 1982 that about one-fifth of its farmland was losing topsoil at a rate likely to diminish the soil's productivity. The country subsequently embarked upon a programme to convert 11% of its cropped land to meadow or forest. Topsoil in India and China is vanishing much faster than in America.

Section D

Government policies have frequently compounded the environmental damage that farming can cause. In the rich countries, subsidies for growing crops and price supports about $250 billion, or more than all World Bank lending in the 1980s. To increase the output of crops per acre, a farmer's easiest option is to use most of the most readily available inputs: fertilisers and pesticides. Fertiliser use doubled in Denmark in the period 1980—1985 and increased in the Netherlands by 150%. The quantity of pesticides applied has risen, too, by 69% in 1985—1984 in Denmark, for example, with a rise of 115% in the frequency of application in the three years from 1981.

In the late 1980s and early 1990s some efforts were made to reduce farm subsidies. The most dramatic example was that of New Zealand, which scrapped most farm support in 1984. A study of the environmental effects, conducted in 1993, found that the end of fertiliser subsidies had been followed by a fall in fertiliser use (a fall compounded by the decline in world commodity prices, which cut farm incomes). The removal of subsidies also stopped land-clearing and over-stocking, which in the past had been the principal causes of erosion. Farms began to diversify. The one kind of subsidy whose removal appeared to have been bad for the environment was the subsidy to manage soil erosion.

In less enlightened countries, and in the European Union, the trend has been to reduce rather than eliminate subsidies, and to introduce new payments to encourage farmers to treat their land in environmentally friendlier ways, or to leave it fallow. It may sound strange but such payments need to be higher than the existing incentives for farmers to grow food crops. Farmers, however, dislike being paid to do nothing. In several countries they have become interested in the possibility of using fuel produced from crop residues either as a replacement for petrol (as ethanol) or as fuel for power stations (as biomass). Such fuels produce far less carbon dioxide than coal or oil, and absorb as they grow. They are therefore less likely to contribute to the greenhouse effect. But they are rarely competitive with fossil unless subsidised — and growing them does no less environmental harm than other crops.

Section E

In poor countries, governments aggravate other sorts of damage. Subsidies for pesticides and artificial fertilisers encourage farmers to use greater quantities than are needed to get the highest economic crop yield. A study by the International Rice Research Institute of Pesticide Use by Farmers in South East Asia found that, with pest-resistant varieties of rice, even moderate applications of pesticide frequently cost farmers more than they saved. Such waste puts farmers on a chemical treadmill: bugs and weeds become resistant to poisons, so next year's poisons must be more lethal. One cost is to human health. Every year some 10,000 people die from pesticide poisoning, almost all of them in the developing counties, and another 400,000 become seriously ill. As for artificial fertilisers, their use world-wide increased by 40% per unit of farmed land between the mid 1970s and late 1980s, mostly in developing countries. Overuse of fertilisers may cause farmers to stop rotating crops or leaving their land fallow. That, in turn, may make soil erosion worse.

Section F

A result of the Uruguay Round of world trade negotiations is likely to be a reduction of 36% in the average levels of farm subsidies paid by the rich countries in 1986—1990. Some of the world's food production will move from Western Europe to regions where subsidies are lower or non-existent, such as the former communist countries and parts of the developing world. Some environmentalists worry about this outcome. It will undoubtedly mean more pressure to convert natural habitat into farmland. But it will also have many desirable environmental effects. The intensity of farming in the rich world should decline, and the use of chemical inputs will diminish. Crops are more likely to be grown in the environments to which they are naturally suited. And more farmers in poor countries will have the money and the incentive to manage their land in ways that are sustainable in the long run. That is important. To feed on increasingly hungry world, farmers need every incentive to use their soil and water effectively and efficiently.

Complete the table below by choosing the correct answers from the box below the table. Write your answers in the spaces given in the box.

Agricultural	**Environmental damage that may result**
● (1) ________	● Deforestation
● (2) ________	● Degraded water supply
● More intensive farming	● (3) ________
● Expansion of monoculture	● (4) ________

A Abandonment of fallow period

B Disappearance of old plant varieties

C Increased use of chemical inputs

D Increased irrigation

E Insurance against pests and diseases

F Soil erosion

G Clearing land for cultivation

【参考答案】

(1) G (2) C (3) F (4) B

5. 阅读下面这篇文章并完成后面的练习。题型与之前的练习略有不同。做完后核对答案，分析为什么做对了或做错了，并且总结出最佳解题方法。

Do Apes Ape?

Recent studies by two famous scientists show that chimpanzees and other apes can learn by imitation.

A The notion that the great apes — chimpanzees and gibbons — can imitate one another might seem unsurprising to anyone who has watched these animals playing at the zoo. But in scientific circles, the question of whether apes really do "ape" has become controversial.

B Consider a young chimpanzee watching his mother crack open a coula nut, as has been observed in the Taï Forest of West Africa. In most cases, the youth will eventually take up the practice himself. Was this because he imitated his mother? Sceptics think perhaps not. They argue that the mother's attention to the nuts encouraged the youngster to focus on them as well. Once his attention had been drawn to the food, the young chimpanzee learned how to open the nut by trial and error, not by imitating his mother.

C Such a distinction has important implications for any discussion of chimpanzee cultures. Some scientists define a cultural trait as one that is passed down not by genetic inheritance but instead when the younger generation copies adult behaviour. If cracking open a coula nut is something that chimpanzees can simply figure out how to do on their own once they hold a hammer stone, then it can't be considered part of their culture. Furthermore, if these animals learn exclusively by trial and error, then chimpanzees must, in a sense, reinvent the wheel each time they tackle a new skill. No cumulative culture can ever develop.

D The clearest way to establish how chimpanzees learn is through laboratory experiments. One of us (Whiten), in collaboration with Deborah M. Custance of Goldsmith's College, University of London, constructed artificial fruits to serve as analogues of those the animals must deal with in the wild. In a typical experiment, one group of chimpanzees watched a complex technique for opening one of the fruits, while a second group observed a very different method; we then recorded the extent to which the chimpanzees had been influenced by the method they observed. We also conducted similar experiments with three-year-old children as subjects. Our results demonstrate that six-year-old chimpanzees show imitative behaviour that is markedly like that seen in the children, although the fidelity of their copying tends to be poorer.

E In a different kind of experiment, one of us (Boesch), along with some co-workers, gave chimpanzees in the Zurich Zoo in Switzerland hammers and nuts similar to those available in the wild. We then monitored the repertoire of behaviour displayed by the captive chimpanzees. As it turned out, the chimpanzees in the zoo exhibited a greater range of activities than the more limited and focused set of actions we had seen in the wild. We interpreted this to mean that a wild chimpanzee's cultural environment channelled the behaviour of youngsters, steering them in the direction of the most useful skills. In the zoo, without the benefit of existing traditions, the chimpanzees experimented with a host of less useful actions.

F Interestingly, some of the results from the experiments involving the artificial fruits converge with this idea. In one study, chimpanzees copied an entire sequence of actions they had witnessed, but did so only after several viewings and after trying some alternatives. In other words, they tended to imitate what they had observed others doing at the expense of their own trial-and-error discoveries.

G In our view, these findings taken together suggest that apes do ape and that this ability forms one strand in cultural transmission. Indeed, it is difficult to imagine how chimpanzees could develop certain geographic variations in activities such as ant-dipping and parasite-handling without copying established traditions. They must be imitating other members of their group.

H We should note, however, that — just as is the case with humans — certain cultural traits are no doubt passed on by a combination of imitation and simpler kinds of social learning, such as having one's attention drawn to useful tools. Either way, learning from elders is crucial to growing up as a competent wild chimpanzee.

The passage has eight paragraphs labelled **A—H**. Which paragraphs contain the following information?

(1) A reference to a variety of ape activities that occur in the wild ( )

(2) The results of research on two different subject groups ( )

(3) An explanation of what opponents view as cultural behaviour ( )

(4) The research question being addressed in the passage ( )

(5) The results of research in two different environments ( )

【参考答案】

(1) G ("ant-dipping" and "parasite-handling")
(2) D ("three-year-old children" and "chimpanzees")
(3) C ("Some scientists define a cultural trait as ...")
(4) A (See the title and the first sentence.)
(5) E ("zoos" and "the wild")

说明：这类题型中有一部分涉及到提取组团信息的技巧，有关方法将在下一章中详细介绍。

13 雅思阅读九类题型分类破解——提取组团信息的题型

雅思阅读中提取组团信息的题型特点是信息覆盖面中等，但集中存在。要破解这类题型，首先要了解总体呈组团形式存在的信息中包含什么具体的内容，即说明文中每个自然段所涵盖的信息，或文中两段及两段以上所涵盖的而又相对独立于文中其他组团信息的信息。

这类题型测试考生的理解能力、提取信息的能力、区分段落中心思想与支持性信息的能力、总结能力、抓住过程和总结要点的能力等，当然同时也考查了考生运用语言的能力。

这类题型包括匹配段落大意题、示意图和流程图题、选择题、简答题、分类题和标题／短语搭配题以及摘要填空题等。

提高提取组团信息的能力是关键，建议先认真学习和研究第 2 章的内容，再进行雅思题型的练习。

13.1 匹配段落大意题

13.1.1 题型分析破解

1. 信息性质：

匹配段落大意题（Choosing from a “Heading Bank” for Identified Paragraphs / Sections of the Text）要求考生把标题与文章的各段进行匹配，其实是要考生理解各段的中心思想，并作出准确的匹配。段落由主要信息和次要信息组成，考生需要读完整段文章，才能分辨出哪个信息主要或哪个信息次要，因此此类信息的性质属于组团信息。（请参看章节 2.2，学会如何提取段落大意。）

2. 出题方式：

1）直接：标题大量引用了原文段落中的主题句或主要信息中的关键词。并不是所有的关键词都有同义词，尤其是专业名词，因此这种没有改写的标题较容易匹配。

2）间接：标题全部根据原文意思进行了改写。这种匹配较难，对考生的词汇和知识结构要求较高。

3）直接＋间接：部分标题大量使用了原文段落中的主题句或主要信息中的关键词，部分标题根据原文意思进行了改写。这种出题方式最普遍，难度相对适中。

3. 提供的标题一般多于需要匹配的段落，几乎达到 2∶1 的比例。考生不但要理解原文的段落大意（要花时间读），还要理解标题的意思，最后还要作出正确的选择，因此这类题难度相当大。每次考试十有八九会出现，可以说此类题是雅思阅读考试的重点题型。

4. 实际操作步骤：

1) 阅读题目中列出的所有标题，对文章大意有一定的了解，并试着记住标题中的关键词（至少有大致印象）。

2) 快速阅读段落。如果有主题句，就试着找出来并进行匹配。

3) 快速阅读段落。如果没有主题句，就阅读段落并自己归纳段落大意，再进行匹配。

13.1.2 练习及解析

下面就匹配段落大意题作具体的个案分析。

1. 下面这篇文章的出题方式比较直接，题目相对容易。

People and Organisations: the Selection Issue

A In 1991, according to the Department of Trade and Industry, a record 48,000 British companies went out of business. When businesses fail, the post-mortem analysis is traditionally undertaken by accountants and market strategists. Unarguably organisations do fail because of undercapitalisation, poor financial management, adverse market conditions etc. Yet, conversely, organisations with sound financial backing, good product ideas and market acumen often underperform and fail to meet shareholders' expectations. The complexity, degree and sustainment of organisational performance requires an explanation which goes beyond the balance sheet and the "paper conversion" of financial inputs into profit-making outputs. A more complete explanation of "what went wrong" necessarily must consider the essence of what an organisation actually is and that one of the financial inputs, the most important and often the most expensive, is people.

B An organisation is only as good as the people it employs. Selecting the right person for the job involves more than identifying the essential or desirable range of skills, educational and professional qualifications necessary to perform the job and then recruiting the candidate who is most likely to possess these skills or at least is perceived to have the ability and predisposition to acquire them. This is a purely person-skills match approach to selection.

C Work invariably takes place in the presence and / or under the direction of others, in a particular organisational setting. The individual has to "fit" in with the work environment, with other employees, with the organisational climate, style of work, organisation and culture of the organisation. Different organisations have different cultures. Working as an engineer at British Aerospace will not necessarily be a similar experience to working in the same capacity at GEC or Plessey.

D Poor selection decisions are expensive. For example, the costs of training a policeman are about £20,000 (approx. US$30,000). The costs of employing an unsuitable technician on an oil rig or in a nuclear plant could, in an emergency, result in millions of pounds of damage or loss of life. The disharmony of a poor person-environment fit (PE-fit) is likely to result in low job satisfaction, lack of organisational commitment and employee stress, which affect organisational outcomes i.e. productivity, high labour turnover and absenteeism, and individual outcomes i.e. physical, psychological and mental well-being.

E However, despite the importance of the recruitment decision and the range of sophisticated and more objective selection techniques available, including the use of psychometric tests, assessment centres etc., many organisations are still prepared to make this decision on the basis of a single 30 to 45 minute unstructured interview. Indeed, research has demonstrated that a selection decision is often made within the first four minutes of the interview. In the remaining time, the interviewer then attends exclusively to information that reinforces the initial "accept" or "reject" decision. Research into the validity of selection methods has consistently demonstrated that the unstructured interview, where the interviewer asks any questions he or she likes, is a poor predictor of future job performance and fares little better than more controversial methods like graphology and astrology. In times of high unemployment, recruitment becomes a "buyer's market" and this was the case in Britain during the 1980s.

F The future, we are told, is likely to be different. Detailed surveys of social and economic trends in the European Community show that Europe's population is falling and getting older. The birth rate in the Community is now only three-quarters of the level needed to ensure replacement of the existing population. By the year 2020, it is predicted that more than one in four Europeans will be aged 60 or more and barely one in five will be under 20. In a five-year period between 1983 and 1988 the Community's female workforce grew by almost six million. As a result, 51% of all women aged 14 to 64 are now economically active in the labour market compared with 78% of men.

G The changing demographics will not only affect selection ratios. They will also make it increasingly important for organisations wishing to maintain their competitive edge to be more responsive and accommodating to the changing needs of their workforce if they are to retain and develop their human resources. More flexible working hours, the opportunity to work from home or job share, the provision of childcare facilities etc., will play a major role in attracting and retaining staff in the future.

Choose the most suitable headings for paragraphs B, C, D, E and G from the list of headings below. Write the appropriate numbers (**A—J**) in the space given after each item.

Note: There are more headings than paragraphs.

List of headings

A The effect of changing demographics on organisations

B Future changes in the European workforce

C The unstructured interview and its validity

D The person-skills match approach to selection

E The implications of a poor person-environment fit

F Some poor selection decisions

G The validity of selection procedures

H The person-environment fit

I Past and future demographic changes in Europe

J Adequate and inadequate explanations of organisational failure

Example:

Paragraph A (*J*)

(1) Paragraph B (   )

(2) Paragraph C (   )

(3) Paragraph D (   )

(4) Paragraph E (   )

(5) Paragraph G (   )

【参考答案】

(1) D　(2) H　(3) E　(4) C　(5) A

分析：读完 B 段，发现 B 段的主题句是该段最后一句 This is a purely person-skills match approach to selection. 该句与选项 D 的意思相同。

读完 C 段，发现 C 段的主题句在该段中间 The individual has to "fit" in with the work environment, with other employees, with the organisational climate, style of work, organisation and culture of the organisation. 该句与选项 H 的意思相同。

读完 D 段，发现 D 段的主题句是该段最后一句 The disharmony of a poor person-environment fit (PE-fit) is likely to result in low job satisfaction, lack of organisational commitment and employee stress, which affect organisational outcomes i.e. productivity, high labour turnover and absenteeism, and individual outcomes i.e. physical, psychological and mental well-being. 该句与选项 E 的意思相符。注意，不要把第一句当作主题句，否则会错误地与选项 F 相匹配，这里突显了读完全段的重要性。

读完 E 段，知道该段谈了两件事情，即 unstructured interview 和 validity of selection methods，与选项 D 相同。

读完 G 段，发现 G 段的主题句是在该段第二句 They will also make it increasingly important for organisations wishing to maintain their competitive edge to be more responsive and accommodating to the changing needs of their workforce if they are to retain and develop their human resources. 这里的 they 指代第一句中的 the changing demographics，因此此段与选项 A 相匹配。

这几道题出得比较直接，因为涉及很多不好替代或改写的专业词汇，所以标题中重复出现文中关键词。虽然文章本身有难度，但做起来反而比较轻松。

13.1.3 专项训练

1. 下面这篇文章出题方式比较间接，相对不太容易做。按照上面的步骤完成文章后面的匹配题，关键是要用略读技巧快速读完整个段落并找出段落的主题句（如果没有主题句，要自己总结出段落大意）。做完后核对答案，再分析为什么做对了或做错了。

Looking for a Market among Adolescents

A In 1992, the most recent year for which data are available, the U.S. tobacco industry spent $5 billion on domestic marketing. That figure represents a huge increase from the approximate £250-million budget in 1971, when tobacco advertising was banned from television and radio. The current expenditure translates to about $75 for every adult smoker, or to $4,500 for every adolescent who became a smoker that year. This apparently high cost to attract a new smoker is very likely recouped over the average 25 years that this teen will smoke.

B In the first half of this century, leaders of the tobacco companies boasted that innovative mass-marketing strategies built the industry. Recently, however, the tobacco business has maintained that its advertising is geared to draw established smokers to particular brands. But public health advocates insist that such advertising plays a role in generating new demand, with adolescents being the primary target. To explore the issue, we examined several marketing campaigns undertaken over the years and correlated them with the ages smokers say they began their habit. We find that, historically, there is considerable evidence that such campaigns led to an increase in cigarette smoking among adolescents of the targeted group.

C National surveys collected the ages at which people started smoking. The 1955 Current Population Survey (CPS) was the first to query respondents for this information, although only summary data survive. Beginning in 1970, however, the National Health Interview Surveys (NHIS) included this question in some polls. Answers from all the surveys were combined to produce a sample of more than 165,000 individuals. Using a respondent's age at the time of the survey and the reported age of initiation (age they started smoking), the year the person began smoking could be determined. Dividing the number of adolescents (defined as those 12 to 17 years old) who started smoking during a particular interval by the number who were "eligible" to begin at the start of the interval set the initiation rate for that group.

D Mass-marketing campaigns began as early as the 1880s, which boosted tobacco consumption sixfold by 1900. Much of the rise was attributed to a greater number of people smoking cigarettes, as opposed to using cigars, pipes, snuff or chewing tobacco. Marketing strategies included painted billboards and an extensive distribution of coupons, which a recipient could redeem for free cigarettes. Some brands included soft-porn pictures of women in the packages. Such tactics inspired outcry from educational leaders concerned about their corrupting influence on teenage boys. Thirteen per cent of the males surveyed in 1955 who reached adolescence between 1890 and 1910 commenced smoking by 18 years of age, compared with almost no females.

E The power of targeted advertising is more apparent if one considers the men born between 1890 and 1899. In 1912, when many of these men were teenagers, the R. J. Reynolds Company launched the Camel brand of cigarettes with a revolutionary approach. Every city in the country was bombarded with print advertising. According to the 1955 CPS, initiation by age 18 for males in tiffs group jumped to 21.6%, a two thirds increase over those born before 1890. The NHIS initiation rate also reflected this change. For adolescent males it went up from 2.9% between 1910 and 1912 to 4.9% between 1918 and 1921.

F It was not until the mid-1920s that social mores permitted cigarette advertising to focus on women. In 1926 a poster depicted women imploring smokers of Chesterfield cigarettes to "Blow Some My Way". The most successful crusade, however, was for Lucky Strikes, which urged women to "Reach for a Lucky instead of a Sweet". The 1955 CPS data showed that 7% of the women who were adolescents during the mid-1920s had started smoking by age 18, compared with only 2% in the preceding generation of female adolescents. Initiation rates from the NHIS data for adolescent girls were observed to increase threefold, from 0.6% between 1922 and 1925 to 1.8% between 1930 and 1933. In contrast, rates for males rose only slightly.

G The next major boost in smoking initiation in adolescent females occurred in the late 1960s. In 1967 the tobacco industry launched "niche" brands aimed exclusively at women. The most popular was Virginia Slims. The visuals of this campaign emphasised a woman who was strong, independent and very thin. Initiation in female adolescents nearly doubled, from 3.7% between 1964 and 1967 to 6.2% between 1972 and 1975 (NHIS data). During the same period, rates for adolescent males remained stable.

H Thus, in four distinct instances over the past 100 years, innovative and directed tobacco marketing campaigns were associated with marked surges in primary demand from adolescents only in the target group. The first two were directed at males and the second two at females. Of course, other factors helped to entrench smoking in society. Yet it is clear from the data that advertising has been an overwhelming force in attracting new users.

This passage has eight paragraphs lablled **A—H**. Choose the most suitable heading for each paragraph from the list of headings below. Write the appropriate numbers (**A—K**) in the space given after each item.

List of headings

A Gathering the information

B Cigarettes produced to match an image

C Financial outlay on marketing

D The first advertising methods

E Pressure causes a drop in sales

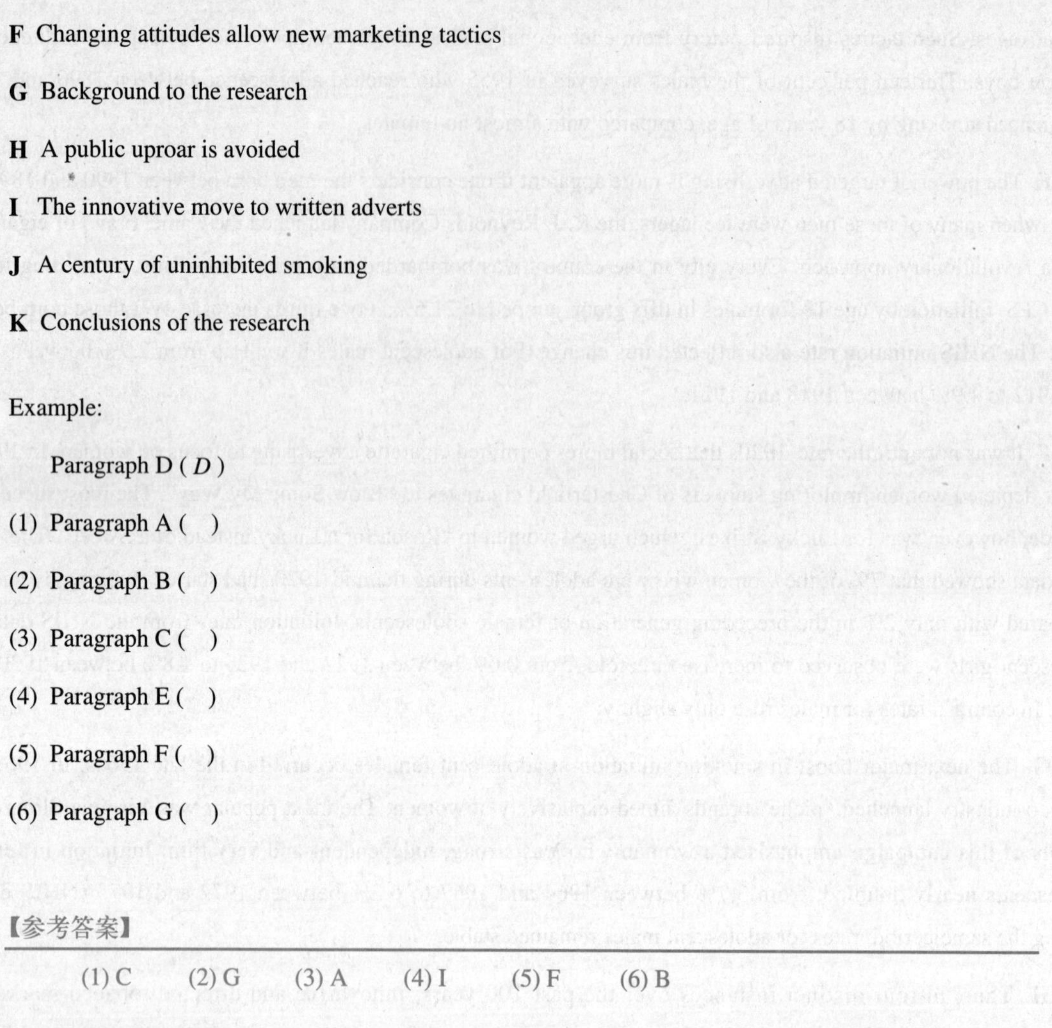

F Changing attitudes allow new marketing tactics

G Background to the research

H A public uproar is avoided

I The innovative move to written adverts

J A century of uninhibited smoking

K Conclusions of the research

Example:

Paragraph D (*D*)

(1) Paragraph A ( )

(2) Paragraph B ( )

(3) Paragraph C ( )

(4) Paragraph E ( )

(5) Paragraph F ( )

(6) Paragraph G ( )

【参考答案】

(1) C (2) G (3) A (4) I (5) F (6) B

2. 下面三篇文章的练习属于间接出题的方式，用常用词汇对原文中核心词汇进行了改写。文章全部段落的主题句都是各段的第一句。英语基础好的考生解决起来一般没问题，不过在做题时要更仔细些。

完成文章后面的匹配题，关键是要用略读技巧快速读完整个段落并找出段落的主题句。（如果没有主题句，需要自己总结出段落大意。）做完后核对答案，再分析为什么做对了或做错了。

Education for the Rural Disadvantaged

1 The vast majority of people in the developing countries live in rural areas, on farms, in villages or in rural market towns. In some countries, such as Rwanda, Burkina Faso and Malawi more than 90% of the total population lives in the rural areas.

2 The projections are that the rural populations of the less-developed countries will increase substantially in the decades to come. The U.N. predicts these will increase from 1.9 billion in 1970 to 2.6 billion by 1990. Thailand's rural population alone will increase from 30.6 million in 1970 to 570 million by the year 2000. Furthermore, because of high birth rates and declining infant mortality rates, more than half of the rural population of developing countries is under 20 years of age. This raises serious implications for education.

3 The main purpose of education is to provide everybody (not only those in urban areas) with relevant knowledge skills, attitudes and ideas which will enable them to lead more fulfilling, productive and satisfying lives. To assert that everyone has a "right" to education has little practical meaning unless this "right" is translated into terms of some "minimum package" of attitudes, knowledge and skills for all people in a given society. To do otherwise is to create a privileged class at the expense of everyone else. Vague objectives such as "giving every child a good basic education" (often defined as four to six or more years of formal schooling) are meaningless when huge sections of the population are getting little or no education at all.

4 People in rural areas suffer from inadequate educational facilities and opportunities. In most rural areas in developing countries the out-of-school group constitutes a vast majority of the whole population of, say, 10 to 20 years old. For all practical purposes, they are beyond the reach of formal education. But no section of the community should be shortchanged by its educational system.

5 Where there are rural primary schools they benefit far fewer rural young people than educational statistics often imply. Primary schools, instead of being the great equalisers of educational opportunity they were meant to be, are the great discriminators. In the rural areas they equip only a small minority of the young for effective and satisfying adulthood. The great majority of rural youngsters are destined to live out the all-too-familiar grind of ignorance and poverty.

6 This vicious circle has to be broken; the goal must be to provide everybody with basic knowledge and skills. Rather than attempt to enroll every child for a seven- or eight-year cycle of primary schooling, which is not financially feasible anyway for many countries for many years to come, the strategy should be a shorter four- to five-year primary cycle to provide every child with the minimum educational needs — literacy, numeracy, health education and those technical and entrepreneurial skills needed to make a decent living. This primary education should be geared for the large majority who will not continue their studies beyond this stage, who will enter straight into productive life.

The passage has six paragraphs. For each paragraph, choose the best heading from the list **A—I** below, and write the letter in the space given after each item. There are more headings than you need. The first one has been done as an example.

List of headings

A Insufficient access to education

B Rural poverty

C Rural populations of developing countries

D Realistic aims

E Education in developing countries

F Rural primary education for the few

G Educational ideals

H Financing education

I A view of the future

Example:

Paragraph 1 (*C*)

(1) Paragraph 2 (   )

(2) Paragraph 3 (   )

(3) Paragraph 4 (   )

(4) Paragraph 5 (   )

(5) Paragraph 6 (   )

【参考答案】

(1) I (2) G (3) A (4) F (5) D

Stay Awake, Stay Alive

Section 1

Sleep laboratories around the world are finding that an alarming number of drivers on motorways may be falling asleep at the wheel. Although researchers have difficulty in knowing for certain whether an accident has been caused by sleepiness, it appears that a driver who is on the road between 4:00 am and 6:00 am is about 10 times as likely to have a sleep-related accident as someone who is driving in the middle of the morning or early in the evening. Some British police forces have become sufficiently concerned to launch campaigns to alert the public to the danger. Leicestershire police, for example, consider sleepiness to be the cause of 20% of accidents on motorways and in the summer of 1990 ran a campaign with the slogan "Stay Awake, Stay Alive". Major motor manufacturers such as Ford and Renault are investigating ways of incorporating sleepiness detectors and alarms into their vehicles.

Section 2

However, British government bodies responsible for road safety have not initiated any studies into the problem of sleepy drivers on motorways. The Department of Transport claims that it is "aware of the problems", but does not regard it as a high-priority issue and is not planning to support any relevant research apart from a general study on "driver behaviour". The department has no figures on the number of accidents caused by driver sleepiness and says it doubts whether reliable statistics can ever be obtained.

Section 3

Unfortunately, the issue is clouded by the fact that many motorway accidents that might be caused by sleepiness are categorised under other headings, such as "inattention", "failed to look or see other vehicle" and "misjudged speed / distance". Figures collected in the 1970s by the Transport and Road Research Laboratory list the cause of 20% of all road accidents as "perceptual errors". "Fatigue" was specified in only 2% of cases. However, few investigators inquire further to discover just why a driver was not attending, failed to look or made errors in perception. For various reasons, including the fear of prosecution and possible difficulties with insurance claims, drivers are reluctant to admit to falling asleep, but are more willing to admit to "inattention". When these rather vague responses are examined thoroughly, sleepiness often emerges as the true culprit.

Section 4

Driving on a road as dull as a motorway exacerbates sleepiness in a driver who is already sleepy. But how can we tell if an accident on a motorway has been caused by sleepiness? There are some very strong pointers. If an accident involves only one vehicle, which runs off the road into the central crash harder, the embankment, a tree or a bridge, then sleepiness is likely to be the cause, especially if there are no skid marks or other signs of braking. A driver who is alert to an impending crash grips the steering wheel and suffers different injuries from someone who is asleep and holding the steering wheel loosely. This pattern of injury, combined with an absence of skid marks on the road, also suggests that the driver was asleep in accidents where one vehicle runs into the back of another, especially if it occurs where traffic is light and vehicles are consequently well-spaced on the road. Under these conditions, the driver's "inattention" must have been more than just momentary.

The passage is divided into four sections. From the list of headings (**A**—**G**) below, choose the best heading for each section and write the corresponding letter in the space given after each item. There are more headings than you need.

List of headings

A Unreliable data

B Sleeping while driving

C Government investigations

D Motorway accidents

E Identifying sleep-related accidents

F The reluctance of drivers to talk

G Lack of government support

(1) Section 1 ( )

(2) Section 2 ( )

(3) Section 3 ( )

(4) Section 4 ( )

【参考答案】

(1) B (2) G (3) A (4) E

Tourism

A Tourism, holiday-making and travel are these days more significant social phenomena than most commentators have considered. On the face of it there could not be a more trivial subject for a book. And indeed since social scientists have had considerable difficulty explaining weightier topics, such as work or politics, it might be thought that they would have great difficulties in accounting for more trivial phenomena such as holiday-making. However, there are interesting parallels with the study of deviance. This involves the investigation of bizarre and idiosyncratic social practices which happen to be defined as deviant in some societies but not necessarily in others. The assumption is that the investigation of deviance can reveal interesting and significant aspects of "normal" societies. It could be said that a similar analysis can be applied to tourism.

B Tourism is a leisure activity which presupposes its opposite namely regulated and organised work. It is one manifestation of how work and leisure are organised as separate and regulated spheres of social practice in modern societies. Indeed acting as a tourist is one of the defining characteristics of being "modern" and the popular concept of tourism is that it is organised within particular places and occurs for regularised periods of time. Tourist relationships arise from a movement of people to, and their stay in, various destinations. This necessarily involves some movement that is the journey and a period of stay in a new place or places. The journey and the stay are by definition outside the normal places of residence and work and are of a short-term and temporary nature and there is a clear intention to return "home" within a relatively short period of time.

C A substantial proportion of the population of modern societies engages in such tourist practices; new socialised forms of provision have developed in order to cope with the mass character of the gazes of tourists, as opposed to the individual character of travel. Places are chosen to be visited and be gazed upon because there is an anticipation, especially through daydreaming and fantasy, of intense pleasures, either on a different scale or involving different senses from those customarily encountered. Such anticipation is constructed and sustained through a variety of non-tourist practices, such as films, TV, literature, magazines, records and videos which construct and reinforce this daydreaming.

D Tourists tend to visit features of landscape and townscape which separate them off from everyday experience. Such aspects are viewed because they are taken to be in some sense out of the ordinary. The viewing of these tourist sights often involves different forms of social patterning, with a much greater sensitivity to visual elements of landscape or townscape than is normally found in everyday life. People linger over these sights in a way that they would not normally do in their home environment and the vision is objectified or captured through photographs, postcards, films and so on which enable the memory to be endlessly reproduced and recaptured.

E One of the earliest dissertations on the subject of tourism is Boorstin's analysis of the "pseudo-event" (1964) where he argues that contemporary Americans cannot experience "reality" directly but thrive on "pseudo-events". Isolated from the host environment and the local people, the mass tourist travels in guided groups and finds pleasure in inauthentic contrived attractions, gullibly enjoying the pseudo-events and disregarding the real world outside. Over time the images generated of different tourist sights come to constitute a closed self-perpetuating system of illusions which provide the tourist with the basis for selecting and evaluating potential places to visit. Such visits are made, says Boorstin, within the "environmental bubble" of the familiar American-style hotel which insulates the tourist from the strangeness of the host environment.

F To service the burgeoning tourist industry, an array of professionals has developed who attempt to reproduce ever-new objects for the tourist to look at. These objects or places are located in a complex and changing hierarchy. This depends upon the interplay between, on the one hand, competition between interests involved in the provision of such objects and, on the other hand, changing class, gender, and generational distinctions of taste within the potential population of visitors. It has been said that to be a tourist is one of the characteristics of the "modern experience". Not to "go away" is like not possessing a car or a nice house. Travel is a marker of status in modern societies and is also thought to be necessary for good health. The role of the professional, therefore, is to cater for the needs and tastes of the tourists in accordance with their class and overall expectations

The passage has 6 paragraphs lablled **A—F**. Choose the most suitable heading for each paragraph from the list of headings below. Write the appropriate numbers (**A—I**) in the space given after each item. Paragraph D has been done for you as an example.

List of headings

A The politics of tourism

B The cost of tourism

C Justifying the study of tourism

D Tourism contrasted with travel

E The essence of modern tourism

F Tourism versus leisure

G The artificiality of modern tourism

H The role of modern tour guides

I Creating an alternative to the everyday experience

Example:

Paragraph D (*I*)

(1) Paragraph A ( )

(2) Paragraph B ( )

(3) Paragraph C ( )

(4) Paragraph E ( )

(5) Paragraph F ( )

【参考答案】

(1) C (2) E (3) D (4) G (5) H

13.2 示意图和流程图题

13.2.1 题型分析破解

示意图和流程图题（Diagram and Flow Chart Completion）的信息在媒体文章中以组团形式呈现。因为媒体文章要面向大众，不能过于专业。面面俱到是这类文章的特点之一。在考试中根据一篇文章从头到尾绘制出一个示意图或流程图的情况非常罕见。

这些图形的信息一般在文中覆盖半段、一段或两段（也有例外，后面会谈到），并以组团形式出现，相对孤立于文本中的其他组团信息。了解了这点，就可以设计出基本的解题方法。

解题方法：建议先用寻读技巧快速定位，把有关图形信息的组团从文本中分离出来，其他的组团可暂且不管。然后快速阅读此组团以获得初步的印象，最后细读每一句以获得信息，完成填空。这是多种阅读技巧的综合和灵活运用。

这种方法可以总结为一个公式：scanning + skimming + careful reading。

下面分别具体分析流程图题和示意图题。

13.2.2 流程图练习及解析

流程图题型的出题方式分为两类：

1）按文本中组团信息的文字叙述顺序绘出（主要考语言之内的能力）。

2）按文本中组团信息的文字逻辑顺序绘出（主要考语言之外的能力，如逻辑分析能力）。

1. 下面这篇文章的流程图属于第一种出题方式——按文本中组团信息的文字叙述顺序绘出。

Falling Asleep

What happens when you are falling asleep? As sleepiness increases, a glazed look comes over the eyes, visual awareness declines and "eye-rolling" begins. The eyes roll up under the slowly closing eyelids, which then slowly open and the eyes roll back down again. One complete eye-roll lasts about two seconds, and is usually followed immediately by another. Such events are called "microsleeps" where consciousness is clouding and the brain is losing contact with reality. It is possible to snap out of this state for a while. Drivers can open the car windows, turn up the radio and sing a song in the hope that all this stimulation will overcome the sleepiness. But for anyone who is really sleepy, such countermeasures are seldom effective for more than a few minutes. Microsleeps and eye-rolling reappear, maybe lasting for many seconds, interspersed with short bursts of greater alertness. Successive microsleeps get longer until true sleep sets in and the head lolls forward, causing, with luck, a startled awakening.

A driver having microsleeps is still vaguely aware of the road but is likely to misperceive events ahead. Limited driving skills can be maintained to keep the vehicle on a fairly straight course or carry out simple steering manoeuvres. Nevertheless, the vehicle may begin to drift sideways and foot-pressure on the accelerator may relax, causing the vehicle to slow down. The driver may still seem to be in control, but as microsleeps particularly impair vision, the immediate danger is one of collision or running off the road. Sleepy drivers tend to drive more slowly, anyway, and try to keep in the slow lane. When the vehicle drifts sideways the main risk is collision with a stationary vehicle on the hard shoulder.

It is known that the brain's 24-hour clock is set to bring sleep twice a day: at night, and in the early afternoon. The early afternoon is therefore a time that can produce a marked feeling of sleepiness, and this is not due to eating lunch. This is the period when sleep-related accidents reach their daytime peak. Many cultures, especially in hot countries, have bowed to the inevitable and adopted the siesta as a way of life. The time of greatest alertness, on the other hand, is in the early evening. Alcohol interacts with this daily rhythm to worsen afternoon sleepiness, which is why many people find that even two units of alcohol (equivalent to a pint of beer) at lunchtime have a strongly soporific effect. While this alcohol intake is unlikely to push drivers over the legal limit, a study showed that at this time of day it clearly impaired simulated motorway driving. The same alcohol intake in the early evening has the same effect on blood alcohol level but can go almost unnoticed, and driving will be less affected. This suggests there is a strong case for setting a lower legal blood alcohol limit for the early afternoon compared with that for the early evening. The more sleepy drivers are feeling, the more alcohol affects them. Tranquillisers can also be soporific, especially at the vulnerable times of the day. Little is known about whether they present a problem for monotonous driving, although many sleep researchers believe they do.

Complete the flow chart below with words from the passage. You should use ONE or TWO words for each answer. Write your answer in the space given.

Alcohol intake works together with *daily rhythm*.

↓

Increased sleepiness if drinking at ______(1)______.

↓

Deterioration in ______(2)______ ability.

↓

Comparison with evening: alcohol has ______(3)______ effect on blood,

______(4)______ effect on driving.

Argument for change in legal limit of ______(5)______.

【参考答案】

(1) lunchtime (2) (motorway) driving (3) (the) same

(4) less (5) blood alcohol

分析：实际解题顺序是：先读流程图的第一步 Alcohol intake works together with daily rhythm. 记住关键词，然后用寻读技巧在文本中快速搜寻，发现 alcohol, daily, rhythm 等关键词在第三段中间出现，在这里做个记号，表明此组团信息由此开始。再读流程图最后一步 Argument for change in legal limit of ______. 记住关键词，然后在组团信息开始的地方继续往下搜寻定位，发现相关信息在此段的倒数第四句，由此表明整个流程图组团信息到此为止。最后细读这中间的每一句，与流程图每一步作比较，进行解答。

注意：这个流程图的题型与完成句子题的填空题型有机地结合在一起了，从中可以看出雅思阅读题型的灵活性。

2. 下面这篇文章的流程图属于第二种出题方式——按文本中组团信息的文字逻辑顺序绘出。

Road Technology since the Romans

Important principles of road building were known to the Romans. How has technology developed since then?

1 Between 43 A.D. and 81 A.D. Roman Britain acquired a 6,000 kilometres network, of technically advanced, hard wearing and straight highways linking towns of importance. Today Britain's motorway system is only half that length; the basic Roman philosophy of building a road to cope with different types and volumes of vehicles and using local materials where possible still applies today.

2 Roman roads were cambered with ditches on either side and built on embankments to give them a properly drained base. A surfacing layer of small stones was used over gravel or larger stones, although some Roman roads were covered with large paving flags, which is where the term "pavement" originates.

3 Once the Romans left Britain, its roads fell into ruin through tack of maintenance. They became run down, dusty highways in the summer and quagmires in the winter. It seems that the next milestone in the history of roads was not until the 18th and 19th centuries, with the advent of the Turnpike Trust. This raised cash for necessary maintenance in local areas to cope with the increasing numbers of wheeled vehicles, coaches and carriages wishing to travel at faster speeds.

4 In 1816 John McAdam observed that it was the native soil that supported the weight of traffic which, when dry, would carry any weight without sinking. He advised that the native soil be made dry and a covering impenetrable to rain be placed over it. However, road maintenance was not given much priority due to the popularity of the railways, until the motor car superseded the horse and cart. Cars, however, accentuated the problem of dust, described by the medical journal *The Lancet* in 1907 as "the greatest modern plague".

5 Like so many other scientific advances, the solution came by accident. Tar mixed with stone had been used in footpaths in certain parts of Britain in 1832, and tarred gravel was applied to roads in Nottingham in 1869, but the biggest breakthrough came in 1901. A surveyor called E. Purnell Hooley was visiting Denby Iron Works near Derby when he noticed a dust-free length of road produced by a burst tar barrel. The resulting pool of tar had been covered with ironworks slag. Hooley experimented with blending hot slag and tar as a by-product from the coal industry and in 1902 patented the process produced by a company known as Tar MacAdam Syndicate Ltd. The company's name was later changed to Tarmac.

6 Nowadays, blacktop materials are made up of bitumen from oil which is blended with rock, gravel or slag. A number of varieties have evolved for different uses in road construction, including hot-rolled asphalt for surfacing major roads, dense bitumen macadam for lower layers of a road and open-textured macadam. Modern surfaces are bituminous-bound, graded stone supplied as a premix. Binders themselves have undergone technical developments. They are customised, ranging from soft to very hard to suit the traffic flow.

7 To accommodate higher traffic levels, either the thickness of the road must be increased or the materials improved. Hence the introduction within the last 10 years of heavy duty macadam in the road base which is three times as stiff as the dense bitumen and aggregrate mix.

8 Alternatively, the structural design can be changed. For example, on an experimental reconstruction section of the M6 at Bescot, West Midlands, the heavy duty "upside-down design" was introduced in the 1980s. Here, rolled asphalt overlays a thinner than normal road-base macadam, over a second rolled asphalt layer, all of which lie on a sub-base which is again thinner than normal. This structure is thought to perform well due to the lower rolled asphalt layer being more resistant to deformation and inhibiting cracking at the bottom of the road base.

9 Another innovative idea is the use of geotextiles. In research geotextiles are being placed between the sub-grade soil and a drainage layer beneath the sub-base. The sub-grade material is often clay and in the absence of the geotextile could, over time, clog the sub-base and reduce its efficiency as a drainage layer. But geotextiles can also have structural uses, and could provide improved resistance to cracking arid rutting in roads.

1) The flow chart below represents the four stages in "the next milestone in the history of roads" mentioned in paragraph 3. For each of the missing stages, match the new problem, action taken and result with the sentences in the boxes below. Write only one letter in each space.

New problem	Body set up	Action taken	Result
(1) ______	formation of the Turnpike Trust	(2) ______	(3) ______

A Roads became run down

B Cash was raised

C Lack of maintenance

D Increasing numbers of wheeled vehicles wanting to go at higher speeds

E Maintenance of roads in local areas

【参考答案】

(1) D　　(2) B　　(3) E

分析：实际解题顺序是：先读懂题目的要求。题目告诉我们，只需关注第三段最后两句，这样就可以避免错选 A 项"Roads became run down"和 C 项"Lack of maintenance"，因为这两个信息出现在第三段的前面两句。这表明了仔细阅读题目要求的重要性。再细读这最后两句，思考它们之间的逻辑关系，发现新问题出现在原文 cope with 后——因为需要处理的正是之前出现的问题。因此按照逻辑，选项 D"Increasing numbers of wheeled vehicles wanting to go at higher speeds"应填入第一个空。后面的题就好做了，按照逻辑，成立公司是解决问题的方法之一，接下来就需要公司筹集资金来维修和保养当地的道路。

注意：这个流程图的题型与标题搭配题型有机地结合在了一起，从中可看出雅思阅读题型的灵活性。

2) Which diagram best illustrates Roman roads? Write A, B, C, or D in the space provided.

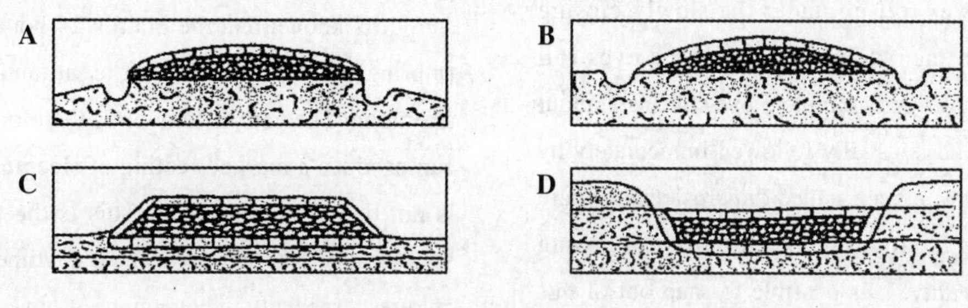

Your answer ( )

【参考答案】

A

这道题属于示意图题。具体做题方法会在下一节中详细讲解。

13.2.3 示意图练习及解析

示意图包括了很多类型的图表，有实物图、循环图、实物图与坐标图的混合和各种平面图等，不一而足，变化极大。因此，提高分析图表的能力就显得尤为重要。只有看懂了图表，才能进一步思考要从文章中提取什么信息填入图表中。这是雅思考试的一大优点，即通过复习考试提高考生的读图能力，以适应以后的学习和社会生活。

这类题型具体的解题方法如 13.2.1 中所述，是 scanning + skimming + careful reading。

下面就不同的示意图题型进行具体分析。

上一节第二篇文章 Road Technology since the Romans 的第二题是示意图与选择题的有机结合。不管题型怎样变化，解题的基本原则不变。

具体的解题步骤是：先用寻读技巧把描述罗马道路怎样修建的组团信息与其他组团信息分隔定位。略读后发现原文第二段整段都是谈罗马道路的具体修建步骤，细读这一段并作出判断，选择 A 图。

1. 下面这篇文章后面的图例也是示意图的一种。解题时先作分析，抓住关键问题，才能做到又快又准。

Falling Asleep

What happens when you are falling asleep? As sleepiness increases, a glazed look comes over the eyes, visual awareness declines and "eye-rolling" begins. The eyes roll up under the slowly closing eyelids, which then slowly open and the eyes roll back down again. One complete eye-roll lasts about two seconds, and is usually followed immediately by another. Such events are called "microsleeps" where consciousness is clouding and the brain is losing contact with reality. It is possible to snap out of this state for a while. Drivers can open the car windows, turn up the radio and sing a song in the hope that all this stimulation will overcome the sleepiness. But for anyone who is really sleepy, such countermeasures are seldom effective for more than a few minutes. Microsleeps and eye-rolling reappear, maybe lasting for many seconds, interspersed with short bursts of greater alertness. Successive microsleeps get longer until true sleep sets in and the head lolls forward, causing, with luck, a startled awakening.

A driver having microsleeps is still vaguely aware of the road but is likely to misperceive events ahead. Limited driving skills can be maintained to keep the vehicle on a fairly straight course or carry out simple steering manoeuvres. Nevertheless, the vehicle may begin to drift sideways and foot-pressure on the accelerator may relax, causing the vehicle to slow down. The driver may still seem to be in control, but as microsleeps particularly impair vision, the immediate danger is one of collision or running off the road. Sleepy drivers tend to drive more slowly, anyway, and try to keep in the slow lane. When the vehicle drifts sideways the main risk is collision with a stationary vehicle on the hard shoulder.

It is known that the brain's 24-hour clock is set to bring sleep twice a day: at night, and in the early afternoon. The early afternoon is therefore a time that can produce a marked feeling of sleepiness, and this is not due to eating lunch. This is the period when sleep-related accidents reach their daytime peak. Many cultures, especially in hot countries, have bowed to the inevitable and adopted the siesta as a way of life. The time of greatest alertness, on the other hand, is in the early evening. Alcohol interacts with this daily rhythm to worsen afternoon sleepiness, which is why many people find that even two units of alcohol (equivalent to a pint of beer) at lunchtime have a strongly soporific effect. While this alcohol intake is unlikely to push drivers over the legal limit, a study showed that at this time of day it clearly impaired simulated motorway driving. The same alcohol intake in the early evening has the same effect on blood alcohol level but can go almost unnoticed, and driving will be less affected. This suggests there is a strong case for setting a lower legal blood alcohol limit for the early afternoon compared with that for the early evening. The more sleepy drivers are feeling, the more alcohol affects them. Tranquillisers can also be soporific, especially at the vulnerable times of the day. Little is known about whether they present a problem for monotonous driving, although many sleep researchers believe they do.

Complete the diagram below by selecting a maximum of four words from the text for each answer. Write your answer in the spaces given.

Effects on eyes	Temporary countermeasures
(example) glazed look (1) ________ (2) ________	(3) ________ (4) ________

MICROSLEEPS AND DRIVERS

Effects on vehicle	Possible accidents
(5) ________ (6) ________	(7) ________ (8) ________

【参考答案】

(1) visual awareness declines (2) eye-rolling begins (3) open the windows
(4) turn up the radio / sing a song (5) drift sideways (6) slow down
(7) collision (8) running off the road

分析：这个示意图与罗马的道路图截然不同，建议先抓中间小方格中的两个关键词 microsleeps 和 drivers，因为中间这个方格影响外围四个方格的内容。换句话说，外围四个方格内的信息围绕着这两个关键词的信息，那么这两个词的上下文中就必然能找到与答案相关的信息。因此先用寻读技巧搜索，发现这两个词在原文第一段和第二段都出现过，也就是说这个图的信息覆盖了两段，于是就确定了大致范围。由于四个大方格里有不少文中的关键词，因此可以充分地利用寻读技巧更快地完成各方格内信息的定位，然后阅读上下文提取相应信息填空。

2. 下面这篇文章的示意图与上一篇文章的截然不同，这是一个蜂箱的实物图。这篇文章与养蜂有关。每个人刚一开始接触一个完全不熟悉的专业都会感到束手无措。考考自己的智慧与能力，结合 scanning + skimming + careful reading 的技巧，看能否又快又准地找出解决办法。

Migratory Beekeeping

Of the 2,000 commercial beekeepers in the United States about half migrate. This pays off in two ways. Moving north in the summer and south in the winter lets bees work a longer blooming season, making more honey — and money — for their keepers. Second, beekeepers can carry their hives to farmers who need bees to pollinate their crops. Every spring a migratory beekeeper in California may move up to 160 million bees to flowering fields in Minnesota and every winter his family may haul the hives back to California, where farmers will rent the bees to pollinate almond and cherry trees.

Migratory beekeeping is nothing new. The ancient Egyptians moved clay hives, probably on rafts, down the Nile to follow the bloom and nectar flow as it moved toward Cairo. In the 1880s North American beekeepers experimented with the same idea, moving bees on barges along the Mississippi and on waterways in Florida, but their lighter, wooden hives kept falling into the water. Other keepers tried the railroad and horse-drawn wagons, but that didn't prove practical. Not until the 1920s when cars and trucks became affordable and roads improved, did migratory beekeeping begin to catch on.

For the Californian beekeeper, the pollination season begins in February. At this time, the beehives are in particular demand by farmers who have almond groves; they need two hives an acre. For the three-week long bloom, beekeepers can hire out their hives for $32 each. It's a bonanza for the bees, too. Most people consider almond honey too bitter to eat so the bees get to keep it for themselves.

By early March it is time to move the bees. It can take up to seven nights to pack the 4,000 or so hives that a beekeeper may own. These are not moved in the middle of the day because too many of the bees would end up homeless. But at night, the hives are stacked onto wooden pallets, back-to-back in sets of four, and lifted onto a truck. It is not necessary to wear gloves or a beekeeper's veil because the hives are not being opened and the bees should remain relatively quiet. Just in case some are still lively, bees can be pacified with a few puffs of smoke blown into each hive's narrow entrance.

In their new location, the beekeeper will pay the farmer to allow his bees to feed in such places as orange groves. The honey produced here is fragrant and sweet and can be sold by the beekeepers. To encourage the bees to produce as much honey as possible during this period, the beekeepers open the hives and stack extra boxes called *supers* on top. These temporary hive extensions contain frames of empty comb for the bees to fill with honey. In the brood chamber below, the bees will stash honey to eat later. To prevent the queen from crawling up to the top and laying eggs, a screen can be inserted between the brood chamber and the supers. Three weeks later the honey can be gathered.

Foul smelling chemicals are often used to irritate the bees and drive them down into the hive's bottom boxes, leaving the honey-filled supers more or less bee free. These can then be pulled off the hive. They are heavy with honey and may weigh up to 90 pounds each. The supers are taken to a warehouse. In the extracting room, the frames are lifted out and lowered into an "uncapper" where rotating blades shave away the wax that covers each cell. The uncapped frames are put in it carousel that sits on the bottom of a large stainless steel drum. The carousel is filled to capacity with 72 frames. A switch is flipped and the frames begin to whirl at 300 revolutions per minute; centrifugal force throws the honey out of the combs. Finally the honey is poured into barrels for shipment.

After this, approximately a quarter of the hives weakened by disease, mites, or an ageing or dead queen will have to be replaced. To create new colonies, a healthy double hive, teeming with bees, can be separated into two boxes. One half will hold the queen and a young, already mated queen can be put in the other half, to make two hives from one. By the time the flowers bloom, the new queens will be laying eggs, filling each hive with young worker bees. The beekeeper's family will then migrate with them to their summer location.

Label the diagram below. Choose ONE or TWO words from the passage for each answer. Write your answers in the space given.

A BEEHIVE

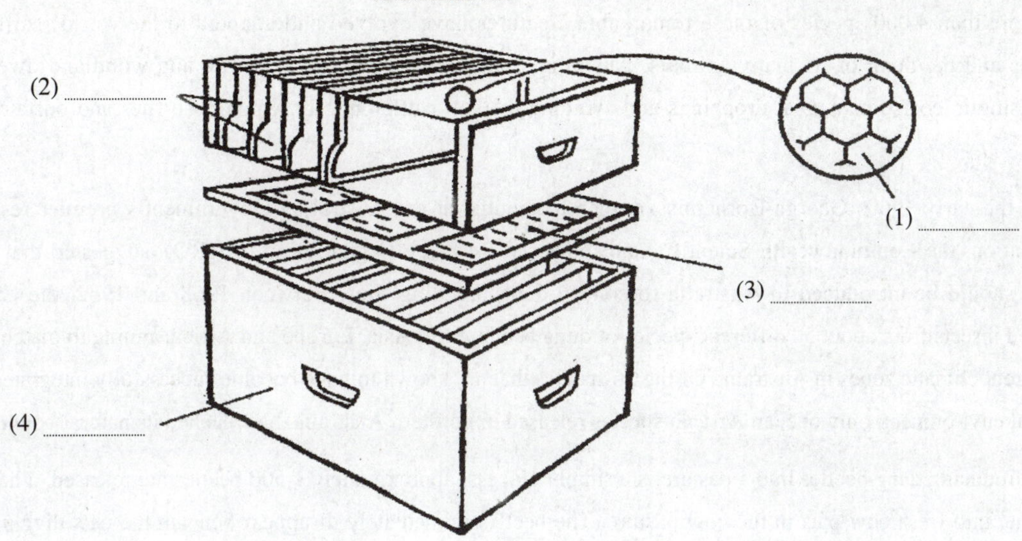

【参考答案】

(1) comb / cells (2) frames (3) screen (4) brood chamber

分析：上图是根据文章内容绘出的。由于考生不熟悉养蜂业，而且整个图没有提供关键词，凭借图无从知道各部分的专业名称，因此会感觉此题很难入手。

这里提供一种解题方法，看看是否与你的方法一样。先看图：这个蜂箱由三层组成，形成了“上、中、下”的关系，由此可以推断出原文的描述必然离不开表示方位关系的名词，如 top，middle，bottom 等，还有表示方位的介词，如 on，between，under，beneath，below 或 in 等，可能还会用到 box，boxes 等名词。想着这几个词，用寻读技巧就可以很快定位，把描述蜂箱的文字组团与其他组团分离开来。整段描述出现在第五段的中间到该段的倒数第二句。细读这几句话，读懂、读透之后问题也就迎刃而解了。

注意：做题的时候还必须细心看图，尤其是第二个空，线条指向箱子内部的片状物，因上题目要求填写这些片状物的名称，而不是这个箱子的名称。

3. 下面这篇文章的示意图与上一篇文章的又有所不同，是实物图与坐标图的混合图。考考自己的智慧与能力，结合 scanning + skimming + careful reading 的技巧，看能否又快又准地找出解决办法。

A Remarkable Beetle

Some of the most remarkable beetles are the dung beetles, which spend almost their whole lives eating and breeding in dung.

More than 4,000 species of these remarkable creatures have evolved and adapted to the world's different climates and the dung of its many animals. Australia's native dung beetles are scrub and woodland dwellers, specialising in coarse marsupial droppings and avoiding the soft cattle dung in which bush flies and buffalo flies breed.

In the early 1960s George Bornemissza, then a scientist at the Australian Government's premier research organisation, the Commonwealth Scientific and Industrial Research Organisation (CSIRO), suggested that dung beetles should be introduced to Australia to control dung-breeding flies. Between 1968 and 1982, the CSIRO imported insects from about 50 different species of dung beetle, from Asia, Europe and Africa, aiming to match them to different climatic zones in Australia. Of the 26 species that are known to have become successfully integrated into the local environment, only one, an African species released in northern Australia, has reached its natural boundary.

Introducing dung beetles into a pasture is a simple process: approximately 1,500 beetles are released, a handful at a time, into fresh cow pats in the cow pasture. The beetles immediately disappear beneath the pats digging and tunnelling and, if they successfully adapt to their new environment, soon become a permanent, self-sustaining part of the local ecology. In time they multiply and within three or four years the benefits to the pasture are obvious.

Dung beetles work from the inside of the pat so they are sheltered from predators such as birds and foxes. Most species burrow into the soil and bury dung in tunnels directly underneath the pats, which are hollowed out from within. Some large species originating from France excavate tunnels to a depth of approximately 30 centimetres below the dung pat. These beetles make sausage-shaped brood chambers along the tunnels. The shallowest tunnels belong to a much smaller Spanish species that buries dung in chambers that hang like fruit from the branches of a pear tree. South African beetles dig narrow tunnels of approximately 20 centimetres below the surface of the pat. Some surface-dwelling beetles, including a South African species, cut perfectly-shaped balls from the pat, which are rolled away and attached to the bases of plants.

For maximum dung burial in spring, summer and autumn, farmers require a variety of species with overlapping periods of activity. In the cooler environments of the state of Victoria, the large French species (2.5 centimetres long) is matched with smaller (half this size), temperate-climate Spanish species. The former are slow to recover from the winter cold and produce only one or two generations of offspring from late spring until autumn. The latter, which multiply rapidly in early spring, produce two to five generations annually. The South African ball-rolling species, being a subtropical beetle, prefers the climate of northern and coastal New South Wales where it commonly works with the

South African tunnelling species. In warmer climates, many species are active for longer periods of the year.

Dung beetles were initially introduced in the late 1960s with a view to controlling buffalo flies by removing the dung within a day or two and so preventing flies from breeding. However, other benefits have become evident. Once the beetle larvae have finished pupation, the residue is a first-rate source of fertiliser. The tunnels abandoned by the beetles provide excellent aeration and water channels for root systems. In addition, when the new generation of beetles has left the nest the abandoned burrows are an attractive habitat for soil-enriching earthworms. The digested dung in these burrows is an excellent food supply for the earthworms, which decompose it further to provide essential soil nutrients. If it were not for the dung beetle, chemical fertiliser and dung would be washed by rain into streams and rivers before it could be absorbed into the hard earth, polluting water courses and causing blooms of blue-green algae. Without the beetles to dispose of the dung, cow pats would litter pastures making grass inedible to cattle and depriving the soil of sunlight. Australia's 30 million cattle each produce 10—12 cow pats a day. This amounts to 1.7 billion tonnes a year, enough to smother about 110,000 square kilometres of pasture, half the area of Victoria.

Dung beetles have become an integral part of the successful management of dairy farms in Australia over the past few decades. A number of species are available from the CSIRO or through a small number of private breeders, most of whom were entomologists with the CSIRO's dung beetle unit who have taken their specialised knowledge of the insect and opened small businesses in direct competition with their former employer.

Label the tunnels on the diagram below. Choose your labels from the list below the diagram. Write your answers in the spaces given.

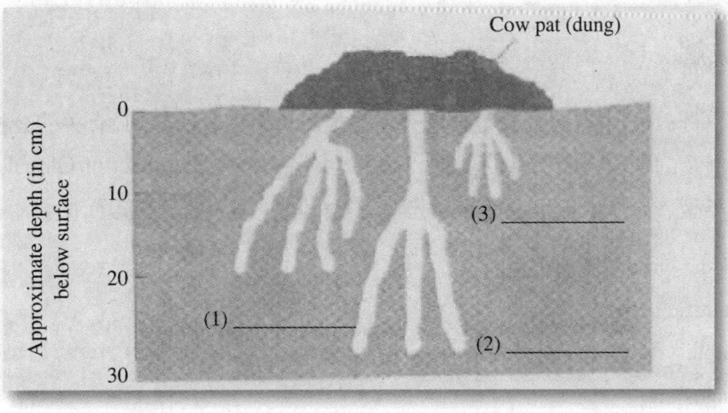

Dung beetle type

French　　Spanish

Mediterranean　　South African

Australian native　　South African ball roller

【参考答案】

(1) South African　(2) French　(3) Spanish

分析：根据坐标所示数字，用寻读技巧很快定位在第五段的中间部分，马上就可以提取信息。

注意：数字 10 在原文中并没出现，但当三者以上进行比较时，一定要用到形容词最高级，因此与 20 centimetres 和 30 centimetres 相比原文中的 the shallowest tunnels 指的就是 10 centimetres。

以上几题反映出此类题型的多样性。做这类题时一定要保持头脑非常清醒。建议平常训练时先分析图形特征，找到突破点之后再动手做题。

掌握基本的解题方法（scanning + skimming + careful reading）的同时，还要根据实际情况灵活处理。如果图中有足够的关键词（包括阿拉伯数字），就可以用寻读技巧更快地完成；如果图中没有任何关键词（如第二篇文章 Migratory Beekeeping），就要自己联想出相应的或其他有关的关键词进行组团信息定位。总之，多动脑筋能力就会提高，才能适应各种变化的题型，这也是雅思考试对考生的要求之一。

13.3 选择题

13.3.1 题型分析破解

选择题（Multiple Choice）中有一部分是要考查考生提取单个信息的能力，有关的分析讲解详见第 12 章。本节要谈谈这类题型涉及的提取组团信息的部分。12.5.2 中第二篇文章 Impact of Global Warming on Climate 的第一题就属于这个类型。要作出正确选择必须先读完第一段，因为信息覆盖面扩大了很多。请看原题：

1) In Paragraph 1 the writer is ________.

A rejecting a scientific belief

B giving an example

C reaching a conclusion

D defending a theory

问题问的是作者在文章第一段写了什么，因此必须读完原文第一段才能知道答案。这就涉及提取组团信息的阅读技巧：灵活运用基本的解题方法 scanning + skimming + careful reading。

13.3.2 练习及解析

下面就具体的选择题进行分析。

The Pursuit of Happiness

New research uncovers some anti-intuitive insights into how many people are happy — and why.

Compared with misery, happiness is relatively unexplored terrain for social scientists. Between 1967 and 1994, 46,380 articles indexed in *Psychological Abstracts* mentioned depression, 36,851 anxiety, and 5,099 anger. Only 2,389 spoke of happiness, 2,340 life satisfaction, and 405 joy.

Recently we and other researchers have begun a systematic study of happiness. During the past two decades, dozens of investigators throughout the world have asked several hundred thousand representatively sampled people to reflect on their happiness and satisfaction with life — or what psychologists call "subjective well-being". In the U.S. the National Opinion Research Center at the University of Chicago has surveyed a representative sample of roughly 1,500 people a year since 1957; the Institute for Social Research at the University of Michigan has carried out similar studies on a less regular basis, as has the Gallup Organization. Government-funded efforts have also probed the moods of European countries.

We have uncovered some surprising findings. People are happier than one might expect, and happiness does not appear to depend significantly on external circumstances. Although viewing life as a tragedy has a long and honorable history, the responses of random samples of people around the world about their happiness paints a much rosier picture. In the University of Chicago surveys, three in ten Americans say they are very happy, for example. Only one in ten chooses the most negative description "not too happy". The majority describe themselves as "pretty happy".

How can social scientists measure something as hard to pin down as happiness? Most researchers simply ask people to report their feelings of happiness or unhappiness and to assess how satisfying their lives are. Such self-reported well-being is moderately consistent over years of retesting. Furthermore, those who say they are happy and satisfied seem happy to their close friends and family members and to a psychologist-interviewer. Their daily mood ratings reveal more positive emotions, and they smile more than those who call themselves unhappy. Self-reported happiness also predicts other indicators of well-being. Compared with the depressed, happy people are less self-focused, less hostile and abusive, and less susceptible to disease.

We have found that the even distribution of happiness cuts across almost all demographic classifications of age, economic class, race and educational level. In addition, almost all strategies for assessing subjective well-being — including those that sample people's experience by polling them at random times with beepers — turn up similar findings.

Interviews with representative samples of people of all ages, for example, reveal that no time of life is notably happier or unhappier. Similarly, men and women are equally likely to declare themselves "very happy" and "satisfied" with life, according to a statistical digest of 146 studies by Marilyn J. Hating, William Stock and Morris A. Okun, all then at Arizona State University.

Wealth is also a poor predictor of happiness. People have not become happier over time as their cultures have become more affluent. Even though Americans earn twice as much in today's dollars as they did in 1957, the proportion of those telling surveyors from the National Opinion Research Center that they are "very happy" has declined from 35%—29%.

Even very rich people — those surveyed among *Forbes* magazine's 100 wealthiest Americans — are only slightly happier than the average American. Those whose income has increased over a 10-year period are not happier than those whose income is stagnant. Indeed, in most nations the correlation between income and happiness is negligible — only in the poorest countries is income a good measure of emotional well-being.

Are people in rich countries happier, by and large, than people in not so rich countries? It appears in general that they are, but the margin may be slim. In Portugal, for example, only one in ten people reports being very happy, whereas in the much more prosperous Netherlands the proportion of very happy is four in ten. Yet there are curious reversals in this correlation between national wealth and well-being — the Irish during the 1980s consistently reported greater life satisfaction than the wealthier West Germans. Furthermore, other factors, such as civil rights, literacy and duration of democratic government, all of which also promote reported life satisfaction, tend to go hand in hand with national wealth. As a result, it is impossible to tell whether the happiness of people in wealthier nations is based on money or is a by-product of other felicities.

Although happiness is not easy to predict from material circumstances, it seems consistent for those who have it. In one National Institute on Aging Study of 5,000 adults, the happiest people in 1973 were still relatively happy a decade later, despite changes in work, residence and family status.

Choose the correct answers for the following questions and write them in the space given.

1) What point are the writers making in the opening paragraph? (　)

A Happiness levels have risen since 1967.
B Journals take a biased view on happiness.
C Happiness is not a well-documented research area.
D People tend to think about themselves negatively.

【参考答案】

C

分析：这道题直接告诉我们答案在第一段，因此不需要定位，直接快速地读完第一段，确定第一段第一句 ... happiness is relatively unexplored terrain for social scientists. 是主题句，与选项 C 意思相符，因此答案是 C。

2) What do the writers say about their research findings? ( )

A They have predicted the results correctly.

B They felt people had responded dishonestly.

C They conflict with those of other researchers.

D Happiness levels are higher than they have believed.

【参考答案】

D

分析：这道题的问题中有关键词 research findings。先用寻读技巧迅速搜索，发现这个关键词出现在第三段，读完这段，确定第二句 People are happier than one might expect, and happiness does not appear to depend significantly on external circumstances. 与选项 D 意思相符，因此答案是 D。

3) In the fourth paragraph, what does the reader learn about the research method used? ( )

A It is new.

B It appears to be reliable.

C It is better than using beepers.

D It reveals additional information.

【参考答案】

B

分析：这道题直接告诉我们答案在第四段，因此不需要定位，直接快速地读完此段，了解到整段都在描述社会学家使用的调查方法。再细读这一段，发现这种方法比较可靠。而整段中都没提到选项 A，C，D 三项中的信息，因此答案是 B。

注意：做这类题时，要先确定是要找单个信息还是组团信息，确定是要用寻读技巧还是用略读技巧。一般来说，如果题目中含有较多的关键词，又涉及到细节信息，那么就可用寻读技巧；如果问题问的是段落大意、作者观点或要从某段描述中推断出作者意图，就要用略读或略读与细读相结合的技巧。

13.4 简答题

13.4.1 题型分析及练习

绝大多数简答题（Short Answer Questions）要求提取的是细节信息（解答方法参看 12.2），但是偶尔也会要求提取组团信息。考哪类信息一般从表面就可看出：一个问题有一个答案的属于前者，一个问题有三个以上答案的属于后者。

这类题基本的解题方法还是对 scanning + skimming + careful reading 技巧的灵活运用。

下面结合具体练习来分析此类题型。

Recycling Britain

1 By 2000, half the recoverable material in Britain's dustbins will be recycled — that, at least, was the target set last November by Chris Patten, Secretary of State for the Environment. But he gave no clues as to how we should go about achieving it. While recycling enthusiasts debate the relative merits of different collection systems, it will largely be new technology, and the opening up of new markets, that makes Patten's target attainable: a recycling scheme is successful only if manufacturers use the recovered materials in new products that people want to buy.

2 About half, by weight, of the contents of the typical British dustbin is made up of combustible materials. These materials comprise 33% paper, 7% plastics (a growing proportion), 4% textiles and 8% miscellaneous combustibles.

3 Of the rest, hard non-combustibles (metals and glass) each make up another 10%, and "putrescibles", such as potato peelings and cabbage stalks, account for 20%, although this proportion is decreasing as people eat more pre-prepared foods. The final fraction is "fines" — nameless dust. This mixture is useless to industry and in Britain most of it is disposed of in landfill-sites — suitable holes, such as worked-out quarries, in which the waste is buried under layers of soil and clay. That still leaves about 40% of the mixture — glass containers, plastics, and some paper and metal containers — as relatively clean when discarded. This clean element is the main target for Britain's recyclers.

4 The first question, then, is how best to separate the clean element from the rest. The method of collection is important because manufacturers will not reuse collected material unless it is clean and available in sufficient quantities. A bewildering assortment of different collection schemes operates in the rest of Europe, and pilot schemes are now under way in many British cities including Leeds, Milton Keynes, Sheffield and Cardiff. Sheffield, Cardiff and Dundee are testing out alternatives as part of a government-monitored recycling project initiated last year by Friends of the earth.

5 A realistic target for recycling mixed refuse is somewhere 15%—25% by weight, according to researchers at the Department of Trade and Industry's Warren Spring Laboratory. This proportion would include metals and perhaps some glass. Statistics compiled by researchers at the University of East Anglia show that we could almost halve the total weight of domestic waste going to landfill by a combination of "collect" schemes (such as doorstep collections for newspapers), "bring" schemes (such as bottle banks) and plants for extracting metals.

6 This estimate makes two important assumptions. One is that the government will bring in legislation to encourage the creation of markers for products made from recycled materials, especially glass, paper and plastics. The other is that industry will continue to introduce new technology that will improve both the products and the techniques used to separate recoverable materials from mixed refuse.

Answer these questions according to the passage.

1. From Paragraph 1, list the British target and the two things it will depend on.

Target ____________ Depends on (1) ____________

(2) ____________

【参考答案】

Target: by 2000 half recoverable material recycled

Depends on: (1) new technology

(2) new market

分析：题目告诉我们需要的信息在第一段，因此不需要定位，直接快速地读完第一段，再通过细读来提取所需信息。

2. What are the FOUR categories of British waste, according to the passage?

(1) ____________ (3) ____________

(2) ____________ (4) ____________

【参考答案】

(1) combustible materials (2) non-combustibles

(3) putrescibles (4) fines

分析：做这道题时要注意信息的覆盖面：第二段和第三段。解答此题的误区是：认为从第二段可以提取全部四个信息。由此可见，细读的过程不可或缺。

13.4.2 简答题——有关省略问题

简答题的一部分题型要求按规定字数回答问题，还有一部分简答题不限制答案的字数，这种题型涉及笔记记录（note-taking）的技能，包括省略、缩略和使用符号等多项技巧。

雅思阅读考试的简答题只涉及省略问题。

1. 语法词（grammar words）在词汇学中叫功能词（function words），包括介词、冠词、系动词、助动词和连接词等。这些词是用来搭建句子结构的，几乎没有实际含义。除了少数词之外，基本可以省略。如介词 by 的意思在表时间概念的时候与 in 的意思是不同的，因此上一节阅读练习第一题的答案 by 2000 ... 中的 by 是不能省的，因为这个介词传达了特殊的含义。而 in 2000 中的 in 是可以省略的。当然，如果答案字数没有超出所规定的范围也可不省略。

关键词（key words）在词汇学中叫实义词（content words），包括名词、动词、数词、形容词、副词和作形容词用的分词等。这些词是用来传达具体意义的，基本不可省略（当然也有例外）。

2. 作定语的形容词绝大多数可省略，当然如果答案词数不超出所规定的范围也可不省略。个别特殊情况下绝对不能省，如上一篇阅读练习第一题答案中的 recoverable materials 的 recoverable 就不能省，省去了就不知道是什么材料了。

作定语的名词基本上是不能省的，因为名词作定语是用来定性的，如 **fashion** design 和 **shutter** design 是两种完全不一样的设计。

作后置定语的短语和从句绝大多数可省，当然也会有例外，这要根据问题的具体要求作出判断。

13.5 分类题和标题 / 短语搭配题

13.5.1 题型分析破解

分类题和标题 / 短语搭配题（Classification; Matching Lists / Phrases）基本是考提取单个信息的能力，部分也会涉及组团信息。本书在章节 12.7 中讲了针对这两种题型如何提取单个信息的方法，现在讲解一下如何提取组团信息的方法。

涉及组团信息的这两种题型的基本解题方法还是对 scanning + skimming + careful reading 技巧的灵活运用。

下面结合具体的练习对涉及组团信息的这两种题型进行分析。

13.5.2 练习及解析

1. 下面这篇文章属于短语搭配题型。

Tourism

A Tourism, holiday-making and travel are these days more significant social phenomena than most commentators have considered. On the face of it there could not be a more trivial subject for a book. And indeed since social scientists have had considerable difficulty explaining weightier topics, such as work or politics, it might be thought that they would have great difficulties in accounting for more trivial phenomena such as holiday-making. However, there are interesting parallels with the study of deviance. This involves the investigation of bizarre and idiosyncratic social practices which happen to be defined as deviant in some societies but not necessarily in others. The assumption is that the investigation of deviance can reveal interesting and significant aspects of "normal" societies. It could be said that a similar analysis can be applied to tourism.

B Tourism is a leisure activity which presupposes its opposite namely regulated and organised work. It is one manifestation of how work and leisure are organised as separate and regulated spheres of social practice in modern societies. Indeed acting as a tourist is one of the defining characteristics of being "modern" and the popular concept of tourism is that it is organised within particular places and occurs for regularised periods of time. Tourist relationships arise from a movement of people to, and their stay in, various destinations. This necessarily involves some movement that is the journey and a period of stay in a new place or places. The journey and the stay are by definition outside the normal places of residence and work and are of a short-term and temporary nature and there is a clear intention to return "home" within a relatively short period of time.

C A substantial proportion of the population of modern societies engages in such tourist practices; new socialised forms of provision have developed in order to cope with the mass character of the gazes of tourists, as opposed to the individual character of travel. Places are chosen to be visited and be gazed upon because there is an anticipation, especially through daydreaming and fantasy, of intense pleasures, either on a different scale or involving different senses from those customarily encountered. Such anticipation is constructed and sustained through a variety of non-tourist practices, such as films, TV, literature, magazines, records and videos which construct and reinforce this daydreaming.

D Tourists tend to visit features of landscape and townscape which separate them off from everyday experience. Such aspects are viewed because they are taken to be in some sense out of the ordinary. The viewing of these tourist sights often involves different forms of social patterning, with a much greater sensitivity to visual elements of landscape or townscape than is normally found in everyday life. People linger over these sights in a way that they would not normally do in their home environment and the vision is objectified or captured through photographs, postcards, films and so on which enable the memory to be endlessly reproduced and recaptured.

E One of the earliest dissertations on the subject of tourism is Boorstin's analysis of the "pseudo event" (1964) where he argues that contemporary Americans cannot experience "reality" directly but thrive on "pseudo-events". Isolated from the host environment and the local people, the mass tourist travels in guided groups and finds pleasure in inauthentic contrived attractions, gullibly enjoying the pseudo-events and disregarding the real world outside. Over time the images generated of different tourist sights come to constitute a closed self-perpetuating system of illusions which provide the tourist with the basis for selecting and evaluating potential places to visit. Such visits are made, says Boorstin, within the "environmental bubble" of the familiar American-style hotel which insulates the tourist from the strangeness of the host environment.

F To service the burgeoning tourist industry, an array of professionals has developed who attempt to reproduce ever-new objects for the tourist to look at. These objects or places are located in a complex and changing hierarchy. This depends upon the interplay between, on the one hand, competition between interests involved in the provision of such objects and, on the other hand changing class, gender, and generational distinctions of taste within the potential population of visitors. It has been said that to be a tourist is one of the characteristics of the "modern experience". Not to "go away" is like not possessing a car or a nice house. Travel is a marker of status in modern societies and is also thought to be necessary for good health. The role of the professional, therefore, is to cater for the needs and tastes of the tourists in accordance with their class and overall expectations.

Choose one phrase (**A**—**H**) from the list of phrases to complete each key point below. Write the appropriate letters (**A**—**H**) in the space given. The information in the completed sentences should be an accurate **SUMMARY** of points made by the writer.

Note: There are more phrases in the list than sentences so you will not use them all.

List of phrases

A local people and their environment

B the expectations of tourists

C the phenomena of holiday-making

D the distinction we make between work and leisure

E the individual character of travel

F places seen in everyday life

G photographs which recapture our holidays

H sights designed specially for tourists

(1) Our concept of tourism arises from ________.

(2) The media can be used to enhance ________.

(3) People view tourist landscapes in a different way from ________.

(4) Group tours encourage participants to look at ________.

【参考答案】

(1) D (2) B (3) F (4) H

分析：建议先快速读一遍方框里的短语，了解各短语的意思，获得一个总体印象。再逐一读题目，用寻读技巧定位。譬如第（1）题在B段，然后用略读技巧快速读这一段，粗略地理解这段的大意。如果略读一遍还不够，就要细读，然后试着与方框中的短语逐个进行匹配，看哪个短语是最佳答案。最后发现第（1）题应该匹配D，而整个句子就是作者对这段要点的总结。

第（1）题定了位，剩下的题目就好解决了，因为题目一般都是按行文顺序出的。于是可推知，第（2）题在C段；第（3）题在D段；第（4）题在E段。

2. 下面这篇文章的练习题要求从题目给出的众多论点中，找出作者在文章中提到的论点。因为题目将原文进行了改写，不容易用寻读技巧发现原文中的原句，建议做这种题时采用略读技巧；在考试中建议考生留到最后再做，因为前面的题做过了，对全文有了较深入的理解，做起这些题来会相对顺利一些。

Penguins Show Signs of Stress

A new argument has been put forward as to whether penguins are disturbed by the presence of tourists in Antarctica.

Previous research by scientists from Kiel University in Germany monitored Adelie penguins and noted that the birds' heart rates increased dramatically at the sight of a human as far as 30 metres away. But new research using an artificial egg, which is equipped to measure heart rates, disputes this. Scientists from the Scott Polar Research Institute at Cambridge say that a slow moving human who does not approach the nest too closely is not perceived as a threat by penguins.

The earlier findings have been used to partly explain the 20% drop in populations of certain types of penguins near tourist sites. However, tour operators have continued to insist that their activities do not adversely affect wildlife in Antarctica, saying they encourage non-disruptive behaviour in tourists, and that the decline in penguin numbers is caused by other factors.

Amanda Nimon of the Scott Polar Research Institute spent three southern hemisphere summers at Cuvervill Island in Antarctica studying penguin behaviour towards humans. "A nesting penguin will react very differently to a person rapidly and closely approaching the nest," says Nimon. "First they exhibit large and prolonged heart rate changes and then they often flee the nest leaving it open for predators to fly in and remove eggs or chicks." The artificial egg, specially developed for the project, monitored both the parent who had been "disturbed" when the egg was placed in the nest and the other parent as they both took it in turns to guard the nest.

However, Boris Culik, who monitored the Adelie penguins, believes that Nimon's findings do not invalidate his own research. He points out that species behave differently — and Nimon's work was with Gentoo penguins. Nimon and her colleagues believe that Culik's research was methodologically flawed because the monitoring of penguins' responses entailed capturing and restraining the birds and fitting them with heart-rate transmitters. Therefore, argues Nimon, it would not be surprising if they became stressed on seeing a human subsequently.

Which THREE of the following arguments are stated in the text? ( )

A Penguins are not afraid of people who behave calmly.

B Penguins need better protection from tourists.

C Not all penguins behave in the same way.

D Tourists are not responsible for the fall in penguin numbers.

E Penguins are harder to research when they have young.

F Tour operators should encourage tourists to avoid Antarctica.

【参考答案】

A, C, D

3. 下面这篇文章后面的练习题与上一篇文章的题目性质相似，但也有所不同：上一篇文章要求从题目给出的众多论点中，找出作者在文章中提到的论点；而这篇文章则要求在文章中找出不同人各自的论点，并与题目给出的众多论点进行匹配。这种题目的难度稍有下降。请看文章后面的分析。

Australia's Growing Disaster

Farming is threatening to destroy the soil and native flora and fauna over vast areas of Australia. What price should be put on conservation?

Australia's National Greenhouse Gas Inventory Committee estimates that burning wood from cleared forests accounts for about 50% of Australia's emissions of carbon dioxide, or 156 million tonnes a year. And water tables are rising beneath cleared land. In the Western Australian wheat belt, estimates suggest that water is rising by up to 1 metre a year. The land is becoming waterlogged and unproductive or is being poisoned by salt, which is brought to the surface. The Australian Conservation Foundation (ACF) reckons that 33 million hectares has been degraded by salination. The federal government estimates the loss in production from salinity at A$200 million a year.

According to Jason Alexandra of the ACF, this list of woes is evidence that Australia is depleting its resources by trading agricultural commodities for manufactured imports. In effect, it sells topsoil for technologies that will be worn out or redundant in a few years. The country needs to get away from the "colonial mentality" of exploiting resources and adopt agricultural practices suited to Australian conditions, he says.

Robert Hadler of the National Farmers' Federation (NFF) does not deny that there is a problem, but says that it is "illogical" to blame farmers. Until the early 1980s, farmers were given tax incentives to clear land because that was what people wanted. If farmers are given tax breaks to manage the land sustainably, they will do so. Hadler argues that the two reports on land clearance do not say anything which was not known before.

Australia is still better off than many other developed countries, says Dean Graetz, an ecologist at the CSIRO, the national research organisation. "A lot of the country is still notionally pristine," he says. "It is not transformed like Europe where almost nothing that is left is natural." Graetz, who analysed the satellite photographs for the second land clearance report, argues that there is now better co-operation between Australian scientists, government officials and farmers than in the past.

But the vulnerable state of the land is now widely understood, and across Australia, schemes have started for promoting environment-friendly farming. In 1989, Prime Minister Bob Hawke set up Landcare, a network of more than 2,000 regional conservation groups. About 30% of landholders are members. "It has become a very significant social movement," says Helen Alexander from the National Landcare Council. "We started out worrying about not much more than erosion and the replanting of trees but it has grown much more diverse and sophisticated."

But the bugbear of all these conservation efforts is money. Landcare's budget is A$110 million a year, of which only A$6 million goes to farmers. Nell Clark, an agricultural consultant from Bendigo in Victoria, says that farmers are not getting enough. "Farmers may want to make more efficient use of water and nutrients and embrace more sustainable practices, but it all costs money and they just don't have the spare funds," he says.

Clark also says scientists are taking too large a share of the money for conservation. Many problems posed by agriculture to the environment have been "researched to death", he says. "We need to divert the money for a while into getting the solutions into place." Australia's chief scientist, Michael Pitman, disagrees. He says that science is increasingly important. Meteorologists, for example, are becoming confident about predicting events which cause droughts in Australia. "If this can be done with accuracy, then it will have immense impact on stocking levels and how much feed to provide," says Pitman. "The end result will be much greater efficiency."

Steve Morton of the CSIRO Division of Wildlife and Ecology says the real challenge facing conservationists is to convince the 85% of Australians who live in cities that they must foot a large part of the bill. "The land is being used to feed the majority and to produce wealth that circulates through the financial markets of the cities," he says. One way would be to offer incentives to extend the idea of stewardship to areas outside the rangelands, so that more land could be protected rather than exploited, Alexander agrees. "The nation will have to debate to what extent it is willing to support rural communities," she says. "It will have to decide to what extent it wants food prices to reflect the true cost of production. That includes the cost of looking after the environment."

Match the views in the left column with the people's names in the right column.

Note: You may have to use some names more than once.

(1) Current conservation schemes are taking many problems into account.

(2) Ordinary people will have to help pay for conservation.

(3) Conserving land is too expensive for farmers.

(4) The Government can encourage farmers to do what it wants them to do.

(5) Australia should review its import / export practices.

(6) More conservation funds should be put into practical projects.

A Jason Alexandra
B Robert Hadler
C Dean Graetz
D Helen Alexander
E Neil Clark
F Michael Pitman
G Steve Morton

(7) Much of the land in Australia is still unspoilt.

(8) Research is necessary to help solve conservation problems.

【参考答案】

(1) D (2) G (3) E (4) B (5) A (6) E (7) C (8) F

分析：这种题目虽然是论点匹配题，但匹配的论点不是作者本人的论点，而是文中不同人的论点，因此可用人名作为关键词去定位，然后细读他（她）的论点，再与某个论点进行匹配。基本做题方法还是要灵活运用 scanning + skimming + careful reading 这一技巧。不过考生对原文题材不一定熟悉，对原文的论点又需要透彻地理解，这就要求考生具备较强的英语理解能力。

4. 下面这篇文章后面的练习题其实是分类题的题目，形式改成了完成句子题。但万变不离其宗，提高分辨题型的能力至关重要，弄清了是什么题型，才能运用适当的方法，从而以不变应万变。请看文章后面的分析。

The Concept of Role Theory

Role set

Any individual in any situation occupies a role in relation to other people. The particular individual with whom one is concerned in the analysis of any situation is usually given the name of *focal person*. He has the *focal role* and can be regarded as sitting in the middle of a group of people, with whom he interacts in some way in that situation. This group of people is called his *role set*. For instance, in the family situation, an individual's role set might be shown as in Figure 6.

The role set should include all those with whom the individual has more than trivial interactions.

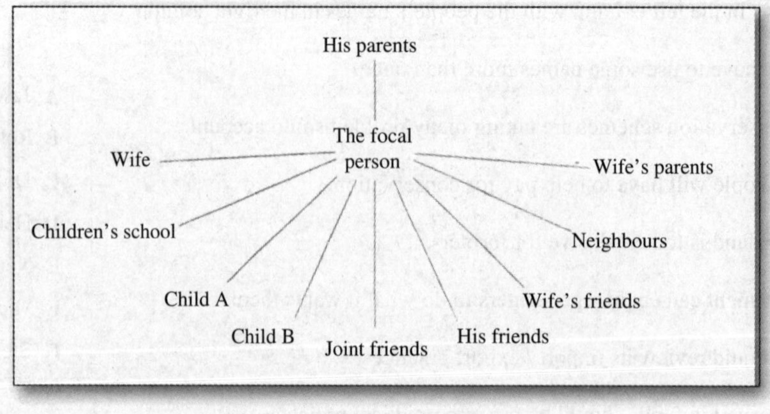

Figure 6

Role definition

The definition of any individual's role in any situation will be a combination of the role expectations that the members of the role set have of the focal role. These expectations are often occupationally defined, sometimes even legally so. The role definitions of lawyers and doctors are fairly clearly defined both in legal and in cultural terms. The role definitions of, say a film star or a bank manager, are also fairly clearly defined in cultural terms, too clearly perhaps.

Individuals often find it hard to escape from the role that cultural traditions have defined for them. Not only with doctors or lawyers is the requited role behaviour so constrained that if you are in that role for long it eventually becomes part of you, part of your personality. Hence, there is some likelihood that all accountants will be alike or that all blondes are similar — they are forced that way by the expectations of their role.

It is often important that you make it clear what your particular role is at a given time. The means of doing this are called, rather obviously, *role signs*. The simplest of role signs is a uniform. The number of stripes on your arm or pops on your shoulder is a very precise role definition which allows you to do certain very prescribed things in certain situations. Imagine yourself questioning a stranger on a dark street at midnight without wearing the role signs of a policeman!

In social circumstances, dress has often been used as a role sign to indicate the nature and degree of formality of any gathering and occasionally the social status of people present. The current trend towards blurring these role signs in dress is probably democratic, but it also makes some people very insecure. Without role signs, who is to know who has what role?

Place is another role sign. Managers often behave very differently outside the office and in it, even to the same person. They use a change of location to indicate a change in role from, say, boss to friend. Indeed, if you wish to change your roles you must find some outward sign that you are doing so or you won't be permitted to change — the subordinate will continue to hear you as his boss no matter how hard you try to be his friend. In very significant cases of role change, e.g. from a soldier in the ranks to officer, from bachelor to married man, the change of role has to have a very obvious *sign*, hence *rituals*. It is interesting to observe, for instance, some decline in the emphasis given to marriage rituals. This could be taken as an indication that there is no longer such a big change in role from single to married person, and therefore no need for a public change in sign.

In organisations, office signs and furniture are often used as role signs. These and other perquisites of status are often frowned upon, but they may serve a purpose as a kind of uniform in a democratic society; roles without signs often lead to confused or differing expectations of the role of the focal person.

Role ambiguity

Role ambiguity results when there is some uncertainty in the minds, either of the focal person or of the members of his role set, as to precisely what his role is at any given time. One of the crucial expectations that shape the role definition is that of the individual, the focal person himself. If his occupation of the role is unclear, or if it differs from that of the others in the role set, there will be a degree of role ambiguity. Is this bad? Not necessarily, for the ability to shape one's own role is one of the freedoms that many people desire, but the ambiguity may lead to role stress which will be discussed later on. The virtue of job descriptions is that they lessen this role ambiguity. Unfortunately, job descriptions are seldom complete role definitions, except at the lower end of the scale. At middle and higher management levels, they are often a list of formal jobs and duties that say little about the more subtle and informal expectations of the role. The result is therefore to give the individual an uncomfortable feeling that there are things left unsaid, i.e. to *heighten* the sense of role ambiguity.

Looking at role ambiguity from the other side, from the point of view of the members of the role set, lack of clarity in the role of the focal person can cause insecurity, lack of confidence, irritation and even anger among members of his role set. One list of the roles of a manager identified the following: executive, planner, policy maker, expert controller of rewards and punishments, counsellor, friend, teacher. If it is not clear, through role signs of one sort or another, which role is currently the operational one, the other party may not react in the appropriate way — we may, in fact, hear quite another message if the focal person speaks to us, for example, as a teacher and we hear her as an executive.

Choose **ONE OR TWO WORDS** from the passage for each answer.

Write your answers in the space given after each statement.

(1) A new headmaster of a school who enlarges his office and puts in expensive carpeting is using the office as a ________ .

(2) The graduation ceremony in many universities is an important ________ .

(3) The wig which judges wear in U.K. courts is a ________ .

(4) The parents of students in a school are part of the headmaster's ________ .

【参考答案】

(1) role sign (2) ritual (3) role sign (4) role set

分析：这些题目看上去是完形填空，其实是要考生结合文章对 role theory 的阐述，对某些社会现象加以归类。这些例子是不能在原文中直接找到的，只是与原文中举出的例子性质相同，因此需要考生把原文对 role theory 的定义搞清楚，把原文所举的例子“吃透”，然后才能归类。这就要进行全文的细读。

13.6 摘要填空题

13.6.1 题型分析破解

要做好摘要填空题（Summary Completion），先要了解它的出题方式。出题方式共有两大类：

1. 文章部分内容的摘要——文章中的某两段或三段内容的摘要。把摘要中任意内容去掉，让考生填写。

2. 全文内容的摘要——整篇文章的摘要。同样是把摘要中任意内容去掉，让考生填写。

需要考生填的缺漏词（missing words）有三种来源，因此从这个角度看，此类题型可细分为三种形式：

1. 所有要填的词从原文中直接提取，不改动。题目中提供或不提供单词表。

2. 要填的词不能从原文中直接提取，而是从所给的单词表中提取，单词表里的词是原文中没有的。题目会提供单词表。

3. 要填的词部分从原文中直接提取，部分从所给的单词表中提取。题目会提供单词表。

这样的出题方式其实是比较多变的，同时也使考生的思维产生了混乱；而且摘要是对原文要点的改写，往往变动很大，这就要求考生有较为坚实的语言基础。但正因如此，才测试出了考生各方面的能力。这些能力包括阅读理解能力、总结能力、分析能力、信息提取能力、阅读技巧运用能力，以及语言（语法结构和词汇意义）运用能力，这种题型能很好地测验考生的综合能力。

本节先谈第一大类摘要填空题，这种题型属于提取组团信息类型。第二大类摘要填空题属于提取整篇信息类型，本书将会在第 14 章中分析。

13.6.2 练习及解析

1. 下面这篇文章的摘要属于部分段落的摘要，题目提供了单词表，而缺漏词不能从原文中直接提取，只能从单词表中选择。

The Pursuit of Happines

New research uncovers some anti-intuitive insights into how many people are happy — and why.

Compared with misery, happiness is relatively unexplored terrain for social scientists. Between 1967 and 1994, 46,380 articles indexed in *Psychological Abstracts* mentioned depression, 36,851 anxiety, and 5,099 anger. Only 2,389 spoke of happiness, 2,340 life satisfaction, and 405 joy.

Recently we and other researchers have begun a systematic study of happiness. During the past two decades, dozens of investigators throughout the world have asked several hundred thousand representatively sampled people to reflect on their happiness and satisfaction with life — or what psychologists call "subjective well-being". In the U.S. the National Opinion Research Center at the University of Chicago has surveyed a representative sample of roughly 1,500 people a year since 1957; the Institute for Social Research at the University of Michigan has carried out similar studies on a less regular basis, as has the Gallup Organization. Government-funded efforts have also probed the moods of European countries.

We have uncovered some surprising findings. People are happier than one might expect, and happiness does not appear to depend significantly on external circumstances. Although viewing life as a tragedy has a long and honorable history, the responses of random samples of people around the world about their happiness paints a much rosier picture. In the University of Chicago surveys, three in ten Americans say they are very happy, for example. Only one in ten chooses the most negative description "not too happy". The majority describe themselves as "pretty happy" .

How can social scientists measure something as hard to pin down as happiness? Most researchers simply ask people to report their feelings of happiness or unhappiness and to assess how satisfying their lives are. Such self-reported well-being is moderately consistent over years of retesting. Furthermore, those who say they are happy and satisfied seem happy to their close friends and family members and to a psychologist-interviewer. Their daily mood ratings reveal more positive emotions, and they smile more than those who call themselves unhappy. Self-reported happiness also predicts other indicators of well-being. Compared with the depressed, happy people are less self-focused, less hostile and abusive, and less susceptible to disease.

We have found that the even distribution of happiness cuts across almost all demographic classifications of age, economic class, race and educational level. In addition, almost all strategies for assessing subjective well-being — including those that sample people's experience by polling them at random times with beepers — turn up similar findings.

Interviews with representative samples of people of all ages, for example, reveal that no time of life is notably happier or unhappier. Similarly, men and women are equally likely to declare themselves "very happy" and "satisfied" with life, according to a statistical digest of 146 studies by Marilyn J. Hating, William Stock and Morris A. Okun, all then at Arizona State University.

Wealth is also a poor predictor of happiness. People have not become happier over time as their cultures have become more affluent. Even though Americans earn twice as much in today's dollars as they did in 1957, the proportion of those telling surveyors from the National Opinion Research Center that they are "very happy" has declined from 35%—29%.

Even very rich people — those surveyed among *Forbes* magazine's 100 wealthiest Americans — are only slightly happier than the average American. Those whose income has increased over a 10-year period are not happier than those whose income is stagnant. Indeed, in most nations the correlation between income and happiness is negligible — only in the poorest countries is income a good measure of emotional well-being.

Are people in rich countries happier, by and large, than people in not so rich countries? It appears in general that they are, but the margin may be slim. In Portugal, for example, only one in 10 people reports being very happy, whereas in the much more prosperous Netherlands the proportion of very happy is four in ten. Yet there are curious reversals in this correlation between national wealth and well-being — the Irish during the 1980s consistently reported greater life satisfaction than the wealthier West Germans. Furthermore, other factors, such as civil rights, literacy and duration of democratic government, all of which also promote reported life satisfaction, tend to go hand in hand with national wealth. As a result, it is impossible to tell whether the happiness of people in wealthier nations is based on money or is a by-product of other felicities.

Although happiness is not easy to predict from material circumstances, it seems consistent for those who have it. In one National Institute on Aging Study of 5,000 adults, the happiest people in 1973 were still relatively happy a decade later, despite changes in work, residence and family status.

Complete the summary of the passage. Choose your answers from the box and fill them in the blanks in the summary.

Note: There are more words than spaces so you will not use them all. You may use some of the words more than once.

stopped	slightly	too	great	doubled	significant	similar
some	stabilised	remarkably	reversed	dropped	no	less
much	affected	crept up	slowed down	more	clearly	

How happy are we?

Our happiness levels are (1) *affected* by relatively few factors. For example, incomes in the States have (2) ________ over the past forty years but happiness levels have (3) ________ over the same period. In fact, people on average incomes are only slightly (4) ________ happy than extremely rich people and a gradual increase in prosperity makes (5) ________ difference to how happy we are. In terms of national wealth, populations of wealthy nations are (6) ________ happier than those who live in poorer countries. Although in some cases this trend is (7) ________ and it appears that other factors need to be considered.

【参考答案】

(2) doubled　(3) dropped　(4) less　(5) no　(6) slightly　(7) reversed

分析：先用寻读技巧定位，发现这个组团在原文倒数第四段至倒数第二段。先略读这三段进行粗略的了解，然后细读，试着找出主题句。如果没有，就自己总结段落大意。再把主题句或自己总结的段落大意跟题目给出的摘要进行比较，在单词表中找一个词性和词义均符合上下文的词填在空格内。

2. 下面这篇文章后的题目看似流程图题，其实本质上是摘要题的第三种形式，即部分缺漏词来自原文，部分来自单词表。该题把流程图题和摘要填空题这两种题型有机地结合在了一起，解题方法还是 scanning + skimming + careful reading。

Migratory Beekeeping

Of the 2,000 commercial beekeepers in the United States about half migrate. This pays off in two ways. Moving north in the summer and south in the winter lets bees work a longer blooming season, making more honey — and money — for their keepers. Second, beekeepers can carry their hives to farmers who need bees to pollinate their crops. Every spring a migratory beekeeper in California may move up to 160 million bees to flowering fields in Minnesota and every winter his family may haul the hives back to California, where farmers will rent the bees to pollinate almond and cherry trees.

Migratory beekeeping is nothing new. The ancient Egyptians moved clay hives, probably on rafts, down the Nile to follow the bloom and nectar flow as it moved toward Cairo. In the 1880s North American beekeepers experimented with the same idea, moving bees on barges along the Mississippi and on waterways in Florida, but their lighter, wooden hives kept falling into the water. Other keepers tried the railroad and horse-drawn wagons, but that didn't prove practical. Not until the 1920s when cars and trucks became affordable and roads improved, did migratory beekeeping begin to catch on.

For the Californian beekeeper, the pollination season begins in February. At this time, the beehives are in particular demand by farmers who have almond groves; they need two hives an acre. For the three-week long bloom, beekeepers can hire out their hives for $32 each. It's a bonanza for the bees, too. Most people consider almond honey too bitter to eat so the bees get to keep it for themselves.

By early March it is time to move the bees. It can take up to seven nights to pack the 4,000 or so hives that a beekeeper may own. These are not moved in the middle of the day because too many of the bees would end up homeless. But at night, the hives are stacked onto wooden pallets, back-to-back in sets of four, and lifted onto a truck. It is not necessary to wear gloves or a beekeeper's veil because the hives are not being opened and the bees should remain relatively quiet. Just in case some are still lively, bees can be pacified with a few puffs of smoke blown into each hive's narrow entrance.

In their new location, the beekeeper will pay the farmer to allow his bees to feed in such places as orange groves. The honey produced here is fragrant and sweet and can be sold by the beekeepers. To encourage the bees to produce as much honey as possible during this period, the beekeepers open the hives and stack extra boxes called *supers* on top. These temporary hive extensions contain frames of empty comb for the bees to fill with honey. In the brood chamber below, the bees will stash honey to eat later. To prevent the queen from crawling up to the top and laying eggs, a screen can be inserted between the brood chamber and the supers. Three weeks later the honey can be gathered.

Foul smelling chemicals are often used to irritate the bees and drive them down into the hive's bottom boxes, leaving the honey-filled supers more or less bee free. These can then be pulled off the hive. They are heavy with honey and may weigh up to 90 pounds each. The supers are taken to a warehouse. In the extracting room, the frames are lifted out and lowered into an "uncapper" where rotating blades shave away the wax that covers each cell. The uncapped frames are put in it carousel that sits on the bottom of a large stainless steel drum. The carousel is filled to capacity with 72 frames. A switch is flipped and the frames begin to whirl at 300 revolutions per minute; centrifugal force throws the honey out of the combs. Finally the honey is poured into barrels for shipment.

After this, approximately a quarter of the hives weakened by disease, mites, or an ageing or dead queen will have to be replaced. To create new colonies, a healthy double hive, teeming with bees, can be separated into two boxes. One half will hold the queen and a young, already mated queen can be put in the other half, to make two hives from one. By the time the flowers bloom, the new queens will be laying eggs, filling each hive with young worker bees. The beekeeper's family will then migrate with them to their summer location.

The flow chart below outlines the movements of the migratory beekeepers as described in the passage. Complete the flow chart. Choose your answers from the box and write them in the spaces given.

smoke	chemicals	pay	barrels	protection	charge
set off	light	split	pollinate	machines	supers
combs	screen	prepare	full	empty	queens

Beekeeper movements

In February, Californian farmers hire bees to help (1) *pollinate* almond trees.

↓

In March, beekeepers (2) ________ for migration at night when the hives are (3) ________ and the bees are generally tranquil. A little (4) ________ can ensure that this is the case.

↓

They transport their hives to orange groves where farmers (5) ________ beekeepers for placing them on their land. Here the bees make honey.

↓

After three weeks, the supers can be taken to a warehouse where (6) ________ are used to remove the wax and extract the honey from the (7) ________.

↓

After the honey collection, the old hives are rejected. Good double hives are (8) ________ and re-queened and the beekeeper will transport them to their summer base.

【参考答案】

(2) prepare (3) full (4) smoke

(5) charge (6) machines (7) combs (8) split

分析：先用寻读技巧搜索，发现第一个方框中的 February 在原文第三段，因此第一个题目就是第三段内容的总结；而第二个方框中的 March 就在原文第四段，因此第二个题目就是第四段内容的总结。依此类推，原文第五段对应第三个方框，原文第六段对应第四个方框，原文第七段对应第五个方框。这样思路就清晰了。然后略读或细读各段，试着找出主题句。如果没有，就自己总结段落大意，再把主题句或自己总结的段落大意跟方框中的摘要进行比照，能从原文中提取单词的就提取，不能从原文中提取的，就从给出的单词表中找一个词性和词义均符合上下文的词填在空格内。

14 雅思阅读九类题型破解——提取整篇信息的题型

提取整篇信息的题型特点是信息覆盖面大，各组团信息连环组成。代表题型是全篇文章摘要题（Summary Completion）。

这类题型跟第 13 章中讲到的题型一样，也是测试考生的理解能力、提取信息的能力、区分段落的中心思想与支持性信息的能力、总结能力、抓住过程和总结要点的能力等，当然同时也考查考生运用语言的能力。

全文摘要与段落摘要题型一样（见 13.6.1），也可分为三种形式：

1. 所有要填的词从原文中直接提取，不改动。题目中提供或不提供单词表。

2. 要填的词不能从原文中直接提取，而是从所给的单词表中提取，单词表里的词是原文中没有的。题目会提供单词表。

3. 要填的词部分从原文中直接提取，部分从所给的单词表中提取。题目会提供单词表。

由于这类摘要填空题是对全篇文章内容的概括，因而解题的具体步骤与文章部分内容摘要有所不同。下面结合具体题型进行分析。

14.1 摘要填空题

14.1.1 缺漏词从原文中直接提取的摘要填空题

针对这种类型的摘要题，建议用以下步骤解题：

1）先读摘要句。

（1）通过这句话的上下文确定缺漏词的词性。

（2）记住这句话的关键词。

2）用关键词快速在原文中定位。由于是全篇内容的摘要，每一段的内容都需要进行总结，大多数情况下是一句话对应一段；又由于缺漏词要从原文中提取，因此摘要中的句子与原文中的原句比较，改动一般不会太大，定位相对容易。

3）定位后细读原文出处上下文，分析句子，选择词性和词义均恰当的词填空。

4）查单词表。如果单词表中包括了你在原文中选择的词，则放心地填空。如果没有，就证明你选错了，再重新从原文中选择。

没有提供单词表的摘要题按照前三个步骤来解题；提供单词表的摘要题则要充分利用所给单词表，用以确认答案，按照四个步骤来解题。

用以上所述步骤来完成下面这篇文章后的练习。

No Word for Anxiety

Psychologists Aruna Mahtani and Afreen Huq look back with mixed feelings on their special project for Bangladeshi women in Britain.

1 Our training as mental-health professional is supposed to be "colour-blind". That sounds fine but in practice it means that people from block and ethnic groups get a raw deal because their particular problems are seldom acknowledged. Even when they are provided for it usually amounts to their being dumped on the few professionals from block and ethnic groups.

2 So we decided to pilot a project involving Bangladeshi women from Tower Hamlets in the East End of London. The largest Bangladeshi community in Britain lives in Tower Hamlets — at least 40,000 people. Most migrated in the 1960s and 1970s. Adjustment was difficult and the transition from a rural to an inner-city setting was hardest for women. They found themselves confined indoors, isolated and without the networks of social support they were used to in Bangladesh.

3 Many of these women turned to their doctors with common symptoms of anxiety, such as palpitations, headaches, tearfulness, sleeping difficulties, chest pains, loss of appetite and lack of energy. They were usually prescribed tranquillisers or even placebos like ascorbic acid (vitamin C). Since the underlying causes remained, the women visited their doctors with increasing frequency. And some were referred on to mental-health professionals like us.

4 We wanted to see how normal Western approaches to anxiety problems might work when applied across cultures. Our first step was to get an anxiety-management package translated. No easy task: there is no colloquial expression in Bangla for "anxiety". We used two approximations, *dushchinta* ("undue worries") and *udhbeg* (a word generally used only in its written form).

5 We knew we had to have a women-only group. A mixed one would have been unacceptable to both the women and their families. Bangladeshi women rarely go out alone. Their cultural background is that of a small rural community where women tend to go out with family members or neighbours. In Britain they are even less likely to go out due to fear of racist abuse and harassment, as well as language difficulties.

6 So many things in the standard approach had to be changed. We had to translate many of the usual examples — we would normally compare learning to relax with learning to drive, for instance, which would not have been culturally appropriate. At first we asked the women to rate, on a scale one to ten, the effect of relaxation on their level of anxiety: they found numbers an odd way of expressing how they were feeling. So we shifted our focus to words and talked of five stages from "very good" to "very bad".

7 It was a pilot project, so there were shortcomings, we looked for too little back-up, naively taking on too much, like driving the women to and from the centre. We did not collect as much objective data as we might have done with a white group. We fell into the white stereotype of assuming that Bangladeshi women would find the use of various checklists and written records foreign. Perhaps racism has conditioned us to a greater extent than we expected.

8 But the rapport between us and the women in the group was instantaneous, probably because we share not just a language and culture but a common experience of racism. The importance of having bilingual and ethnic staff is clear.

9 We found that using of Western model across cultures has potential. But it needs political, financial and personal commitment. And the lack of response by the authorities in Tower Hamlets leads us to conclude that "institutional" racism is very much alive and kicking.

The passage below is a summary of the reading passage. Decide which word should go in each gap and then write the letter in the space provided. Note that there are more words than gaps. Write only one letter in each space. The first one has been done as an example.

A conditioned	**B** data	**C** allowance
D acknowledged	**E** statistic	**F** rapport
G transition	**H** urban	**I** inform
J translate	**K** records	**L** ratc
M exposed	**N** symptoms	**O** rural

People from black and ethnic groups frequently find that their problems are not (1) ___*D*___ . A project was piloted involving Bangladeshi women in inner-city London. Most came to the U.K. in the 1960s and 1970s from a (2) ________ background. Particularly for women, this (3) ________ has been very difficult to adjust to. Many of the women experienced common anxiety (4) ________ and after visiting their doctors some were referred to clinical psychologists. First, the psychologists had to (5) ________ an anxiety-management package. Then a women-only group was established. They asked the women to (6) ________ in numbers the effect of relaxation on their anxiety level, but this was an odd concept for them so words were used instead. Being a pilot scheme, there were problems such as not having sufficient back-up and working too hard. They ended up with less (7) ________ than with a white group. They made assumptions about Bangladeshi women's approach to keeping (8) ________ and wondered if they were more (9) ________ by racism than they expected. However, being of an ethnic group themselves led to a good (10) ________ due to a shared language and exposure to racism.

【参考答案】

(1) D (2) O (3) G (4) N (5) J (6) L (7) B (8) K (9) A (10) F

2. 下面这篇文章属于没有提供单词表的摘要题，请按前面所述的解题步聚的前三步来做。没有了单词表，解题的难度会增加，因为不能利用单词表来验证自己的答案。

The Greenhouse Effect

The greenhouse effect is not a new phenomenon. Scientists have known for centuries that a layer of gases naturally surrounds the earth like an insulating blanket, trapping the reflected energy of the sun and preventing it from escaping into space. That's what makes the earth warm enough for people, plants and animals. However, recent human activity has boosted concentrations of greenhouse gases and enhanced their heat-trapping ability. The main culprit is carbon dioxide (CO_2), which scientists estimate accounts for nearly half of global warming. CO_2 is released from burning fossil fuels (coal, oil and gas) and from clearing and burning forests.

There are other important greenhouse gases too, and they cannot be ignored — CFCs, for example, may account for 25% of global warming in the next century if their production is not scaled back. But carbon dioxide is the pivotal one. The U.N. International Panel on Climatic Change now says that CO_2 levels could double within 40 years if present rates of fossil-fuel burning and deforestation continue. That could mean an average temperature increase between two and four degrees centigrade and a sea-level rise of perhaps a foot by 2050.

No one knows for certain how local weather will change as a result of this warming. But one thing is clear — it will be no picnic. Indications are that the earth will be warmer than at any time since the start of the last ice age nearly 100,000 years ago. But there's one major difference. This temperature increase will take place not over thousands of years, but over decades. And it is the speed of the change which makes the precise impact so difficult to predict.

The most sophisticated computerised climate models, in the U.S. and Britain, agree that weather around the world will become more erratic and more extreme. In general, temperatures will rise more towards the poles than at the equator. Overall rainfall will also increase as higher temperatures boost evaporation from the seas. But the distribution of precipitation will shift. Some areas will become wetter, others will be drier. In middle latitudes, climate zones will march pole-wards, Saskatchewan may become like Kansas, southern England like southern France. In tropical and sub-tropical parts of the Third World, warming will be less but the impact on a relatively stable climate will be greater. Tropical storms and droughts could both increase. The pattern of the monsoons may shift.

Global warming will also cause ocean levels to rise — though not, as popular wisdom has it, due to the Antarctic ice cap melting. If this catastrophe occurs it will not be for at least another century.

Instead, sea levels will rise simply because water expands as it warms. People living in low-lying coastal regions from New York and London to Jakarta and Dacca will be in danger. The world's great river deltas, home to millions in Asia and Latin America and containing some of the Third World's richest food-growing land, could become brackish graveyards.

The passage below is a summary of the reading passage. Complete this summary by writing **ONE OR TWO WORDS** in each space. These words must be taken from the reading passage. The first one has been done as an example.

It has long been known that earth is (1) _warm enough_ to support life because of an (2) ________ layer of greenhouse gases which trap the sun's (3) ________ . Recently, increased production of one of these gases, (4) ________ by mankind's (5) ________ of wood and fossil fuels, has been the main cause of (6) ________ . If the (7) ________ of CO_2 continue to increase, both temperature and (8) ________ could rise significantly by 2050. The (9) ________ of this change has made predictions about the effect on the world's (10) ________ uncertain. However, computers forecast greater unpredictability and a more (11) ________ climate. And with the temperature rise will come a corresponding expansion of (12) ________ and rising sea-levels, threatening (13) ________ cities and fertile land alike.

【参考答案】

(2) insulating (3) (reflected) energy (4) CO_2 (5) burning
(6) global warming (7) levels (8) sea-level (9) speed
(10) weather (11) extreme (12) water (13) low-lying coastal

3. 下面这篇文章也属于没有提供单词表的摘要题，解题步骤同上一篇文章。

Johnson's Dictionary

For the century before *Johnson's Dictionary* was published in 1775, there had been concern about the state of the English language. There was no standard way of speaking or writing and no agreement as to the best way of bringing some order to the chaos of English spelling. Dr. Johnson provided the solution.

There had, of course, been dictionaries in the past, the first of these being a little book of some 120 pages, compiled by a certain Robert Cawdray, published in 1604 under the title *A Table Alphabetical of Hard Usual English Words*. Like the various dictionaries that came after it during the seventeenth century, Cawdray's tended to concentrate on "scholarly" words; one function of the dictionary was to enable its student to convey an impression of fine learning.

Beyond the practical need to make order out of chaos, the rise of dictionaries is associated with the rise of the English middle class, who were anxious to define and circumscribe the various words to conquer — lexical as well as social and commercial. It is highly appropriate that Dr. Samuel Johnson, the very model of an eighteenth-century literary man, as famous in his own time as in ours, should have published his Dictionary at the very beginning of the heyday of the middle class.

Johnson was a poet and critic who raised common sense to the heights of genius. His approach to the problems that had worried writers throughout the late seventeenth and early eighteenth centuries was intensely practical. Up until his time, the task of producing a dictionary on such a large scale had seemed impossible without the establishment of an academy to make decisions about right and wrong usage. Johnson decided he did not need an academy to settle arguments about language; he would write a dictionary himself, and he would do it single-handed. Johnson signed the contract for the Dictionary with the bookseller Robert Dosley at a breakfast held at the Golden Anchor Inn near Holborn Bar on 18 June, 1764. He was to be paid £1,575 in instalments, and from this he took money to rent 17 Gough Square, in which he set up his "dictionary workshop".

James Boswell, his biographer described the garret where Johnson worked as "fitted up like a counting house" with a long desk running down the middle at which the copying clerks would work standing up. Johnson himself was stationed on a rickety chair at an "old crazy deal table" surrounded by a chaos of borrowed books. He was also helped by six assistants, two of whom died whilst the Dictionary was still in preparation.

The work was immense; filling about eighty large notebooks (and without a library to hand), Johnson wrote the definitions of over 40,000 words, and illustrated their many meanings with some 114,000 quotations drawn from English writing on every subject, from the Elizabethans to his own time. He did not expect to achieve complete originality. Working to a deadline, he had to draw on the best of all previous dictionaries, and to make his work one of heroic synthesis. In fact, it was very much more. Unlike his predecessors, Johnson treated English very practically, as a living language, with many different shades of meaning. He adopted his definitions on the principle of English common law — according to precedent. After its publication, his Dictionary was not seriously rivalled for over a century.

After many vicissitudes the Dictionary was finally published on 15 April, 1775. It was instantly recognised as a landmark throughout Europe. "This very noble work," wrote the leading Italian lexicographer, "will be a perpetual monument of fame to the author, an honour to his own country in particular, and a general benefit to the republic of letters throughout Europe. The fact that Johnson had taken on the academics of Europe and matched them (everyone knew that forty French academics had taken forty years to produce the first French national dictionary) was cause for much English celebration."

Johnson had worked for nine years, "with little assistance of the learned, and without any patronage of the great; not in the soft obscurities of retirement, or under the shelter of academic bowers, but amidst inconvenience and distraction, in sickness and in sorrow". For all its faults and eccentricities his two-volume work is a masterpiece and a landmark, in his own words, "setting the orthography, displaying the analogy regulating the structures, and ascertaining the significations of English words". It is the cornerstone of Standard English, an achievement which, in James Boswell's words, "conferred stability on the language of his country".

The Dictionary, together with his other writing, made Johnson famous and so well esteemed that his friends were able to prevail upon King George III to offer him a pension. From then on, he was to become the Johnson of folklore.

The passage below is a summary of the reading passage. Complete this summary by writing **ONE OR TWO WORDS** in each space. These words must be taken from the reading passage.

In 1764 Dr. Johnson accepted the contract to produce a dictionary. Having rented a garret, he took on a number of (1) ________ who stood at a long central desk. Johnson did not have a (2) ________ available to him, but eventually produced definitions of in excess of 40,000 words written down in 80 large notebooks. On publication, the Dictionary was immediately hailed in many European countries as a landmark. According to his biographer, James Boswell, Johnson's principal achievement was to bring (3) ________ to the English language. As a reward for his hard work, he was granted a (4) ________ by the king.

【参考答案】

(1) clerks / copying clerks (2) library (3) stability (4) pension

分析：这篇摘要虽然不是全篇文章的摘要，但覆盖了文章大部分段落。建议先通过 In 1764 在原文中定位，发现该摘要涵盖了从第四段开始至最后一段的内容。然后，按照前面所述的解题步骤的前三步来做。

14.1.2 缺漏词从原文中间接提取的摘要填空题

下面这几篇文章的题目属于第二种类型的摘要填空题。其实所有的有关全文内容的摘要都是原文各段大意的相加，因此用略读技巧找出各段大意，提高提取组团信息的能力是关键。

由于第一种类型的全文摘要直接从原文中提取缺漏词，不作任何改动，摘要的行文与原文原句的结构差异不能太大，因此相对限制了出题者的自由。

第二种类型的全文摘要不直接从原文中提取缺漏词，而是从所给的单词表中选取，这就给了出题者很大的改动自由，摘要的行文与句子结构变化会很大，因此建议这种类型的摘要题用下列步骤完成：

1. 通读摘要，并且理解大意。

2. 略读或细读文章各段，试着找出主题句，并且理解它；如果没有主题句，自己总结段落大意。

3. 将摘要中的句子与原文的主题句或自己总结的段落大意进行比较，找出异同，判断摘要中的句子缺了什么意思或词。

4. 最后在单词表中找出词性与词义均符合上下文逻辑的词填入空格内。

需要提醒的是，这种题型难度较大，重在考查考生的阅读理解和逻辑能力。

下面用此步骤完成下列文章的摘要填空题。

1. 下面这篇文章是关于利用史前昆虫生产新型抗生素的研究的，这一题材对大多数考生来说比较陌生，且行文较难，做起来不容易。希望上面介绍的解题步骤能助考生一臂之力。

Prehistoric Insects Spawn New Drugs

A Insects entombed in fossilised amber for tens of millions of years have provided the key to creating a new generation of antibiotic drugs that could wage war on modern diseases. Scientists have isolated the antibiotics from microbes found either inside the intestines of the amber-encased insects or in soil particles trapped with them when they were caught by sticky tree resin up to 130 million years ago. Spores of the microbes have survived an unprecedented period of suspended animation, enabling scientists to revive them in the laboratory.

B Research over the past two years has uncovered at least four antibiotics from the microbes and one has been able to kill modern drug-resistant bacteria that can cause potentially deadly diseases in humans. Present-day antibiotics have nearly all been isolated from micro-organisms that use them as a form of defence against their predators or competitors. But since the introduction of antibiotics into medicine 50 years ago, an alarming number have become ineffective because many bacteria have developed resistance to the drugs. The antibiotics that were in use millions of years ago may prove more deadly against drug-resistant modern strains of disease-causing bacteria.

C Paul Cano, who has pioneered the research at the California Polytechnic State University at San Luis Obispo, said the ancient antibiotics had been successful in fighting drug-resistant strains of staphylococcus bacteria, a "superbug" that has threatened the health of patients in hospitals throughout the world. He now intends to establish whether the antibiotics might have harmful side effects. "The problem is how toxic it is to other cells and how easy it is to purify," said Cano.

D A biotechnology company, Ambergene, has been set up to develop the antibiotics into drugs. If any ancient microbes are revived that resemble present-day diseases, they will be destroyed in case they escape and cause new epidemics. Drug companies will be anxious to study the chemical structures of the prehistoric antibiotics to see how they differ from modern drugs. They hope that one ancient antibiotic molecule could be used as a basis to synthesise a range of drugs.

E There have been several attempts to extract material such as DNA from fossilised life-forms ranging from Egyptian mummies to dinosaurs but many were subsequently shown to be contaminated. Cano's findings have been hailed as a breakthrough by scientists. Edward Golenberg, an expert on extracting DNA from fossilised life-forms at Wayne State University in Detroit, said: "They appear to be verifiable, ancient spores. They do seem to be real." Richard Lenski, professor of microbial ecology at Michigan State University, said the fight against antibiotic-resistant strains of bacteria, such as tuberculosis and staphylococcus, could be helped by the discovery.

F However, even the discovery of ancient antibiotics may not halt the rise of drug-resistant bacteria. Stuart Levy, a micro-biologist at Tufts University in Boston, warned that the bacteria would eventually evolve to fight hack against the new drugs. "There might also be an enzyme already out there that can degrade it. So the only way to keep the life of that antibiotic going is to use it sensibly and not excessively," he said.

The passage below is a summary of the reading passage. Complete this summary by choosing the words from the box.

deadly	resistant	responding	modern
safe	significant	preserved	single
unsuccessful	successful	careful	prehistoric
combined	particular	contributing	lifetime
unusual	placed	serious	excited

Microbes that may supply new antibiotic drugs have been (1) ________ in the bodies of fossilised insects. The discovery may help destroy bacteria that are no longer (2) ________ to modern medicine. What needs to be done now is to find out how (3) ________ the antibiotics will be. Microbes that seem to have the characteristics of (4) ________ diseases will have to be killed. It is thought that a (5) ________ molecule could lead to a whole series of drugs. Other scientists who have tried to produce antibiotics in a similar way have been (6) ________ . This work is considered a (7) ________ achievement. It is necessary to be (8) ________ about maintaining the life of the antibiotics.

【参考答案】

(1) preserved　(2) responding　(3) safe　(4) modern
(5) single　(6) unsuccessful　(7) significant　(8) careful

2. 下面这篇文章的题目也属于第二种类型的摘要题，虽然不是全文内容的摘要，但却是对作者观点的概括，亦涉及全文内容。

The Truth about the Environment

For many environmentalists, the world seems to be getting worse. They have developed a hit-list of our main fears: that natural resources are running out; that the population is ever growing, leaving less and less to eat; that species are becoming extinct in vast numbers, and that the planet's air and water are becoming ever more polluted.

But a quick look at the facts shows a different picture. First, energy and other natural resources have become more abundant, not less, since the book *The Limits to Growth* was published in 1972 by a group of scientists. Second, more food is now produced per head of the world's population than at any time in history. Fewer people are starving. Third, although species are indeed becoming extinct, only about 0.7% of them are expected to disappear in the next 50 years, not 25%—50%, as has so often been predicted. And finally, most forms of environmental pollution either appear to have been exaggerated, or are transient — associated with the early phases of industrialisation and therefore best cured not by restricting economic growth, but by accelerating it. One form of pollution — the release of greenhouse gases that causes global warming — does appear to be a phenomenon that is going to extend well into our future, but its total impact is unlikely to pose a devastating problem. A bigger problem may well turn out to be an inappropriate response to it.

Yet opinion polls suggest that many people nurture the belief that environmental standards are declining and four factors seem to cause this disjunction between perception and reality.

One is the lopsidedness built into scientific research. Scientific funding goes mainly to areas with many problems. That may be wise policy, but it will also create an impression that many more potential problems exist than is the case.

Secondly, environmental groups need to be noticed by the mass media. They also need to keep the money rolling in. Understandably, perhaps, they sometimes overstate their arguments. In 1997, for example, the World Wide Fund for Nature issued a press release entitled "Two-Thirds of the World's Forests Lost Forever". The truth turns out to be nearly 20%.

Though these groups are run overwhelmingly by selfless folk, they nevertheless share many of the characteristics of other lobby groups. That would matter less if people applied the same degree of scepticism to environmental lobbying as they do to lobby groups in other fields. A trade organisation arguing for, say, weaker pollution controls is instantly seen as self-interested. Yet a green organisation opposing such a weakening is seen as altruistic, even if an impartial view of the controls in question might suggest they are doing more harm than good.

A third source of confusion is the attitude of the media. People are clearly more curious about bad news than good. Newspapers and broadcasters are there to provide what the public wants. That, however, can lead to significant distortions of perception. An example was America's encounter with El niño in 1997 and 1998. This climatic phenomenon was accused of wrecking tourism, causing allergies, melting the ski-slopes and causing 22 deaths. However, according to an article in the Bulletin of the American Meteorological Society, the damage it did was estimated at US$4 billion but the benefits amounted to some US$19 billion. These came from higher winter temperatures (which saved an estimated 850 lives, reduced heating costs and diminished spring floods caused by melt waters).

The fourth factor is poor individual perception. People worry that the endless rise in the amount of stuff everyone throws away will cause the world to run out of places to dispose of waste. Yet, even if America's trash output continues to rise as it has done in the past, and even if the American population doubles by 2100, all the rubbish America produces through the entire 21st century will still take up only one 12,000th of the area of the entire United States.

So what of global warming? As we know, carbon dioxide emissions are causing the planet to warm. The best estimates are that the temperatures will rise by 2 °C—3 °C in this century, causing considerable problems, at a total cost of US$5,000 billion.

Despite the intuition that something drastic needs to be done about such a costly problem, economic analyses clearly show it will be far more expensive to cut carbon dioxide emissions radically than to pay the costs of adaptation to the increased temperatures. A model by one of the main authors of the United Nations Climate Change Panel shows how an expected temperature increase of 2.1 degrees in 2100 would only be diminished to an increase of 1.9 degrees. Or to put it another way, the temperature increase that the planet would have experienced in 2094 would be postponed to 2100.

So this does not prevent global warming, but merely buys the world six years. Yet the cost of reducing carbon dioxide emissions, for the United States alone, will be higher than the cost of solving the world's single, most pressing health problem: providing universal access to clean drinking water and sanitation. Such measures would avoid 2 million deaths every year, and prevent half a billion people from becoming seriously ill.

It is crucial that we look at the facts if we want to make the best possible decisions for the future. It may be costly to be overly optimistic — but more costly still to be too pessimistic.

Complete the summary with the words in the box. Write the correct letter **A**—**I** in the spaces given.

A unrealistic	**B** agreed	**C** expensive	**D** right	**E** long-term
F usual	**G** surprising	**H** personal	**I** urgent	

Global warming

The writer admits that global warming is a (1) _______ challenge, but says that it will not have a catastrophic impact on our future, if we deal with it in the (2) _______ way. If we try to reduce the levels of greenhouse gases, he believes that it would only have a minimal impact on rising temperatures. He feels it would be better to spend money on the more (3) _______ health problem of providing the world's population with clean drinking water.

【参考答案】

(1) E　　(2) D　　(3) I

分析：如果这个摘要是这篇文章的第一题，那么先不要做这道题，而是先做其他题目。待其他题目都做完之后，对这篇文章的内容也就已经有了一个较为全面和深入的了解，此时再做这道题就会得心应手了。

3. 下面这篇文章的题目也属于第二种类型，虽然不是全文内容的摘要，但却是对大部分段落大意的总结，覆盖面也很广。

对于这篇文章，可先按组团信息处理，解题方法仍旧是 scanning + skimming + careful reading，再参照本节一开始提到的解题的四个步骤来做。

Flawed Beauty: the Problem with Toughened Glass

On 2nd August, 1999, a particularly hot day in the town of Cirencester in the U.K., a large pane of toughened glass in the roof of a shopping centre at Bishops Walk shattered without warning and fell from its frame. When fragments were analysed by experts at the giant glass manufacturer Pilkington, which had made the pane, they found that minute crystals of nickel sulphide trapped inside the glass had almost certainly caused the failure.

"The glass industry is aware of the issue," says Brian Waldron, chairman of the standards committee at the Glass and Glazing Federation, a British trade association, and standards development officer at Pilkington. But he insists that cases are few and far between. "It's a very rare phenomenon," he says.

Others disagree. "On average I see about one or two buildings a month suffering from nickel sulphide related failures," says Barrie Josie, a consultant engineer involved in the Bishops Walk investigation. Other experts tell of similar experiences. Tony Wilmott of London-based consulting engineers Sandberg, and Simon Armstrong at CladTech Associates in Hampshire both say they know of hundreds of cases. "What you hear is only the tip of the iceberg," says Trevor Ford, a glass expert at Resolve Engineering in Brisbane, Queensland. He believes the reason is simple: "No one wants bad press."

Toughened glass is found everywhere, from cars and bus shelters to the windows, walls and roofs of thousands of buildings around the world. It's easy to see why. This glass has five times the strength of standard glass, and when it does break it shatters into tiny cubes rather than large, razor-sharp shards. Architects love it because large panels can be bolted together to make transparent walls, and turning it into ceilings and floors is almost as easy.

It is made by heating a sheet of ordinary glass to about 620 °C to soften it slightly, allowing its structure to expand, and then cooling it rapidly with jets of cold air. This causes the outer layer of the pane to contract and solidify before the interior. When the interior finally solidifies and shrinks, it exerts a pull on the outer layer that leaves it in permanent compression and produces a tensile force inside the glass. As cracks propagate best in materials under tension, the compressive force on the surface must be overcome before the pane will break, making it more resistant to cracking.

The problem starts when glass contains nickel sulphide impurities. Trace amounts of nickel and sulphur are usually present in the raw materials used to make glass, and nickel can also be introduced by fragments of nickel alloys falling into the molten glass. As the glass is heated, these atoms react to form tiny crystals of nickel sulphide. Just a tenth of a gram of nickel in the furnace can create up to 50,000 crystals.

These crystals can exist in two forms: a dense form called the alpha phase, which is stable at high temperatures, and a less dense form called the beta phase, which is stable at room temperatures. The high temperatures used in the toughening process convert all the crystals to the dense, compact alpha form. But the subsequent cooling is so rapid that the crystals don't have time to change back to the beta phase. This leaves unstable alpha crystals in the glass, primed like a coiled spring, ready to revert to the beta phase without warning.

When this happens, the crystals expand by up to 4%. And if they are within the central, tensile region of the pane, the stresses this unleashes can shatter the whole sheet. The time that elapses before failure occurs is unpredictable. It could happen just months after manufacture, or decades later, although if the glass is heated — by sunlight, for example — the process is speeded up. Ironically, says Graham Dodd, of consulting engineers Arup in London, the oldest pane of toughened glass known to have failed due to nickel sulphide inclusions was in Pilkington's glass research building in Lathom, Lancashire. The pane was 27 years old.

Data showing the scale of the nickel sulphide problem is almost impossible to find. The picture is made more complicated by the fact that these crystals occur in batches. So even if, on average, there is only one inclusion in 7 tonnes of glass, if you experience one nickel sulphide failure in your building, that probably means you've got a problem in more than one pane. Josie says that in the last decade he has worked on over 15 buildings with the number of failures into double figures.

One of the worst examples of this is Waterfront Place, which was completed in 1990. Over the following decade the 40-storey Brisbane block suffered a rash of failures. Eighty panes of its toughened glass shattered due to inclusions before experts were finally called in. John Barry, an expert in nickel sulphide contamination at the University of Queensland, analysed every glass pane in the building. Using a studio camera, a photographer went up in a cradle to take photos of every pane. These were scanned under a modified microfiche reader for signs of nickel sulphide crystals. "We discovered at least another 120 panes with potentially dangerous inclusions which were then replaced," says Barry. "It was a very expensive and time-consuming process that took around six months to complete." Though the project cost US$1.6 million (nearly £700,000), the alternative — re-cladding the entire building — would have cost ten times as much.

Complete the summary with the words in the box. Write your answers in the spaces given.

A numerous	**B** delected	**C** quickly	**D** agreed	**E** warm	**F** sharp
G expands	**H** slowly	**I** unexpectedly	**J** removed	**K** contracts	**L** disputed
M cold	**N** moved	**O** small	**P** calculated		

Toughened glass

Toughened glass is favoured by architects because it is much stronger than ordinary glass, and the fragments are not as (1) ________ when it breaks. However, it has one disadvantage: it can shatter (2) ________ . This fault is a result of the manufacturing process. Ordinary glass is first heated, then cooled very (3) ________ . The outer layer

(4) ________ before the inner layer, and the tension between the two layers which is created because of this makes the glass stronger. However, if the glass contains nickel sulphide impurities, crystals of nickel sulphide are formed. These are unstable, and can expand suddenly, particularly if the weather is (5) ________. If this happens, the pane of glass may break. The frequency with which such problems occur is (6) ________ by glass experts. Furthermore, the crystals cannot be detected without sophisticated equipment.

【参考答案】

(1) F (2) I (3) C (4) K (5) E (6) L

分析：如果这个题目是这篇文章的第一题，那么先不要做这道题，而是先做其他题目。待其他题都做完之后，对这篇文章的内容也就已经有了一个较为全面和深入的了解，此时再做这道题就会得心应手了。

后　记

原打算在书中不仅要阐述如何把阅读技巧运用到雅思阅读考试中，还要兼顾其他种类的阅读考试（包括英语高考、大学英语考试、英语专业考试和新托福等不同类型的阅读考试）以及课外阅读的实践。不过在编写过程中，书变得越来越厚，篇幅越来越长，只好就此打住。

然而，科学的阅读技巧适用于任何类型的阅读考试，纵使不同的阅读考试中具体的题型有所变化，题目要求有差异，阅读技巧却是万变不离其宗的。本书所阐述、分析、运用和实践的技能，对其他类型的阅读考试也具有参考价值。另外，科学的阅读技巧同样适用于课外阅读的实践。

雅思考生在学习完前九章的阅读技巧后，再进入后五章的雅思阅读题型破解，进行实践。后五章的阅读材料主要来源于“外研社·剑桥雅思考试培训教程”系列材料。要想进一步实践，建议使用英国或澳大利亚作者编写的雅思备考书籍。请记住：每份雅思阅读试卷都是独一无二的，难度也是不同的。多花些时间巩固英语基础，才是应付雅思考试的万全之策。